The
Death
of an
American
Jewish
Community

THE FREE PRESS
A Division of Macmillan, Inc. · *New York*

MAXWELL MACMILLAN CANADA
Toronto

MAXWELL MACMILLAN INTERNATIONAL
New York · *Oxford* · *Singapore* · *Sydney*

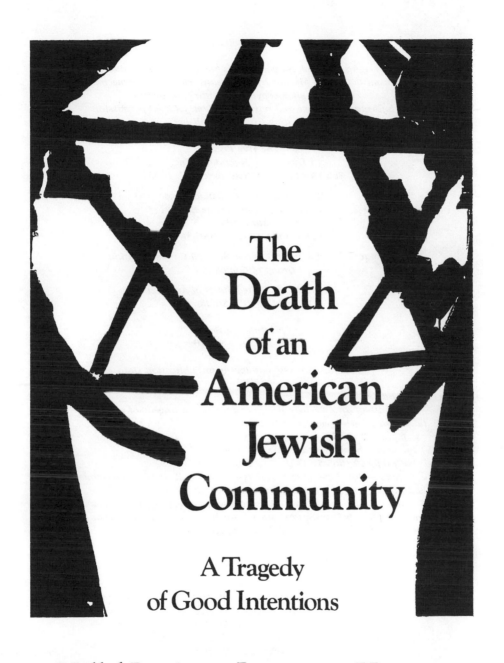

The
Death
of an
American
Jewish
Community

A Tragedy
of Good Intentions

Hillel Levine • Lawrence Harmon

Copyright © 1992 by Hillel Levine and Lawrence Harmon

The Free Press
A Division of Macmillan, Inc.
866 Third Avenue, New York, N.Y. 10022

Maxwell Macmillan Canada, Inc.
1200 Eglinton Avenue East
Suite 200
Don Mills, Ontario M3C 3N1

Macmillan, Inc. is part of the Maxwell Communication
Group of Companies.

Printed in the United States of America
Designed by REM Studio, Inc.

printing number
1 2 3 4 5 6 7 8 9 10

Library of Congress Cataloging-in-Publication Data

Levine, Hillel.
    The death of an American Jewish community: a tragedy of good
intentions / Hillel Levine and Lawrence Harmon.
        p.   cm.
    Includes bibliographical references and index.
    ISBN 0-02-913865-5
        1. Jews—Housing—Massachusetts—Boston.   2. Jews—Massachusetts—
Boston—History.   3. Afro-Americans—Housing—Massachusetts—
Boston.   4. Afro-Americans—Massachusetts—Boston—Relations with
Jews.   5. Dorchester (Boston, Mass.)—Ethnic relations.   6. Boston
(Mass.)—Ethnic relations.   I. Harmon, Lawrence.   II. Title.
F73.9.J5L48   1992
974.4'61004924—dc20   91-28161
                                                                        CIP

Portions of this book appeared in substantially different form in
the article "Profits and Prophets: Overcoming Civil Rights in
Boston" published in the July/August 1988 issue of TIKKUN: A
Bimonthly Jewish Critique of Politics, Culture & Society
(Oakland, California).

*In memory of Professor Albert Kahn,
lawyer, entrepreneur, and educator's educator,
whose integration of intention and action
was singularly inspiring.*

Contents

Preface

In the spring of 1987, we took a lengthy drive through three Boston neighborhoods—Roxbury, Dorchester, and Mattapan—that had once been home to 90,000 Jews and today are still home to the overwhelming majority of the city's 120,000 black residents. Hillel Levine, a professor of sociology and religion at Boston University, had been invited to lecture in a town ten miles south of Boston by members of the Dorchester/Roxbury/Mattapan Association. The group comprised mostly middle-aged Jews who had left Boston for the suburbs more than twenty years earlier but continued to meet regularly to recall the street life of their beloved inner-city neighborhoods. The meetings, as it would turn out, were rooted in more than mere nostalgia. For many members, a free-standing home in the suburbs had carried a hidden cost: the loss of a deep-rooted sense of community. These former residents of changing neighborhoods found little solace in knowing they'd made it in conventional terms. Instead, their nostalgia provided but a thin cover to inchoate rage and mistrust.

Though a long-time resident of Boston, Levine was unable to follow the driving directions via Boston's black neighborhoods provided by his hosts. He consulted his friend Lawrence Harmon, then managing editor of Boston's *Jewish Advocate* weekly newspaper, who had grown up in those neighborhoods when they were largely Jewish. Curious to see what this group was all about, Harmon offered to accompany Levine to the meeting. Harmon suggested that they leave early to tour the old neighborhood. He was somewhat unsure if the map in his memory still corresponded to real streets and spatial relations.

The two of us drove past a dozen buildings that had once been home to Jewish congregations and now served as African-American churches, mosques, or community centers. Along Blue Hill Avenue, the neighborhood's main thoroughfare, we identified sites of former kosher butchers, Judaica bookstores, and Jewish wedding halls. Many of the storefronts were now boarded or bricked up, save for an occasional Chinese takeout restaurant, check cashing service, or mini-market. It was a sight familiar to Jews who had grown up in Philadelphia's Mt. Airy, New York's East Flatbush, Los Angeles's Boyle Heights, or any of scores of other inner-city neighborhoods. Conventional wisdom, after all, dictated that blacks would take over inner-city neighborhoods abandoned by Jews.

As a sociologist, Levine was aware of the "succession" theory that accounts for changing neighborhoods: It was all but taken for granted that Jews, breaking into once forbidden occupational and social bastions, would find their new social reality inconsistent with continuing to reside in an inner-city ethnic neighborhood. Everyone who could escape the old neighborhood did so and, according to the theory, would sell to blacks. Those Jews who kept an interest in the community, it was believed, were largely slumlords and shopkeepers.

Levine had rarely considered what additional forces contributed to rapid neighborhood change. During the 1960s, he studied in rabbinical school and later did graduate work in comparative history and sociology. His teacher at Jewish Theological Seminary, Rabbi Abraham Joshua Heschel, inspired his disciples to personal involvement in the plight of the blacks, much as he inspired them in spirituality. Levine tried to combine the two by visiting and becoming active in the black Jewish communities of Harlem, where he so much admired the members' fervor. On his Saturday morning walks through Harlem, he often thought of his great-great-grandparents living in those very streets more than a half century before. Subsequently moving to Cambridge, he joined friends who were trying to create new Jewish communal forms. In the confrontational style of the 1960s, they pressed the Jewish federations for greater support of substantive Jewish experiences and for broader participation in the governance of Jewish communal life. While making these demands, Levine was oblivious to the fact that a substantive Jewish experience was being systematically dismantled by bankers and real estate agents just a few miles from his Harvard office. In some ways this book is meant to acknowledge that oversight.

Lawrence Harmon was born and raised in Dorchester. As a high school student in the late 1960s, he experienced firsthand the racial changes that took place in that neighborhood. More than a decade later, while working as an editor for the *Jewish Advocate,* Harmon encountered a reservoir of intense bitterness among former Jewish residents of Dorchester, Mattapan, and Roxbury. This book is also an attempt to uncover the sources of that bitterness.

Our research consisted of documents available in libraries, in archives, and in private hands, as well as hundreds of hours of interviews conducted by one or both of us between 1987 and 1990. Dialogue quoted in the book is based on the recollection of at least one participant, sometimes more. Wherever possible, we have corroborated interview material with printed sources.

To the many people who gave so generously of their time and insights to help us unravel this exceedingly complex story we hereby express our deepest appreciation. Throughout we have attempted to be accurate in the presentation of historical events, fair in the depiction of personalities, and compassionate when it came to that most elusive level of analysis, human motives.

The works of journalists J. Anthony Lukas and Alan Lupo have been of utmost importance in providing insight into the politics and people of Boston.

We would like to thank especially the staffs of the library and photography departments at the *Boston Globe,* the Boston Public Library, Boston University's Mugar Library, Harvard's Widener Library, the national offices of the Anti-Defamation League of B'nai B'rith, and the Council of Jewish Federations. Bernard Wax and Nathan Kaganoff of the American Jewish Historical Society were especially helpful in regard to sharing material and insights. While all of our interview subjects provided illumination, we were especially grateful to Marvin Antelman, Sumner and Janice Bernstein, Rachel Bratt, Hubert Jones, Elma Lewis, Sylvia Rothchild, Robert Segal, Lawrence Shubow, Otto and Muriel Snowden, and Chuck Turner.

Friends and colleagues have read sections of this book in various drafts. We would like to thank the following for their helpful and erudite comments: Yaron Ezrahi, Ronald Garet, Yitzhak Nebenzahl, Richard Rabinowitz, Ester Shapiro, and Glenn Wallach. With the joy in remembering and the sadness of loss, we especially acknowledge the generous attention to this book given by the late Samuel Schafler, president of Boston's Hebrew College. His learnedness and mastery of style contributed greatly to this work. We are also indebted to Brigitte and Peter Berger, Leonard Fein, Bernard Frieden, Nathan Glazer, Irving Levine, Dan and Joanna Rose, Emily Rose, John Ruskay, Steven Shaw, and William Julius Wilson for their encouragement and insight.

At The Free Press, Erwin Glikes, Adam Bellow, Noreen O'Connor, and Edith Lewis have handled this project with skill, commitment, and professionalism.

We thank Mildred Marmur, our literary agent, for her assistance and wise counsel at every stage of this project. Julius Marmur made us regulars of his clipping service, for which we are grateful.

We extend special thanks to Emily and Leo Kahn for their encouragement and support. Their commitment to social justice was an inspiration for us throughout this project.

Lauri Slawsby, program director of the Boston University Center for Judaic Studies, has coordinated many of the technical aspects of this research. She and her husband, Alan Slawsby, checked facts with the determination of detectives and the thirst for truth of scholars. We thank them for their friendship.

Our families have had to put up with not only our lengthy search for elusive forces but our own elusiveness. We thank our wives, Shulamith Levine and Susannah Sirkin, for their support and understanding. Our children, Leah, Hephzibah, Tiferet, Haninah, Ana, and Naomi, have given us more joy than we deserve in view of the troubled world that we bequeath to them. We share with them our hope that each will find a creative way to contribute to America and to Judaism, to bring harmony to their thoughts and actions, and to overcome the many tragedies of good intentions.

The
Death
of an
American
Jewish
Community

Introduction

The family, though a durable human grouping . . . possesses few
barriers save a front door and little capital to protect it from disaster.
—SAM BASS WARNER, JR., *The Way We Live:*
Social Change in Metropolitan Boston Since 1920, 1977

Gone—a viable Jewish community with a special "tam" and heart-
beat of its own. Where shall we find its replacement? Is this nostalgia
which I feel or is it quiet rage?
—MRS. CONCERNED URBANITE, *Jewish Advocate,*
May 18, 1972

In May 1987 an anonymous author writing in a real estate trade
journal offered the following insights into how he sold homes in
several Boston neighborhoods during the late 1960s:

I first heard about blockbusting when I decided I wanted to buy and sell property in Dorchester. So I went to local real estate agents. I got friendly with one fellow who worked in a particular office. We went out to lunch a couple of times, and he said, "I like you. You ought to come to work here. You can make a ton of money. . . ."

He explained to me that the banks had decided to take a certain area and designate it with a red pen . . . Mattapan and parts of Dorchester. We're going to finance minorities in this particular area, so they can get a house with no money down. That's how it all began. Of course, I personally wasn't out to help any minorities. I was out to make a buck for myself, and, seeing all those clients lining up out the door, I thought a fortune was certainly there. For a lot of people already in the business, it was a boon to them. And a lot of people who weren't in the business said, gee, this looks really good. . . .

The big area at that time was River Street [Mattapan]. Back towards Woodhaven, Colorado, Alabama Streets, that whole area, it was primarily a Jewish community. And they were all newer homes. They were affluent people, for living in the city of Boston, they were mostly people who owned their own small businesses. They weren't filthy rich, but they weren't hurting either. And that's more or less where it began; after a while, it expanded. The banks didn't expand the area; the brokers did. . . .

We were told, you get the listings any way you can. It's pretty easy to do: just scare the hell out of them! And that's what we did.

We were not only making money, we were having fun doing what we were doing. We all liked selling real estate—if you want to call what we were doing back then selling real estate. And it got to a point that, to have fun while we were working, we would try to outdo each other with the most outlandish threats that people would believe, and chuckle about them at the end of the day. Some of the milder things were: property values are going down, you're going to get a thousand dollars less next month than this. Market values really didn't decline that much. They did decline slightly, but the thousand dollars a month, or whatever figure you picked— that was something you pulled out of the air. . . .

We weren't subtle about it. You'd say, how would you like it if they rape your daughter, and you've got a mulatto grandchild? I remember one particular family where this little girl was about twelve years old and blonde, she was a very pretty little kid. And I used that on them, and it did sway them. They sure as hell sold! I even used it once on a son, the little boy would get raped. Whatever worked, I would try to use.

The office I worked in had ten full-time sales people, and I would say seven of us did it. The other three, if they did do it, they were quiet about it. There was one fellow, he was such a nice guy, he wouldn't do it at all. He didn't make the big cash the other people did. . . .

I had direct contact with people who were more blatant than I ever dreamed of being. There were instances of house-breaks that were arranged only to scare people out. That was the worst. I thought that was a bit much. I don't think anybody to this day is aware that anybody arranged this. Nobody was ever arrested for it, convicted of it, or anything else. . . .

Under these federal programs, many of the buyers shouldn't have owned a house. Anyone who doesn't have *any* equity in a house is a high risk. I've sold houses to people who never made a first payment. Why should they? It never cost them a thing to get in. In some cases, the seller paid the closing costs, the first year's insurance, and moving costs. It cost them nothing to move in, so they just waited for foreclosure. . . .

What we did back then, I don't really consider that bad. We hurt people who were asking to be hurt. They were bigoted, and they asked for everything they got. It was their idea to run. We fueled the fire. In my own defense, I lived in Dorchester and sold the house next door to a black family, and then I lived there for the next five years. The black family left, though, after the white kids in the neighborhood got together and stoned their house night after night.

Stonings happened so often that if I had a choice, I'd say to the buyer, let's take your car, not mine. I would tell them it was broken or out of gas. The car would get stoned about once a week, more often when we weren't in it, but occasionally when we were. Kids would look at the car and see a whole family of black people and one white guy in a suit and tie with a clipboard, and they knew what was going on. . . .

Whole areas went from white to black in a matter of months then . . . I'm retired now, and enjoying it very much. I look back, and I realize I've mellowed in my retirement.[1]

There are no winners in this story. But there are big losers— mainly the black and Jewish residents whose lives once revolved around the institutions and thoroughfares of these communities and those who still reside there. Their struggles provide insights into the current breakdown of the historic black–Jewish civil rights alliance, a subject of much recent debate and analysis.

Conventional theories attribute much of the alliance's breakdown to forces intrinsic to the black and Jewish communities. Blacks and Jews blame each other for this breakdown. They cite such factors as Jewry's reluctance to accept corporate responsibility for Jewish slumlords, demands for black community control and affirmative action that challenge universalist principles on which many Jews staked their achievements and for which they felt they were being forced to pay a disproportionate part of the cost, racism, and the rise of black antisemitism and anti-Zionism that went largely unchallenged in the black community. But there is growing evidence that elusive forces external to the black and Jewish communities also played a role in undermining their relationship, and that opportunities were lost for positive contact between blacks and Jews at the neighborhood level.

It was not black–Jewish relations, however, that were of paramount concern to Boston's civic leaders during the 1960s. Committed to their city's economic development, the leaders worried about how potential investors would view the threat of black ghettoes burning at the periphery of downtown. Throughout the early 1960s, poorly conceived and poorly administered federal urban renewal programs had contributed to rather than eased the housing shortage for Boston's growing black population. By the late 1960s, the city's bankers, eager to be "good citizens," saw in these housing issues an opportunity to respond to America's urban and racial crisis while accepting no risks. Using federal programs that guaranteed housing loans for low-income residents, the bankers unilaterally redefined these programs such that funds were to be made available almost exclusively to blacks.

The most important role was that of the consortium established by these bankers, the Boston Banks Urban Renewal Group (B-BURG). Unlike classic "redlining," wherein banks and insurance companies withhold housing loans and other financial vehicles from residents in older, less prosperous neighborhoods, the Boston experiment provided a bizarre new twist. Under the guise of expanding homeownership opportunities for the city's black community, the heads of twenty-two Boston savings banks were complicit in establishing a carefully limited and well-defined inner-city district within which, and only within which, blacks could obtain the attractive, federally insured housing loans. Incredibly, the area selected for heightened loan activity skirted the predominantly Irish and Italian working-class neighborhoods and, less surprisingly, the suburbs where the bankers themselves lived. Falling exclusively within the B-BURG line, however, was almost the entirety of Boston's Jewish community, an unprofitable neighborhood for the city's bankers because so many of the residents had paid off their mortgages.

By forcing blacks with homeownership aspirations to compete in a limited geographic area, the B-BURG bankers created an eruption of panic selling, blockbusting, street violence, and rage. How this happened in Boston and other cities across America, how blacks, Jews, and their leaders responded, the damage done, and how it might have been averted are what this book is about.

The actors in this story included not only residents of the affected neighborhoods of Roxbury, Dorchester, and Mattapan but also bankers, bureaucrats, politicians, real estate agents, and religious leaders. Many, such as the "blockbusters" who played on racial fears and prejudices to turn a profit, were motivated solely by greed and venality. Others, such as bankers and community leaders, seemingly acted with good intentions. Yet their activities, too, led to the radical, often violent transformation of inner-city neighborhoods. Instead of planning healthily integrated neighborhoods in a way that might have strengthened alliances between the two communities, black and Jewish leaders in Boston looked on helplessly as larger economic forces intensified the tendency toward conflict and mutual hostility.

These elusive economic forces were clearly at work in many cities across the country. Harvard government professor Edward Banfield has emphasized how Federal Housing Authority and Veterans Administration programs "have subsidized the movement of the white middle class out of the central cities and older suburbs while at the same time penalizing investment in the rehabilitation of the rundown neighborhoods of these older cities. The poor—especially the Negro poor—have not received any direct benefits from these programs."[2] Banfield's controversial study might well have underestimated the power of prejudice in forcing blacks to live in separate neighborhoods, but he was correct in assuming that more subtle forces also contribute to this separatism.

America's foremost neighborhood organizer, Saul Alinsky, once observed that "integration is the time between when the first black family moves in and the last white family moves out." The interim condition is generally described as a "changing neighborhood." This book may explain some of the reasons why Alinsky's observations cannot be dismissed as mere sarcasm. Roxbury, Dorchester, and Mattapan, once home to 90,000 Jews, today are home to the overwhelming majority of the city's 120,000 black residents. In much of the district, more than fifty years of Jewish settlement were overturned during a two-year period from 1968 to 1970. Jews sold their homes to unscrupulous speculators for less than market value while blacks, eager to participate in the "American Dream," were forced to pay inflated prices.

The Boston Banks Urban Renewal Group program was to housing what court-ordered desegregation was to education: while creating the impression of fairness, in reality it created more problems than it solved. Today few middle-class white students attend the Boston public schools, having fled to private and parochial schools. Despite many noble efforts by faculty and students, the public school system in Boston is woefully substandard. The few black students lucky enough to be bused to suburban systems in numbers large enough not to be wholly isolated flourish academically while their urban cousins, in many cases, manage just the most basic skills. The sons and daughters of stable communities, not just of stable families, are on the fast track. Many whites who have moved from the city see race as a factor in their departure. The housing within the B-BURG line is mostly dilapidated. Neighborhoods are "resegregated," unstable, and crime-ridden, the home of those that sociologist William Julius Wilson calls "the truly disadvantaged." Yet the largely black neighborhoods just outside the B-BURG line are well maintained and viable, and foster a sense of community.

While this is indeed a local story, ample evidence of similar communities in crisis precipitated a national response among observers of changing neighborhoods and ultimately led to legislative remedies such as the "anti-redlining laws" and community reinvestment acts of the 1970s. Within the Jewish community itself, organizations and federations such as the Cleveland Jewish Federation learned the lessons of Boston. Jewish flight from Cleveland Heights was successfully prevented through community organizing, and a modicum of integration was achieved. Efforts to stabilize neighborhoods were less successful in Philadelphia.[3]

What, unfortunately, might come as a surprise are some implications of this study to sociologists and leaders of the American Jewish community. While American Jewry may be more than Boston Jewry writ large, in fact (because of the stringent census laws of the commonwealth resulting in an unmatched data base) much of what researchers tell us about American Jewry is based upon generalizations from Massachusetts. Yet these scholars have demonstrated an obliviousness to social structural factors—such as those involved in what the federal government officials, politicians, and bankers are up to—preferring to focus with ever-greater methodological sophistication on the social psychological factors involved in identity, assimilation, intermarriage, and the like. This study should make the perils of that limited field of vision amply clear.

The terms "neighborhood" and "community" are often used interchangeably in the urban studies literature. But neighborhoods have to do with natural topographic transitions highlighted by administrative boundaries and even transportation lines. Community refers to the delicate lattice of human networks and social institutions. Community also represents the shared meaning of residents, a moral order and ideals, memory and expectations; it satisfies emotional needs for understanding and control over structures of power and the forces that govern us—needs that are upheld, if only in the breach, in streets and homes, businesses and public institutions. More than the benefits of specific rights and entitlements, communities provide citizens with a sense of control and empowerment.

In recent years—perhaps as a result of incidents such as those we describe in this book taking place across the country—the importance of community has risen among legislators, social theorists, and social workers. And the loss of community is disorienting in more ways than we may think. The characters in this story who long to reconnect with their former communities are motivated not by nostalgia alone. For many, "the old neighborhood" not only is perceived as better—it was better in fact.

Community has another face—a dangerous one—which serves purposes other than strengthening the mental health and democratic sentiments of its participants. Many Americans continue to hold the concept of community in far greater esteem than they do the concept of equal opportunity. Unfortunately, their sense of community is more important for what it excludes than what it includes. This predilection has taken ugly forms, such as the white on black racial attacks at Howard Beach and Bensonhurst. But the promotion of equality as the supreme value has also failed us.

More than twenty years after the death of an American Jewish community in Boston, it is difficult to invoke the subject of black–Jewish relations without reference to two great visionaries, Reverend Martin Luther King, Jr. and Rabbi Abraham Joshua Heschel. Yet many Jews and blacks cannot share in the romantic memories of the civil rights movement of the 1960s. It is not the voices of great spiritual leaders that they recall. It is, instead, the voices of blockbusters who phoned with veiled threats at midnight; the voices of loan officers telling applicants where one could and could not live; the voices of angry and violent youths and bitter and bigoted elderly.

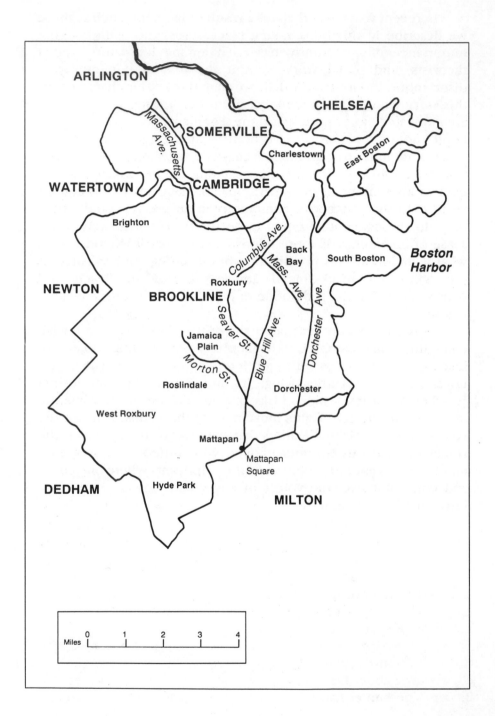

ARLINGTON

CHELSEA

Massachusetts Ave.

SOMERVILLE

Charlestown

East Boston

WATERTOWN

CAMBRIDGE

Brighton

Columbus Ave.

Back Bay

Mass. Ave.

South Boston

Boston Harbor

NEWTON

Roxbury

BROOKLINE

Seaver St.

Blue Hill Ave.

Dorchester Ave.

Jamaica Plain

Morton St.

Roslindale

Dorchester

West Roxbury

Mattapan

Mattapan Square

DEDHAM

Hyde Park

MILTON

Miles

0   1   2   3   4

Blue Hill Avenue

The Glory Years

Boston City Councilor Julius Ansel was in pursuit of hippopotamus in the summer of 1951. Ansel, the most beloved politician in Jewish Boston, was not the kind of man to stand idly by while neighborhood children stared disconsolately into the empty cage once occupied by "Happy the Hippo" in Roxbury's Franklin Park Zoo, a taste of the jungle in the midst of a staid middle-class Jewish neighborhood. After scores of inquiries he had secured the services of a big-game hunter from Capetown, South Africa, who, as luck would have it, was in America on business. The man had promised to trap a first-class river beast. Ansel would settle for nothing less when it came to his constituents in Ward 14.

Ansel relished any opportunity to show a visitor around his turf; no adventurer who led safaris on the veldts of Africa was more chauvinistic about his domain than Julius Ansel was about Jewish Boston. The hunter had reluctantly agreed to accompany Ansel on

11

a fund-raising tour of the ward. It had not even occurred to the politician to seek authorization or funds for the animal from the city's parks commissioner; advocacy and getting things through budget hearings and bureaucracies were not his style. And besides, what did the *goyyim* in city hall know about his people? He would appeal directly to Boston's working-class Jews of Ward 14, the city's most populous.

The first stop on Ansel's tour was the cavernous G&G delicatessen on Blue Hill Avenue, where he introduced the hunter to the regulars. An enormous vertical sign in blue and red extended over the entrance, a provocation to the city's code enforcers and a beacon to the lunch and dinner trade who worked, shopped, gossiped, and ceaselessly traversed the Avenue. In the early 1950s more than ninety thousand Jews lived within a three-square-mile area including the neighborhoods of Roxbury, Dorchester, and Mattapan. Blue Hill Avenue, dubbed "Jew Hill Avenue" by some forgotten Bostonian, cut a four-mile-long swath through the Jewish district before being swallowed up south of the city limits in a saddleback range favored by suburban trekkers. Few of Boston's Jews had ever hiked to the top of Big Blue or skied down its modest slopes. These sons and daughters of Vilna, Lodz, and Odessa were content to toil, shop, and gossip on the flatlands. Most believed that Blue Hill Avenue rivaled Manhattan's Lower East Side or the Bronx's Grand Concourse. There was little reason even to travel downtown. Blue Hill Avenue was, in the words of a local novelist, "a mighty river of traffic, a double helix of asphalt around which the tributaries, the life of the Jews in Boston, spun, cohered, developed."[1]

The big-game hunter stood by in silence while Ansel, dapper in bow tie and sports jacket, made his back-slapping rounds. Although it was at least an hour before lunchtime, the patrons of the G&G deli were wolfing thick sandwiches and slurping coffee and soft drinks. Convulsive chatter rose from the deli's north wall, where a dozen countermen sliced, crammed, and spread behind a display case packed with rolled beef, stuffed *kishke,* and briskets. The Yiddish conversations of nearby salesmen were unintelligible to a visitor, save for occasional utterings of "linoleum" and "Formica." The English conversations were almost as difficult to follow. A group of cabdrivers, whose empty trip logs indicated that they spent more time drinking coffee than driving hack, were dispatching a skinny teenager to place an order: "For Inky, *kasha varnitchkes*. For Eleval, a slice of *kishke*. For Cockeye, tongue on a roll. Don't forget the borscht, bagel, and a *shmeer.*" Then, pointing to a particularly obese driver, one of the drivers warned, "Nothing for Skinny. He's digging his grave with his teeth." The cabbies convulsed with laughter.

The G&G, at 1106 Blue Hill Avenue, stood almost exactly midway between the Jewish district's northern border in Grove Hall and its southern border in Mattapan Square. If asked to free-associate about Jewish Boston, former residents invariably utter "the G&G," referring to Irving Green and Charlie Goldstein's eatery. One wall of the deli consisted of glass display cases and steam tables resplendent with smoked meats and kosher-style prepared dishes over which customers shouted orders to aproned countermen. The booths hugging the walls were favored for business lunches. The tables in the open space at the deli's center were popular with tradesmen, cops, and cabbies, who ate with gusto and traded barbs at inappropriate decibel levels. A small private dining room tucked in the back was available for lodge meetings and officer installations. The delicatessen, in short, meant for the working-class Jews of Boston what the private downtown Algonquin Club meant for the Boston Brahmins: a place to dine, cut deals, and evaluate prospective sons-in-law. But the G&G did not serve crabs amandine, and the Algonquin Club did not serve Jews.

That a delicatessen enjoyed the greatest drawing power of any institution in the Jewish community never sat well with proper Jewish Bostonians. Those charged with shaping the community struggled for ways to get people off the Avenue and into the classroom or clubhouse. Since 1921 the Hebrew Teacher's College on Roxbury's Crawford Street had offered not only professional training but also adult education courses by an acclaimed staff. Classes, to be sure, were well attended, but few former residents think first of Hebrew College when reminiscing of the old neighborhood.

No one could work the crowd at the G&G like Julius Ansel. The sole Jew on the twenty-four-member city council, "Julie" could do no wrong in Dorchester. The son of a Roxbury cigar maker, Ansel was Jewish Dorchester incarnate—brash, streetwise, and not overly clever. He might have had a successful Hollywood career had he not chosen a career in politics. Dubbed by the press the "lion of Dorchester" for his silver mane, Ansel had been known to wrap his head in phony bandages before going out on the hustings to accuse his opponents of hiring political muscle. A veteran of five campaigns during World War II and a Bronze Star recipient, he could never quite bring himself to reject a mother's tearful request to intercede with Selective Service officials on behalf of a "sickly" son. War heroes were far more likely to win admiration from voters over in South Boston's Irish pubs. Julie's war exploits were notable for nonviolent *chutzpah,* such as the time he impersonated a German officer, when surprised on reconnaissance by a Nazi patrol in the Hurtgen Forest, and managed to convince the enemy that he was merely masquerading in an American uniform.

The regulars at the G&G regaled each other for hours with tales of the exploits of their favorite councilor. Ansel had an amazing gift for imitating voices, which he used in the service of and for the amusement of his constituents. It was said that he had even managed to place scores of Jews in city jobs by mimicking the telephone voice of Boston Mayor James Michael Curley. Ansel was obsessed with Curley—a Robin Hood figure who was reelected from a jail cell by loyal voters—and had even taken to imitating the former mayor's dress and gait; in winter, following heavy snows, it was not uncommon to see Ansel, dressed in a cutaway coat and pinstripe trousers, walking behind the snow plow and tipping his hat to constituents as they peered from the windows of their wooden triple deckers.

Ansel was always involved in one half-baked project or another to enhance the image of his ward. No one, therefore, thought twice when he started to drum up the down payment for the hippo by introducing the big-game hunter around the neighborhood. Had anyone cared to query the visitor, they might easily have learned that he was a shipping agent specializing in sea transport from Africa. But if Julie said he was an intrepid hunter, so be it. "We're going to name the hippo Putzi," Ansel told his benefactors with a wink when they pitched in with pocket change and one-dollar bills.

It fell to Ansel, as the preeminent politician of Ward 14, to carry messages across the multidimensional matrix of neighborhood institutions: morning coffee klatches at the delis, officer installations at meetings of any one of dozens of temple brotherhoods and sisterhoods, Tuesday and Thursday night dances at the Hecht House Jewish Community Center, speeches at gatherings of the Jewish War Veterans, and late-night poker games with favor seekers and political hopefuls. It seemed at times that no one in Jewish Dorchester during the 1950s had heard the news that group affiliation was voluntary. Adults, with few exceptions, donated time to several special charities or volunteer organizations; the Jewish War Veterans boasted an incredible thirteen chapters in Roxbury, Dorchester, and Mattapan alone. Children marched the streets collecting coins in the blue and white tin *pushkes,* or charity boxes, distributed by the Jewish National Fund. Even the bookies had adopted a favorite charity: a local workshop for handicapped youngsters. Politicians were required to join practically everything. In this ward where civic participation exceeded even de Tocqueville's dreams, a goodly portion of a public official's salary could be eaten away by multiple synagogue memberships, club dues, and greetings in temple ad books.

Sometimes, on his rounds, Ansel encountered a discreetly passed envelope intended to push a name to the top of a civil service list or to guarantee some other political favor. Putting cash in Julie's hands, however, was always something of a crapshoot. Often, the money was passed on to a needy resident before it found its way to the necessary official. Like Curley, who died broke, the "lion of Dorchester" had minimal interest in personal profit. When Ansel invited too many of "the boys" over to his Wales Street home for dinner and cards, his wife was reduced to knocking on neighbors' doors to borrow flatware. In 1954, while a state legislator, Ansel would bounce a series of checks for campaign expenses, and in 1956 he would be fined for larceny in connection with an illegal payment to secure a liquor license for a South End cafe owner. As always, Dorchester residents would bail out their beloved legislator.

Ansel loved to walk the streets of his ward. Like many Dorchester residents, he had picked up the inexplicable habit of walking down the median line, particularly on broad Blue Hill Avenue where often as many as three lanes of northbound motorists sped to jobs downtown. The seasoned Irish cops who patrolled the Avenue begged the Jews on their beat to use the sidewalks; this was not, the officers reminded them, some two-bit village in

Poland. Predictably, there were accidents when careless drivers clipped distracted pedestrians. "Hey, Goldstein," a cop would warn, "you're going to get killed out there." And the Jews would purse their lips and reply sarcastically, "Hey, Kelly, go catch a thief."

During the 1940s (and as would be true throughout the 1950s) an aging Boston police officer couldn't ask for an easier beat than Boston's Jewish neighborhood. At Morton Street's Station 19, a small brick fortress overlooking the Midland Railroad tracks, cops had plenty of time to calculate their retirement pay. After twenty years on the job, no one was in the mood to match foot speed with juvenile delinquents or break up barroom brawls. In Jewish Dorchester and Roxbury, it was a given that parents kept their kids in line and there was hardly a bar in sight. Potbellied cops angled for Station 19, where, the saying went, a cop "who couldn't find a Jew in a synagogue" could still hang on for a few more years. An exciting night, recalled a former Station 19 sergeant, was "playing dominoes in the guard room." Clerks at the neighborhood drugstores uniformly honored instructions from their bosses regarding the tradition of free cigarettes for "Boston's finest." These Jews respected the badge. There were other easy beats in the city, such as West Roxbury and Roslindale, where lace-curtain Irish meticulously maintained single-family ranch-style homes. But those neighborhoods were dull in comparison, lacking fruit stands, herring hawkers, and the smell of floating chicken feathers from a dozen kosher butcher stores.

Ansel and the big-game hunter kept to the sidewalk on their fifteen-block trek to the Franklin Park Zoo. The distance normally could be covered in twenty minutes but took more than an hour, given the number of people Ansel met on the street—old classmates from Dorchester Evening High, lodge brothers from the Knights of Pythias, and colleagues from the Roxbury–Dorchester Zionist District. Many Dorchester Jews couldn't walk past three storefronts without running into an acquaintance or former tenant. With the addition of sidewalk vendors, shoppers, and deliverymen, it was little wonder why some risked the passing Chevrolets and Ramblers in the center of the avenue when it became necessary to keep an appointment or rush home to feed a hungry family. Ansel had to deal with supplicants to boot: housewives appealed to the councilor to find jobs for unemployed or underemployed husbands, and parking tickets materialized from extended hands. Ansel promised that they would be taken care of, with reminders to "remember me on Election Day." Fixing parking tickets, in fact, took up the lion's share of a Dorchester politician's duties. Scores of times each week Ansel and other area representatives were on the phone with the police captain at Station 19. Some weeks the police brass tore up all of the tickets in the district in order to keep their phone lines free for more serious police business.

Ansel and the hunter encountered heavy foot traffic on the 1000 block of Blue Hill Avenue, where shoppers dashed between Richard's Kiddie Shop, the Mattapan Baking Corporation, Leshner's Creamery, Willie and Eddie's Fruit, Rosalie's Hosiery, and the New Deal Fish Market. Ansel pointed out neighborhood shops and services along the way with the reverence tour guides reserve for the most exotic shrines. Had the big-game hunter, he queried, ever seen so many pharmacies on one street? Outsiders could never quite figure out the need for so many drugstores along the Avenue—Alaska Drug, Ross Pharmacy, Harris Pharmacy, Feinsches Pharmacy, Twin Pharmacy, and Rothenberg's, to name a few.

The proliferation of pharmacies dated back to the days of Prohibition. In Irish neighborhoods across town, speakeasies were the order of the day. In Jewish Dorchester, however, valued customers could look forward to a stiff shot poured discreetly into a fountain Coke. Most of the stores had retained their fountains, complete with pink Formica counters and round swivel seats, where youngsters now gorged on sundaes, ice cream frappes and cones. (Into the early 1960s scores of young drugstore cowboys would be found hanging out at these fountains despite sharp warnings from parents. The fountains would prove so compelling to neighborhood youths that innovative social workers at the nearby Hecht House Jewish Community Center on American Legion Highway would even replicate a full soda fountain in the center's youth room in the hope of luring the youngsters off of the Avenue.) The adults favored the area around the prescription counters. In stores with sufficient space, proprietors even provided easy chairs in which to relax and exchange gossip while prescriptions were filled. In Irish South Boston or Charlestown, it was the parish priest to whom the locals confessed; in Jewish

Roxbury and Dorchester, it was the pharmacist who offered dispensation in the form of penicillin or "blue butter" ointment for embarassing conditions.

In front of Max Platt's fish store, a woman buttonholed Ansel with a tale of woe. Her son had been arrested for fighting with an Irish boy on nearby Talbot Avenue and was scheduled to appear in Dorchester District Court. He was such a good boy, she told Ansel, and had been merely defending Jewish honor. Her son would never have kicked the other boy and never in the groin, God forbid, had it not been for the antisemitic insult. The woman offered to go directly to a nearby credit union and borrow enough money to set things right with the court officers. "Save your money," Ansel told her, jotting down the miscreant's name. The frantic woman insisted that Ansel accompany her to the Morton Building, where she could secure a small loan "just to make sure." Ansel gently extricated himself and patted the woman's arm reassuringly. "I've got business in the court tomorrow," he told her. "Forget the credit union. Relax and remember me on Election Day."

For many of the area's working-class Jews, the credit union was the difference between a lower-class lifestyle and middle-class respectability. With few exceptions, major Boston savings and commercial banks dismissed the slim pickings in the working-class Jewish district. In their place were some eighty small credit unions, legal and illegal, operating throughout Jewish Dorchester and Mattapan in the 1940s and 1950s. The center of the credit union activity took place in the Morton Building at 1165 Blue Hill Avenue. In the dusty offices above the Morton Theatre, a popular neighborhood movie house, more than twenty credit unions with comforting names like Mohliver Credit and Friendship Credit were interspersed with union locals composed largely of Jewish plumbers, carpenters, and cap makers. When state bank examiner Meyer Finkel ventured into Dorchester to ensure that the credit unions did not overstep their charters, particularly the rule limiting home mortgage loans to $10,000, he rarely knew what to expect: some credit unions were meticulously managed, others were little more than fronts for local loan sharks, and still others were run by small groups of Yiddish-speaking widows who loaned one another sums at whatever interest rates caught their fancy. The latter often posed the greatest challenge to Finkel's authority. When Finkel presented his credentials and explained the terms of fair competition, he was usually met with a rejoinder along the lines, *"Narrishkeit* [foolishness], sonny, go away."[2]

Finkel loved to watch the warm interchange between the credit union customers and the loan officers. Back in the office of the bank commissioner, he rankled at the stiff collars and dour demeanors. In the early 1950s, Finkel went over to the other side, signing on as manager of the Blue Hill Credit Union, one of the neighborhood's largest. On his first day Finkel, a religious man, sat down at his new desk, opened his briefcase, and placed a copy of the humash *(Five Books of Moses) squarely in the middle of his desk. He was ready for business. The first lesson that Finkel learned in Dorchester's* aktsya, *or credit union, was that one kissed good-bye the common practice of requiring two additional cosigners for loans; if a family lacked the assets to marry off a daughter or send a child to college, it was certainly not the business of one's friends or relatives. The collateral in the Jewish financial district was one's good name. Besides loans for dowries and tuition, loans for cars and vacations were also in demand. (In Dorchester that usually meant the opportunity to pack the kids into the family sedan and head off to rent a small efficiency apartment for a few weeks at Nantasket Beach, twenty miles south of Boston. A visitor to the lower end of the beach, dubbed Little Israel by the locals, found thousands of Dorchester residents frolicking in the chilly surf. Wading into the Atlantic, elderly women vigorously splashed water on their wrists and necks and uttered "a gesund tzu de aktsya," translated roughly as "God bless the credit unions.") Finkel particularly loved providing these small loans for summer vacations. Back in town old colleagues from the banking commission would ask him when he was going to finish slumming. "I've found joy in banking," Finkel responded, dismissing his detractors with a wave.*

The crowds thinned out a bit as Ansel and the big-game hunter continued northward on the Avenue. The councilor stopped to fund-raise with patrons coming out of Davidson's Hebrew Bookstore and with shopkeepers who stood sunning themselves in their doorways. A few blocks further north Ansel and the hunter saw the food and clothing stores give way to grimy shops specializing in heating and burner equipment, auto parts, paints, and wallpaper. Next came Franklin Field, a pendant in the "emerald necklace" of parks surrounding Greater Boston. The two men finally rested by leaning on a low stone wall, almost four hundred yards long, that framed the portion of the field facing Blue Hill Avenue. A few old women from the nearby housing project gossiped on plastic beach chairs in the middle of the broad sidewalk. Every few yards, a knot of elderly men sat on the wall watching the passing traffic. Behind them, young boys competed relentlessly on makeshift baseball diamonds, sliding into large stones used as bases. It was only a matter of days before the children would once again be behind their desks at one of the many Dorchester five-day-a-week afternoon Hebrew schools that local youths dutifully attended after a full day of secular studies.

There was plenty of room on the wall on a late summer day. But in early fall, with the advent of Rosh Hashanah, the Jewish New Year, wall space would be at a premium. All commerce along Blue Hill Avenue came to a halt on the High Holy Days. Sidewalks usually crammed with food stalls and dry goods would soon be cleared for a parade ground for the legions of men in dark suits and fedoras, the women in silk dresses and stylish hats, and boys and girls stiffly attired in new holiday outfits. Most of the crowd would arrive from the direction of Woodrow Avenue, where several popular Orthodox synagogues were located. Police would reroute traffic away from more than a dozen *shuls* to protect the sensibilities of the observant, who shunned driving and the kindling of lights on holy days. At the end of services synagogue goers would descend on the wall from all directions, some muttering that the apostates who avoided synagogue had already secured the best spots. The wall at Franklin Field was the one opportunity for all of the disparate neighborhood characters to connect. The members of the socialist Workmen's Circle, which ran a popular Kinder Ring summer camp for neighborhood youth, would share wall space with followers of the Hasidic Bostoner Rebbe, Levi Horowitz. Even the modest *rebbitzins* (rabbis' wives) would nod to the prostitutes who made their living in the back room of a barber shop on Erie Street. By early afternoon, the field would be filled with Jews. The grown-ups would censor their conversations to avoid unholy talk of business, sports, or stock market prices, which might interfere with reflection and repentance. Despite the solemnity of the holy days, it would be impossible for even pious parents to keep their children from play. Little ones would push nuts along the ground with sticks. Preadolescent boys would knot their pocket handkerchiefs and flick them at the silk stockings of young girls practicing in their first high heels. Adolescents would take over a portion of the field furthest from public view for spirited games of "buck buck," in which a team of jumpers would catapult themselves onto the backs of a row of defensive players in an attempt to topple the human bridge.

Ansel and his guest continued toward the zoo, past the popular Liberty Theatre, where Ansel enthused about featured headliners from New York's Yiddish stage. They passed the Chinese laundry, a shoe shine stand, and the ornate Franklin Park Theater. At Blue Hill Avenue and Columbia Road, they crossed the street and entered Franklin Park—427 acres thick with oak, hickory, and hemlock. The park had been designed as a working-class paradise in 1879 by social visionary and renowned landscape architect Frederick Law Olmsted. The largest jewel in Olmsted's "emerald necklace" surrounding Boston, Franklin Park boasted zoological gardens, a municipal golf course, and a toboggan run. On rows of benches, reminiscent of the upper deck of a ferry boat and placed strategically at the gates of the park, sat scores of mostly elderly Jews, sunning themselves, reading papers, arguing politics, and unwinding from dead-end jobs in the needle trades. Exuberant children paused at the zoo's stone arches only long enough to eye the venders' balloons and plastic animals before tugging their *bubahs* (grandmothers) and *zadehs* (grandfathers) into the zoo. Inside, tropical birds shared the aviary and sculpted ponds with lazy mallards and freeloading park pigeons. The monkey and elephant houses were a must-see before venturing out on the veldt to view antelopes and camels. Sharp-eyed children could catch a glimpse of lovers, too, entangled on the grass in several cozy glens.

The park served a purpose larger than entertainment and spiritual renewal. For decades Franklin Park had proved the perfect geographic separator for Boston's xenophobic ethnic groups. Lifelong Bostonians understood that their city consisted of invisible lines across which one might shop and visit but not sink roots. The Irish had put up little fuss about leaving middle Roxbury in the 1920s; larger homes and yards awaited just a few blocks west in Jamaica Plain. No one had to waste breath telling the Jews that they were unwanted west of Franklin Park. It was widely known as well that blacks were free to stake their claims to the rundown neighborhoods north of the park provided they steered clear of the Jewish regions to the south and the Irish areas to the east and west. The invisible lines reflected the spirit of Massachusetts. Regardless of whether one's roots were in County Cork, Liberia or Galicia, Bostonians shared the Puritans' tendency to panic at the sight of strangers. And as in many border areas, warfare was not unknown in Franklin Park. Irish youth, in particular, displayed violent contempt for Dorchester's Jews; interviews with Jewish residents who were adolescents in the 1940s and 1950s almost always include detailed descriptions of gang fights in the park. Irish youths from the southern districts of Dorchester and contiguous sections of Roxbury had found the park ideal for staging elaborate ambushes on "kikes" and "sheenies." Spurred by the antisemitic radio broadcasts of Father Charles Coughlin, they occasionally roamed the park and its environs on missions against the "Christ killers." Sometimes, they underestimated their enemies' numerical and tactical strength.

Officials of the Anti-Defamation League of B'nai B'rith kept careful records of the confrontations. The reports reveal a pattern that generally began with an assault by a large group on a smaller group of young men; this was followed by a series of retaliatory strikes that often escalated to more than a hundred youths fighting pitched battles with sticks, knives, and garrison belts. A report on an incident that took place on April 21, 1951, reads as follows: "Two Christian boys exchanged words with a group of Jewish youths in the Park. A fight started and the Christian boys were beaten. Later that night, a group of 15 Christian boys entered the park seeking the assailants of the two youths beaten earlier . . . this group of Christian boys was immediately attacked by a group of 30 to 40 Jewish boys. The Christian youths, outnumbered, took a terrific beating. One of them was so badly hurt that the Jewish youths offered to rush him to the hospital."[3]

Boston police rarely extended themselves when the Irish lads came out on top, which was generally the case. When the Jews prevailed, however, there were court appearances and arraignments for assault and battery. Novelist Mark Mirsky, who, like conductor Leonard Bernstein and journalist Nat Hentoff, had experienced a face scraping on Dorchester sidewalks at the hands of Irish toughs, gave vent to his rage in a passage that described the venomous feelings that many Jews developed toward Boston's *goyyim:* "Boston is a city of grotesques, of midgets, morons, half-wits. A holy city full of maddened, desperate, punch-drunk pilgrims. The faces of the old are worn away by anger and fear into the cruelest expressions. The bodies hunch protectively like turtles, eyes water with disgust. Everyone aspires to be ancient, gnarled."[4] The border skirmishes, however, were almost exclusively the domain of youth. Parish priests and Jewish social workers counseled the combatants to keep the episodes in check. Since injuries were rarely more serious than black eyes or bruised ribs, retaliatory violence was of little concern. The skirmishes never kept the children, the middle-aged, or the elderly out of the park. If testosterone-driven teens wanted to smack each other around, fine; they never bothered anyone else.

Entering Franklin Park's zoological gardens, Ansel became as excited as a child and pointed out the various species of the Roxbury wilds to the big-game hunter. At the park's northeast edge, the councilor gushed, residents in the attached brick apartment houses along Seaver Street could even set their watches by the lion roars of those *balebateshe* (stolid) beasts at feeding time. But Ansel's mood changed when they stood before the empty hippo cage. "The children miss Happy the Hippo, may he rest in peace," he said.

The taciturn visitor finally spoke. "Going price for that kind of wild animal is six thousand dollars."

Ansel stared misty-eyed into the empty cage for a minute before responding. "Three thousand five hundred," he whispered.

"Won't even cover shipping," the hunter responded.

"Forty five hundred, final offer," the lion of Dorchester roared.

"Deal," said the stranger.

Boston's Jews were obsessed with grassroots politics in the 1950s. Decades before former Speaker of the House Thomas "Tip" O'Neill's famous utterance "All politics are local," the Jews of Ward 14 lived the message. Ansel's campaign slogan, "My heart belongs to Ward 14," said it all. As a councilor, and later as a state legislator, he rarely sought entry to the downtown party leadership or seats on shadow committees. His marching orders came from Dorchester's ward bosses, and his main office was a corner table at the G&G. Ironically, the fierce allegiance to local community issues provided Dorchester's Jews with a national reputation. Jewish leaders and lobbyists did not need to advance their causes by having breakfast with their senator in the Senate Dining Room. The national leaders, instead, came to the G&G.

With their growing numbers, Boston's Jews felt increasingly confident about asserting their political will. Candidates for national, state, and local offices had early on recognized the political significance of the ward. Jews, with their historical memories of repression and political impotence, were not about to squander their right to vote. Some had maintained a nostalgic attachment to socialism, but most longed for a place in the political mainstream. Back in 1932 the nation's immigrant Jews responded resoundingly to the message of social justice explicit in the Democratic party of Franklin Delano Roosevelt. Dorchester's Jews adored Roosevelt: they hung on every word of his radio "fireside chats." On the Avenue they named shops, such as the New Deal Fish Market, for the president's policies. In 1936 Roosevelt's limousine traveled down Roxbury's Seaver Street as thousands of cheering residents showered the leader of the free world with rose petals. Turning onto Blue Hill Avenue, the procession was met by more ecstatic throngs. In little more than three decades Boston's Jewish community had grown both large and vibrant enough to rate a prominent campaign stop in the reelection bid of the most powerful man in the Western world.

The G&G stood at the epicenter of Ward 14's political life. Almost since its founding, few candidates felt confident of capturing the increasingly important Jewish vote without tasting the fare and pressing the flesh at the G&G. The restaurant was positively electric on the eve of local and national elections. An enormous wooden bandstand was erected outside the delicatessen, where recorded jingles and live political pitches from scores of soundtrucks competed at a deafening volume for the precious votes of tailors, mechanics, rabbis, pharmacists, and bookies. This candidate for attorney general was good for the Jews; that candidate for Congress favored a Jewish state in Palestine. Each candidate for state Senate or House of Representatives boasted sufficient vision to lead the messiah by the hand down Blue Hill Avenue. For familiar Democratic candidates, Jewish Dorchester was a guaranteed claque and opportunity to be photographed and recorded in friendly territory; for others, it was a proving ground. A dashing hopeful for a seat in Congress, John Fitzgerald Kennedy, had no trouble winning Irish hearts in Charlestown and South Boston. At the G&G the future president made eye contact and munched french fries smothered in *kishke* grease with the best of them, proving in the process that his golden touch extended beyond the city's traditional Catholic wards. Republican presidential candidate Dwight Eisenhower, too, made direct appeals for the Jewish vote at the G&G.

Over coffee and knishes at 2 A.M., regulars would recall in minute detail the torchlight parades for Roosevelt, Eisenhower, and other national luminaries. The most passionate debates, however, centered not on national figures but on the local races, particularly those for city council and the state legislature. With World War II behind them, many ambitious men were determined to make a mark in politics. Pundits hunkered down in the G&G booths and predicted political futures. Young Danny Rudsten, for example, had done the neighborhood proud as a first lieutenant in the U.S. Marine Corps but seemed headstrong and disrespectful of local ward heelers. Blind George Greene had won his seat at the statehouse while a lot of the boys were overseas fighting. Could the popular representative, who had learned to read braille at the Perkins School for the Blind and gone on to Northeastern Law School, hold back tough political challengers? And what about Wilfred Mirsky, the intellectual Polish-born lawyer who distinguished himself in the House as chairman of the state committee on education and author of the Fair Employment Bill? It was one thing to get in tight with the downtown Democratic leadership, but a man could still lose a lot of constituents if he missed too many breakfasts at the G&G; and Mirsky, it seemed, had found some new dining partners.

The exalted place of local politics in Ward 14 could be measured by the fantasies of the patients at the nearby Mattapan State Hospital for the mentally ill. Patients were often found wandering between tables at the G&G in an attempt to garner sufficient signatures to place their names in nomination for state treasurer, senator, or representative. Somehow, the *meshuganahs*, as they were referred to in Yiddish, usually collected sufficient signatures to make the ballot. Inevitable defeats were accepted gracefully, although a hothead or two had been known to fling a cylindrical sugar container at the successful candidate, and on one unfortunate occasion a patient spurned by the voters burned the victor's storefront campaign office to the ground.

Dorchester's Jews suffered fools gladly, just as their fathers and grandfathers had done in the shtetls of Poland and Russia. Fully two decades before state-run departments of mental health implemented programs to mainstream the mentally ill into community settings, Dorchester and Mattapan served as an unself-conscious model. Local bar mitzvah bands played free concerts for the back wards of the Mattapan State Hospital, neighborhood teens sent patients on simple down-and-out patterns during pickup football games on the institution's broad lawn fronting Morton Street, and sympathetic housewives sent used but serviceable clothing to the wards of Mattapan State Hospital (sitting by the window seats at the G&G, husbands watched schizophrenics wander by in familiar suits and hats). In Dorchester charity began at home. The *meshuganahs* generally had free reign of Blue Hill Avenue provided they posed no immediate threat to themselves or others. Those with a dollar to spend preferred the sandwich line at the Parkview or the New Yorker deli to the tranquilizer line back at the nurses' station. Those with nothing could usually coax a few french fries or half-sour pickle slices from the Aleph Tzaddik Aleph boys, who favored the privacy of booths at the G&G while plotting their sexual strategies for upcoming socials with B'nai B'rith girls.

Had Samuel "Chief" Levine determined that one of the Mattapan State patients was to be the ward's newest state representative, it would likely have come to pass. The Chief was a short, burly ward heeler with a broken nose who was rarely seen without an enormous smoldering Garcia Vega cigar extending from the right side of his mouth. The Chief not only breathed life into political allies in the city's Jewish ward but buried many of them as well at his funeral home on Dorchester's Washington Street. Back in the 1920s and 1930s Levine had been a perfect choice for precinct captain for populist Mayor James Michael Curley's ethnic neighborhood armies. Not only was the Chief known by practically every Jew in Ward 14 who had suffered a loss in the family but he also got along famously with the Irish politicians citywide, who respected both his loyalty and uncanny ability for knocking men out with a single punch.

In the 1930s Curley and his precinct bosses like Sam Levine symbolized the weakening grasp of the Boston Brahmins and the rise to power of new ethnic groups. With Curley the Massachusetts Irish served notice that the political dominance of the Brahmins would never again go unchallenged. The mayor was bold and fearless; when the First National Bank of Boston refused the city a loan for a building project, Curley threatened to open a water main under the bank's vault. Even Franklin Roosevelt recognized Curley's power and proffered an ambassadorship back in the early 1930s in exchange for the mayor's support. Curley also elevated political patronage to an art form; the mayor and his minions could extract money from building contractors with the same ease that a diner at a Jewish deli plucks out the savory filling from a *knish*. And no one had learned more about the art of politics from "Hizzoner" than Chief Levine.

Levine had grown up in the North End of Boston, a predominantly Italian district with a liberal sprinkling of Jews. An early knife fight with an Italian youth caused some nerve damage to his arm, making it difficult for him to shave and button his collar in later years. The Chief's formal education was terminated in his junior year at English High School when he coldcocked a teacher who had reportedly taunted him with antisemitic remarks. In 1912, at the age of 19, he was offered a contract to catch for the Boston Red Sox, an idea that was quickly abandoned when the Chief's father, Jacob, learned that his son wouldn't be dismissed from duties on the Jewish Sabbath. A short stint as a sheet metal worker at the Quincy Shipyard during World War I was also called on account of a knockout—of the foreman. The time came to absorb the Chief into the family funeral home business, where he could be expected at least to refrain from clobbering distraught mourners.[5]

The Chief started his day by checking the criminal docket for Jewish names at the Dorchester District Court. A good word from Levine to an assistant district attorney was usually enough to convince the prosecution that a rambunctious Jewish kid should be let off. When fixing court cases, the Chief followed one general rule: if the Jewish kid arrived in court with his mother, he was probably worth saving. If he came alone, even the old lady had given up on him, and the Chief would let the system run its course. Politics usually absorbed the rest of the day. At the Chief's apartment over the Dorchester mortuary, which resembled in miniature Mayor Curley's own office at city hall, people stood in line to secure a few dollars for groceries or a delivery of coal. The needy were always supplied after careful instruction on which candidates deserved their support in upcoming elections. After the passage of the Social Security Act of 1935, the seekers continued to arrive but with different requests. Some sought help in locating apartments roomy enough for large families, others hoped to be graced with thirty-day municipal jobs to take the sting out of a recent layoff, and still others hoped to smooth the entrance for a child into a state university or simply to fix a parking ticket.

Levine relished the role of ward heeler and played it to the hilt. Silk suits, a flashy diamond ring, and a sixteen-cylinder Cadillac were perfect fits for the man who controlled the city's most populous ward. During the 1940s and 1950s the Chief held court in rented space over the Franklin Park Theater with other members of Roxbury's Brunswick Civic Club. There they planned political strategies and hand-lettered political signs for favorites like Ansel, State Representative Benjamin Klebanow, and Judge A. Frank Foster. Phil Briss, a young butcher who courted and later married the Chief's only daughter in 1940, recalled his first visit to the Brunswick Club. The ward bosses, barely visible through the thick cigar smoke, were hard at work on campaign signs. Briss had received a speeding ticket and had been instructed by his sweetheart to bring it to her father. The Chief looked at the ticket briefly, handed it back to Briss, and instructed him to return it to the cop with the following message: "The Chief says to stick this ticket up your ass." Briss found the cop down on Warren Street in Roxbury and, bracing himself for a night stick in the solar plexis, delivered the Chief's message. A broad grin swept across the cop's face as he took the ticket from Briss and ripped it into small pieces.

That blunt approach to neighborhood problem solving began to change during the mayoralty race of 1949, when Curley's political career was eclipsed by a veteran municipal bureaucrat. City Clerk John Hynes was a dignified Irish Catholic whose soft-spoken demeanor had earned him the sobriquet "whispering Johnny." In Hynes, Boston's Brahmins perceived a candidate who would be at once friendly to the business interests of old New Englanders and attractive to the growing cadre of upper-middle-class Irish. Chief Levine sensed that Curley had run his course, but loyalty dictated that he throw the weight of Ward 14 behind his old hero. Hynes, nevertheless, was elected by a narrow margin. Particularly rankling to Levine was the fact that the "Youth for Hynes" campaign was led by a Jewish Harvard Law School graduate and native New Yorker, Jerome Lyle Rappaport.

Even with Curley in defeat, Levine rededicated himself to Curley's vision of providing for the "little people." During the weeks before Passover, Thanksgiving, and Christmas, the Chief and his fellow Brunswick Club members served Jewish shops along Blue Hill Avenue with a nonnegotiable list of the items needed to provide festive holiday baskets for the needy of all races. No one had to be asked twice. When the burly Chief told a local butcher that an eighteen-pound turkey would greatly enhance the holiday season for a local family, he didn't mean fourteen pounds and he didn't mean maybe.

None of the largesse ever found its way into the pockets of the Chief. In fact, the Chief was forced to limit his public appearances for the sake of economic survival. "I wouldn't know when the hell I was going to stick my hand in my pocket to dish out a twenty dollar bill for some guy in trouble," Levine told a reporter. "It always cost me from day to day. It was spontaneous and I always gave with a smile. Votes cost me money and they cost me favors. I got jobs. I got housing. I got anything they asked me for. I expected the same in return. If Chief Levine told them to vote for Mickey Mouse, then they voted for Mickey Mouse. I paid for and was accorded that kind of loyalty."[6]

With Curley no longer running interference, the style of the Chief and other ward bosses clashed with that of the new reformists in Hynes's city hall. Jerome Rappaport and his reform-driven college activists joined forces with Yankee Republican Henry Shattuck to form the New Boston Committee, which aimed to weed out "Curleyism" from the city council and school committee. A charter reform reduced the number of city councilors from twenty-four ward representatives to nine at-large members, thus weakening the position of old guard power brokers. The ambitious Rappaport, who served as Hynes's chief assistant, pressed forward with a vision of a revitalized Boston. National magazines tracked the career of the brash young lawyer, and a whisper campaign began that the native New Yorker might even be slated to replace Hynes, thus becoming the city's first Jewish mayor. The Chief doubled his efforts to maintain a grip on Ward 14. Levine's funeral chapel was always empty on Saturdays owing to the Jewish prohibition against burying the dead on the Sabbath. Each Saturday morning, therefore, the Chief and his cronies set up folding tables at the back of the chapel and piled them high with sandwiches, coffee, and schnapps for an open reception for friendly city politicians. Throughout the decade and into the early 1960s, handpicked local candidates had the opportunity to rub shoulders with elected and appointed officials from neighboring wards. Rising stars, like Massachusetts Secretary of State Kevin White, a future mayor, were introduced around. Even U.S. Representative John W. McCormack, who would go on to serve as Speaker of the House from 1962–1971 dispensed political wisdom at the mortuary. The Chief was quick to let everyone know that his cherished Ward 14 still had the numbers.

The sight of Rappaport and his uppity reformers sickened the Chief. Why, he wondered, couldn't the editorial writers see through the phony Harvard accents and self-righteous palaver about good government? The first Jewish mayor of Boston indeed! If the city was ever to elect a Jewish mayor, Levine vowed, it would be Julius Ansel, not Jerome Lyle Rappaport.

Community building in the nation's Hub (the locals' term for Boston) had never been an easy task for Boston's Jews. They had been forced to play catch-up with their cousins who had settled in other urban centers like Philadelphia, which claimed a significant Jewish community in colonial times, and New York, where Jews had arrived at the major port of entry since 1654. Boston had only a marginal Jewish presence before the great immigration waves of the 1880s. To be sure, the Pilgrims had expressed a profound fascination with the Hebrew faith, but it did not extend to living, breathing Jews. William Bradford, one of the original passengers on the Mayflower in 1620, was stricken by the very notion of the Hebrew language: "I have had a longing desire to see with my own eyes, something of that most ancient language, the holy tongue, in which the Law and Oracles of God were written, and in which God and angels spoke to the holy patriarchs of old time."[7] But Jews, like Quakers and Papists, knew enough to steer a wide berth of the

Massachusetts Bay Colony, where public burnings of heretics were not uncommon.

The first Jew to rise to prominence in Boston managed to do so by accepting conversion. Judah Monis, an Italian-born peddler, delighted the Harvard faculty in 1720 when he submitted an original manuscript on Hebrew grammar. Harvard Professor Harry Wolfson, who would examine the manuscript more than 200 years later, found it "full of grammatical errors from title page to the end," a flaw that easily escaped the notice of Harvard President Increase Mather and his son, Cotton Mather, who both longed to convert Monis as a step to "make ready the Jewish people for the Lord."[8] Monis, who made up in prudence what he lacked in integrity, readily accepted the offer of conversion with full knowledge that Harvard faculty positions were reserved for Christians. In 1722 before a large assemblage in Harvard's Common Hall, he received his baptism and, a short time later, his instructorship.

Other notable early Boston Jews, like Judah Touro, also kept their public distance from the Jewish community, preferring to be known for philanthropic work with churches and general charities rather than with comparable Jewish institutions. In later years Touro, who was responsible for providing funds in 1839 to construct the Bunker Hill Monument, relented and provided large grants to New York's Mt. Sinai Hospital and even helped fund the construction of an early Jewish settlement outside the walls of Jerusalem's Old City.

Jews would not come to Boston in any significant numbers until 1840, when several hundred arrived by sea with a larger group of German immigrants. The German Jews founded the city's first synagogue in 1852, Ohabei Shalom, on Warrenton Street. Within weeks the congregation split along ethnic lines, with the "real" Germans taking umbrage at the presence of the "Polish" Germans originally from the province of Posen. The ethnic stratification between Germans, however, became irrelevant with the arrival in the 1880s of the "Russians." From 1880 to 1914 almost three million Jews fled the Russian Empire for the United States to escape the pogroms and infamous May Laws, which forced them into ghettoes in the Pale of Settlement. Of that number, approximately seventy-five thousand found their way to Boston. As in cities nationwide, the newcomers to Boston were greeted with suspicion, particularly by the city's increasingly prosperous German Jews. These fastidious German Jews perceived that their privileged positions were secure only to the extent that their community remained small and inoffensive. In just three decades many German Jews had moved from small flats in the North End to larger units in the South End and Roxbury. In 1877 they had even presented a successful candidate for the U.S. House of Representatives: Leopold Morse. These early assimiliated Jews believed that the "Russian" newcomers, unwashed and uncouth, would surely provoke hatred toward Jews and in the process diminish their own stock. Rabbi Solomon Schindler of Temple Israel, the city's second synagogue, led the assault against the "Russians" by promoting the prevailing notion that the refugees were "a bane to the country and a curse to the Jews."[9] Regardless of whether the immigrants were pious Poles, educated Litvaks, Roumanian merchants, or Galician peasants, their coreligionists sought any means to cut them off. That included denying the newcomers charity from already established Jewish social services, an act that prompted a shipload of 415 "Russians" in 1882 to be turned around in the port of Boston and rerouted to New York. That same winter seventy-five "Russians" made public their desire to return to their motherland, based largely on the inhospitable reception by German Jews. Reports of the "Russians" sitting idly in alms houses and waiting for Christian charity created the first of many public relations disasters for Boston's early Jewish community. Only the ancient fear of *ma yommru hagoyyim* ("What will the Gentiles say?") finally compelled the leaders of the community to take minimal action to absorb the newcomers.[10]

But "Russians" continued to pour into the East Boston Immigration Building, where they faced an immediate barrage of tests the results of which would determine rejection or sanctuary. The average "Russian" carried only nine dollars to the "golden land," a sum that hardly convinced many immigration officials that they would not wind up wards of the state. Others tried desperately to convince medical officers that troublesome cases of conjunctivitis were not chronic but merely the temporary result of washing with sea water. Most, however, made it through processing, settled in tenements near their point of disembarkation, and thrived. In 1900 Boston's Irish Catholics pointed proudly to a birthrate almost double that of the national average of 16.40 per thousand, but the "Russians" put the Papists to shame on their own turf, recording an astounding birthrate of 94.6 per thousand.

At the turn of the century Jews and Italians made up more than 80 percent of the city's North End, and tens of thousands of Jews flocked to nearby Chelsea, an industrial town just north of Boston. Chelsea's Jews crowded into wooden tenements and worked at menial tasks shunned by earlier immigrants, largely the buying and selling of junk. On Palm Sunday of 1908 fire broke out in the back of one of the mile-and-a-half-square city's numerous junkyards. High spring winds propelled the blaze, which spread to nearby tenements. In a few hours 492 acres were scorched, and seventeen thousand Jews were left homeless. Most of the displaced citizens of Chelsea migrated across the Mystic River into Roxbury and Dorchester, where the extension of the streetcar lines from the center of the Hub encouraged the new immigrants to explore Boston's outer neighborhoods.

The coming of the Jews to Roxbury and Dorchester would eventually send many Yankees and Irish trudging down the paths of neighborhood change. The process, however, was gradual. Historian Theodore White, chronicler of U.S. presidents, grew up on Dorchester's Erie Street in the 1920s. As a boy, White loved to rummage through the discarded items left in the attic by former Yankee owners. It was, for him, a connection to old New England. Surrounded by old brass bedsteads and stained glass lamps, the young White would pore over pages of old Scribner's and National Geographic magazines. In the musty attic White relived the exciting exploits of Admiral Farragut and General Grant. He descended from his attic into another world: Erie Street was a favorite haunt of horse-cart peddlers who had established an active marketplace ancillary to the main action on Blue Hill Avenue. Yiddish-speaking newcomers from Eastern Europe stared curiously at never-before-seen fruits, such as bananas, pineapples, and the enormous twenty-five–cent watermelons that the peddlers had bought in bulk at the Faneuil Hall marketplace. White was mesmerized by the cries and yodels of the peddlers. The sales pitches fell silent only on Friday evening with the advent of the Jewish Sabbath. At sundown on Saturday the cacophony resumed as peddlers reappeared with carts piled high with factory seconds on socks, shirts, and underwear.

For White, neighborhood change was an artistic admixture of conventionalized poses and flowing movements:

There is an ethnic ballet; slow yet certain, in every big American city that I have reported, which underlies its politics. The ballet is different in each city. In the larger cosmopolitan cities of the Eastern Seaboard, old stock Protestants gave way to the Irish, who gave way in turn to Italians or Jews, who gave way in turn to blacks. Chicago's lower six wards also passed from Irish to Jewish to black; the old Jewish synagogues, still engraved with the commandments in Hebrew, converted to black churches. So, too, did Harlem pass from Irish to Jewish to black. Even in Los Angeles, Boyle Heights became Jewish, then black. In the Midwest and along the Great Lakes, the ethnic ballet involves other groups—Poles, Slavs, Germans, Scandinavians. But in Boston, specifically, the Jews leapfrogged the Irish, moving from the West End of the core city to Dorchester, which the old stock Protestants were leaving for the southern suburbs.[11]

Another Boston historian, Francis Russell, grew up nearby on Mattapan's Wellington Hill, a Protestant stronghold, during the same period. "To live on Wellington Hill then was like living on top of the world. The only roots I have are there, somewhere under the twelve-winded sky between the stone wall and the pignut trees," he would wax eloquently many years later.[12] Five miles from the center of Brahmin aristocracy on Beacon Hill, middle-class Protestant families like Russell's had found their own divine heights. From Wellington Hill they enjoyed the views of the densely-wooded Blue Hills to the south and on a clear day could even glimpse the obelisk of the Custom House to the north. The standard patterns of the one- and two-family homes might not have impressed the Coolidges or Lowells, but they suited the bank clerks, salesmen, and teachers named Dodd, Blair, and Kent. It was a strictly Republican enclave, free of the Roman Catholic Church and Boston Irish who were then beginning to tighten their grip on municipal jobs and services. Jews, Russell recalled, if considered at all were thought of only in "medieval" terms.

During his boyhood Russell loved to knock about the Avenue —staring at the old bearded men in their long black coats and black skullcaps and glancing timidly at the older women in their modest shawls. Frequently, he would pass early summer afternoons by standing outside the open windows of the area Hebrew schools, from which the unusual murmur of the pupils mixed intoxicatingly with the aromas of lime trees, nickel loaves of bread, poppyseed cakes, and unusual smoked fish.

Wellington Hill had been developed at the turn of the century by Wellington Holbrook, a ne'er-do-well who inherited the land shortly after his graduation from Harvard. Holbrook, who scored the winning touchdown in the Harvard–Yale football game of 1898, was still living on past gridiron glory when his luck changed in 1906. It was then that the Boston Elevated Street Railway Company extended its services roughly two miles, from Grove Hall to Mattapan Square. Holbrook's inheritance suddenly acquired value as a potential streetcar suburb. Streets were cut and sections divided into house lots, usually of minimum legal dimension. Dorchester realtors advertised Wellington Hill as a "clerical," rather than an "executive," neighborhood.[13] On a clerk's weekly salary of $20, it was possible to buy a home for $2,500 on Wellington Hill, even if one was forced to carry a second or even third mortgage.

Wellington Hill would face profound changes with the coming of the Jews. The newcomers took the lowlands along Blue Hill Avenue, the failed toll road formerly operated by the Brush Hill Turnpike in the mid-nineteenth century. Speculative builders were quick to welcome the Jews by constructing three-deckers, usually spaced apart by the minimum fourteen feet required by law. From the summit of Wellington Hill, Russell and his fellow Protestants watched as "Kosher" signs and odd wares appeared in the storefronts along the "Avenue of Jewville." The Protestant hill dwellers viewed "Jewville" from a distance until shortly after the end of World War I, when one of their own sold a two-family house (which he had purchased in 1915 for $3,500) to a Jewish fur trader named Isadore White for double the original price. The sale was viewed as undermining the neighborhood's Puritan foundation, and the Robinson family, the first to sell to the newcomers, were no longer welcome at the tennis club and retreated behind closed shades for their last month on the Hill. But as postwar inflation escalated housing costs, "for sale" signs appeared in the yards of other clever Yankees. The transition, nevertheless, was gradual. Jew and Gentile rarely exchanged a heated word. The Protestant remnant grew accustomed to the sight of the newcomers and grudgingly came to respect their talent for acculturation. Although the young sons and daughters of the immigrants who arrived at the Martha Baker School were unable to speak a word of English, they mastered their subjects before the end of the school year. Many would pass the admissions test for the competitive Latin School, which each year sent more students on to Harvard College than any other public school in the nation.

Each year, as the Norway maples on the Hill grew another few inches, a few more of the neighborhood's original Protestant inhabitants retreated. They sold their homes for a handsome profit and relocated, for the most part, to the leafy towns west and south of Boston. Throughout the 1950s and early 1960s, Russell often returned for nostalgic walks around the Hill. The bearded old men and the women in shawls—the Jews popularized in the images of Roman Vishniac—had long since vanished. The Hill was once again a bourgeois neighborhood, populated now by Feldmans, Goldmans, and Hymans. As Russell retraced the paths of his childhood, he recalled passing by a two-family brick house guarded by two small cement lions. Young couples, drinks in hand, stood chatting under the breezeway. A young Jewish housewife half-smiled at Russell as he ambled by; he wished that she would ask him to stop and share a drink. The Boston historian longed to share with the new Hill residents "a placid, timeless moment, before the first stars came out."[14]

In 1930 Dorchester would boast almost one quarter of a million residents, roughly one-third of the city's entire population. To satisfy the demand for housing, builders had erected more than five thousand wooden triple-deckers by 1925. The triple-decker soon became synonymous with Dorchester. The unique housing style offered a compromise between a worker's cottage and crowded wooden apartment buildings. For the most part, they were designed not by architects but by entrepreneurial builders. The earliest of the species were built without balconies or ornamentation, but by the turn of the century the style had shifted to towered bays and balconies with fanciful cornices. By the late 1920s, when the last of the triple-deckers were built, the style had once again shifted back to the minimalism of the Prairie-Modern period. Regardless of style, the triple-deckers appeared to be a sound investment for newly arriving Jewish immigrants. Owner-occupants could live in one unit, lodge extended family in a second, and rent the third. The style also contributed greatly to neighborhood cohesion. With their homes set close together with small setbacks, parents easily kept watch on children playing in the streets below and neighbors casually exchanged information across balconies.

The northern border of Jewish Boston was Grove Hall, a busy residential and commercial center eight blocks beyond the Franklin Park Zoo. The area presented a visitor with an immediate contrast in housing styles, ranging from handsome Victorians and solid brick apartment buildings to wooden triple-deckers. A few blocks further north, in lower Roxbury, surface blight was advancing upon the small frame houses built for workers in the late-nineteenth century. Lower Roxbury had long served as a way station for various ethnic groups. The Irish ruled in the 1870s and 1880s, staying long enough to save for homes in more desirable sections of the city. Canadians, mostly Nova Scotians in the building trades, followed. By the early 1930s, however, the Jews had already established a three-decade presence in much of Roxbury and Dorchester. By the early 1950s the majority of the city's forty thousand blacks lived between lower Roxbury and the South End at the edge of Boston's business and financial district.[15]

Since they arrived en masse at the turn of the century, Boston's Jews had served as a convenient buffer between black neighborhoods in lower Roxbury and the Irish neighborhoods in the eastern section of nearby Dorchester. It was, for most concerned, a cozy decades-long arrangement. The "two-toilet" Irish, who had replaced the Yankee estate owners at the turn of the century, lavished care on their handsome Victorians in the eastern reaches of Dorchester and did not welcome strangers who might drive down property values. The "block park" landscaping characteristic of Irish Dorchester had proved conducive to both privacy and community building: on one hand, spacious homes were surrounded by sufficient open ground to offer the advantages of family estates, and, on the other, the absence of boundary fences, walls, and vegetation encouraged contact with neighbors. With the expansion of the streetcar lines, the Irish residents of Jones Hill and Mount Bowdoin in Dorchester commuted happily to jobs in the city center just a few miles to the north.[16] The Jews, too,

found life comfortable in the spacious two-family homes characteristic of middle and upper Roxbury. It was expected that the
Jews, as latecomers to the city, would live next to the ramshackle
houses in lower Roxbury, where many of the city's small black
population (only 2 percent of the city's 560,000 residents at the
turn of the century) resided. The occasional "Black Brahmin" who
fancied a house in upper Roxbury could expect no resistance from
the Jews, newcomers themselves. Similar incursions, however,
were unthinkable in Irish strongholds. In Boston, arguably the
country's most insular city, nothing was more important than
finding one's niche.

In xenophobic and largely Catholic Boston, however, antisemitism was never far from the surface. It boiled over in the 1940s
when a virulently antisemitic Jesuit priest, Father Leonard Feeney,
derided Jews as "horrid, degenerate hook-nosed perverts" during
his sermons on Boston Common. Interdenominational cooperation was advanced, however, by no less a figure than the city's
enormously popular Cardinal Richard J. Cushing. The South
Boston native's elevation to cardinal in 1944 heartened the city's
Jews. He not only boasted several Jewish friends who had helped
him with fund-raising for the Archdiocese but his own sister had
married a Jew, whom the cardinal called "the best Christian I
know."[17] Jewish representatives who approached the cardinal
during the early 1950s were also assured that he would take a
personal interest in putting an end to the assaults in Franklin Park.
He was true to his word. When the cardinal took the further step of
stripping Feeney of his priestly authority, the Jews were sure
they'd found a friend.

The spiritual life of Boston Jewry also changed dramatically
shortly before World War II. Many of the Jews who reached
America's shores before the turn of the century had been anxious
to dispose of their immigrant baggage. Largely merchants and
tradesmen, they had made a conscious decision to trade their
Orthodox traditions for more Americanized practices and customs.
The city's earliest synagogues, like those nationwide, conformed
to Protestant models, placing emphasis on English services, family
pews, and decorum.[18] Later arrivals, however, included deeply
religious Jews who had lost all hope of religious freedom in
Eastern Europe. With their arrival, it was no longer possible to

pretend that American Judaism was practiced solely in the sanitized Reform temples. In Boston, Orthodox Jews soon developed dozens of *shtibels* (unpretentious synagogues usually located in converted houses) throughout Roxbury and Dorchester, consecrating them with the names of once-beloved Eastern European villages or provinces. Among the new arrivals were internationally renowned rabbis who steeped themselves in Jewish learning and cared little for taking on the appearances of "regule [regular] Yankees."

Rabbi Mordecai Savitsky, the spiritual leader of Congregation Chevra Shas on Ashton Street in Dorchester, was reputed by patriots of Jewish Boston to possess the greatest memory of any living rabbi. Savitsky amazed his disciples with his ability to flawlessly memorize hundreds of pages of the Babylonian Talmud. Letters from religious Jews worldwide arrived at the sage's modest apartment asking for rulings on fine points of Jewish law. In the spirit of American enterprise, Rabbi Savitsky parlayed his steel-trap mind and knowledge of ritual slaughter into impressive profits. "Sioux City Savitsky," as he was called by neighborhood wags, began to exert his authority over the religious inspectors of a large number of kosher slaughtering houses throughout the Midwest and by the 1950s had earned both a place in neighborhood legend as well as unusual scrutiny of his consulting practice from inquisitive IRS agents.

No religious leader in Roxbury, however, surpassed Rabbi Joseph Soloveitchik, the rabbi's rabbi. The scion of a line of Lithuanian rabbis, Soloveitchik emigrated to the United States and settled on Ruthven Street in Roxbury in 1932. By the 1950s he would be regarded worldwide as the unchallenged leader of modern Orthodoxy. Soloveitchik, despite his disregard for publicity, quickly established his reputation as the foremost authority on Jewish law and commuted several times each week to New York's Yeshiva University to teach advanced students for rabbinic ordination. Soloveitchik, however, was never a prophet in his own city. Internecine conflicts between the Eastern European Jews exceeded at times those between the newcomers and the already established. The "Russians" condemned the Litvaks, who in turn dismissed the Poles as oafs. For their part, the Poles kept a wary eye on the thieving Rumanians who, in turn, rejected the abject

Galicians.[19] Almost all, however, adhered to the tenets of Orthodox Judaism. Shortly after his arrival in Boston, Soloveitchik was recommended by national rabbinic organizations to assume the title of Chief Rabbi of Boston. That appointment, as well as other attempts to establish Soloveitchik as a central authority, was blocked by a group of local Orthodox rabbis who resented their brilliant colleague and jealously guarded their control over the provision of kosher certificates to local shops and restaurants. Soloveitchik would never assume a permanent pulpit in Boston, choosing instead to ride the circuit of local Orthodox synagogues. Outside of Boston Soloveitchik's oral discourses attracted thousands of devotees from across the United States, including unconventional scholars, truth seekers, and a variety of students and theologians. For them, the "Rav" was the voice of authenticity and sophistication. But back in the city, Soloveitchik's lectures drew surprisingly few.

Locally, the Rav directed his energy and authority into the cause of Jewish education. In 1937 Soloveitchik and his wife Tonya founded the first Jewish day school in New England. It was named the Maimonides School in honor of the twelfth-century rabbinic authority, codifier, and royal physician. Convinced that the "most wholesome type of Jew is one within whom is integrated the secular knowledge that fits him for the American scene and the religious and spiritual wealth of his own tradition," the Rav began to recruit boys and girls of elementary school age. But opposition to the school soon surfaced from wealthy Jewish businessmen who believed parochial schools would hinder the integration of American Jews into the mainstream. Louis Kirstein, vice president of Filene's Department Store and a board member of Bloomingdale's, Abraham and Strauss, and a number of Jewish organizations, tried unsuccessfully to convince Soloveitchik to abandon his plans.

The great rabbis like Soloveitchik and Savitsky exerted little political leadership in Ward 14. Because the main gathering places, such as the G&G, were not kosher, no Orthodox rabbi would be seen setting foot on the premises. In other areas of life the Orthodox rabbis held tremendous sway over their congregants, providing guidance on mates, charitable gifts, dietary laws, and even the proper time of the month for marital relations. Rulings from both Soloveitchik and Savitsky were actively sought out by members of Israel's religious parties, but on the local political scene the rabbis had little influence.

The contrapuntal melodies of Jewish Dorchester were heard most clearly in the hours before sundown on Friday, the advent of the Jewish Sabbath. Traditional Jews speak of a unique peacefulness that descends with *Shabbat,* the twenty-four hours during which there will be no business problems, no intrusion by radio or television, and no distractions by spirit-numbing tasks. But the hours before sundown are a frantic race to secure the festive foods necessary to welcome the Sabbath "queen." Along Blue Hill Avenue, Jewish housewives frantically searched for the freshest chicken or the perfect braided *hallah* (bread) to set upon a clean white tablecloth. Husbands rushed home from work to change their clothes for Friday night services, where they would praise the King of the Universe who, "with wisdom, opens the gates of heaven, changes the times and causes the seasons to alternate."

Friday afternoons, too, were special for the neighborhood's self-proclaimed "intown degenerates." It was then that grown men would skip off from day jobs to converge on the nearby schoolboy stadium in Franklin Park for the afternoon high school football matchups. As their fathers prepared for *shul,* the "degenerates" gathered high above the stadium's fifty-yard line and wagered not only on the outcome of the game but on the outcome of a half, a quarter, and even a single play. Most Boston schoolboys were too lackadaisical to attend the contests, leaving the wise guys as the most animated spectators. More than once, a grown-up in a sharkskin suit had to be restrained by coaches after rushing the field to berate a halfback from Boston Technical or Boston English who would have been amazed to learn that the pass dropped coming out of the backfield had cost a spectator an entire week's paycheck.

Their appetites whetted, the "degenerates" moved on to the candlepin bowling alleys. Congregating behind groups of adolescent bowlers, they would wager on the outcome of attempts at spares and total pinfall. It was possible to drift between four bowling alleys along Blue Hill Avenue, but the favorite spot was Sam's in Mattapan, which also offered the possibility of action on eight pool tables. Savvy gamblers factored in the odd behavior of the one-legged proprietor, who was given to hobbling away from his cash register to ceremoniously ban a player for some real or imagined breach of bowling etiquette.

While most of Dorchester's Jews sat down to partake of the traditional Sabbath meal, the "degenerates" would hole up in Ye Ole Brown Jug, an incongruously named bar and Chinese restaurant. There they would consume huge platters of lobster sauce and pore over racing sheets. A side trip to the market for cigarettes usually meant an opportunity to put a dollar on the illegal number, contemptuously referred to as the "nigger pool."

The "degenerates," like the great rabbis, held a cherished place in the community. Pegged as unaggressive and bookish, Jews worldwide have taken special pleasure in relating tales of their criminal element. Even the great poet laureate of Palestine, Hayyim Nahman Bialik, was reported to be rapturous in the years before the establishment of the Jewish state on learning of the arrest of a Jewish second-story man. Others repeated with gusto an apocryphal tale of a synagogue for pickpockets in Warsaw where a sign warned worshippers to exert extra caution when shutting their eyes to recite the *shema.* An authentic community, after all, boasted a few thieves and con men along with scholars, statesmen, and proper burghers. But the seedier elements in Dorchester, Roxbury, and Mattapan could not compete for the minds and hearts of the neighborhood youth. The goal in Jewish Boston was still acceptance at Harvard College, not distinguishing oneself in eight ball at Cutler's poolroom. The "degenerates" were considered neither heroes nor villains. They were, in the popular parlance, "a bunch of harmless schmucks."

It is of little surprise that Dorchester's Jews so easily accepted both scholars and bookmakers. Cut off from religious and ethnic diversity by sociopolitical boundaries, Boston Jews heralded the diversity of class and personality in their insular neighborhoods. As Julius Ansel knew, there was no zoo without both range animals and river beasts. And there was no community without at least the strong perception of diversity.

But Ansel would not succeed in bringing his hippo to the Franklin Park Zoo. "Putzi" would indeed arrive in Boston, but city port authorities would seize the animal because the politician had not secured the needed documentation. The high-handed bureau-

crats instead sold the beast to a private zoo in western Massachusetts. In a few short years the downtown politicians would betray
the faith of Boston's inner-city Jews as well. By the 1960s, the
traditional Jewish prayer of gratitude exclaiming *meshane
habriyot* ("who makes the creatures so very different") would fall
silent along Blue Hill Avenue.

Movers and Shakers

The Early Exodus to the Suburbs, *1951–1954*

In the spring of 1930 Lewis Weinstein, a 25-year-old student at Harvard Law School, was hard at work on his thesis in the basement of the college's Landgell Hall. Weinstein's research focused on the intricacies of federal jurisdiction, a subject he studied under his favorite professor, Felix Frankfurter. Lately, however, Weinstein had been distracted from his thesis work. He kept returning, instead, to a nearby open shelf that was crammed with transcripts of the 1916 Senate Judiciary Committee's confirmation of Supreme Court Justice Louis Brandeis. The promising law student was thoroughly intrigued by Brandeis, arguably America's most brilliant Supreme Court Justice and the country's foremost Jewish leader.

Weinstein pored over hundreds of pages of transcripts that detailed the bitter struggle between pro- and anti-Brandeis forces. Leading the battle against confirmation was the Boston Brahmin community, led by Massachusetts's Senator Henry Cabot Lodge. Brandeis's detractors, citing lack of "judicial temperament" and unprofessional conduct before the Boston Bar, sought to block the appointment. Arguing in favor of confirmation were union leaders, students, and university faculty members who perceived in Brandeis the future of American legal reform. Supporters, like the Reverend A. A. Berle, lashed out at Brandeis's critics. "Long and unchallenged control of everything in the Commonwealth has given many of these gentlemen the perfectly natural feeling that whoever is not approved by them is ipso facto a person who is either 'dangerous' or lacking in 'judicial temperament' . . . They simply cannot realize, and do not, that a long New England ancestry is not prima facie a trusteeship for everything in New England."[1]

Harvard law students knew that Brandeis's academic record at the school was unsurpassed. Ambitious Jewish law students like Weinstein also knew that Brandeis had managed, at least for a time, to cross profitably between the disparate worlds of Brahmin and Jewish society. That the Brahmins would turn so totally against one whom they had previously embraced was a lesson carefully noted by a clever student who believed he too possessed unusual qualities of leadership. With the patience of the successful lawyer he would later become, Lew Weinstein searched through the paper trail left by Brandeis researchers to determine the smooth spots and pitfalls on the road to success.

Jewish leaders in Massachusetts have long been intoxicated with the stature and brilliance of Louis Dembitz Brandeis. But few, if any, have chosen to follow his exhortations for a democratized Jewish community. Brandeis, the son of prosperous German-Jewish immigrants, arrived at Harvard Law School from Louisville, Kentucky, in 1875. For an outsider, it was the most opportune of times to discover Boston. Xenophobia was out of fashion and Eastern European Jews, with their strange garb and stranger habits, had yet to arrive and to interfere with the social position of the city's German Jews. The Boston Brahmin community had rejected Jew hatred as irrational, lumping it together with other ills of society including slavery and child labor. Philosopher William James, upon learning that Jews were not allowed at one of his favorite New England hotels, had sent the proprietor a message stating, "I propose to return the boycott."[2]

There was little in Brandeis's background that would suggest his eventual devotion to populist causes. His preparatory studies took place largely at the elite Annen-Realschule in Dresden, Germany. His classmates at Harvard Law School were, almost without exception, the wealthy sons of New England patrician families. But Brandeis quickly fell under the sway of Brahmin intellectuals like Edward Everett Hale and Julia Ward Howe who waged public campaigns to welcome immigrants into the intellectual life of the city. His biographers have noted Brandeis's penchant for copying inspirational passages from the work of his favorite author, Ralph Waldo Emerson, during this period. Among his favorites: "Every man takes care that his neighbor shall not cheat him. But a day comes when he begins to care that he does not cheat his neighbor. Then all goes well. He has changed his market cart into a chariot of the sun."[3] Brandeis won almost immediate acceptance as an honorary Brahmin. Although destined for enormous wealth, he disdained, in solid Brahmin tradition, the open pursuit of money in favor of public service and self-reliance.

After graduation the young lawyer crossed easily between the worlds of Brahmin gentility and Jewish commerce. With law partner Samuel Warren, the son of a prominent New England family, Brandeis was introduced to the social world of the Union Boat Club and Dedham Polo Club. Brandeis was also the darling of the city's German-Jewish elite. Jacob Hecht, a wealthy merchant and leader of the Boston Jewish community, brought the young lawyer the first case he would argue before the Massachusetts Supreme Judicial Court. Other prominent Jewish businesses, including the Filene and Eisemann merchant families, Lehman Pickert and Company, and Jacob Dreyfus and Son, quickly sought his counsel.

From the perspective of Jewish leadership, Brandeis had the good fortune to reach his prime in the early part of the twentieth century. It was a period when, as historian Melvin Urofsky noted, "there were giants on the earth."[4] One of the most compelling and bitterly debated issues in this pre-Holocaust period, was the democratization of the American Jewish community. At one end of the spectrum were the prosperous and Americanized German Jews who sought to maintain their control of Jewish affairs through wealth and political connections. High on their agenda were the abrogation of the Russo-American commerce treaty and the protection of the civil and religious rights of American Jews. At the other end of the spectrum was the Jewish labor movement, particularly the Eastern European–dominated garment unions. In open and democratic elections union members elected hundreds of functionaries to advance the causes of medical care, cooperative housing, and worker education.

Brandeis stood at the epicenter of a war between "the masses and the classes" in America's Jewish community. Spokesmen for the self-selected and elitist German Jewish leaders, including jurist Louis Marshall and financier Jacob Schiff, clashed mightily with Brandeis and Rabbi Stephen Wise, who sought to advance the working class agendas of the Eastern European immigrants.

In 1915 Schiff, the German-Jewish founder of the American Jewish Committee, gave expression in the pages of *American Hebrew* magazine to an almost dizzyingly undemocratic vision of national Jewish leadership:

> At all times in Jewish life there have risen men who have endeavored to lead the masses for their own purposes. It began at the dawn of history, it began when our forefathers were about to enter the land of promise, when Korach arose and said to Moses and Aaron—"We are all leaders, we are all prophets"—and what was the consequence? Our forefathers were on the border line of the promised land, and just as they were to enter it, God in his wisdom ordained "you shall stay forty years, a full generation, in the desert until the present generation shall have gone out of existence and a united Israel alone shall enter the promised land." And so it is now again here with us. Do we really want, just as we are on the borderland and have actually gone across the border line . . . [to] the United States of America . . . do we want again to have this firebrand thrown into our midst, this firebrand that says we do not trust our old leaders, we want new leaders chosen upon a democratic basis? If you really want to do this, I say to you, leaders cannot be elected. True leaders must develop, true leaders must have proven their value. Office holders can be

elected, but we Jews, to gain what we must obtain, not for ourselves but for our unhappy and miserable brethren in Europe, must have proven leaders, and not office holders.[5]

Four days prior to his nomination to the Supreme Court in 1916, Brandeis offered an alternate vision for the selection of Jewish leaders during a lecture before an overflow crowd at Carnegie Hall. Brandeis suggested the creation of an American Jewish congress that aimed to forge America's Jews into a permanent, democratic ethnic polity.[6] He insisted that "the rights of the Jewish people can be gained only by traveling the same road as other peoples travel—the road of democracy—through the people's asserting their own authority in their own interest. The demand for democracy in the consideration of the Jewish problem is not a matter of form—it is of the essence. It is a fundamental Jewish conception, as it is the basic American method."[7]

Over subsequent decades, Brandeis developed into the model of a Jewish leader, distinguishing himself in both the Jewish and non-Jewish worlds, altering Jewish history for decades through his espousal of Zionism, and working out a meaningful approach to being Jewish and American.[8] Few Jewish leaders have shown greater talent for political brinksmanship than Brandeis, who managed to amass a fortune in legal fees from corporate clients while simultaneously fighting political patronage, advocating election law reform, and supporting trade unionism. One of the boldest positions staked out by Brandeis was his insistence that strong ethnic self-interest need never be at odds with basic tenets of American equality. The message was hardly appreciated by proponents of Reform Judaism, who had sought by all means to "de-ethnicize" their religion.

On a sweltering July 4th afternoon in 1915 Brandeis pounded home this message at Boston's Independence Day celebration at Faneuil Hall. "The new nationalism adopted by America proclaims that each race or people, like each individual, has the right and duty to develop, and that only through such differentiated development will high civilization be attained. Not until these principles of nationalism, like those of democracy, are generally accepted will liberty be fully attained and minorities be secure in their rights. Not until then can the foundation be laid for a lasting peace among the nations."[9] Although Brandeis made no specific reference to Zionism, many of the Jews in the audience perceived the message that absolute loyalty to the United States was consistent with support for a Jewish state in Palestine. Others in the audience, including his host, Mayor Curley, concluded that Brandeis meant "hyphenated" Americans need never take a back seat to patrician interests.

Old-line Bostonians, who had staked out their own sections of the historic hall to hear the gaunt and passionate speaker, felt betrayed. Decades before, they had conferred on Brandeis an honorary membership in Brahmin society. In return, he had prepared legal attacks on Brahmin-owned insurance companies and the New Haven Railroad, siding openly with labor and consumers against the financial security of landed families. In writings with titles such as "Other People's Money" and the "Curse of Bigness," he had pointed to the dangers of elusive economic forces that undermine collectivities, good people's best intentions notwithstanding. The Brahmins would not forget the slight. The following year anti-Brandeis petitions would reach the nation's capital at the height of the nominating proceedings for Brandeis's elevation to the Supreme Court. The petitions bore the venerable Brahmin names of Lowell, Adams, Sargent, Peabody, Putnam, and Coolidge. Brandeis would nevertheless emerge victorious in his quest for a seat on the Supreme Court.

Brandeis died on October 5, 1941, having ushered in a new era in liberal jurisprudence. Lewis Weinstein was already well on his way to a prominent leadership position in Boston's Jewish community when he heard the news of Brandeis's death. That night he wrote a poem in honor of his hero, which included effusive terms of praise:

> People's lawyer . . . fighting fallacy with fact . . . armed with figures, mathematically exact/Foe of bigness, wealth entrenched . . . /Champion of the public weal . . . /Broad his vision for the future. . . .[10]

Jewish historians have noted that the age of outstanding pre-Holocaust Jewish leadership in America ended with extraordinarily talented individuals like Brandeis, Louis Marshall, Abba Hillel Silver, Henrietta Szold, and Jacob Schiff. The reasons are mysterious. Some hold that only periods of intense crisis can bring

forth charismatic leaders, others that a united American Jewry
demands organizational skills rather than compelling personalities. What is clear is that since World War II American Jews have
been led by a managerial class rather than by personalities like the
titans of old. And while today's Jewish leaders may resemble the
prominent German Jews of fifty years ago in style and ego, few
would argue that they equal their predecessors in substance,
mediation skills, statesman-like authority, and moral courage.
Throughout the 1940s and 1950s Lewis Weinstein would come to
represent this new methodical and managerial style of Jewish
leadership. Despite his early fascination with Brandeis, Weinstein
would never test his skills at standing up to the city's controlling
interest. Nor is it likely that a future Harvard student will write a
paean to Weinstein as the "foe of bigness, wealth entrenched."
Weinstein would, however, greatly advance organizational causes
and earn a national reputation as an advocate for Soviet Jewry and
Israel. In Boston from 1941 to 1990, Lew Weinstein's name was
synonymous with Jewish leadership.

Weinstein's road to Harvard Law School had been somewhat
rockier than his hero's. At the age of eighteen months Weinstein
had been brought by his parents from Lithuania to Portland,
Maine. In 1918, when Lewis was thirteen, his father died in an
automobile accident, leaving the family's small bottling company
in the hands of a "trusted" employee who wasted no time loading
the company truck with bottles, syrups, and equipment—and
driving off never to be seen again. Weinstein managed to make his
way through law school on loans and in 1930 moved with his new
bride Selma into a comfortable apartment on Roxbury's Humboldt
Avenue. Selma loved to stroll through Franklin Park in the summer
and cross-country ski its gentle hills in the winter. She also taught
afternoon Hebrew School around the corner at Temple Mishkan
Tefila, where she doted on talented students like Leonard Bernstein, who already was showing the musical abilities that would
bring him international acclaim.

Lewis Weinstein, however, did not share his wife's fascination
with the affairs of Boston's Jewish ghetto. He preferred to involve
himself in international issues like the growing Zionist movement.
For almost three decades Boston had been a hotbed of American
Zionism. Elihu Stone, the city's foremost Zionist leader and a
distant relation, handpicked Weinstein to head the Roxbury/

Dorchester Zionist Association. Weinstein's Zionist activities led to participation in the Jewish National Fund and Associated Jewish Philanthropies, where he hobnobbed with the city's Jewish leaders, including Louis Kirstein of Filene's and Judge Lewis Goldberg. Weinstein, an FDR Democrat, also supported the mayoral campaign of reformer Maurice Tobin, who in 1937 upset Mayor Curley. But by 1938 Weinstein had his fill of Roxbury and moved his family across town to Brighton, the neighborhood favored by wealthier members of the Jewish community.

Weinstein's reputation as a winner was greatly enhanced during World War II. The war exploits of men like Julius Ansel were related by former residents of Jewish Boston with deprecating humor—"Julie" duping the Nazi patrol with German double-talk or missing an important battle because he had taken a sleeping pill and fallen asleep under a pile of leaves. Weinstein, on the other hand, was the darling of society columnists from the local dailies. As liaison officer assigned to Charles de Gaulle during the liberation of Paris in 1944, Major Weinstein impressed all with his fluency in French, Spanish, and even sufficient Arabic to be admitted as an honorary member of the Moslem Bar of North Africa. Reporters described in detail the sumptuous billets of Major Weinstein and fellow officers in the Cherbourg peninsula, quarters resplendent with parquet floors, black marble fireplaces, mahogany beds, and carvings of fat naked angels. Readers back home on Blue Hill Avenue could hardly miss the contrast with the letters they had received from sons and husbands that described their awakening in dank pup tents, their hair crawling with lice and their boots filled with snails. But Weinstein, too, had seen more than his share of carnage. In April 1945 he was present at the liberation of Nazi death camps at Ohrdruf, Buchenwald, and Dachau. He had spoken softly, in Yiddish, to dying prisoners and recited *kaddish* over their bodies.

Weinstein returned from the war with great energy and enthusiasm, much of which he directed into Boston's Jewish communal affairs. In the postwar years he was a textbook example of what Jewish sociologists described as the "cosmopolitan volunteer," a leader for whom communal activities become, in effect, a religion. Unlike synagogue and club officers whose activities are concentrated in one institution or neighborhood, the cosmopolitan volunteer sought to maintain involvements across the entire matrix of the Jewish community—religious, cultural, community welfare, and overseas.[11] During the 1950s alone Weinstein served as president of Boston's Hebrew Teachers College, vice president of the Associated Jewish Philanthropies (later the Combined Jewish Philanthropies), and president of the Jewish Community Council.

The first federated Jewish charity in America had been founded in Boston in 1895 by German Jews and served as a model for the United Way and other secular philanthropic organizations. German Jews, however, had never had much to do with Roxbury and Dorchester, preferring the leafy suburbs west of the city. Dorchester's Jews knew they were expected to contribute to the annual United Jewish Appeal campaign but had no illusions that they they would be welcome on any of the federation's leadership committees, generally reserved for the big givers. (The Jewish Community Council and the other instruments of the organized community, housed at 72 Franklin Street, at the periphery of Boston's financial district, were the meeting ground for the rising lawyers and the declining shoe and textile manufacturers.) Dorchester natives had set their own standards for membership in elite clubs: at the respected King Solomon Lodge of B'nai B'rith, for example, members overhwelmingly rejected landlords with reputations for providing insufficient heat and frowned on applications from shopkeepers who failed to honor warranties.

Weinstein enjoyed being close to the center of power. In Boston, as in all other major Jewish communities, that meant holding high office in the Associated Jewish Philanthropies—called, simply, "the federation." Boston's Jews proudly proclaimed that they had organized the first Federation of Jewish Charities in 1895; the establishment of a similar organization followed in Chicago, Detroit, New York, and Philadelphia. By the outbreak of World War I approximately twenty-five local federations existed in Jewish communities across the country. The original federations consisted almost entirely of social welfare organizations, including Jewish orphanages, old age homes, and Hebrew Relief Societies. Synagogue activities and Hebrew schools rarely, if ever, came under the purview of the federation.[12] The federations were formed primarily to link these existing Jewish social service and philanthropic organizations and to focus on improved fund-raising.

By the 1950s the federations had taken on the additional role of fund-raising for overseas ventures, particularly, through the United Jewish Appeal, for Israel. The single-drive fund-raising campaign proved so successful in generating both money and volunteers that it was soon adopted by secular charitable organizations. By 1960 most of the federations were involved in community planning as well, touting themselves as the "central address" for educational, cultural, overseas, and defense needs of the Jews. Jewish power and wealth were concentrated in the federations. Throughout the 1960s and into the 1970s the federations and their constituent agencies controlled about 75 percent of the public expenditure by the American Jewish community.[13]

Brandeis, who had exhorted America's Jews to "organize, organize, organize," would clearly have been impressed by the organizational accomplishments of the modern federation. The "people's lawyer," however, would likely frown on the system by which the major Jewish organizations select their officers. Federation elections, to this day, rarely serve more purpose than to ratify the handpicked choices of nominating committees. The highest offices, too, are generally reserved for the biggest contributors. And on the rare occasion when more than one candidate stands for office, the choice is usually between personalities rather than points of view or organizational vision. The vision of Jacob Schiff, by and large, has come to pass. And with Brandeis gone, there is no longer an authoritative voice urging democratization of the Jewish community.

As an attorney with expertise in housing law and urban renewal, Lew Weinstein played a significant role in the restructuring of the skyline of Boston. Before that, however, he conducted a mini dress rehearsal in Jewish Roxbury. In 1951, fueled partially by a vision of suburban lifestyles, Weinstein, then president of Hebrew College, convinced the leadership of Boston's federation to relocate the college from Crawford Street in Roxbury to the western suburb of Brookline, an action that would have profound effects on the community. For Weinstein, his beloved institution was no longer well situated, based in large part on its proximity to a contiguous black census tract. In 1950 the area of Roxbury now known as Washington Park was home to some thirty thousand residents, almost two-thirds of whom were Jews living in the southern portion of the district bordering Franklin Park. Since the 1920s upper-middle-class blacks had lived side by side with Jews in the district that city planners compared with Harlem's desirable Sugar Hill. The northern neighborhoods of Washington Park comprised mostly poor and less educated blacks, a source of some suspicion to the Jews and "Negro elite."

Although he often boasted to friends of his efforts to fight segregation in the armed forces, Weinstein lacked confidence that Jews and blacks could live successfully in integrated areas. His beliefs were based largely on his experience at the New York–based National Community Relations Advisory Council, an umbrella group formed in the 1940s to coordinate the activities of disparate national and local Jewish organizations. Shortly after the end of the war, Weinstein headed a study team on "changing neighborhoods." The group advanced the theory that demobilized black GIs would no longer stand for the substandard housing of the prewar days. By virtue of the fact that blacks and Jews lived in contiguous areas throughout much of the northeast and because Jews related so easily to the problems of other embattled ethnic groups, it was naturally assumed that blacks would take over Jewish neighborhoods.[14]

Because Hebrew College received a major portion of its funding from the Associated Jewish Philanthropies, Weinstein would need the Jewish federation's permission to buy a new site in the western suburb of Brookline. Armed with almost $100,000 in pledges from four prominent families, Weinstein met in the fall of 1951 with the federation's executive committee at the group's downtown headquarters in the financial district. Weinstein came prepared, "armed with figures," much like his hero Brandeis. He arranged three charts before the federation leadership: one depicted the number of blacks living in the Crawford Street census tract in 1947, another the number in 1951, and a third projections for 1957. "Now, this area is about 30 percent black," Weinstein told the Jewish leaders. "Based on my experience in the national area, I can tell you that this area will be almost 100 percent black in five years. This is inevitable."[15]

Several of the constituent agency heads raised their voices to object. The most vigorous protest came from Benjamin Shevach, the head of Boston's Bureau of Jewish Education. "By moving

Hebrew College, you'll be selling out the Jews of Roxbury," Shevach insisted. Weinstein dismissed the argument as naive. "Whatever we do as a community will help very, very little," he told Shevach. "Demographic change is inevitable." The lawyer's arguments and visual presentations were convincing. It had not occurred to Weinstein that his hero Brandeis, the "champion of the public weal" with his "broad . . . vision for the future," might have confronted this situation armed with more than "figures, mathematically exact." On September 12 Lew Weinstein reported back to the Hebrew College trustees that permission was granted to move to Brookline.

Weinstein's prediction, though not his schedule, proved to be correct. But whether it was inevitable or desirable is still a subject of debate. Marshall Sklare, a sociologist of American Jewry, commented, "It may be highly American to be so mobile but there may be greater ethnic wisdom in standing ground and defending turf."[16] But whatever position might be taken in this controversy, the very decision to relocate Hebrew College proved instructive for both Jews and blacks in Roxbury. For Jewish residents of the area the Hebrew College move was both self-fulfilling prophecy and a reflection of the gulf between the lay leadership of Jewish organizations and working-class residents of the area. For black residents, particularly members of the middle class who hoped to maintain an integrated Roxbury, the plan showed a gaping hole in the black–Jewish alliance. Jewish leaders were perceived as verbally and financially supportive of black social integration efforts yet capable of writing off neighborhoods merely because of proximity to blue-collar blacks. The average "cosmopolitan" leader in a national Jewish organization in the 1950s, however, seemed to perceive no hypocrisy in maintaining such a position. Striving Jewish professionals were discovering new opportunities in once off-limits law offices and hospitals. Ready mortgage money was available in the suburbs. New highways smoothed the ride. The blacks, it was assumed, would have their chance in the future.

Not all Jews, however, were in a hurry to leave. Rabbi Joseph Soloveitchik, the sage and teacher whose name opened doors everywhere but in his own hometown, wanted to stay in Roxbury. The founder of the Maimonides School dispatched members of his own board to investigate the Hebrew College site on Crawford Street as the possible new home for the school, which was operating in cramped headquarters on nearby Columbia Road. For several weeks emissaries from the two institutions negotiated around the asking price of $40,000. Each time they seemed near agreement, however, the Maimonides representatives failed to receive the expected donations necessary to seal the arrangement.

Boston's major black social policy center, Freedom House, was also expressing keen interest in buying Hebrew College. Freedom House had been founded only three years earlier by Otto and Muriel Snowden, two of the black community's most respected leaders. Muriel, the daughter of a successful dentist, had grown up in the lone black family of a New Jersey suburb. She'd come to Boston to attend Radcliffe College and study Romance languages. Otto Snowden, as a youngster in Roxbury, had functioned as a *shabbos goy,* turning on and off lights for sabbath-observant Jewish neighbors. He believed then and continued to believe that blacks would do well to adopt Jewish attitudes about education and industriousness.

In their efforts to raise money to buy Hebrew College, the Snowdens turned first to several of Boston's wealthier Jewish philanthropists. For almost five decades Jews had been among the most generous and ardent supporters of black organizations and institutions nationwide, including the NAACP and Booker T. Washington's Tuskegee Institute. The philanthropic motives were not based solely on altruism; Jews needed little imagination to see their own struggle against antisemitism in the black struggle against racism. Victims of the May Laws and, later, of the Holocaust understood intrinsically the power of alliances and the danger of isolation. If the great American experiment should ever go sour, if soldiers should once again come for the Jews, there would at least be black allies in the resistance.[17]

Several Jewish philanthropists responded immediately to the Snowdens' requests, including brothers Joe and Kivie Kaplan, cosmetics tycoon Al Green, and travel agency owner Joel Krensky. Encouraged, Muriel Snowden also tried her hand at reaching prominent members of Boston's Irish Catholic community. Then U.S. Rep. John Kennedy made a small donation that gave Muriel Snowden courage to approach the Kennedy patriarch, Ambassador Joseph Kennedy. "Young lady, you're talking to a busy man. Sell me only what you think I'll buy," barked the Ambassador. Snowden hesitated as she grappled with a figure. "What did my son give?" Kennedy asked impatiently. "I'll match it." Muriel turned next to Cardinal Richard J. Cushing, a prolific fund-raiser who was worshipped by the city's Irish Catholic majority. The cardinal instructed Snowden on everything from the intense need in the city's Irish parishes to the work of the church in African missions. A few years later the cardinal helped establish the first church for the city's roughly one thousand black Catholics. But in 1951 Cushing had little sympathy for the integrationist views of Freedom House. "My dear, it's diversity that holds us together," the cardinal told Muriel Snowden as he showed her the door.[18]

The Snowdens managed to raise $15,000 from their Jewish supporters for a down payment, considerably more than Rabbi Soloveitchik was able to raise for the Maimonides School. But they were disturbed that liberal Jewish philanthropists, so kind to them, seemed hardened to the appeals of the Orthodox school. At one point in the negotiations Otto Snowden decided to withdraw the offer because he felt it was creating too much discord among his Jewish neighbors. But Lewis Weinstein soothed him, stressing that the future of the neighborhood lay in black, not Jewish, hands. "You want it, you've got it," Weinstein promised the reluctant Snowdens.[19]

The Snowdens moved into the former site of Hebrew College during the Christmas/Hanukah season of 1952. Otto Snowden's first act was to fashion a makeshift menorah and place it in the building's front window as a symbol of his willingness to coexist with his Jewish neighbors. Every day for the next eight days Otto and Muriel placed a Hanukah candle in the Freedom House menorah.

From their base in Freedom House the Snowdens vowed to do everything in their power to keep upper Roxbury integrated and to prevent it from becoming another Northeast slum. Their most ambitious efforts included the establishment of block organizations to deal with neighborhood services including public safety, recreation, trash removal, and street cleaning. The Snowdens were also careful to plan programs with both blacks and Jews in mind. A preschool program catered, for a time, to both black and Jewish youngsters from the neighborhood. Two professional models, one black and one Jewish, held sessions for the neighborhood's adolescent girls on how to impress prospective employers at job interviews, offering special advice on the best clothes and makeup for their complexions and body types. The Snowdens also planned joint programs with the Hecht House Jewish Community Center on American Legion Highway in nearby Mattapan even though they did not have the happiest memories of Hecht House—in the 1940s blacks were clearly not welcome at the Jewish community center—and a popular Jewish youth worker had recently been reprimanded by the Hecht House board for dancing with Muriel at a joint function. But the Snowdens believed that their efforts would stabilize the area. The black middle class and the Jews of Roxbury and Dorchester, they were convinced, had every reason to grow closer in a city controlled by white Anglo-Saxon bankers and Irish politicians and policemen.

The Snowdens' vision, however, could not have been further from reality. The sale of Hebrew College sent a message to other Jewish institutions in the area that it was time to pack up. It was, in essence, the same message sent by the federal government through its subsidy programs for homeownership and highway development outside the city. The call was quickly taken up by the area's most stately and influential synagogue: Temple Mishkan Tefila.

Mishkan Tefila, the oldest Conservative synagogue in Massachusetts, was founded in 1895 by immigrants from East Prussia. From its inception it was considered a *stadt shul,* the dominant synagogue in a metropolitan community and one whose appeal and influence transcended both personal and geographic boundaries. In 1925, after eight moves, the congregation built its neoclassical building of Indiana limestone on Roxbury's Seaver Street, the very heart of Boston's Jewish community. Mishkan Tefila lived up to its advance billing: youngsters from nearby Dorchester and Mattapan were bused to its central Hebrew school and more than a dozen Zionist and fraternal organizations soon were flourishing in meeting space supplied by the temple.

In 1946 temple officers recruited Rabbi Israel Kazis, a graduate of the Jewish Theological Seminary who had earned a PhD at Harvard University. With great pride the temple announced the appointment of their new rabbi, a man blessed with "qualities of leadership, oratory, and scholastic ability."[20] Kazis's arrival coincided with an unacknowledged but dramatic revolution in class composition in the Mishkan Tefila community. The temple's

wealthier members, including lawyers who were just beginning to
penetrate the city's largest firms, were drawn in increasing numbers to the streetcar suburbs west of Boston, particularly the towns
of Brookline and Newton. By the early 1950s half of the approximately eight hundred member families lived in the suburbs and
commuted back to Roxbury for religious services and Hebrew
school. But the synagogue's thirty-member executive committee
did not reflect the fifty-fifty split: only two of the committee
members lived in Roxbury; the remaining twenty-eight made their
homes in Brookline, Newton, and downtown Boston.

Kazis understood early on that he could look to the Roxbury
brotherhood to keep the daily *minyan* going and to man volunteer
committees and that the sisterhood could be relied upon for its
covered dishes. But the money, by his accurate calculations, was
moving west. Kazis eyed the suburban shift with some trepidation.
Although the immediate vicinity of the synagogue was more than
90 percent Jewish, the two census tracts closest to Mishkan Tefila
were 56 percent and 25 percent black.[21] Kazis prided himself on
his liberal politics and took no satisfaction in the thought of his
congregation turning their backs on integration. It would be less
satisfying, however, if Mishkan Tefila's congregants left to join one
of the large Conservative or Reform synagogues in Brookline. By
1951 Rabbi Kazis had positioned himself squarely in the camp of
congregants who believed Mishkan Tefila's future lay outside the
city limits of Boston. Rising at the annual board meeting, he
expressed to his leadership that they could count on him in any
future power struggle between Roxbury members and those who
were tiring of the seven-mile commute from their large suburban
homes back to the old neighborhood for Sabbath services and
holiday observances. "The migration toward Newton was an
inevitable geographical phenomenon," he declared. Finding a
new site "would be an act of foresighted religious statemanship
that would decide the continued existence of Temple Mishkan
Tefila as the greatest religious center of Greater Boston."[22]

Kazis was prepared for a backlash from Roxbury boosters, but
the assault came from an unexpected direction. Three Conservative congregations, Temples Emeth, Emanuel, and Reyim, were
already serving Jews in Newton and South Brookline, and each
would have been more than happy to add new, well-off congregants to their own membership lists. Citing the Jewish proscrip-

tion against *hasagat gevul* ("encroachment"), the rabbis of the three synagogues appealed to the national leadership of the Conservative movement to block Kazis's attempt to establish a suburban annex to Mishkan Tefila's popular Hebrew School. Administrators at the New York–based Jewish Theological Seminary agreed that the interests of Jewish education were already being well served by the existing synagogues and upheld the protest of the offended synagogues.

Kazis and Mishkan Tefila's Newton members continued to press their point. The matter was referred for arbitration to a rabbinic court convened by the Conservative Movement's Rabbinical Assembly. In December of 1953 Rabbi Kazis, weighed down by scores of documents and information sheets, approached the court and its head judge, Simon Greenberg. Kazis conducted himself with the confidence of a successful trial attorney. He reeled off precedents from Europe and America of synagogues in close physical proximity that had thrived and complemented one another. He then began a measured description of the demographic changes in Roxbury, referring briefly to a phrase in his notes— "temple surrounded by Negroes."[23] The arbiters were impressed by Kazis's presentation, particularly his knowledge of historic Jewish communities. In their decision, which went in Mishkan Tefila's favor, the judges noted briefly that "the neighborhood in which Mishkan Tefila is located is rapidly changing its character." The synagogue was given free rein to relocate to Newton, with the provision that it "find a site at a maximum distance from the existing congregations in order to avoid even the appearance of competition or rivalry."[24] The rabbinic court made no mention of the synagogue's future responsibility to its members who were unwilling or unable to move to the suburbs. Nor did it raise the question of Jewish commitment to integration.

Kazis and his committee were buoyed by the ruling and quietly began their search for an appropriate site. The most desirable location was a twenty-three–acre tract of undeveloped land, then owned by the state's Metropolitan District Commission, along Newton's Hammond Pond Parkway. Shortly after the synagogue leaders and the state began to negotiate for the land, rumblings were heard among the Roxbury members of Mishkan Tefila. Fearful that the Roxbury resistance might become embarrassingly loud, Kazis and pro-Newton members of the congregation asked the board of directors to postpone their annual meeting in order that they might first secure title to the land. But in April 1954, faced with growing anger at the grass roots level, the board instead voted to appoint a committee, composed in equal parts of Roxbury and Newton members, "to study the best method of . . . insuring the perpetuation" of the congregation.[25] The minutes of that committee's meeting present the aspirations and plans of the Newton group in considerable detail but offer no insight into the plans and objections of the Roxbury supporters. The Newton position, though couched in weighty verbiage, boiled down to the following proposal: "Temple Mishkan Tefila cannot exist for any length of time in Roxbury. . . . there must always be only one Temple Mishkan Tefila," and it is therefore recommended to "move all of Temple Mishkan Tefila to Newton."[26]

The annual meeting of the congregation in April 1955 found open hostility between the two groups. Roxbury members decried the decision-making process, which had included a select few members meeting off the temple grounds. The congregation's president, attorney Nathan Yamins, finally addressed the issue before the congregation:

> A lot of rumors have been circulated that the temple and school house will be sold and that the Newton temple will be available only to Newton residents. I want to take this opportunity of stating emphatically that the present administration has no thought of selling or otherwise disposing of the existing temple and schoolhouse building. . . . As for membership in the new Mishkan Tefila, it will be open to everyone who wants to become affiliated. Naturally, the present members of Mishkan Tefila in Roxbury or elsewhere will be particularly welcome, but it is only fair to expect that everyone joining in this wonderful venture will be expected to contribute to the cost of its erection in accordance with his means.[27]

Yamins's promises sounded hollow and impractical to the Roxbury group. It was all well and good to pay lip service to egalitarianism but membership in the new congregation demanded a minimum $1,000 contribution to the building fund. Roxbury members met to discuss the possibility of blocking the move in court and of securing the assets of the building, which was no longer mortgaged. But the building-drive chairman scoffed at the absurdity of a dwindling group of working-class Jews filing suit against their wealthier professional cousins. "If no members remain in Roxbury," he told them, "Newton temple takes all. If Roxbury organizes as a new congregation, Newton temple still takes all."[28] The temple chairman's pronouncement had a familiar ring to congregants with roots in Eastern Europe. Back in Russia, the saying went as follows: "You give me all your wood in exchange for which I'll take all your fish."

American synagogues, though oligarchic in nature like all religious entities, are considered the height of participatory democracy when compared with federations. But even organizational planners who make their livings preparing slates for rubber stamp approval would have been jolted by the experience of Mishkan Tefila. With little further discussion and no vote of the general membership, the board elected to purchase the desired land and hired an executive director to lead a fund-raising drive for the new building. By December 1956 approximately $700,000 was pledged to the Mishkan Tefila building drive. Of that total, 40 percent came from thirteen individuals none of whom lived in Roxbury. The dues structure of Mishkan Tefila was further altered to accommodate the building drive. Minimum dues for both Roxbury and Newton members were set at $100 per year, a sum that many of the inner city congregants could not afford. The executive committee eventually lowered dues to $60 per year with the stipulation that those who paid less would find seating in the adjacent schoolhouse rather than in the main sanctuary during the High Holy Days. The decision proved deeply humiliating to the poorer congregants.

The next two years were a time of relentless fund-raising and frenetic activity for the Newton group. The country's leading synagogue architect, Percival Goodman, was hired and construction began. A fund-raising brochure promised that "In our new temple windows open on nature and the soul finds repose through a long vista of trees and sky. Here the child, while learning the book lesson, lifts his eyes to see the living fact of the Creator's design in every leaf and blade of grass or snow-clad knoll."[29] The brochure, gushing as it did over a few acres of undeveloped suburban land, stunned the Roxbury members. The old Mishkan Tefila sat on the edge of Franklin Park, the crown jewel in the "emerald necklace" designed by the country's greatest landscape architect. Why, they wondered, couldn't the synagogue's young students contemplate one of the hundreds of maples or oaks in magnificent Franklin Park?

The Roxbury membership, ignored and demoralized, soon dwindled to only two hundred families. They themselves estimated that they would need at least five hundred families to maintain the Roxbury structure. Mishkan Tefila's officers, no longer fearful of litigation from their poorer cousins, voted in April 1958 to sell the Seaver Street buildings to a group of Orthodox Lubavitcher Jews for $80,000. Roxbury had lost its Conservative *stadt shul.*

The area near Mishkan Tefila had undergone cataclysmic change from 1950 to 1960. In 1950, a decade before communal leaders like Weinstein and Kazis had declared the neighborhood unfit for Jews, the Jewish population of the greater Roxbury-Dorchester-Mattapan area within walking distance of Mishkan Tefila exceeded fifty thousand. By 1960 the number of Jews living in the neighborhood contiguous to the synagogue and Hebrew College had dropped from roughly twenty thousand to seventy-five hundred. The neighborhood turned from two-thirds white to 71 percent black. As the Snowdens had feared, many of the new black arrivals came with little to offer by way of educational or professional skills. Crime and juvenile delinquency increased. The loss of professional workers was three times as high as the net population loss. Income and education levels, higher than the city average in 1950, slipped well below the Boston median only one decade later.[30] The younger, wealthier, more upwardly mobile, and generally less traditional of Roxbury's Jews followed Mishkan Tefila and Hebrew College to the western suburbs. The majority, however—and not necessarily those who could not have afforded otherwise—merely moved a mile south into Jewish sections of Dorchester and Mattapan. Many of them purchased their own homes—triple-deckers or, as was becoming more fashionable among their cousins in the suburbs, ranch homes with front and rear gardens. By 1957 Dorchester's Jewish population had swelled to more than forty thousand, with an additional ten thousand Jews in Mattapan.

Resettled in new homes, former residents of Roxbury struggled to understand the previous decade's history Had major institutions like Hebrew College and Mishkan Tefila merely responded in a rational manner to "inevitable demographic change?" Or had their boards in essence *created* cataclysmic change by pulling up stakes and unilaterally removing the most prominent neighborhood institutions? While Jewish leaders argue the former, it is clear that the actions of the major Jewish institutions signaled a different message—that Roxbury was a bad risk—to federal, state, and local officials, as well as to bankers, developers, and realtors.

Those left behind—both blacks and Jews—felt lingering bitterness. The Snowdens and other members of the "Negro elite," whose suburban dreams had been all but smothered by racial barriers in real estate and mortgage lending, had little choice but to stay on in upper Roxbury. They fought to hold on to white members of the community, who were largely elderly and suspicious. A redevelopment expert who later studied the movement out of Roxbury in the 1950s found no overt hostility between the blacks and Jews but little communication. "This in part stems from the fact that those Jews that have remained are not the outgoing community type. . . . There are no Jewish block associations . . . with little sense of future, there is not much incentive for neighborhood renewal. There is a desire for city projects for the elderly . . . and for better city services . . . but probably little contribution to a self-help rehabilitation program could be expected."[31]

In December 1958 a proud group of upper-middle-class Jews celebrated the one hundredth anniversary of Mishkan Tefila in their sparkling new building in Newton. At the open house and gala ball, they congratulated themselves on how far they'd come from the old neighborhood. Other messages of congratulations poured in from across the country, including a telegram from President Eisenhower. At the official dedication ceremony Mishkan Tefila's lay leaders, the men who led their people out of Roxbury, walked down the center aisle of the new sanctuary, each solemnly clutching in his arms the beloved Torah. The sons of the lay leaders appeared proudly at their fathers' sides. Then, in a touching ceremony conducted by Rabbi Kazis, each father passed the scroll, recently removed from the inner city synagogue, to his son, thus forming in Kazis' words, "a historical link to the synagogue of the future."

Thus the trek westward, already begun in the 1930s for individual Jews like Lew Weinstein, was firmly established in the 1950s; "Moving up" correlated with "moving out." The pattern was repeated in major urban areas across America. What might have been the largest exodus since Moses led the Jews out of Egypt was now under way. But this exodus was not led by men of the caliber of Moses or, for that matter, Louis Brandeis. The Jewish lower middle class was being abandoned. And before too long, upper-middle-class Jewish liberals would respond to slogans of black power by calling for the transfer of Jewish shopkeepers out of the areas of the expanding black ghettos, the very areas once revered by their parents and grandparents.

Wheeling and Dealing

The Politics of Urban Renewal,
1955–1965

In the mid-1950s, both John Collins and the city of Boston were struggling against paralysis. Only a few years earlier, things had seemed far more hopeful. John Hynes, the newly elected mayor of Boston, had captured the mayoralty race on the promise of reform and good government, and Collins, an energetic state legislator from Roxbury's Ward 12, had been swept up in the Hynes campaign. He'd scoffed at the cynics who insisted that the "New Boston" would be nothing more than a profitable plaything for the wealthy. James Michael Curley, the "neighborhood mayor," had built parks, fire stations, and swimming pools on graft and, in the process, drove the city to the brink of bankruptcy. It was time for some fiscal common sense. Even a chauffeur's son like Collins, who had grown up on Roxbury's Elmore Street, just three houses away from the elevated railway, could see that.

Collins was a tireless worker. It was a trait characteristic of his classmates at Roxbury Memorial High School, including Eddie Pellagrini, the catcher for the Boston Red Sox who hit a home run his first time at bat; Albert "Dapper" O'Neil, who would later gain notoriety as a pistol-packing city councilor and vociferous critic of school desegregation; and Al Schlossberg, who made quite a living for himself in funeral homes and was a leader in the Jewish community. Like his classmates from poor families, Collins was proud of his "bootstrap elevation" in life. Back in 1937 he had enrolled at Suffolk Law School and supported himself by working as an usher at the Franklin Park Theatre on Blue Hill Avenue. Each morning, Collins would take the trolley downtown for classes, return home at noon, eat a fast lunch, and jog across Franklin Park to work the afternoon show. At suppertime, he'd jog home, grab a bite, and hit the books for an hour before the jog back for the evening show. Only by day's end did Collins feel he'd earned the right to spend a nickel on the trolley ride home.

Collins had served two terms in the Massachusetts House of Representatives and one in the Senate by 1954, when he decided to make a bid for state attorney general. The effort fell short. It had been a disappointing winter and spring for an ambitious man who thrived on responsibility and authority. Collins's wife, Mary, a shy and devoted woman, determined that nothing would take the edge off a narrow political loss like a few weeks on Cape Cod's Silver Beach, where the family could unwind and chart a new course. Occasionally, Collins's political advisers would drop by the small beach cottage for clams and conversation. "Statewide politics is not what I want right now," Collins would tell them. "I'm considering a run for Boston City Council. I can make a contribution to this city." Invariably, they would tell Collins that he was squandering a promising political career in the cesspit of Boston politics and would end up like any run-of-the-mill Irish pol. "I'm going to prove that every Irish politician isn't stupid, crooked, or drunk," Collins shot back. "With the right people, this city can be managed effectively and honestly."[1]

Even from the perspective of his beach chair on the sun-swept shore, the city's economic future at mid-decade looked dark and cloudy. Only one new private office building had appeared on the skyline since 1929. The tax rate escalated at confiscatory rates while the city's appearance grew seedier and services deteriorated. One in five of the city's housing units was classified as dilapidated or deteriorating. Wooden tenements across the city had been pulverized only to be replaced by drab public housing units, breeding grounds for crime and discord. Manufacturing jobs, too, were leaving the city as mill owners moved south, attracted by cheap labor and low taxes. While the nation's Hub ranked lowest in new building starts, no major city was higher in number of municipal employees per capita. The city's only growth industries were government and universities. Expansion efforts by college administrators became land-grabbing juggernauts through Beacon Hill, Brighton, and the Back Bay. Together, the expanding colleges and government offices succeeded only in further eroding a diminishing tax base. Boston's Brahmin financial institutions seemed satisfied to stand by and watch the Irish-dominated political dinosaur wallow in the tar pit. No one blinked an eye when Moody's investor service rated Boston's municipal bond the lowest of any major city in the nation.[2]

It was difficult for Collins and other observers to know if the actions of the federal government would help or hurt. During the early 1950s federal bulldozers were deployed at the gates of American cities, fueled by funds for the federal urban renewal program. A new crusade against Babylon was being launched, committed to overcoming the slums, poverty, inequality, the breakdown of family life, and the depersonalization of social relations—all viewed as the inevitable consequences of urban existence.[3] And the operators of the federal bulldozers were not shy about wielding the law of eminent domain when the appeal to progress did not evoke the right response.

Urban dwellers, particularly the poor and nonwhite, had every reason to be suspicious of the housing arms of the federal government. For most of the years since its founding in 1934 the Federal Housing Administration had taken an unusually callous approach to home building and mortgage lending. Through the provision of federal insurance to lending institutions, the federal government could have required a nondiscrimination policy. Instead, it played the role of protector of all-white neighborhoods.[4] In the early days of the agency FHA agents were constantly on the lookout for "inharmonious" racial or nationality groups,[5] the prevention of "infiltration" by such groups into Christian, all-white neighborhoods being a priority for FHA employees. FHA appraisers followed the same dictum utilized by real estate brokers nationwide—Gresham's Law of Neighborhoods: as surely as bad dollars drive out good ones, people of the wrong complexion or status drive out "good" people and depress neighborhood values.[6] Evidence for this belief ran deep in the manuals with which thousands of brokers had been educated. Particular focus was placed on blacks. "There is a natural inclination of the colored people to live together in their own communities," explained one supposedly authoritative source. "With the increase of colored people coming to many Northern cities they have overrun their old districts and swept into adjoining ones or passed to other sections and formed new ones. This has had a decidedly detrimental effect on land values, for few white people, however inclined to be sympathetic with the problem of the colored race, care to live near them. Property values have been sadly depreciated by having a single colored family settle down on a street occupied exclusively by white residents."[7]

The only solution, according to these real estate authorities, was segregation. "The colored people certainly have a right to life, liberty and pursuit of happiness," it was argued, "but they must recognize the economic disturbance which their presence in a white neighborhood causes and forego their desire to split off from the established district where the rest of their race lives."[8] A hierarchy of races and nationalities was also presented in real estate texts and accepted, in large measure, by leading economists and real estate schools. The most common list, from most desirable as neighbors to least desirable, read as follows:

1. English, Germans, Scotch, Irish, Scandinavians
2. North Italians
3. Bohemians or Czechs
4. Poles
5. Lithuanians
6. Greeks

7. Russian Jews ("lower class")
8. South Italians
9. Negroes
10. Mexicans[9]

During the 1930s and 1940s restrictive covenants were encouraged by FHA officials to exclude groups on the lower end of the scale. One model frequently in use required that builders and lenders pledge that "no persons of any race other than [race to be inserted] shall use or occupy any building or any lot, except that this covenant shall not prevent occupancy by domestic servants of a different race domiciled with an owner or tenant."[10] Despite protests by the National Association for the Advancement of Colored People (NAACP) and civil rights groups, the FHA continued its support for such practices, even after 1948, when the Supreme Court held racial covenants unenforceable. Under intense pressure the FHA finally began to relent. The 1949 edition of the FHA manual omitted references to mortgages in areas faced with infiltration by minorities. In December of the same year the FHA agreed not to insure mortgages on properties subject to restrictive covenants. As sociologist Charles Abrams would later note, "The fight to bring the FHA within the Constitution was beginning to show results."[11]

But Abrams also noted that the official use and sanction of racial covenants had an enduring character. The concept of heterogeneous communities was permanently undermined, giving way to racially segregated neighborhoods from coast to coast. Private builders who had never considered the use of covenants were trained in implementation as a contingency of receiving FHA insurance. Most damaging, however, was the housing deprivation in the inner cities: Blacks were excluded from FHA developments, and realtors perceived neighborhoods contiguous with black districts as undesirable. As Abrams would later point out, FHA policies went further than endorsing the "separate but equal" doctrine found in southern states; its policy was separate for whites and nothing for blacks. The result, Abrams wrote, "was accentuation of housing shortages for the people who needed housing most, concentration of minorities into older deteriorated sections, pressure upon newer areas by minorities seeking space, chaotic competition for dwellings between majority and minority, and deepening of tensions between classes—one of the most sensitive aspects of American neighborhoods today."[12]

White Bostonians, like their urban counterparts nationwide, found prosperity in the suburbs. From 1950 to 1960 the city's population would tumble from 801,000 to 697,000. New Deal money under Franklin Delano Roosevelt and aid-for-housing under Harry Truman had helped create the radial roads, parks, and water and sewage systems needed to develop the large tracts of land between the old neighborhoods like Roxbury and the semirural towns to the north and west. Wealthy Yankees were not the only ones who benefited. Demobilized soldiers armed with veterans' loans received an unanticipated boost when anti-covenant court rulings prohibited real estate appraisers for government-backed mortgages from giving positive weight to the Gentleman's Agreement to maintain segregation in a neighborhood. A formidable barrier was seemingly removed from the upward social mobility of many Americans, including second-generation Jews, who could now penetrate more deeply into the attractive and forbidden sylvan reserves of the landed Brahmins.

In Massachusetts and across America new plasterboard houses arose—made affordable by low interest rates and mass production building techniques. Suddenly, the American dream of the private family home fell within the economic reach of many. Jobs were available in suburban industrial parks, an architectural concept pioneered in 1951 by Boston real estate mogul Gerald Blakely of Cabot, Cabot, and Forbes. Government-sponsored electronics research at MIT and Harvard spawned scores of start-up ventures along the federally built Route 128 beltway.[13] Suddenly, a solidly middle-class younger generation who might otherwise have carefully scraped away at the peeling paint of a Dorchester tripledecker on a Sunday afternoon were mowing lawns and hosting barbeques a few miles down the road. The new highways that carelessly carved up the cityscape eased the access of the suburbanites to their sprawling shopping centers while in downtown Boston hotels and department stores were closing. The five newspapers in town would soon decrease to three and then two, and few would mourn the passing of those lost. The newly landed aristocracy was far too busy worshipping at their newly-acquired totems—the shiny automobile in the driveway and the evocative wagon wheel on the lawn.

When he'd represented Roxbury's Ward 14 in the statehouse, John Collins had felt powerless to compete with suburban legislators and lobbyists. Boston's elected officials could not raise taxes or even appoint a new police commissioner without the approval of legislators from neighboring cities and towns, and Boston's legislators rarely got the better of their suburban counterparts. Boston's Finance Commission—to take only one example—was funded through city taxes but the governor appointed all of its members.

The Collins family returned home from Cape Cod shortly after Labor Day. In a matter of days each Collins child in turn developed a high fever and fell gravely ill. John Collins sat day and night at the bedside of his children, aged two, four, and six, at Boston's Floating Hospital. He feared the worst. During the summer of 1955 a polio epidemic was sweeping across the eastern United States. A defective batch of vaccine had been released into the population just months before. Due to the subsequent massive recall, no vaccine was available during the summer and early fall. As doctors tapped into the spines of the Collins children with their long needles, John Collins held them and gently wiped away the tears and perspiration from their faces with his pocket handkerchief. Then, dabbing his own brow, he would return the handkerchief to the pocket of his suit. Collins was unaware that polio was easily transmitted through perspiration.

On September 15 Collins awoke with a terrible pain in his back. Fearing that he'd panic his neighbors, he refused to call an ambulance. Instead, he drove himself to the medical center and collapsed. The next day a doctor informed Mary Collins that her husband had a fever of 105 degrees and that his chance for survival was slim. The diagnosis was polio. Over the next two months the Collins children began to show a steady recovery. All survived without lasting or permanent residual effects from the disease. John Collins also survived, confined to a wheelchair for life.

Despite his paralysis, Collins believed that he could mount a successful campaign for city council from his hospital room. He first made an audiotape from his bedside and released it to the radio stations. He delivered what seemed at first to be an exaggerated campaign promise. "If elected," he declared, "I will attend the first meeting of the council and every session thereafter."[14] In a crowded field Collins placed a strong fourth in the race for the nine-member council. True to his promise, he attended the first meeting, which featured hours of speeches by the councilors on the choices facing the "New Boston." Throughout his term on the council and later as register of probate, Collins studied Boston from every angle. He was certain that with good management the city could be turned around. He looked at the gin mills, burlesque houses, and tattoo parlors in Scollay Square and envisioned office buildings, fine restaurants, and fine shops. He looked at the fish shacks rotting on Atlantic Avenue and envisioned a revitalized harbor front with pleasant parks and tourist attractions. But first, he concluded, Boston needed a man like John Collins as its mayor.

In 1959, when Collins announced his intention to join the crowded mayoral field, the smart money was on John Powers, the Massachusetts Senate president. Powers's backers included then U.S. Senator John F. Kennedy, Cardinal Richard J. Cushing, the adored leader of the city's Catholic majority, and a bevy of powerful bankers and industrialists. Nor did the drivers of the federally fueled bulldozers have reason to support the crippled candidate. Shortly before the primary a Massachusetts Superior Court justice took Collins aside to explain the impudence of challenging the Senate president. "The next mayor of Boston will be a young man from the legislature," the judge gently explained, pointing out that Powers's election would be little more than a formality. "What you're telling me is very interesting," Collins responded. "I come from the legislature and I'm not an old man. And I'm going to run no matter what. I don't get out under any circumstances."[15]

For Collins, who dreamed of downtown revitalization, it was especially painful to be cut off from the institutional support of bankers and businessmen. With the city stumbling to the edge of bankruptcy, even a Roxbury native like Collins gave little thought to the social effects of development on individual neighborhoods. Such disregard was most widely in evidence in the city's West End. Shortly before the primary, in 1958, the city had seized by eminent domain a forty-eight–acre tract along the Charles River in Boston's West End. The developer for the site was Jerome Rappaport, Hynes's former chief assistant and leader of the New Boston Committee. The decks had been cleared for a new "first-class residential neighborhood," a marked contrast to the tight-knit ethnic neighborhood.

Rappaport's West End Project would be the swan song for the city's most ethnically diverse neighborhood, where Italians, Irish, and Jews—more than twenty-six hundred families in total—had lived harmoniously for decades in crowded tenements. They were told, and most believed, that the wrecking ball would bring salvation in the form of modern middle-income housing. As developers set about studying plans for luxury high rises instead, a weak neighborhood coalition, Save-the-West-End, tried to stop the evictions. The rudimentary opposition of these "urban villagers," too little, too late, to policies so detrimental to their collective interests would provide little more than an influential case study for urban planners on working-class behavior.[16]

Soon the wrecking ball was in full swing, and a community was transformed into rubble. Although 54 percent of the West Enders had incomes sufficiently low to qualify for relocation in federally subsidized housing, only 19 percent received aid. For more than a decade social scientists would keep tabs on the scattered residents, monitoring their adjustment to new homes and communities, and identifying the signs and symptoms of deep trauma.

John Collins did not mourn for the West End. He had no desire to be perceived as a shrill populist like James Curley. The next Irish mayor of Boston should be a practical administrator, long on municipal experience and short on histrionics. Collins was sure that was what the people wanted, and he was ready to test his theories in the neighborhoods. In Ward 14 Collins knew the road to the city's Jewish voters passed through power brokers Sam Levine and Julius Ansel. Both had been strong Curley supporters and now supported Powers. Collins also knew that Dorchester's bookies made him a ten-to-one underdog.

Collins sought out a second tier of Jewish leaders who he hoped could help deliver Wards 12 and 14. Collins could at least count on his old friend Louis Nathanson, a diminutive, cigar-smoking former state representative. Nathanson knew the best places to politick in the Jewish districts off of Seaver Street— namely, the scores of poker and pinochle games that the men played until they limped off exhausted or broke. "I'll be in there fighting for you, John," Nathanson promised the candidate. "Remember the race for legislature in Ward 12. They voted for you like you were a Jew." Collins also courted members of the respected Brier family, who certified kosher meat in butcher shops across the ward. Collins dangled a plum in front of one of the sons, Jacob Brier, who expressed an interest in running the city's housing authority, but Collins was cut off quickly by the man's elderly father. "A job he wants to give him," the elder Brier complained. "A wife he needs."[17] Collins knew he would never be taken seriously in Ward 14 without a campaign appearance at the G&G delicatessen. During the height of the campaign the mayoral hopeful, accompanied by his wife Mary, wheeled a sound truck down Blue Hill Avenue and delivered his message of a revitalized Boston under honest and capable leadership. State Rep. Julie Ansel, firmly in Powers's camp, pulled up behind Collins in a second truck and drowned out the candidate's message. But Mary Collins, who had toughened up considerably in the years of reclaiming her family from poliomyelitis, was not going to see her husband humiliated by Ansel or anyone else. Jumping off her husband's sound truck, she strode up to Ansel, who was working the crowd at an ear-splitting decibel. Standing within an inch of Ansel's face, Mary Collins shouted out her lesson in political science: "Julius Ansel, if you don't turn the volume down on that sound truck so that my husband has an opportunity to talk, I'll never forget it, and I'll make sure he'll never forget it and he's going to be elected mayor." Ansel appeared stunned by the reaction of the usually reticent Mary Collins; he turned the microphone off and drove silently down Blue Hill Avenue.

Collins also sensed the growing political importance of the city's black population. Black laborers were streaming into northern cities from the south while middle-class whites were rushing to the suburbs. From 1950 to 1960 the number of blacks in Boston would almost double from forty thousand to about seventy-five thousand at a time when the city's overall population had declined 12 percent. Collins looked to Edward Brooke for inroads into the black community. Brooke, a highly competent and amiable politician, suffered many early setbacks as a Democrat. As a Republican, however, he would enjoy greater success, going on to serve in the mid-1960s as Massachusett's first black Attorney General and in the early 1970s as U.S. Senator from Massachusetts. In 1959 Brooke was the president of Amvets, a "thinking man's VFW" that supported progressive political candidates. Brooke pledged his support to Collins but couldn't resist needling his old political contact. "John, you're so bad off that you need a black Amvets commander to sign your ads," he joked.[18]

No one was laughing when the votes were counted on election day. John Collins scored a stunning upset over Powers. Even in Ward 14, Collins narrowly missed upsetting Powers, by only thirty-one votes. The unexpected Powers defeat was an early example of the power of the "alienated voter." Collins had been correct in assuming that the romance between Curley-style politicians and average Bostonians was over. The newly elected mayor had pulled off his victory with only about $15,000 in campaign funds. If that was possible, John Collins's shabby city could also be transformed into the "New Boston" of polished steel and glass. The new mayor set about formulating a master plan, one that would radically change the rotation of the nation's Hub.

Before taking office in January 1960, Collins began a nationwide search for a new director of the Boston Redevelopment Authority, the state-authorized agency responsible for the planning, development, and administration of neighborhood programs. He needed a candidate who possessed not only the vision of a "New Boston" but one who could also convince the downtown bankers, notably the First National Bank, to invest in their own city's future rather than funding bailout schemes for the Hollywood movie projects that now captured their attention. At the beginning of the search process, Collins took an unusual step for a Boston Irish politician: he sought the advice of academics at Harvard and the Massachusetts Institute of Technology. The professors believed that as much as 50 percent of the city's neighborhoods would eventually need to be brought under urban renewal. That would take an unusually able administrator. The name that came up most often was Edward Logue, a brash lawyer who was doing a superb job as urban renewal chief under Mayor Dick Lee in New Haven.

Logue, of Philadelphia Irish stock, shared the mayor's enormous capacity for hard work. Socially, they had little in common. The grey-flanneled Logue, a graduate of Yale, favored elitist gatherings at places like the Tavern Club. Collins was a graduate of working-class Suffolk University who preferred family life over the clubhouse. But Logue viewed the chance to head the Redevelopment Authority as an exciting challenge and told Collins that an annual salary of $30,000 would be enough to tempt him away from New Haven. "I only make $20,000 myself," a stunned Collins answered. But Logue was adamant. "I'm not proud," Collins responded, in a rare moment of self-effacement. "What's $10,000 when you're trying to turn a city around?"[19]

Collins and Logue set about to formulate a plan to rebuild Boston. The plan would eventually call for the construction of thirty-seven thousand new units of housing and the rehabilitation of an additional thirty-two thousand. Planners at the Redevelopment Authority predicted that twenty-nine thousand dilapidated units would likely face demolition. Given the tight credit situation and general economic malaise in the city, the two figured that private developers would be in short supply. To turn that situation around, they knew they would have to crack "the Vault."

In Boston the financial high ground was held by a dozen banks, insurance companies, and utilities, notably the State Street Bank and Trust, the National Shawmut Bank, the First National Bank of Boston, Eastern Gas and Fuel Associates, and Liberty Mutual Insurance Company. In the late 1950s leaders of these institutions, along with the presidents of major retail stores, including Jordan Marsh and Filenes, had formed a "Coordinating Committee" ostensibly to link Yankee commerce and the rough-and-tumble world of Boston politics. The committee members held their meetings in the boardroom of the Boston Safe Deposit and Trust Company. Secrecy and discretion were valued above all else; absent members could not send replacements and no minutes were ever kept. The group's penchant for secrecy and choice of venue for meetings earned them the sobriquet "the Vault" in the local press.

The tycoons dreamed of forging a powerful political and civic unit along the lines of the Allegheny Conference, which had revitalized downtown Pittsburgh shortly after World War II. No one wanted to face the uncertainty of a bankrupt Boston, but Vault members privately began to contemplate their potential role as receivers. Sitting around the Vault's conference table were powerful representatives from banking and insurance, retail business, real estate, and hotel development. The loss of manufacturing jobs, they believed, could be adequately compensated for by the expansion of the very service industries represented on their committee. With John F. Kennedy entering the White House and John McCormack serving as the Speaker of the House, Massachusetts' capital city could be assured of getting a lion's share of federal aid.

Collins was on good terms with at least one Vault member— Charles Coolidge, a senior partner in the prestigious law firm Ropes and Gray. Although a lifelong Republican, Coolidge had been impressed by Collins, giving rise to speculation during the campaign that the Vault and Collins could do business. When Collins asked for access to the Vault, Coolidge complied. The new mayor was determined to keep his pitch simple. He'd thought to himself that "banks and insurance companies don't give a shit about cities," but he felt that he could reach the Vault on its own level. Straightening himself in his wheelchair, Collins began: "There are a lot of theories about why your organization came into being—one being that you supported my opponent but actually dreaded his election and you're together now to deal with the possibility of having to pump the city into bankruptcy. I don't believe that was your purpose because anyone who did that would be engaged in a criminal conspiracy. Naturally, I will give anybody engaged in such conspiracy a chance to testify before a grand jury. But I know people like you would never engage in a conspiracy, and that rumor must be dispelled. I'd like to suggest a way to work it out. You all like to deal in structured environments and you're all busy. Let's meet every two weeks at four o'clock on Thursday. I'll create the agenda. I'll identify the problems which the city has that affect you. I'll tell you what the city can do and I'll tell you what I want you to do. I'll give the agenda items to Mr. Coolidge and if he wants to improve on them he'll tell me—won't you, Mr. Coolidge?" The Vault members had found a fellow traveler on the road to downtown revitalization. "Yes, mayor," Coolidge nodded. "I will."[20]

The implementation of the master plan for the New Boston would require an expert team of lawyers and housing specialists. As special counsel to the Redevelopment Authority, Logue chose Lewis Weinstein. In Logue's opinion, the New Boston would be well represented by Weinstein, the urbane partner from Foley, Hoag, and Eliot and counsel to the housing authorities in more than a dozen Massachusetts cities. Weinstein had proven so adept at steering public housing legislation through the statehouse that he had attracted national attention. Rumors were even circulating that President Kennedy was considering Weinstein for a top position at Housing and Urban Development. To Collins, Weinstein represented a clean break from the shenanigans of Jewish politicians like Julie Ansel and "Chief" Levine. Here, at last, was a prominent Jewish leader who understood progress. The man who had helped initiate the decline of a neighborhood with the sale of Roxbury's Hebrew College was now, ironically, slated to play a major role in the attempted revitalization of the city.

Weinstein had proved a quick study on the subject of eminent domain. His analysis of relevant statutes convinced him, and Logue, that they need not fear legal constraints regarding either the use of public money to seize vacant, "blighted" land or the selling or leasing to private persons of cleared land acquired by eminent domain. Writing in a major law journal, Weinstein announced, "[t]he courts almost unanimously upheld the validity of the redevelopment statutes on the theory that the primary objective was slum clearance, not the taking of the property of one individual and turning it over to another, and that disposition of the land after clearance is incidental to that basic public purpose."[21]

Collins and Logue, aided by their special counsel, began their transformation of Boston. Collins's successive tax cuts stimulated investor interest in downtown building projects. The Massachusetts Port Authority was given powers of eminent domain and tax-free properties to expand Logan International Airport. Lifelong residents suffered vertigo as they watched the construction of twenty-four hundred luxury high-rise apartments, dubbed Charles River Park, that rose from the rubble on the once-beloved turf of the West End. A modernistic city hall broke through the scarred earth that had only a short time before comprised the city's red light district. Ground, too, was broken for new federal and state office buildings in Government Center.

But Weinstein's greatest contribution to the "New Boston" came through the expansion of profitable and tax-yielding downtown real estate in an unanticipated direction, thereby strengthening ties with the wealthy western suburbs. At Copley Square, the Back Bay formed a narrow corridor constituted largely of nineteenth-century landfill, the old New Haven railway yards, and a few seedy hotels. One of Logue's most ambitious ideas was to develop this run-down section. Although Logue and executives from the Prudential Insurance Company agreed that the site might be perfect for a modern high-rise office complex, the Redevelopment Authority had been hamstrung by several advisory opinions that development on that scale was forbidden for an area zoned for mixed use. Weinstein studied the proposal. With the same self-confidence but with considerably more imagination than he'd mustered a decade earlier in analyzing the borders of Boston's inner-city Jewish community, Weinstein reassured his redevelopment colleagues. "I think we can draw legislation to make that kosher," he told Logue.[22] Weinstein proved true to his word and beamed proudly as the Prudential broke ground for its new fifty-two–story headquarters, commercial offices, and residential complex, which was erected largely on the basis of air rights and eliminated the eyesores of the railroad yards and turnpike right-of-way. Weinstein's innovations in the sale of "blighted" land and the legislation that it initiated contributed mightily to the revitalization of Boston and provided a significant precedent for urban renewal across the country.

Friends and foes alike agreed that Logue showed a particular genius for attracting federal rehabilitation funds. When the Boston Redevelopment Authority (BRA) chief arrived, the city had begun only four urban renewal projects covering an area of 75 acres. After only five years with Logue at the helm, an additional eight projects, worth $150 million and covering 2,667 acres, had been approved. By comparison, New York City, with roughly thirteen times the population of Boston, had managed to attract only enough federal money to redevelop 2,785 acres.[23] From his office on the top floor of city hall, with its stark white walls and colorful maps of projects in process, Ed Logue surveyed the New Boston. With the full support of his mayor, his excellent ties to funding sources in Washington, and his clever Jewish legal advisor, nothing could hinder his plans.

One of Logue's earliest undertakings was the Washington Park Project, the rehabilitation of 186 acres in Roxbury. It played wonderfully in both the press and the neighborhoods. A master of public relations, Logue touted his "planning with people" program, which brought BRA officials into contact with residents of renewal areas, be they Irish dockworkers, black housewives, or recently arrived Chinese. Since his arrival in Boston, Logue had carefully wooed what the city's tabloids called the "tea-drinking Negroes." NAACP branch president Melinea Cass had pledged publicly that the black community would "work with Logue and his staff family so that we might have the kind of city he is trying to bring us." Otto and Muriel Snowden, the founders of Freedom House, got on famously with the new BRA head and were chosen by Logue to take on all community organization responsibilities for the renewal programs through a funded-project office in Freedom House, the former site of Hebrew College. For the Snowdens and other mainstream black leaders in Roxbury, rehabilitation with federal funds was looked upon as the magic wand that could sanitize a decade of upheaval.[24] It was the federal government, in the form of the FHA, that had been responsible for the creation of so many slums prior to 1950. It was therefore fitting that the federal Urban Renewal Administration should raze or rehabilitate those crumbling tenements now populated by low-income blacks. Decisive action, they believed, would not only send a message to the remaining whites that it was safe to stay but encourage others to move into the area as well.

Throughout the early 1960s Logue had advanced rehabilitation as an alternative to razings. It soon became apparent, however, that almost 10 percent of Washington Park's twenty-seven thousand housing units were beyond repair and, indeed, would not be spared a visit from the federal bulldozer. Boston planners had noted the amazing passivity with which the eviction notices were received. The Snowdens were particularly effective in calming the fears of residents who would shortly be forced from their homes with promises of abundant affordable housing. The quiet ambience of block meetings in Roxbury were a far cry from those in Irish Charlestown, where BRA planners were met with catcalls and even flying objects.

In the name of progress, the wrecking balls obliterated twenty-five hundred dwellings in Washington Park, the heart of Roxbury. But the eight hundred new units built to replace the slum dwellings went on the market at rents too high for the former residents. Growing numbers of the city's blacks began to fear that Boston-style urban renewal was, as elsewhere, synonymous with

"Negro removal." As entire black neighborhoods crumbled under earth-moving equipment, Boston's black population continued to swell, driven mainly by recent migration from the south. Muriel Snowden, for one, was no longer arranging fashion shows for local ingenues; she was far too busy teaching new arrivals about parking regulations and garbage disposal. Without adequate relocation funds, many of the Washington Park refugees searched frantically for new apartments. Further north, slum clearance was also under way in the black community at the edge of the downtown business district. To the east lay the overtly hostile Irish sections of Dorchester. To the west was Jamaica Plain, where John Collins and other politicians and city workers now lived comfortably in large Victorian homes. By and large, the relocatees had only one direction remaining: southward into Jewish Dorchester. The invisible line demarcating Boston's ethnic neighborhoods had suddenly shifted without comment or organized protest. Jewish leaders matched blacks in their passive response to neighborhood change. Such passivity would be well noted by future planners of the new Boston.

Julius Ansel did not live long enough to see the full fruition of the ambitious development program. On March 15, 1965, the 57-year-old politician died of a heart attack. Ansel would have approved of the funeral arrangements. More than three thousand people filled the sidewalks and packed into Congregation Agudas Israel on Woodrow Avenue. Colleagues from the Massachusetts Senate and House of Representatives attended en masse. Governor John Volpe was joined in a front pew by former governors Endicott Peabody and Foster Furcolo. President Lyndon Johnson even sent a telegram bidding farewell to his "valued friend" who could always be counted on to deliver the Democratic vote. But mostly it was Ansel's beloved "little people" who pressed into the synagogue—the men and women for whom "Julie" had fixed tickets, secured jobs, and committed petty crimes and venial sins. Ansel was eulogized by Agudas Israel's Polish-born rabbi, Meyer Strassfeld. "Julius Ansel always heard the voice of God in the cry of the poor, sick, downtrodden and oppressed," the rabbi intoned. "He was willing to battle established procedures, prejudices and any action which he felt endangered the dignity of man and the respectability of an individual."[25] The eulogy was vintage Strassfeld, placing heavy emphasis on the Jewish obligation of "healing the world." The congregants of Agudas Israel had heard it all before. Some may have wondered what it had to do with Ansel, the enchanting con artist who made a public mockery of respectability and could hardly qualify as a citizen of the world. His heart, they knew, belonged exclusively to the blue-collar Jews of Ward 14.

The dignitaries who came to pay their last respects to Ansel could not have known that a deep schism had developed in the early 1960s between Rabbi Strassfeld and his congregants. Nor could they know that it was indicative of an even deeper rift between American Jewish leaders and blue-collar Jews across the country. For more than a decade the rabbi and his congregation had been growing further apart. Strassfeld felt a special calling to the Judaic principle of *tikkun,* the obligation to heal the world of social ills. Almost alone among the city's Orthodox rabbis, he had directed his energy into what he considered the greatest moral issue of the time: the struggle of the nation's blacks for equal rights under the law. While a student, Strassfeld had felt torn between his Talmudic study sessions at a New York yeshiva and the liberal ideology he encountered in the classroom at Brooklyn College. When he arrived at Agudas Israel in 1952, he was ritually in sync with the synagogue's six hundred observant families but politically at odds with them. The congregation was largely working-class—butchers, carpet layers, plasterers, and masons, with an occasional insurance salesman or shopkeeper. Among the most notable of the congregants was Irving Green, co-owner of the G&G delicatessen. Each Sabbath, Rabbi Strassfeld delivered in fluent Yiddish his *derashah,* or commentary on the weekly Torah portion. Only on High Holy Days, when grown children would return from the suburbs to attend services with their parents, would he switch to English. Invariably, he would be upbraided by his *balabatim,* the synagogue officers, for whom the use of English during services was little short of sacrilege. "It's not my fault, it's your fault," he'd shoot back. "If you'd taught your children Yiddish, they'd understand."[26]

Only one week before Ansel's funeral, Strassfeld had responded to the Reverend Martin Luther King's nationwide appeal to American clergy to march for black voting rights in Selma, Alabama. He was one of only two Orthodox rabbis in Massachusetts to do so. Scores of Reform and Conservative rabbis had answered the call, even chartering aircraft to Alabama. But Strassfeld had met only with blank stares when he asked administrators of the Union of Orthodox Congregations to defray even a small part of his travel expenses. The leaders of Orthodoxy reasoned that a rabbi's place was with his congregation. After witnessing the attacks on King and his supporters at the Pettus bridge by white mobs and the subsequent gassing of the civil rights demonstrators by police, Strassfeld could only shake his head at their narrow and parochial mentality. Unlike many of Rev. King's Jewish supporters, whose Jewishness was incidental to their liberal beliefs, Strassfeld felt compelled *halakhically*—by virtue of Jewish law—to enter the civil rights struggle. The love of God, he argued, was not complete without the love of one's fellow citizen. In King's march for voting rights, the rabbi saw the fulfilled promise of Psalm 145: "The Lord lifts up all who are falling, and raises up all who are bowed down. . . ." The following August, when President Johnson signed the Voting Rights Act, Strassfeld saw the promise of the psalmist fulfilled: "The Lord is near to all who call upon him; he hears their cry and saves them."

After the Selma march Strassfeld returned invigorated, determined to expand his own contacts in the black community and to challenge his aging congregation's commitment to justice and mercy. Back in Boston he deepened his acquaintance with Rev. Virgil Wood, a close aide to Rev. King and the regional representative of the Southern Christian Leadership Conference. Rev. Wood had earned his stripes in the civil rights movement as pastor at the Diamond Hill Baptist Church in Lynchburg, Virginia. In that small southern city of fundamentalist churches and manufacturing plants, Wood had led several sit-ins and demonstrations against Lynchburg's segregation ordinances. Unlike those of other southern municipalities, Lynchburg's officials and employees sought accommodation with the black clergymen. Wood had earned accolades from whites and blacks alike for helping to open manufacturing jobs to blacks, thereby advancing peaceful integration.

That spring Wood's family joined Strassfeld's for the traditional Passover seder in which Jews read from the illustrated *Haggadah* a vivid retelling of the story of the Israelites' exodus from slavery in Egypt. Together the two men seized on the idea of a similar holiday for America's blacks that would emphasize the enslavement of Africans and their struggle for independence in the West. In place of the unleavened matzoh hurriedly baked by the fleeing ancient Israelites, the men spoke animatedly about traditional slave dishes made from sweet potatoes. At the center of the black seder table they envisioned not the symbol of the pascal lamb but a miniature finely crafted slave block depicting scenes of cruelty and ultimate redemption.

Following the voting rights march, Wood lobbied King strenuously to come to Boston. Issues for Boston's blacks, he argued, might lack the glamour of the struggle in the south but were no less substantive. Wood was correct. On April 20, 1965, only two days before King touched down at Logan International Airport, the Boston branch of the NAACP had filed suit in Federal District Court seeking the desegregation of the Boston Public Schools. To the delight of Boston's Jewish leaders, the visit from the man described as "the black Moses" also coincided with the Passover holiday. King's visit to Boston proved less opportune for Mayor Collins. On the day before King's arrival Collins received what he remembers as a "nonnegotiable demand" from Virgil Wood: "We demand that Mayor Collins meet Dr. King, the Nobel Prize winner, at Logan Airport." Collins didn't appreciate the tone and responded with characteristic bluntness. "I don't meet visitors at the airport unless they're guests of the State Department." Wood hung tough. "Then you'll meet him at the Carter Playground in Roxbury. That is also nonnegotiable," is how Collins recalled the conversation. Collins struggled to regain control of his emotions. "There is nobody I would rather meet than Dr. King. He is a distinguished visitor and I meet all distinguished visitors at city hall. I hope to see him here."[27]

King's first day in Boston was hectic. It began with a short press conference, then proceeded to a tour of Roxbury's urban renewal area, a visit at the statehouse with Governor John Volpe, and an address before a joint session of the legislature. King's day ended at Boston's most distinguished synagogue, Temple Israel, where Rabbi Roland Gitelsohn and his Reform congregation had asked the civil rights leader to attend Passover services.

Temple Israel (on Boston's Riverway, bordering Brookline) was a natural to host Martin Luther King. Its congregants consisted mostly of liberal and affluent professionals, many of whom worked at nearby major medical centers. The temple had always been proud of its reputation for pushing the edges of Judaism. Back in the late 1800s, Rabbi Solomon Schindler introduced Sunday services with an eye toward changing the very day of Judaism's most treasured symbol, the Sabbath. Schindler was followed at Temple Israel by an even more radical theologian, Rabbi Charles Fleischer, who encouraged his flock to intermarry as a means to bring forth a "new nation." By 1965 Temple Israel was solidly modern Reform. Social action committees had replaced theological experimentation as the correct path for liberal Jews. Rabbi Gitelsohn led several attempts to establish joint programs with black churches in Roxbury. The relationships, however, were never truly reciprocal. Temple Israel members were only too happy to play host to blacks at their synagogue, but it was always difficult for the rabbi to find sufficient numbers of his own congregants to visit the black churches in Roxbury. Although tens of thousands of Boston's less affluent Jews lived in areas contiguous to the black neighborhoods, the trip across town was considered too dangerous for many of Temple Israel's members. The gulf between the rhetoric of the social action committees and the personal concerns of the members was further evidenced by a study commissioned by the temple's board shortly before King's arrival. Worried by the rapidity of neighborhood change in Roxbury, the board hired a demographic expert to determine if the growing black population was likely to push further west toward the temple. The congregation was relieved to learn that the city's major medical institutions, including Harvard Medical School and Children's Hospital, served as a permanent buffer between Temple Israel and the black community.

Rabbi Strassfeld could not help but think that King would have found more in common with the emotive and traditional Judaism practiced in the *shtibels* on Blue Hill Avenue. He understood, however, that the movement depended on appearances at progressive and wealthy Jewish institutions. In the mid-1960s Jews nationwide were contributing as much as 75 percent of the operating funds of the Student Nonviolent Coordinating Committee, the Southern Christian Leadership Conference, and the Congress of Racial Equality.[28] New York businessman Stanley Levinson was serving as Rev. King's fund-raiser and adviser. In Dorchester the tight charitable dollar rarely found its way outside intrinsically Jewish causes.

The morning after King's appearance at Temple Israel, thousands of Bostonians gathered to greet King at the Carter Playground in Roxbury, the point of origin for his first massive march in a northern city. By the time the marchers arrived downtown at the Boston Common, the crowd had swelled to twenty thousand. King, who had done graduate work at the Boston University School of Theology, immediately challenged the righteousness of the New Boston. "The vision of the New Boston must extend into the heart of Roxbury," he told his rapt audience. "Boston must become a testing ground for the ideals of freedom. . . . We must not become a nation of onlookers. This fight is not for the sake of the Negro alone, but rather for the aspirations of America itself. All Americans must take a stand against evil."

John Collins, the major architect of the New Boston, was not at the Carter Playground or at Boston Common to hear King. He'd felt handcuffed and insulted by Wood's demands. He wanted to meet the civil rights leader, but he would not allow one of King's advance men to place him in a position of weakness. Collins resolved to remain at his desk at city hall up until the moment that King departed the city for the airport; then no one could accuse him of snubbing the civil rights leader. By 6:30 P.M. most of the workers in the mayor's office had gone home, and Collins was catching up on paperwork and chatting with the police officer assigned as his bodyguard. The officer went to the foyer when he heard a commotion in the stairwell and returned with King and his entourage. Collins was not a man who warmed up to people easily, but it took him less than ten minutes to succumb to King's charm. The two men spoke of the urban renewal program in Roxbury, with Collins emphasizing the need to raze blighted areas and King emphasizing the need to find replacement housing for the black poor. Collins expressed his willingness to work with any federal agencies that might provide rent subsidies and other alternatives to public housing for the city's poor. Collins recalled that he might have been swept away by King's courtliness had it not been for continuous icy glares emanating from Virgil Wood. "Listen, Dr. King, I do the best I can and I'm not afraid to ask for help," Collins said. "But your man there, Virgil Wood, is impossible to get along with, absolutely impossible." Wood, Collins recalled, nearly flew off his chair. "That's the mayor," Wood shouted. "Divide and conquer." King's closest adviser and colleague, Ralph Abernathy, moved quickly from where he was seated on a windowsill and wordlessly placed one hand on Wood's shoulder. To Collins, Wood seemed to wilt under the powerful touch of Abernathy. But the outburst seemed to make the need for diplomacy unnecessary. "I don't expect there will be a new mayor in this town for some time," King reportedly said. "I don't think you'll be having any further trouble from my staff."[29] John Collins, the pragmatist, and Martin Luther King, the visionary, understood one another.

After King's visit to Boston, Strassfeld began to believe that his congregation could serve as a role model for cooperation with the nearby black community. He urged his congregants to welcome the blacks from the Washington Park urban renewal areas who now sought housing in the wooden triple-deckers in the Woodrow Avenue–Norfolk Street area nearest to the synagogue. Invariably, the response was that the arrival of the blacks meant only two things: a decline in property values and an increase in street crime. The rabbi countered with descriptions of black and Jewish Freedom Riders who were changing the face of the south, but the congregants scoffed at the southern exploits. They suggested that the rabbi look instead just a few blocks to the north where congregants of once-majestic synagogues, like Adath Jeshurun on Blue Hill Avenue, were now besieged by violent street crime and struggled to survive behind security fences. But Strassfeld was undeterred. On the Jewish New Year, a time when Jews reflect on the year gone by and repent, Strassfeld prepared a Rosh Hashanah *derashah* (sermon) that, he hoped, would appeal to the consciences of his followers. "Dorchester, indeed America, was not always our community. We, too, were allowed to move here. Decent black families are moving to our area. Let us remain firm and work with our new neighbors. Blacks and Jews share a history of persecution and oppression. It is time they shared neighborhoods as well."[30] The congregants of Agudas Israel looked at the rabbi as if he'd grown a second head. "What do you want with the *schwartzes?*" one man demanded at the conclusion of the sermon. "They'll stab you in the back."

Rabbi Strassfeld began to feel like an outcast in his own community. As he became increasingly absorbed with social issues, including his growing opposition to the Vietnam War, he could feel his bonds to Orthodox Judaism beginning to weaken. For several months a Conservative congregation in Marblehead, on Massachusetts' North Shore, had been conducting an unsuccessful search for a rabbi. Quietly, Strassfeld began to negotiate with the temple's board. Although less than twenty miles north of Boston, Marblehead and Dorchester were worlds apart. Dotted with homes of sea captains crowned by widows' walks, Marblehead offered ocean breezes, sailing regattas, and a small but growing Jewish community committed to the liberal causes of the day. In historic Marblehead one could at last teach and serve fellow Jews whose minds were not clouded by obsessive mistrust of the *goyim*. What his new congregation lacked in adherence to Jewish ritual, Strassfeld reasoned, they would more than make up for in political sophistication. Strassfeld prepared to depart for the shore.

Large black families, ineligible for return to the rehabbed one- and two-bedroom Washington Park units, continued to spread out into North Dorchester throughout the mid-1960s. Jewish landlords grudgingly rented their apartments to the newcomers, just as they had done in Washington Park a decade before. Tenants, however, were not enamored of life in the triple-deckers, particularly the older houses along Norfolk Street. Many of the aging Jewish homeowners had been unable or unwilling to put improvements into their properties. Decrepit gas-stack hot water heating systems, largely gone from most neighborhoods across the city, were still the rule rather than the exception in much of Jewish Dorchester. Even in 1960, according to U.S. Census data, 22 percent of the housing in the Norfolk Street area was already characterized as "deteriorated." Housing built at the same time in Irish Savin Hill, on the other hand, showed a zero percent rating in the "deteriorated" category.

If the blacks came to generalize Jews as slumlords, the Jews, particularly the elderly, perceived the black newcomers as violent criminals. Unsupervised youths cut a swath through the neighborhood and stunned the elderly Jews with the callousness of their crimes. A purse snatching on the Avenue was regularly followed with a knockdown and a sharp kick to the face. With the growing demands for black power and community control, many young black hoodlums fancied themselves as freedom fighters. An assault on an elderly pensioner was elevated to an attack on capitalism itself. Beating an old man on his way to an

*evening service at one of the Woodrow Avenue shuls and then
yanking his pants down around his ankles translated as payback
for hundreds of years of humiliating servitude. By 1966 the
conversation at the G&G was slowly turning from local politics to
hospital updates for the latest mugging victim.*

In 1966 Rabbi Strassfeld put up for sale his home on
Mattapan's Hazelton Street, a broad street barely a half mile south
of Agudas Israel. The large single and two-family homes were of
sounder construction and had larger rooms and more amenities
than the houses in North Dorchester. Few blacks had moved into
Mattapan beyond the intersection of Blue Hill Avenue and Morton
Street. The 1960 census had shown only 473 nonwhites among a
population of 10,000 in Mattapan. Over the next five years, despite
the pressures of urban renewal, the community had remained
largely unchanged. A black couple, both professionals, was the
first to respond to the rabbi's listing. The house suited them
perfectly. The Marblehead-bound rabbi encouraged the buyers,
anxious both for a quick sale and an opportunity to assert his own
belief in equal housing opportunity. During the weeks in which
the potential buyers sought financing, a night rarely passed without a troubling phone call. "Why are you selling us out to the
blacks?" asked one congregant. "You're leaving us for a fancy
synagogue somewhere else," shouted another hysterical congregant during a late night phone call. "We're left here with the
blacks. You're always telling us about integration. Do you want
your daughter to marry a black?" The rabbi was shaken by the
overt racism of the callers as well as by a nagging recognition of the
hypocritical nature of preaching racial equality and moving to a
swanky North Shore town with few minorities. "Their attitudes are
wrong," he reasoned, "but I simply can't do this to my congregation." Anxious to resolve the growing dilemma, the board members of Agudas Israel offered to buy Strassfeld's house as a
parsonage for his successor. Saddened and confused, the rabbi
agreed and called the black couple and told them that the house
was no longer for sale.

As Strassfeld packed away his books and personal effects, he
contemplated the final irony of his twelve years as a spiritual leader
to the Jewish community of Dorchester. For years he had negotiated with the congregation for a proper housing allowance. The
best congregations, he told them, offer their rabbis homes as an

incentive to remain in the community. "Too expensive," had been the standard reply. His successor would now receive the benefit for which he had fought unsuccessfully for more than a decade. It seemed to the departing rabbi that nothing short of offering to sell his home to a black would have been sufficient to bring about that change.

Carrying the Message

Ethnic Conflict and Urban Renewal in the Mid-60s

"What's new and exciting?" It was the phrase that Eli Goldston, president of Eastern Gas and Fuel Associates, used to open almost every conversation. Regardless of whether the greeting was directed toward a gas meter reader or a colleague on the powerful Vault, Goldston always seemed to presume the existence of an innovative project and was ready with genuine words of encouragement. That his 1967 partnership in the country's largest urban renewal project had results for Boston's blacks that were neither new nor exciting would eventually confound Goldston and the city's other leading liberals.

Boston had never seen a corporate executive like Goldston and has not seen one like him since. The sole Jewish member of the Vault during the 1960s, Goldston was a devotee of "doing well by doing good." Goldston did well through the creative management of thirteen subsidiary companies engaged in the production,

92

sale, and transportation (including river and ocean barge lines) of the raw materials of energy—principally bituminous coal, coke, and gas. Goldston was energy incarnate, managing not only his own corporate empire but serving as director of a number of the city's largest firms, including John Hancock Mutual Life Insurance Company, the First National Bank of Boston, and Raytheon Company.

It was through doing good, however, that Goldston developed a national reputation in the 1960s as "the man who taught the corporate elephant to dance." Goldston's favorite role was that of the *shadhan,* the traditional Jewish matchmaker. During numerous speeches to associations of manufacturers and business executives, he loved to soften up his audiences with the folk wisdom and humor characteristic of Yiddish literature. His toughest match, he'd tell them, was trying to marry off "Miss Urban Crisis" to "Mr. Industrial Free Enterprise." Goldston frequently offered the executives a personalized glimpse of the enigmatic world of matchmaking through the following scenario:

"But you said she was a beautiful girl," whispered the wealthy young man who recoils in dismay when the *shadhan* introduces him to his prospective bride. "She's at least fifty years old and she has a face like a duck. You said she was shapely but she's fat enough for two women."

"Oh, you don't have to whisper," replied the *shadhan.* "She's also very hard of hearing."

At this point the lady stood up and began to walk painfully toward the two men. "Oh my," the young man said. "She limps, too."

"But only when she walks," replied the *shadhan.*

Goldston would then challenge the snickering manufacturers to change their mental picture of a desirable mate. Why, he asked rhetorically, should business marry a girl like that? "Because you, the business community, made her what she is today, and you, the business community, are the only bridegroom left."[1]

Eli Goldston arrived by train in Boston from the small town of Warren, Ohio, in 1938 to attend Harvard College. His high school teachers had taken a special interest in their earnest student and encouraged him to go east for higher education. He would not disappoint them, eventually graduating from both Harvard Law School and Harvard Business School. From the moment he'd arrived in the city, Goldston began to make connections. Barely able to drag his steamer trunk up the stairs at the Harvard subway kiosk, he enlisted the help of another arriving student, Endicott Peabody. Twenty-five years later Peabody would be elected governor of Massachusetts and Goldston would be among the state's most prominent citizens.

Goldston proved to be the perfect candidate to help lift Boston out of the economic slump. An ardent devotee of American success stories as relayed by popular writers such as Dale Carnegie and Norman Vincent Peale, Goldston radiated confidence. Many of the entrenched Brahmin executives at Eastern Gas were suspicious of the beefy midwesterner. Their judgment was confirmed when Goldston took the unprecedented step of promoting talented Irish and black workers to management positions. Goldston easily disarmed his critics with his self-effacing humor, and his innovations were trumpeted in the national business press. Jealous underlings knew better than to disturb an active volcano. Boston's business elite believed they had found a precious asset in Goldston. His "can do" midwestern attitude was particularly refreshing. Charles Coolidge, a Vault founder and senior partner in the law firm of Ropes and Gray, offered Goldston an introduction to Mayor John Collins in 1962. "John, meet Eli. He's a very attractive and useful fellow."[2] The mayor and the utility executive took an immediate liking to one another. They, together with urban renewal chief Ed Logue, quickly formed a troika determined to turn Boston into a success-oriented metropolis.

In many ways the three encompassed much of the *traditional* American ethos of success and progress. For Logue, redevelopment rested on the belief that most Americans had the ambition to move up—to make the journey from rundown inner city, to better city neighborhood, to suburban development, and, with perseverance, eventually to a home with a commanding view on some sublime hilltop. Logue chafed at the demands of community activists who insisted that all displaced persons in urban renewal areas be allowed to move back into rehabilitated units. For Logue, there was something un-American about returning where you had already been. Moreover, he was confident that residents of Roxbury and other urban renewal areas would, in time, understand that they were involved in a historic national experiment upon which the progress of America depended. "Bostonians love their city. I believe they are ready to do their share toward making it a better place," he wrote shortly after coming to the Redevelopment Authority. "Once started on its way toward rebuilding, Boston will find all America cheering it on and ready to help. There is, after all, a little bit of Boston in everyone who calls himself an American."[3]

For John Collins, success was linked with tireless striving and the overcoming of adversity. Surely, if he could run a successful mayoralty campaign from a wheelchair, the city could lift itself out of economic paralysis. In many respects Collins's election represented the triumph of good character over charisma in Boston leadership. The city had seen enough of flamboyant political personalities like James Michael Curley. The successful transformation of Boston would require the endowments of a man like Collins: hard work, thrift, courage, self-reliance, honesty, and patient plodding.[4] In this regard, being born into modest circumstances was actually an advantage in that it provided opportunities to transcend obstacles that were unavailable to children of the rich. If Irish John Collins could make the journey from a working-class apartment in Roxbury to the corner office at City hall, surely a poor black could do the same.

In Eli Goldston the American idea of success had been given full expression. In many ways Goldston was a throwback to the gilded age of the nineteenth century, when the acquisition of great wealth was considered a noble pursuit. Like industrialist Andrew Carnegie, Goldston preached that the wealthy and successful were duty-bound to assist those less fortunate—to "do well by doing good." Only through acts of social responsibility and community service could the wealthy develop the nobility of character and peace of mind necessary for "true success." There was a religious component as well to Goldston's worldview. Back in Warren, Ohio, his father had founded a Reform synagogue as an alternative to the town's small Orthodox house of prayer.[5] When Goldston arrived in Boston, he gravitated to Temple Israel, where social action committees provided ample opportunity for members to feel virtuous. Eli Goldston, like John Kennedy and John Collins—all "outsiders"—was now donning the mantle of leadership that had been worn exclusively by Boston's Brahmins.

Goldston made friends in the black community as easily as he did in the business community. Elma Lewis, Roxbury's fiery arts patron, whose lifelong dream was the establishment of an Afro-American school for the performing arts, formed a deep friendship with Goldston after the two met at various charity events. To Lewis, Goldston represented the best in Boston's philanthropists: generous but practical, gracious without a hint of paternalism. Lewis and Goldston did not so much converse as trade monologues on the arts, business, government, and social policy. It was not uncommon to find the stocky Lewis speaking directly to Goldston for more than an hour while the rapt executive did little more than nod or utter, "I see." Goldston would then launch into his own hour-long analysis while Lewis, never known for her patience, hung on every word. To Goldston, Elma Lewis represented that most vital but underrated of all players in a great struggle — the messenger.

Few who knew Goldston had not been treated to his dramatic reading of "A Message to Garcia," an inspirational success essay written in 1899 by soap salesman turned journalist Elbert Hubbard. During the early part of the century, as many as forty million copies of the essay were thought to be in distribution in some fifty languages. The inspiration for "A Message to Garcia" was the story of a young soldier ordered by President McKinley to fight his way across Cuba with a message for the leader of the Cuban insurgents. The true hero, Hubbard insisted, is the one who "carries the message," a phrase symbolizing any job done efficiently without fuss and self-importance. It is the "messenger" types who are capable of great enterprise, who work without an eye on the clock, and who grow old struggling against indifference. Lewis fit this description of messenger. She had started teaching dance in a one-room Roxbury studio. She demanded great discipline and devotion from her students and offered unqualified support in return. She would not, however, be content to limit her vision, which encompassed a national center for Afro-American arts in Roxbury. That was the no-nonsense message that she carried to her friend Eli Goldston.

Lewis and other black leaders respected Goldston's motives in Boston's black community precisely because his interests, by his own admission, were not purely altruistic. Other major Jewish figures in business and philanthropy, notably leather manufacturer Kivie Kaplan, were engaged in the financial backing of black civil rights groups, including the NAACP. Privately, black leaders resented the perceived moral smugness of these philanthropists who seemed motivated as much by publicity and honors as by the desire for distributive justice. Goldston, however, not only talked about the danger of stereotypes, he shattered them. Shortly after arriving at Eastern, he challenged the utility's practice of prompt shutoffs for nonpayment in poor, largely black neighborhoods. When challenged, Goldston did not present the image of poor, shivering children in inner-city neighborhoods; instead, he produced documentation showing even greater rates of nonpayment in suburban neighborhoods populated by transient executives. If the gas company should redline any neighborhood, he reasoned, it should be those suburban areas. Goldston also saw in the city's black community an unprecedented opportunity to expand the franchise for Boston Gas, one of Eastern Gas and Fuel's largest franchises. Goldston knew that Eastern, as a utility locked into a product and a franchise area, would suffer economically if a major portion of its central territory were to descend into decay or demolition. In Roxbury, Eli Goldston knew that hundreds, if not thousands, of talented individuals awaited their chance to carry a "message to Garcia." Better, he thought, that they receive that chance at the same time that Boston Gas made a significant addition to its gas load.

On Friday, June 2, 1967, Bostonians opened their afternoon papers and learned that Massachusetts Attorney General Elliot Richardson planned to reopen the Boston Strangler case. It was shocking news. Over the course of two years the city had been deeply scarred by reports of the strangulation of thirteen women. Detectives had combed their files for suspects while terrified single women raced to locksmiths to reinforce the security of their apartments. Suspicion came to rest on Albert DeSalvo, an intermittently employed handyman and former patient at the Mattapan State Hospital. By the beginning of 1967 officials had gathered sufficient evidence to convict DeSalvo of the murders. The court testimony had been particularly lurid: psychiatric experts described a compulsive killer whose enormous sexual drive could be satisfied only by strangling his victims with their pantyhose—after which he would tie intricate little bows in the murder weapons.

Bostonians had believed that the terror had finally ended when DeSalvo was sent away for life to the maximum security state prison in suburban Walpole. Now it appeared that the attorney general was not totally convinced that they had the right man.

In the brouhaha over the strangler, it was easy to overlook a small news item toward the back of the papers that described a sit-in and silent vigil by thirty black welfare mothers in the drab Grove Hall welfare office in Roxbury. The mothers vowed to remain until their demands were satisfied by official responses to the following issues: work training programs, representation on welfare decision-making boards, and a "policy on politeness" for welfare office workers who, the mothers claimed, treated recipients with open contempt. There would be no dramatic developments on the reopening of the Boston Strangler case, but the repercussions of the small sit-in would capture the attention of an entire city for weeks to come.

Urban warfare had arrived late in Boston. Roxbury had lagged considerably behind Harlem, Detroit, and Watts in the outbreak of major urban uprisings, and that was just fine with Thomas Atkins and especially with Paul Parks, a close associate of Martin Luther King. Neither man had much patience with the strident calls for black power and community control now emanating from the Black United Front and other radical groups in Boston. "What you want is absolute control of the caboose," Atkins would chide the city's black radicals. "I want access to the whole train."[6]

Atkins and Parks, two of the city's most promising black leaders, were monitoring Boston's first race riot from the Operation Exodus office at 378 Blue Hill Avenue shortly after 2:00 A.M. on June 3 when a burst of gunfire shattered the police-imposed curfew. A few hours earlier the two men had congratulated a small group of black street workers for implementing Atkins's plan to limit the effects of the previous night's violence. Atkins, the vice-chairman of the NAACP, had convinced Boston police superintendent Edmund McNamara of the need to place well-known black leaders at the site of rioting in order to provide a counterbalance to the radicals intent on escalating the troubles. To angry young blacks, Atkins's plan smacked of complicity with despised city authorities. Secretly, however, Atkins had instructed his observers to keep an eye open for incidents of police overreaction and to document any instances of police brutality. The plan had been carried out at considerable personal risk, for the fusillade of bricks, soda bottles, and rocks along Blue Hill Avenue grew so intense that observers spent more time with their heads down than up.

The riot had started at 5:00 P.M. on Friday when the protesters from Mothers for Adequate Welfare not only refused to leave the Grove Hall Welfare Office but chained the doors from the inside, denying egress to fifty-eight office workers and social workers. A weary Mayor Collins, who had returned from a trip to Ireland the night before, received a call from the police commissioner reporting that one of the captive office workers had taken ill, possibly with heart trouble. Collins, who had hoped to wait out the demonstrators, ordered the police to enter the building by any means possible, remove the workers, and arrest the protesters. Hundreds of the neighborhood's black residents watched as Boston patrolmen smashed through plate glass and cut through the bicycle chains used by the protesters to secure the building. Curses, taunts, and the sounds of shattering glass filled the welfare office as the police tried to arrest the trespassers and free their hostages. One of the demonstrators who evaded capture rushed from the building. "They're beating people in there. It's terrible," she cried.[7] As police tried to escort the welfare employees from the building, they were met by another fusillade of bricks and bottles. Soon more than seven hundred angry blacks squared off with one hundred police reinforcements. As if on signal, seventy or eighty black youths engaged the police officers amid supporting cries of "Black power!" from the next human wave. The politics of violence had found its voice. "No Viet Cong ever clubbed me,"[8] cried out one wounded rioter as he attempted to staunch the flow of blood from a gash on his head inflicted by a police nightstick.

Pitched battles continued until 8:30 P.M., when riot-helmeted police, their short-sleeved white shirts spattered with blood, formed a flying wedge and led the welfare workers toward Seaver Street and safety. After the arrest of the welfare mothers and the release of their captives, the rioting spread through a five-block area contiguous to Grove Hall. Cohen's Furniture store, on the 300 block of Blue Hill Avenue, was among the first to be torched. Rioters then burned and looted several hardware and shoe stores, also Jewish-owned. Whites caught either on foot or in passing cars were subject to beatings and cuts from flying shards of glass from shattered windshields. The police commissioner activated the entire seventeen-hundred–man force after his officers came under intense sniper fire at the corner of Intervale Street and Blue Hill Avenue. Armed with .30 caliber carbines, the reinforcements mustered at the high school football stadium in Franklin Park. By 9:30 P.M., when police had successfully cordoned off the area of the worst rioting, thirty people had been seriously injured and more than $500,000 in property damage committed. By the early hours of Saturday morning, most of the rioters had gone home to bed, leaving the fire department to deal with dozens of gasoline-fed grass fires and the work crews to contend with gaping storefronts. Atkins, Parks, and fifteen other black leaders in the Operation Exodus office knew the rioters would return in force the next day and considered ways to minimize injuries and property damage.

Both Atkins and Parks came from Indiana—Atkins from Elkhart and Parks from Indianapolis. Like Goldston, these midwesterners were perceived as principled and pragmatic. And in Boston's competitive black community there was a distinct advantage to "out of town" status, provided that "out of town" did not mean recent arrivals from agrarian southern states. Atkins had arrived in Boston in 1961 to attend graduate school in Middle Eastern studies at Harvard University. A superb student at Indiana University, he earned Phi Beta Kappa in his junior year. At Harvard he'd written a scathing research paper on the organizational failings of the local branch of the NAACP. The paper was shown to NAACP branch president Ken Guscott, who, instead of turning defensive, correctly gauged Atkins's energy and intelligence and offered him a job in the organization. "It's pretty easy to criticize," Guscott told Atkins. "Let's see you do better." It would be the end of Atkins's formal studies in Arabic and Middle East politics. "What I was doing at the NAACP seemed more relevant than sitting over at Harvard discussing somebody's theory about somebody's theory," he recalled.[9]

Atkins's reputation in Boston was further enhanced through his friendship with Bill Russell, the player-coach of the Boston Celtics. Boston's professional sports teams had long employed a higher percentage of white players than was normally found on other professional teams across the nation. In Boston, it was widely believed, white spectators simply would not pay to watch a team comprised mainly of blacks, and Russell had always been expected to adapt. "I play them (blacks) two at a time when we're at home, three when we're on the road—and five when we're behind," he later told a reporter.[10] Russell, however, would not be denied the opportunities a sports-mad town offered its greatest white competitors and set about to master the boardroom with the same tenacity he'd displayed on the basketball court. Like his rival, Philadelphia's center Wilt Chamberlain, the Boston basketball legend was diversifying in the 1960s. But even a legend has difficulty balancing a position as player-coach, a book contract, a basketball shoe endorsement, and a rubber plantation in Liberia. Russell hired Atkins to serve as general manager of Bill Russell Enterprises. After only one year, however, Atkins wearied of the business world, deciding instead on a legal career. In June 1966 Atkins presented himself at the admissions office of Harvard Law School. He had not only neglected to take the necessary aptitude exam but was several months late in applying for the coming fall semester. Atkins's persuasive powers, however, were not lost on the admissions officer. After an impassioned presentation lasting several hours, Atkins left the admissions office with a place assured for September.

In the early hours of June 3, the world of torts and contracts could not have seemed further away as Atkins huddled with other black leaders in the cramped Blue Hill Avenue office trying to predict the course of the next day's events. The sudden burst of gunfire had seriously threatened their careful plans to defuse the situation. Against the advice of his colleagues, Atkins decided to venture out to the sidewalk to determine the source of firing. He asked Parks to keep an eye out for him from the doorway of Operation Exodus.

Paul Parks was an engineer who had met Martin Luther King through his church ties during the early 1960s. King had been so impressed with Parks's breadth of experience that he'd convinced the Indianapolis native to serve as one of his negotiators, carrying demands to white officials in southern towns slated for civil rights demonstrations. More to the point, Paul Parks was the kind of man you wanted to watch your back. No stranger to horror, a mere urban riot was not likely to shake him.

As a young soldier in 1941, Parks and another black soldier had left their base in Louisiana to pick up company supplies in Mississippi. Parks entered the store, leaving his companion to watch the truck. A group of whites surrounded the vehicle, dragged Park's companion from the cab, and tied him to the back of the truck. Hiding beneath the porch, Parks stared out in terror as members of the white mob pushed the truck into gear and sped down the road, eventually killing the trussed soldier. In 1945 Paul Parks again bore witness to the depths of pathological hatred. As a soldier in an all-black engineering platoon, Parks was among the first U.S. troops to liberate the concentration camp at Dachau. The shriveled survivors and the stunned liberators sat together on the death camp's road. "It doesn't make sense. Why were they killed?" Parks queried a survivor. "They were killed because they were Jews," the man said flatly. "I understand that," Parks replied. "I've seen people lynched just because they were black."[11]

Tom Atkins edged cautiously out on to Blue Hill Avenue. Barely five yards away a solitary black man, reporter's notebook in hand, was being questioned by a group of police officers. Invoking the curfew, a police officer told the man he was under arrest despite the reporter's protest that his job required his presence on the street. Atkins felt it was time for a little of his persuasive charm. "Officer, let him go. He's welcome to wait out the curfew in here," Atkins told the lead officer. The reporter quickly accepted the offer and ducked past the police into the Operation Exodus storefront. The police officer attempted to push past Atkins to retrieve the reporter as Atkins quickly backed into the doorway. "You're not going inside here," Atkins snapped. The police officer grabbed Atkins's neck tie at the knot and twisted hard. Atkins responded instinctively with a well-placed karate chop that knocked the wind out of the policeman. As the officer collapsed against the wall, Atkins frantically reached out to hold him up. "Oh shit, please don't go down," Atkins thought to himself as several officers broke his grasp and pinned him to the wall. Atkins was placed under arrest and led to a paddy wagon just as the breathless police officer regained his composure. When Atkins stepped up to enter the vehicle, the officer settled the score by body slamming Atkins face first into the floor. Blood flowed from a split lip of the NAACP leader who earlier in that day had met with the police commissioner to search for ways to mitigate violence. Tom Atkins, Boston's rising black star, was on his way to district headquarters to be booked for assault and battery on a police officer.

The riot in Grove Hall was perceived by most of the city's political analysts and columnists as a manifestation of nationwide black frustration. But Atkins saw in the roots of the riot the failure of a local political system that had long kept blacks from achieving citywide office. Black Bostonians had been the victims of gerry-mandering for decades. As early as 1896 redistricting had stripped seats away from two black representatives in the Massachusetts House. In 1949 the lone black city councilor failed to win reelection when an amendment to the city charter replaced ward-based elections with an at-large system; suddenly the city council was pared down from twenty-two members chosen by ward to just nine chosen by a city-wide vote. And since Boston's black population comprised only five percent of the city's popula-tion in 1950, black candidates accurately came to perceive themselves as unelectable. Similar fears coursed through Jewish neighborhoods. Boston's lone Jewish city councilor, Julius Ansel, knew that Ward 14 would diminish in power as a result of charter reform and switched his sights to state office.

Even without redistricting headaches, the city's blacks had experienced major difficulties getting off the political mark. Throughout the 1920s and 1930s, Mayor Curley had kept tabs on the black community through his favorite black ward boss, Silas "Shag" Taylor, an astute politician who supplemented his job as a pharmacist with the income from several legendary after-hours speakeasies in Roxbury. Taylor's first role was to woo Boston's blacks in Wards 9 and 12 away from the Republican party, which many still associated historically with the party of Abraham Lincoln. It was a role similar to the one played by Sam "Chief" Levine in Ward 14. But Taylor had considerably less success at securing state and city jobs for his constituents than did the Chief. Enterprising blacks deeply resented the fact that Taylor could provide the best bootleg whiskey in the city but couldn't make a dent in local black unemployment, which in the early 1930s ran higher than 30 percent.[12] Black ward bosses, too, did not have sufficient influence to advance the careers of talented black candidates for public office. Such candidates, it seemed, could always be dissuaded from running with the promise of a secure position on the Parole Board or Governor's Council, the rare agencies where blacks served prominently at the state or city level.

Internecine suspicions also played a significant role in blocking black progress. Boston's black community consisted historically of three groups, as different in terms of class characteristics as the German and "Russian" Jews. Sociologists applied the labels "Negro elite," "blue-collar Negro," and "black proletariat"[13] to the nation's northern black communities. Bostonians, however, spoke of black Brahmins, "Turks," and "homies."

The black Brahmins could make no claims to the Mayflower but pointed proudly instead to the First African Baptist Church on the north slope of Beacon Hill, which had been financed and crafted in 1806 by African-born free men. The oldest black church building in the United States, known widely as the African Meeting House, had served as the *stadt shul* of the black settlement on Beacon Hill. Even in the deepest south, runaway slaves knew help was at hand if they could elude the slave catchers long enough to reach sanctuary at the African Meeting House.[14]

The unsophisticated "homies" entering the South End were comtemned by Boston's black Brahmins in much the same way the newly arriving Jews of Eastern Europe were snubbed by the well-established Jews from Germany. The city's South End, particularly the neighborhoods within walking distance of the Boston and Albany Railroad yard, had been a magnet for sharecroppers arriving from the south early in the century in search of porter jobs or service positions in the nearby Copley Square hotels. Housing opportunities were plentiful in the New York–style row houses and shabby rooming houses that lined the broad thoroughfares along Tremont Street and Columbus Avenue. The Ebenezer Baptist Church on West Concord Street in the South End was the central institution for the southern migrants. The newcomers, at first, attracted more sympathy from white coreligionists than from blacks. The white reverend at the downtown Clarendon Baptist Church offered use of his facility for a "Colored Baptism" to the Ebenezer congregation, which then had no pool for baptism rites. The invitation, however, was withdrawn when the newcomers got "happy in the water," creating a very un-New England–like spectacle.[15] The black Brahmins sought to put as much space as possible between themselves and the newcomers. Many set their sights on Upper Roxbury, where they nestled in during the 1930s among the Jews who inhabitated the spacious homes along the tree-lined streets bordering Franklin Park. The brain drain from the loss of several prominent Jewish families to nearby towns was more than made up for by the advance of black Brahmins. A Boston urban planner had summed it up with the following remark: "There are more black brains between Seaver and Townsend Street than anywhere else in Massachusetts."[16] Ambitious homies, too, were never far behind. One of the most prominent was Eugene Clinton Roundtree, a Mississippi native who supplemented his job as a Pullman porter with savvy real estate deals until he had amassed a considerable fortune. Roundtree built a home in the Roxbury highlands and then set about helping other southern migrants do the same. "He would deliver bottles of whiskey to City Hall and grease the wheels," Roundtree's daughter Josephine Roundtree Brice told a reporter. "So, when he sent people downtown and they said, 'Mr. Roundtree sent me,' they got attention."[17]

The third group in the black community were the industrious sons and daughters of Barbados and Jamaica who arrived in Boston shortly after World War I. Referred to as "black Jews," "monkey chasers," and "Turks," the West Indians quickly set themselves apart from both the homies and the black Brahmins. Dressed in silk shirts, straw hats, and white flannel pants, the "Turks" strove to maintain the genteel English traditions of Barbados despite hoots from "homies" and hrumphs from Brahmins. The cultural distinction of the West Indians did little to impress their fellow Episcopalians in white churches. The West Indians, cramped for space for services, were at first given permission to worship in Boston's white Church of the Ascension late on Sunday afternoons. It was an arrangement that was suitable to the white parishioners —provided only that the sanctuary be thoroughly fumigated after the black worshippers left. Outraged at the insult, the "Turks" founded their own church, St. Cyprian's Episcopal Church on Tremont Street. There, at least, proper ladies "in-service" as maids and cooks, and underemployed black artisans making ends meet as porters and hotel workers could savor a taste of home through musical teas and literary societies.

The black community divided along ideological as well as class lines. Following World War I many of the city's blacks could be found in one of four camps: the separatist movement of Marcus Garvey; the NAACP; political action groups led by populist newspaper publisher William Monroe Trotter; and the campaigns of white politicians, including Curley.

Garvey, a native of Jamaica, was successful in attracting many of the city's leading West Indian families with his forceful early messages of black power. Every Sunday at 4:00 P.M. Garvey's local supporters gathered in the United Negro Improvement Association meeting hall on Walpole Street in the South End, where they heard local Garvey-ites urge them forward with the movement's stunning motto: "Up you mighty race, up you mighty people; you can what you will." The "black Jews" label pinned on the West Indians stemmed mostly from their preference for quality education but was reinforced by Garvey's nationalistic philosophy. In a forceful 1920 speech Garvey declared, "A new spirit, a new courage, has come to us simultaneously as it came to other people of the world. It came to us at the same time it came to the Jew. When the Jew said, 'We shall have Palestine,' the same sentiment came to us when we said, 'We shall have Africa.' "[18]

Many children of West Indian families whose surnames are now synonymous with black achievement in Boston—Batson, Bynoe, Lewis—wore the uniforms of the girl guides and boy cadets in the Garvey movement during the late 1920s. Elma Lewis, who would later build a major Afro-American arts center in Roxbury, first performed as a 3-year-old on stage at a Garvey rally at which she recited a poem from the NAACP publication "The Crisis."[19] Garvey's movement captured imaginations but failed to translate into elected offices. The movement was, in essence, separatist and did not encourage activism on local issues. Garvey's imprisonment on mail fraud in 1923 also deeply embarrassed local chapters, although many believed the charges were trumped up by Republicans sore over the desertion of black supporters.

The city's black Brahmins and upwardly striving "homies" found little to their liking in the Garvey movement. Their aspirations were better expressed in the political activism of Boston's most eminent black leader, William Monroe Trotter. In the pages of his newspaper, *The Guardian,* the Harvard-educated Trotter lashed out at all enemies of black advancement on both the local and national levels. Trotter was effective at fighting on many fronts. He excoriated the complacency of black southern leader Booker T. Washington; agitated against local screenings of D. W. Griffith's *Birth of a Nation,* which glorified the Ku Klux Klan; and lambasted attempts to build an all-black hospital in Boston. In 1922 Trotter took on his alma mater when the president of Harvard College excluded black freshmen from college residence halls. "If President Lowell is responsible for race exclusion in the freshman dormitory he is making Harvard turn from democracy and freedom to race oppression, prejudice and hypocrisy," Trotter wrote in the *Guardian.*[20] Trotter's popularity stemmed from his courage to address local issues. The Boston branch of the NAACP throughout the period spoke forcefully on national issues but shied away from local controversy. NAACP campaigns during the period focused on anti-lynching campaigns, voting rights, and oppression of Southern blacks—none of which affected the daily life of black Bostonians. Trotter's combative local stances gained circulation for his *Guardian,* which grew into a community paper in the truest sense: readers were not only treated to gutsy broadsides and insightful opinion pieces but a faithful listing of marriages, births, and graduations. Trotter's star began to wane when the NAACP took a more activist stance, particularly in the 1930s, when it became more involved in local issues, including well-organized protests against discriminatory hiring practices in local insurance companies and public utilities.

Blacks finally began to make small inroads in the election process. In 1946 Roxbury attorney Lawrence Banks, whom friends invariably described as passive and gentle, won election to the Massachusetts House as a Republican, the first black to serve in the body since 1902. Three years later Banks made a bid for Boston City Council from Ward 9 in the South End. Banks lost by six votes and suspected vote tampering—a charge later justified by a Massachusetts judge. But the city councilors voted to leave Banks's opponent in office until the final outcome of an appeal to the state Supreme Court, a process that continued for twenty-one months. Banks was finally seated, but only for the three months remaining in his term. He subsequently lost seven straight runs for statewide office, prompting Ruth Batson, another of the city's prominent black activists, to comment: "Poor Lawrence Banks. . . . To me, he always appeared to be a very tragic figure . . . a very brave man. . . . It was just the saddest thing."[21]

During the 1950s a 57 percent increase in the black population of the city made the potential for statewide office more practical. The at-large city council, however, was still out of reach. Several black legislators came to prominence during this period, including two particularly talented leaders—Lincoln Pope and Royal Bolling. Pope, a confidante of ward boss "Shag" Taylor, was witty and debonair. The Boston University graduate had seen his share of job discrimination and was waiting tables for local caterers in 1956 while conducting his successful campaign for representative from Ward 9. The affable Pope was well loved by his constituents but rarely took an aggressive stand at the statehouse. That role was left to Royal Bolling, an equally dashing native of Virginia whose experience as a real estate broker in Boston led him to seek political reform. "I had plenty of black customers interested in homes but when I went to the downtown banks for financing I got turndown after turndown," Bolling recalls of his post–World War II efforts. "Everyone was reluctant about taking care of the mortgage needs of black clients."[22] Bolling seethed over the constant rejection of his clients, particularly when it affected returning black GIs. As in other cities across the United States, Boston's financial institutions had effectively redlined many older urban neighborhoods (literally drawing red lines on maps around neighborhoods that were either denied mortgage funds and insurance or charged higher rates). Members of the black middle class, like Bolling, were thus doubly thwarted in their social climbing. Inner city housing continued to remain out of their reach despite the softening market created by the Jewish exodus to the suburbs. In the very neighborhoods where blacks might have moved up from renters to owners, the banks were reluctant to administer government subsidies in the form of FHA and VHA loans to blacks. There was little sense, too, in looking toward the suburbs, where prejudice was enduring despite the legal eradication of the realtors' gentleman's agreement a decade earlier.

In 1958 Bolling decided he could address the city's inequities best by running for state representative. He knew he would have to attract a significant number of Jewish votes in Ward 12. He consulted a Jewish calendar and sent holiday greetings to Jewish voters in the district, many of whom, he knew, were prone to pull the lever next to any name that was not distinguishably Irish. Bolling was narrowly defeated in his first bid by incumbent George Greene, a blind Jew who lived just a few houses away from Bolling on Roxbury's Schuyler Street. In 1960, as the Jewish population of Ward 12 moved south into Dorchester and Mattapan, Bolling ran against Greene again and this time succeeded. Bolling took considerable care to serve his Jewish constituents. Like Otto and Muriel Snowden, he placed a high priority on maintaining an integrated Roxbury. His first priority, however, was to force his fellow legislators to confront discriminatory lending patterns in the city.

The first piece of legislation introduced by Bolling in 1961 was a bill requiring Massachusetts banks to maintain a minimum 40 percent of their mortgage portfolios in the cities where their main branches were located. The bill was roundly defeated but attracted the attention of area bankers, particularly Robert Morgan, president of the Boston Five Cents Savings Bank. Bolling organized black brokers to testify at several hearings of the banking committee at the statehouse. While his banking colleagues parried the criticism, the civic-minded Morgan readily admitted that the banking community had been derelict in its responsibilities to predominantly black neighborhoods. A short time later, Morgan and the chief officers of a dozen other savings banks formed a loose consortium—the Boston Bank Urban Renewal Group (B-BURG) —ostensibly to make mortgage money available for minority clients. Although the consortium's pool reached several million dollars in the early 1960s, little publicity attended the program and few buyers were directed to the new mortgage source. Housing issues remained focused mainly on the expansion of the rental market through federal urban renewal programs. Throughout the mid-1960s the B-BURG mortgage pool was all but forgotten.

By 1967 housing issues in the black community were being subsumed by a host of other issues, including minority-owned business, education, and welfare reform, all of which fell under the banner "community control." That call was infused with the passion of black nationalism but was bolstered by rationales provided by Lyndon Johnson's War on Poverty. In Boston and elsewhere, the programs generated under the rubrics "community action" and "community development" were derived from compelling but untested theories that located the sources of crime and dysfunction in a weakened sense of community and limited economic opportunities. The crusader-bureaucrats in the Office of Economic Opportunity circumvented state and municipal governments by lending direct support for small, decentralized antipoverty programs run by local people, often inexperienced in administration. Old-line and loyal Democratic leaders, such as Chicago's Mayor Richard Daley, were incensed by this encroachment on their turf. And as these programs focused more on efforts to eradicate racism, their many critics pointed to real and imagined links between federally funded programs and black militancy.[23]

The cries for community control in Boston focused largely on local businesses. Only one week after the June welfare mothers' riot, Rev. Virgil Wood led one hundred marchers down Blue Hill Avenue bearing a wooden coffin that they said symbolized Jim Crow. At a vacant lot the demonstrators set the coffin ablaze. "We have shown our burning power. Now we must exercise our brain power," Wood told the crowd. Blacks, he continued, must no longer spend their dollars in white-owned businesses and instead "exercise control through the selective use of our dollars spent only with community-approved businesses." As the flames consumed the word *racism* scrawled on the coffin, Wood shouted, "We want to take over every inch of this community."[24] Wood, who two years earlier had planned the intricacies of a black freedom seder with his friend Rabbi Meyer Strassfeld, was no longer in an integrationist mood. The white, largely Jewish storeowners and landlords who had remained in Roxbury after the neighborhood change were standing in the way of black economic emancipation.

One member of the black community who perceived a certain naïveté in the strident calls for community control was Tom Atkins. Real power, he believed, required a role for blacks in every aspect of the city's political and financial operation. By 1967 Boston's black population had grown to almost ninety thousand, roughly 15 percent of the city. Victory would be gained in stages, and the first battle would be fought in the city council, where no black had been seated since the election was stolen from Lawrence Banks more than sixteen years earlier. Atkins knew that his prominent peace-keeping role during the riot made him an attractive candidate to the many white voters who perceived him as a responsible leader with a healthy appreciation for public safety. He realized, too, that his confrontation with police during the curfew also sent a clear message to black voters that Tom Atkins was a man who could only be pushed so far.

With the aid of fellow students at Harvard Law School, many of them Jewish, Atkins set about to build a campaign organization and a war chest. He knew that he must campaign throughout the city if he hoped to win a place on the nine-member city council. One of Atkins's earliest campaign stops was in South Boston, an insular neighborhood of working-class Irish and Poles abutting Boston Harbor, a neighborhood where it was generally understood that blacks had no business.

The closest black concentration to the South Boston peninsula was the Columbia Point public housing projects, a drab series of sickly yellow high rises adjacent to the city dump. Although South Boston's public beach on L Street was just a few minutes' walk from the project, the black residents accurately anticipated that a beach trip was more likely to result in tauntings and even beatings from "Southie" toughs than a relaxing day in the sun. Fears of hassles on public trains and buses also kept many black workers from seeking jobs in the factories in Southie's industrial section. Those who risked the commute were often greeted with contempt by white workers.

But Atkins also understood that an insistence on fair play often transcended racism in Boston's white insular neighborhoods. It was one thing if a minority member was accosted, even assaulted, by a lone tormenter. If two or more assailants were involved, however, it was bad sportsmanship. One high school student who worked the swing shift in a South Boston sportswear factory in 1967 recalled a similarly emblematic Boston experience: After a black worker's paycheck failed to arrive on payday due to an administrative snafu, the same white workers who had resisted an integrated work force called an immediate work stoppage. A burly cloth cutter known for his open contempt for blacks laid down the law to management in blunt language: "Nobody returns to the shop floor until the nigger gets his fuckin' paycheck."[25]

Atkins believed he could tap this deep though blighted sense of distributive justice in Boston voters. On his first foray into South Boston, he handed out campaign literature and introduced himself to voters near the South Boston District Court on East Broadway. When the foot traffic at the courthouse slowed, he decided to do some campaigning in one of the neighborhood's numerous taverns. Though well before noon, the bar was filled with patrons. "Hi, I'm Tom Atkins and I'm running for city council," he said as he worked his way down the bar extending his hand to the stunned trade. "I know who you are," slurred one patron who had several empty glasses aligned in a row before him. "Why the hell would I vote for you? You won't do a damn thing for me." Atkins was ready with his response: "You might be right because the guys in the council are doing absolutely nothing for me and my people. But you know as well as I do that we need representation in this city, too." The quarrelsome drinker looked Atkins over from head to toe and muttered, "I'll say one thing for you; You've got a lot of balls coming in here."[26]

Atkins and his fellow Harvard students worked with intensity throughout the city's twenty-two wards. When the smoke had cleared on Election Day, Atkins had placed seventh in a large field, good enough for a seat on the nine-member council. In addition to carrying the four black wards, Atkins had topped the ticket in Jewish Ward 14 and showed surprising support even in the "lace curtain" Irish sections of Hyde Park and West Roxbury. It was a heady time for an ambitious black politician; landmark legislation and court rulings proclaimed that times were indeed changing for America's blacks, and attitudes among whites, even in insular Boston, hinted at a greater acceptance of integration. There was ample evidence to believe that America, despite the grim conclusion of the Kerner Commission report, would not forever remain two distinct societies—separate and unequal.

The election of a black to Boston City Council for the first time in sixteen years was overshadowed by the election of a new mayor, Kevin Hagan White. The White name ran deep in Boston politics. The new mayor's father, Joe, had held numerous elected and appointed posts during the 1950s. When the New Boston Committee first put together its reform slate in 1951, Joe White was the only incumbent on the city council considered clean enough to receive an endorsement. White could also count on Jewish votes in Wards 12 and 14 largely on the basis of his deep-rooted friendship with ward boss Sam Levine and his activities with the National Conference of Christians and Jews. But Joe White was never able to gather sufficient forces to pursue his greatest dream, a run for mayor. That task was left to his clever, if unpredictable, eldest son.

Kevin White had his father's knack for hooking up with the right crowd. White's first foray into politics came as a member of the Ward Five Democratic Committee, a liberal group consisting mainly of Jews and Yankees who in 1960 presented a reform slate to the voters on Beacon Hill. Kevin White then went on to win election as Massachusett's Secretary of State, a job that, in Boston's political parlance, required "no heavy lifting." But White squeezed every conceivable ounce of political juice out of that statewide office by making a personal visit during his first years in office to every one of the Bay State's 351 cities and towns. In 1966 White and his family felt that the political career of Mayor Collins was in decline and that the door to the main office in city hall was wide open. Collins did indeed decide not to run again, throwing his weight behind redevelopment czar Ed Logue. Also expected to pose a strong challenge was Louise Day Hicks, a hefty daughter of South Boston whose unapologetic support for working-class whites and their insular neighborhoods and schools earned her the sobriquet "Bull Connor of the North."

The campaign was lackluster until September 1967 when one Richard Iantosca, a man later discovered to be an obscure Logue operative, announced that he'd discovered 701 false signatures on White's nomination papers. When White demanded to meet his accuser, Iantosca was nowhere to be found. Amid escalating charges and countercharges, it became clear that Logue was having trouble playing the hand he'd dealt himself whereas White was bluffing and improvising with great skill. White's staff discovered a connection between Iantosca and two of the city's major corporate law firms, including that of Logue's rehabilitation counsel, Lewis Weinstein. White quickly called a press conference at the statehouse. "Suddenly this obscure person [Iantosca] of limited means emerges as a client of an expensive and prestigious firm with additional assets to pay not one but two handwriting experts," White said with raised brow and a look of utter sarcasm. "And how did Mr. Iantosca get to [the law firm of] Hale and Dorr? He was sent there by the law firm of Foley, Hoag and Eliot, equally expensive, equally prestigious, which represents Edward Logue and the Boston Redevelopment Authority."[27] Back at his desk at Foley, Hoag, and Eliot, senior partner Lewis Weinstein contemplated the fallout of backing the wrong horse. Kevin White, not Ed Logue, would be the next mayor of Boston.

Tom Atkins and Boston's black community welcomed the election of Kevin White. After eight years of John Collins and downtown development, Boston needed a mayor who promised equal time to the neighborhoods. Atkins, like most black leaders, believed that urban renewal under Logue had been merely "Negro removal." As evidence, he cited the historic failures of renewal planners to relocate evicted tenants in quality housing in their former neighborhoods. During his tenure at the NAACP, Atkins had clashed with Logue and Collins around the development czar's plan to set up a "Model Cities Area Department" throughout Roxbury and North Dorchester that would, in effect, have sole power to administer federally aided neighborhood programs. Atkins fiercely, and successfully, lobbied city council to reject the new department unless it included an elected board from the community. Now, as chairman of the city council's urban renewal committee, Atkins had, or so he thought, the insider's view he had longed for.

Unbeknownst to Atkins, as well as other city officials, the largest housing rehabilitation program in the nation was being implemented in Roxbury during the final months of the mayoral campaign. The Boston Rehabilitation Program, which would become known by the acronym BURP, aimed to rehabilitate two thousand units of substandard housing in Roxbury. The success of the program, its federal authors were convinced, depended on keeping the details and scope of the project strictly under wraps and away from the scrutiny of public officials, the press, and, most importantly, Roxbury landlords. What was required was a core group of experienced developers who were capable of keeping the project in strict secrecy, for if word got out that the government planned a major show project, it would surely drive up the acquisition costs. The winter of 1967 was the perfect time for secret negotiations. As an urban specialist would later point out, the city of Boston was in "a state of interregnum."[28] John Collins was preparing to retire, White was not yet in office, and the Boston Redevelopment Authority's Logue, a careful "fed watcher," had stepped down to seek the mayorality. Even the fire and building departments, upon which such a massive rehabilitation program would depend, were preoccupied with the highly charged political races. It was a perfect operating environment for the FHA, which traditionally preferred dealing with the banking and construction community rather than city officials.

The federal housing programs desperately needed a success. BURP had developed out of escalating pressure on Robert Weaver, Secretary of the Department of Housing and Urban Development (HUD). Since the riots that rocked Watts, Detroit, and the nation's capital, the Johnson Administration had turned to the highest appointed black in the executive branch to originate a bold plan to rehabilitate blighted urban neighborhoods. Bulldozers, this time, would not be the weapon of choice. For a variety of reasons, Boston seemed to Weaver to be the best place for a major rehabilitation project. Party politics played a major role in Weaver's site selection. Massachusetts Senator Edward Brooke, the highest elected black in the Republican party, was one of the nation's harshest critics of the performance of governmental agencies in older urban neighborhoods. He'd publicly lambasted the highly touted 221 (d) (3) program, the housing rehabilitation scheme for people with moderate incomes sponsored by the Federal Housing Administration, which, he had been quick to point out, had not succeeded in rehabilitating even five thousand units nationwide. In fact, for all the Johnson Administration's talk about the War on Poverty, only sixty-eight thousand housing units had been reclaimed under all federal urban renewal programs. The Democrats appeared seriously vulnerable on the issue of the urban crisis.[29]

Secretary Weaver also had much to prove to his colleagues. He had inherited a seemingly unmanageable fiefdom that included the Federal Housing Administration. As the agency responsible for the lion's share of HUD's rehabilitation projects, the FHA operated in a state of semiautonomy. Additionally, more than seventy insuring agencies operated under the FHA umbrella, and each guarded its independence with as much ferocity as did the FHA in regard to its own relationship with HUD. The FHA's executive assistant commissioner, Edwin G. Callahan, took a generally dim view of rehabilitation programs. But even that widely respected and grizzled veteran of thirty-three years of government service was starting to sense an urgency in the growing clamor for an increased federal role in the inner city. Secretary Weaver and Philip Brownstein, the FHA's assistant secretary for mortgage credit, were not sanguine that the project could succeed without both the blessing and direct participation of Callahan. When the FHA commissioner signed on, there were audible sighs of relief at HUD that the conditions leading to the Grove Hall welfare mothers' riot and others like it were at last being addressed.

Callahan conducted a site suitability tour of Roxbury early in the summer of 1967 and liked what he saw. Boston boasted several developers who had worked successfully in the past with the FHA. One, Maurice Simon, who, like Eli Goldston, was a prominent member of Boston's Temple Israel, had already received a commitment from the FHA on a major rent-supplement rehabilitation package. Callahan was also impressed with the housing stock in Roxbury. On his tours through Humboldt Avenue, Seaver Street, and Blue Hill Avenue he encountered many sound three- and four-story brick buildings that appeared to be excellent candidates for rehabilitation. The buildings, for the most part, had been built in the 1920s to accommodate the large numbers of Jews moving into the area. As recently as 1960 the units had been inhabited mainly by Jewish owner-occupants who rented to other Jews. Roxbury rents had always run slightly ahead of the rest of the city, the housing units offering tenants the beauty of Franklin Park and an easy commute downtown. As racial change set in, many of the old-time landlords kept their rents artificially low to retain their Jewish tenants. But this attempt at neighborhood "stabilization" were short-lived. The loss of beloved Jewish institutions and rising street crime in contiguous black neighborhoods had already sent all but the poor elderly and the recalcitrant into southward retreat down Blue Hill Avenue to Dorchester and Mattapan.

When Callahan arrived for the inspection tour, many of the units on his lists were still owned by old-time Jewish landlords, although the majority no longer lived in the buildings. Many Jewish landlords, rather than sell in panic, had decided to manage buildings from a distance with the assistance of lawyers and black rent collectors; some even increased their holdings in Roxbury, using higher rentals to compensate for declining property values. The new black tenants faced immediate rent increases; in many cases families doubled up to make ends meet. The increased density placed further strain on the facilities.

By 1967 the two communities, Jewish and black, had come to perceive each other through hardened images: the criminally greedy and apathetic Jewish slumlord, and the criminally destructive and lazy black tenant. Through a vicious cycle of neglect and vandalism, each side seemed to have ample evidence for its beliefs. For many Jewish property owners, it was proving easier and less costly to deal with city building inspectors than with bankers: there were always channels through which to fix a fine for the violation of the housing code; bank loans for renovations were harder to come by. Diminishing cash returns from increasingly recalcitrant black tenants hardly encouraged the Jewish landlords along Seaver Street and Blue Hill Avenue to provide necessary services and repairs. When they did tend to the needs of their property, financial investment and weeks of work could be undone in minutes by marauding teenagers. "You can't believe how those people live," became the familiar refrain of property owners in Roxbury.

As early as 1964 Boston's chapter of the Congress of Racial Equality (CORE) had made headlines when it organized twenty-one black families in the city's first rent strike, against absentee landlord Joel Rubin, owner of several rental properties on Waumbeck and Warren Streets in Roxbury. Angry tenants, backed by CORE, drew extensive media attention when they picketed their own dwellings holding signs that read, "Get Rid of Rats, Roaches, and Rubin." The Rubin-owned units were found in multiple violation of building codes, including roof leaks, sagging porches, and defective electrical fixtures. But to Jews, particularly those who were familiar with the Goebbels-inspired Nazi propaganda films such as "Jews, Lice, and Bedbugs," the linking of a Jewish property owner and vermin set off dangerous and familiar alarms. After the 1967 Grove Hall riot and with the growing militance within the black community, these same landlords were beginning to reevaluate the price of doing business in the black community. The buildings began to appear on

*the speculative market, with greater second and third mortgages
and decreasing equity involved in each transfer. HUD believed it
could, with proper planning, turn the presence of speculators and
absentee landlords to its own advantage: the old-time Jewish
landlords would sell cheaply to HUD to avoid the further head-
ache of doing business in a hostile community, and since the
agency had no emotional cards to play with the speculators, they
could easily be expected to fall in line with adequate bids.*

Callahan reported back to HUD's Weaver that all systems
seemed operable. In an agency known for protracted bureaucratic
delays, Weaver's response came back with blinding speed: $24.5
million was immediately authorized for the rehabilitation of more
than two thousand units in Boston. Callahan's next move was to
find the developers in the city with the best track record of
rehabilitating multifamily buildings. In exchange for the developers' agreement to acquire and rehabilitate the buildings in six
months, he offered a top total mortgage price of $12,000 per unit
and a swift FHA commitment. After dozens of private meetings and
inquiries, Callahan came to terms with five developers and rehab
specialists, Maurice Simon, Gerald Schuster, Harold Brown, Irwin
Cantor, and Joseph Kelly—four Jews and an Irishman, all but one
of whom had previous experience with the FHA. With his team
assembled, Callahan and his field staff roamed through Roxbury
and parts of North Dorchester by day and night and throughout the
weekends, making architectural evaluations of buildings for possible inclusion in the program. The entire staff of Boston's FHA office
was utilized to process the paperwork. All of the buildings were
committed by the end of November. The largest share of the BURP
package, fifteen hundred units, went to Schuster and Simon.

Redemption, nonetheless, was starting to look like a long shot.
Despite the efforts of the Snowdens and other community leaders,
much of Roxbury was becoming shabby. Street lights, replaced
more irregularly than in "good neighborhoods," no longer illumi-
nated fading facades. Abandoned cars lined streets that were now
less frequently visited by inspectors and sanitation services. The
accumulation of rubbish, the neglect of snow removal, the inatten-
tion to potholes, and the decay of park benches were but a few of
the ways in which City hall demonstrated to the residents the
acceptability of destructive norms of behavior in their new neighborhood. Rumors circulated of tacit agreements between the

police and dope pushers who had been forced out of the South End to make way for white urban pioneers. The pushers were now proliferating in the playgrounds and on the street corners of Roxbury. The dwindling number of whites who lived in Roxbury recall that not-so-subtle change. Harvey Cox, ordained by the Yale Divinity School, moved with his wife and three children to Roxbury in the early 1960s. They wanted to live in an integrated community. There he wrote *The Secular City: A Celebration of Its Liberties and an Invitation to Its Discipline,* a seminal work hotly contested among theologians and social scientists for a decade and more. By the mid-1960s, Cox began to notice the drug peddlers as he walked his children to school. He and his wife decided to celebrate the city's liberties on the other side of the Charles River, closer to the Harvard Divinity School in Cambridge where Cox had been invited to teach.

Eli Goldston, characteristically, was keeping the faith. The Washington Park area of Roxbury might be looking a little frayed along the edges, but its development, after all, was another opportunity to "do well by doing good." The Eastern Gas chief was one of the few nondevelopers let in on the secret of BURP. Goldston, who was growing in influence in Democratic circles in Massachusetts, was friendly with Charles Haar and Ralph Taylor, both assistant secretaries at HUD, and through them had met on several occasions with Secretary Weaver. Goldston was wildly enthusiastic about the potential of BURP. He recognized that the BURP rehabilitation program could provide a major expansion of Eastern's pipeline and directed his company to purchase a 10 percent limited partnership in Simon's BURP package. Throughout October and November, Goldston immersed himself in research on the expanded gas load and spillover tax benefits. His instincts were correct. By becoming a limited partner, Eastern could specify gas as the primary fuel. In addition, the company would earn a portion of the depreciation credit as tax shelter to be applied against income tax charges. Goldston, like Weaver, could hardly wait for the announcement of BURP to the public. He was so convinced that the program would not only prove profitable but would become a national model for the amelioration of social ills through a partnership of private enterprise and government that he directed his public relations staff to find the best way to highlight the link between Boston Gas and the new program. The staff prepared several proposals, but none appealed to the earthy chief executive officer. Goldston finally settled on his own creation: "When you BURP, think gas."

On December 3, 1967, Secretary Weaver arrived in Boston to announce the nation's largest single housing rehabilitation program. Weaver chose Freedom House as the site of the luncheon and press conference. It seemed particularly appropriate: no one in the black community had been more supportive of urban renewal than Freedom House founders Otto and Muriel Snowden. Even in the face of growing criticism from younger black radicals, who mocked Freedom House as "Uncle Tom's cabin in the woods," the Snowdens stood steadfastly for integration and middle-class respectability.

There would be no public relations coup for HUD. Instead of the anticipated warm reception from city and neighborhood leaders, Weaver's speech was interrupted almost immediately by Bryant Rollins, a local black militant. At first Weaver refused to yield. But each effort to begin his speech was met by Rollins's cry that BURP was nothing more than "a robbery of the Roxbury community." The Freedom House audience grew increasingly agitated. Since the situation appeared as if it might escalate out of control, Weaver yielded the floor to Rollins. "The program being dedicated has given no consideration to local developers, nonprofit developers, cooperative ownership, or local management," Rollins began. "It has been marred by racial discrimination in employment and inadequate relocation procedures. The FHA has shown that it can move with unprecedented speed—to give high profits to developers from outside the community and to establish a huge preserve for exploitation by absentee landlords. Apparently, Secretary Weaver's department can move quickly only when it is operating against community interest."[30]

Rollins's charges captured the next day's headlines, deflated BURP's supporters, and encouraged community control activists. Melvin King, director of Boston's New Urban League and one of the black community's most clever political strategists, dashed off a letter to Weaver that coincided with his arrival back in Washington. "Black people now are demanding that the equity coming out of programs be put into the hands of the community. . . . The alternative to such an approach—an alternative which you have selected in regards to the new $24.5 million program—

represents a continuation of the method of operating which has so badly failed to bring about the needed change."[31]

No one was more disappointed or determined to turn around the Freedom House disaster than Eli Goldston. The attack on BURP was also an attack on Goldston's treasured personal philosophy. While Goldston struggled with the issues raised by Rollins and the black militants, he instructed Robert Tracy, his special assistant, to write to Weaver reaffirming Eastern's commitment to the project. "On the one hand," Tracy wrote, "we believe quite strongly that the Negro community must develop the competence and sophisticated tools and understanding of American business. On the other hand, we believe it makes business sense to obtain a significant portion of the gas revenues in what is going to be the largest market in our franchise area, Boston's ghetto. Add to this, that if Roxbury burns, we all suffer tragically, and one has our motivations."[32]

Goldston no longer had confidence in BURP's success without a role for black developers. He began a city-wide search that yielded four prominent blacks: real estate entrepeneurs Jack Robinson and Sam McCoy; respected contractor Lester Clemente; and Tom Sanders, a Boston Celtics forward who could provide both high name recognition and much of the cash to meet equity requirements. The members of the new black development team became frequent guests at the celebrated soirees at Goldston's home in Cambridge. The utility director particularly delighted in arranging parties where bankers, basketball players, and Harvard professors could mingle and exchange ideas. Honored guests were invited into Goldston's study, where he proudly showed them his collection of porcelain character jugs bearing the images of renowned literary personages.

The prominent bankers and insurance executives on Goldston's guest list, however, did not share his enthusiasm for the black development team. It was only after Eastern's offer to provide an irrevocable letter of credit that necessary insurance bonding and construction financing materialized. On March 20, 1968, the black team, called Sanders Associates, received a FHA commitment of $996,000 for the rehabilitation of eighty-three units in Roxbury. Goldston again displayed his genius for public relations by arranging the FHA signing on a day when the announcement could be scooped by Boston's leading black weekly newspaper, *The Bay State Banner*. The *Banner* responded in kind with a page-one article and a favorable editorial.

Even with the addition of Sanders and other black developers, the greatest share of the BURP units remained in white, and largely Jewish, hands. Maurice Simon and his partner, Sydney Insoft, were responsible for a full 50 percent of the BURP package. Simon's holdings were located in the census tracts with the highest numbers of substandard housing units, and he quickly became a favorite target for the hostility of black labor and black community activists. More than the property of any other BURP participant, the Simon–Insoft units were plagued by robbers and vandals. Simon was finding it almost impossible to keep copper fixtures on any of the rehabilitated units, and at the height of the project an estimated 50 percent of the windows in newly rehabilitated units were broken. According to an FHA report on BURP, stealing and pilfering from Simon projects became "institutionalized and legitimized" because it was perceived as a protest against enemies of the black community.[33]

Boston's other newspapers readily advanced the Simon–Insoft image of white slumlords exploiting black tenants. In January 1968 a severe cold snap hit Boston. The breakdown of aging heating systems at Insoft-owned buildings on Humboldt Avenue landed the developer in court to face ten charges of failure to provide heat to tenants. Judge Elwood McKenney, who found Insoft guilty on two of the charges, ordered him to provide one month free rent to seven tenants rather than pay the usual court fines. Officials of the Housing Inspection Department could not recall a similar verdict, and headline writers quickly dubbed Insoft the "no heat landlord."

Cost overruns, pilferage, and labor problems plagued Simon and Insoft's BURP package. The two men became increasingly obsessed with saving their properties from looters and vandals. Copper flashing was soon replaced with aluminum; copper pipes were coated with sticky substances to make them more difficult to steal. Simon naively clung to the view that everything would work out—he'd make a respectable profit and appreciative blacks would improve their living conditions. A native of Lawrence, Massachusetts, and a resident of the upscale suburb of Newton, he seemed to have little knowledge of the historic tensions between blacks and Jews in Roxbury and Dorchester and little understanding of the growing black militant movement. In the eyes of the black community, Simon could do no right. An animal lover, he often brought his pet poodle with him when he inspected rehabilitated units. Black workers soon grumbled that Simon was no better than the white Southern sheriffs who turned their German shepherds on black civil rights marchers. His was the world of golf at the Belmont Country Club, not bowling at Mickey's or Sam's Bowladrome on Blue Hill Avenue. Even when he was seized by a craving for a corned beef sandwich while inspecting one of his 1,030 units, he'd race off for Jack and Marion's fancy delicatessen in Brookline's Coolidge Corner rather than try the traditional fare at the nearby G&G.

In February 1968 a group of twenty black workers and community leaders, led by Mel King, cornered Simon in his downtown office. There they presented a two-page list of demands and a document from the Massachusetts Commission Against Discrimination ordering Simon to rehire twenty-four laid-off black workers. Simon angrily threw the document to the floor. The black workers overturned several of Simon's file cabinets and threatened to burn down all of his BURP units. Three police officers tried to quell the disturbance but only succeeded in raising tensions. At the height of the disturbance, activist William Lee beseeched Simon to deal with the composed and articulate King. "Deal with this man because he is a man of peace," Lee urged. Under psychological duress and physical threat, Simon agreed to the entire list of demands. King, who believed Simon had reneged on many promises in the past, ordered the furious developer to initial each item with the phrase, "I agree. M. Simon."

Simon's wife urged him to terminate the project, arguing that no amount of money was worth the aggravation of threats and having his name dragged through the papers, but Simon was determined to complete the project. One recourse was to bring in additional partners. Simon had approached Norman Leventhal, one of the city's rising developers, during a chance meeting at the Parker House. Leventhal's Beacon Company had recently developed a thousand federally subsidized housing units in Hyde Park, a largely Irish Catholic neighborhood on the city's southern outskirts. Over subsequent decades Leventhal's downtown office buildings would set the pace in architecture and quality of construction. But in 1967 his planners were busy trying to determine the best use of the wooded Hyde Park site for affordable housing. The Beacon Company marketing division had predicted that the projected Hyde Park apartments would attract largely middle-class Irish from the southern sections of Dorchester. Leventhal subsequently would be surprised to discover that, in fact, 60 to 70 percent of the new residents were Jews from North Dorchester.

When Simon approached Leventhal, he wasted few words. "Norman, I've got 1,000–1,200 units and federal funds for this project. Want to be a partner with me?" Years later, Leventhal would reiterate his unequivocal response: "I said no, I don't want any part of it. Just like that. Why did I respond that way? I felt the housing would be all black and I didn't want to be involved with all the problems."[34] Simon went back to the FHA and asked for additional funds to offset his costs. The FHA, which had no desire to own the increasingly troublesome properties as a result of foreclosure, reluctantly agreed. But as the black community embellished its image of the profiteering Jewish slumlord, several of the other BURP developers were drawing their own conclusions, which they argued before FHA officials: no amount of money, would make it worthwhile to do rehabilitation work and manage property in Roxbury.

Simultaneous efforts by nonprofit organizations to advance black development teams were also meeting with little success. Virgil Wood and Ralph Abernathy of the Southern Christian Leadership Conference approached Allan Moore, Jr., an idealistic young architect who they believed would be the perfect team player on an otherwise all-black development team. Moore, a Nashville native, was a proponent of "professional tithing" who had dedicated several years to designing workers' housing in the West Indies. He responded enthusiastically to the invitation to help rehabilitate several abandoned buildings in the Grove Hall area. The young architect, however, quickly noted that "the infrastructure had just gone adrift. The area of Grove Hall to Blue Hill Avenue was heavily assaulted by drug users. When we came into buildings to do existing conditions drawings, we would find areas of a building that had been plywooded off, mattresses lugged in, and we would find syringes and needles in the corner. It was clearly a combat zone."[35]

The Wood–Abernathy development team struggled with their

site plans for an adult educational center, a child-care center, and a baby carriage factory. Like the BURP efforts, these projects were beset by problems from the very beginning, especially the theft of building materials. Unlike the Simon case, however, there could be no fallback on the notion of "legitimized" thefts directed against enemies of the black community. The new black developers, skilled as they were as craftsmen, were overwhelmed. City sponsorship for the model project was beginning to wane. Moore would later note that the attitude of city officials was "like pouring water on a flashfire. Here are some buildings, here is some money, let's see what you can do."[36] The mood of the new black developers darkened with the withdrawal of city support. Reflecting two decades later, Moore said the disappointment was based, in part, on the expectation that "they would move into the upper echelons of the construction industry. They were given jobs without proper training and backing, they were also given salaries that were fairly high and then, when the funding and the commitment ran out, they were left with a life style and an income level that was no longer supported."[37]

What began with Eli Goldston's ubiquitous "What's new and exciting?" ultimately left the community no better off than it was before. The unfulfilled expectations of talented and ambitious blacks did not lead to an improvement in their relations with whites, and particularly with Jews, who were prominently represented among the urban renewal developers. Eli Goldston's worldview was, for the first time in his life, becoming foggy. "Doing well" and "doing good" were, after all, not quite so clearly compatible.

BURP was making its presence felt further south, down Blue Hill Avenue, in the Jewish working-class neighborhoods of Dorchester. The FHA officials responsible for the rehabilitation program stressed at first that since tenants were being evicted by private owners, there was no public responsibility for relocation. When that response was met with an outcry by black community activists, the federal officials attempted to switch relocation responsibility to the Boston Redevelopment Authority (BRA). Displaced families, particularly large families in need of three or four bedrooms, were the most desperate. As they had in Roxbury, small

Jewish landlords in Dorchester now found that they could rent the same apartments at a premium by allowing displaced black families to "double up." By the time a coordinated relocation program was in place, FHA and BRA officials had lost track of more than half of the BURP evictees. A consortium of Roxbury community groups, including the Roxbury Multi-Service Center, The New Urban League, and Fair Housing Inc., pressed for an appeals process for evictees who were denied access to their rehabilitated units. Social scientists and government bureaucrats hoped to interview BURP tenants to learn something new about the Great Society. Most, however, could not be found.

The countermen at the G&G delicatessen knew precisely where the BURP evictees were moving—to the Jewish sections of North Dorchester, the same area chosen by those displaced by previous urban renewal efforts. Once again locked out of hostile Irish neighborhoods to the east and west, evictees saw Jewish Dorchester as the only option. The shift in population was reflected in the change of fare at the G&G. "When a guy walked in and ordered a roast beef with mayonnaise, I knew it was over," explained one former sandwich maker. The conversation among Jewish diners again shifted from the school and job accomplishments of their children to the increasing amounts of time between visits. "His wife doesn't want him driving down here . . . too dangerous." Reports of the latest street crimes, particularly the muggings and purse snatchings, were on practically everyone's lips.

Young black hoodlums in Dorchester had developed a bizarre marksmanship ritual in which they would razor-slash the back pants pockets of the elderly Jewish men so that their wallets would fall to the ground. The less skillful thugs inflicted flesh wounds, which proved more embarrassing than life-threatening. Each fresh assault caused Dorchester's Jews to harden their hearts to the city's blacks and to the suburban Jews who supported their causes. The old saw "The definition of a conservative is a liberal who has been mugged" held more than a grain of truth in Dorchester. The experience of lying face down on a hospital gurney while an intern sutured one's backside was hardly conducive to progressive thinking.

The Gift

Black–Jewish Exchanges, 1968

Marvin Gilmore had developed a good eye for real estate from his mother, who owned several rooming houses in Cambridge. The Gilmores often boarded promising black students, including Martin Luther King, Jr., who was studying for his doctorate in theology at Boston University. In 1968, Gilmore chartered the Unity Bank and Trust, Boston's first black-owned bank.

One of Gilmore's closest friends was Kivie Kaplan, a millionaire manufacturer of patent leather with a habit of passing out "Keep Smiling" cards. Since 1945 Kaplan had contributed hundreds of thousands of dollars to the NAACP, and he had ascended to the organization's national presidency in 1966. By 1968, however, the perceived paternalistic leadership style of Kaplan and other prominent Jews in the civil rights movement was coming under increasingly sharp attack. Activists called for his resignation; Kaplan refused.

Kivie Kaplan died of a heart attack in an airport phone booth in 1975; he was in transit between meetings of the Union of American Hebrew Congregations and the NAACP. Fifteen years after his friend's death, Gilmore recalled how much he still cherished a fine silk tie that Kaplan passed on to him. But when asked why Kaplan had never opened an account in the fledgling Unity Bank, Gilmore was suddenly silent. "Never thought about it," he said. "Never thought about it."[1]

During the torrid days after the Grove Hall riot in June 1967, attorney Lawrence Shubow drove along the thoroughfares and back roads of Jewish Dorchester and Roxbury in his late-model Buick Electra. At his side was his close friend and client, Elma Lewis. Shubow, the nephew of a prominent local rabbi, pulled up in front of a dozen Jewish institutions—synagogues, catering halls, and cultural centers. Lewis, a 45-year-old heavyset woman of Barbadian descent who favored dresses of lime green set off by a circular hairpiece on her crown that gave her the appearance of African royalty, carefully studied each one. Elma Lewis was a queen in search of a castle.

Since 1950, when she began operating out of her Roxbury home with $300 and a secondhand piano, Lewis's dream was to provide quality education in the arts for black children in Boston. Such a goal required a building capable of housing classrooms, administrative offices, and, most importantly, a large performance hall. During the 1950s and early 1960s Lewis and her performing arts students had outgrown four separate Roxbury headquarters. Her next move, she knew, would be critical. A clever fund-raiser, Lewis knew the time was right to implement her dream of a thriving performance center and a national center for Afro-American artists. She had every reason to expect a successful outcome. Old alliances with wealthy and liberal Jews could be tapped for political and financial support. The leaders of WASP institutions seemed, like the Jews, to be vulnerable to the Lewis one-two punch of righteous anger and veiled threats delivered with wit and charm. Lewis, after all, had actually come out on top of an exchange with directors of the Museum of Fine Arts during a fund-raising drive after telling them, as quoted in the *Boston*

Globe, "I stopped looking at your pictures a long time ago. I'm looking now at all that pretty green money you have."

Unlike many of the city's black leaders, Lewis refused to burn her bridges with the Boston Irish. It was true that many local politicians, like City Councilor Albert "Dapper" O'Neil, were hardly discreet regarding their opposition to school and neighborhood integration. But Lewis would not accept that entire sections of a major American city would present monolithic opposition to black advancement, and she was determined to maintain her contacts in the Irish political strongholds. "If I had only considered racist neighborhood leaders, I would have lost my mind," she recalled in an interview twenty years later. "But those people who make the linen and those people who make Irish whiskey and those people who go down to the sea in ships have a core of something different."[2]

Shubow and Lewis drove slowly past the low, drab Orthodox synagogues situated along the side streets perpendicular to Blue Hill Avenue, but they rarely stopped. At the area's larger synagogues—Agudas Israel on Woodrow Avenue, Chai Odom on Nightingale Street and Beth El on Fowler Street—they left their car only long enough to note dimensions and make a quick mental appraisal of a building's condition. None of the synagogues had sufficient grandeur or square footage to contain Lewis's dream. Shubow wheeled onto American Legion Highway, a ragged and undeveloped swath bisecting several cemeteries and property of the Mattapan State Hospital, and pulled over in front of the Hecht House. Thousands of Jewish immigrants during the 1920s and 1930s had absorbed American culture at the Hecht House Jewish Community Center, learning everything from prepositional phrases to outside shots on the basketball court. The Hecht House was big enough to contain Lewis's vision but singularly unattractive. Arsenal-like in red brick, it was appropriately protective for new immigrants but unsuitable for black artists who, Lewis believed, were ready to form a national movement.

Lewis and Shubow continued east on American Legion Highway toward Franklin Park. They pulled to a stop across from the park's rose garden, in front of Temple Mishkan Tefila on Seaver Street. No expense had been spared when the temple was constructed in 1925. Its authoritative columns and towering copper dome advertised to all that Jews had arrived in Boston. Elma Lewis was determined to carry the identical message for black Bostonians. She and Shubow walked up the flight of granite stairs leading to a portico with a terra cotta ceiling. At the entrance to the main foyer were three monumental doors framed in rare Bottocino and Siena marble carved in Italy. The walls and floors of the foyer were decorated liberally with mosaics. Eight immense variegated marble columns supported the foyer's vaulted ceiling. Lewis and Shubow toured the synagogue's ground floor, which consisted of an assembly hall, dining hall, kitchen, rest rooms, and daily chapel. But it was the synagogue's upper floor that intrigued Lewis. The main chapel, beneath an ornamental plaster ceiling in the pattern of a star of David, had the capacity to seat almost two thousand. It was a perfect showcase for the talents of Boston's young black artists. The pair continued their tour in the brick schoolhouse used for afternoon Hebrew classes, which stood adjacent to the temple on Elm Hill Avenue. With parking spaces, the temple complex covered more than two acres. "The new home of the Elma Lewis School of Fine Arts," said Shubow, smiling broadly.

Lewis was seized with a strong sense of ironic justice. For most of her life, she had lived on Homestead Street, just a few blocks from the synagogue. Throughout her adolescence she had watched her Jewish neighbors, the proper burghers who lived in the large two-family homes behind the synagogue, stroll leisurely to Sabbath services at Temple Mishkan Tefila. Lewis had always felt a kinship to her Jewish neighbors. Like many of Boston's leading black citizens, she prided herself on her family's origins in the small Caribbean island that claimed one of the highest literacy rates in the world. Lewis recalled being confused, then offended, when Jews began pulling up roots on Homestead Street. She could not forget her bitterness when her Jewish tenants knocked on her door to terminate their lease. "We're moving to Milton," they'd whispered, astonished that they could find housing in a suburb that had long been regarded as hostile territory for Jews. Years later, with an indignation that came as if from fresh wounds, she would speak of her disappointment in Jews for having abandoned her. Jews, she learned, might have been victims of discrimination but their white skin allowed them passage through doors still closed to black Bostonians. Despite her middle-class upbringing and special skills, Elma Lewis had no delusions regarding the obstacles facing blacks in Boston. Her own earliest memories dated to age three, when she sought any opportunity to perform her poems and mimicry. "I seemed to be born to the arts," she'd later tell friends, and, indeed, when Lewis discovered and examined her school records from nursery school, she found the following memo from the school psychologist: "This bright precocious little negro girl, as is usual with members of her race, will test at a much lower level as she gets older. Therefore, train her to use her hands."[3]

With a facility like Mishkan Tefila's, thought Lewis, no black child whose hands were destined for sculpting or whose feet were meant for classical dance need use them in the performance of spirit-numbing dead-end tasks. A temple for the arts was certainly a legitimate use for a beautiful building in a neighborhood that Jews had rejected in recent years in favor of suburban lifestyles.

All that stood between Lewis and her dream of a first-class Afro-American center for the arts was a group of suspicious and strangely clothed men who hovered protectively over a handful of ragged schoolchildren. Members of the Lubavitcher Hasidim, an Orthodox sect characterized by their austere black garb, marched not to the step of wealthy Boston philanthropists or enlightened liberals but rather to the messianic strains of Rabbi Menahem Schneerson, a Brooklyn-based old-world *Rebbe* who encouraged Jews to trust God and lobby City hall. The *Rebbe,* amid intense ethnic conflict and white flight from the Crown Heights section of Brooklyn, had decided to stake his ground. His message to followers across the United States was to maintain the sanctity and exclusivity of inner-city neighborhoods.

Eager to expand beyond their small schoolhouse on Bradshaw Street in Dorchester, the Lubavitcher group bought the temple and school building in 1954 for $80,000 when Mishkan Tefila's board voted to pull up roots in the "changing neighborhood" and move their congregation to the suburb of Newton. The Lubavitchers, poor and without funds from the Jewish federation, had quickly abandoned hope of fully maintaining the facility. They used the school annex for services and elementary school classes and the main sanctuary only on the high holidays, when neighborhood Jews craved religious authenticity and flocked back to Mishkan Tefila. With little money for maintenance, the Lubavitchers were unable to prevent the synagogue building from developing structural problems—a leaking roof, drafty walls, and wet rot. Furniture and building materials had been stripped from the main synagogue in order to furnish and repair the school annex. The Lubavitch group paid little attention to the condition of the main sanctuary, with the exception of the memorial plaques that Mishkan Tefila members had left in their trust during their rush to the suburbs.

Boston's Lubavitcher leader, Rabbi Joshua Kastel, seemed content to plod along at the head of the small yeshivah. The Lubavitchers paid little mind to their black neighbors. Unlike their less Orthodox cousins, they were openly disdainful of the world of interfaith activities. For them, improving race relations had no purpose, since it did not advance their overriding objective—to usher in the kingdom of the messiah. Neighborhood blacks, too, seemed to have no use for the reclusive and somberly attired Jews. By the early 1960s Lubavitcher worshippers and students were facing increasing hostility from black neighbors. Teachers stood guard over their charges in the schoolyard, scurrying at times to protect them from rocks and other missiles hurled from the street by black adolescents. Although tens of thousands of Boston Jews lived just one mile south in neighboring Mattapan and Dorchester, the Lubavitcher yeshivah in Roxbury increasingly took on the appearance of a military outpost. Falling deeper into debt and watching their physical plant deteriorate rapidly, many Lubavitchers began to wonder if it would be just the same to the messiah if they awaited his return in the suburbs.

"Crazy as bedbugs,"[4] thought Elma Lewis as she watched a bearded rabbi lead his young charges through the school annex. Where was justice if a group of xenophobic fanatics could block black advancement? Shubow, however, could barely suppress a smile at the sight of the young Hasidim. Their dangling earlocks and curious glances reminded him of pictures he had seen of Jews in the Warsaw Ghetto before it was destroyed. These youngsters, however, chattered in the excited way he remembered from his own childhood, growing up in Dorchester.

Since early childhood Larry Shubow believed he was destined for a special role in life. Growing up in Jewish Dorchester, Shubow was the only Lawrence in a neighborhood of Seymours, Irvings, and Melvins. "Ma, Pa, where did you get this name from?"[5] he finally asked his parents. They produced a picture book with a portrait of Lorenzo de' Medici, the wealthy patron of Michelangelo. Reading the volume, Shubow learned that de' Medici, dubbed "Il Magnifico," supported the great artist when he sculpted his famous rendering of David. Lawrence David Shubow received early messages that with the name came opportunity.

After World War II Shubow worked for a time for the Boston office of the American Jewish Congress, the progressive Jewish defense organization that would later take an active role in the civil rights movement. Throughout the 1950s Shubow, after attending law school, hurled himself into legal efforts to block local political witch-hunts inspired by right-wing supporters of Wisconsin Senator Joseph McCarthy. Few clients could afford to pay; "In those days we worked on promises of rubles after the revolution," he later joked.[6] Shubow was so intense a defender of those accused of Communist sympathies that his friends were amazed that he did not himself become one of the hunted. But Shubow was no one-dimensional limousine liberal. He was equally at home talking world revolution with left-wing intellectuals or sitting at all-night poker games with lowbrow Ward 14 politicos whose vision often extended no further than traffic court. In the early 1960s Shubow and his law partners represented scores of criminal defendants in Boston's black community. Radical defendants, in particular, sought his counsel; nevertheless, his advice and friendship were still cherished by the law-and-order crowd down in the district courts. Friends marveled at how Shubow managed to operate in disparate political worlds. "I'm unassailable by staying in the eye of the storm," he would tell them. "In every goddamn political controversy there are always a few people who are allowed to function in a no-man's-land between the two enemy camps. Certain people operate in the dusk. That's me."[7]

The friendship between Shubow and Lewis dated back to the early 1950s when Larry's wife, Lillian, began studying dance in Lewis's small Roxbury studio. The Shubows were always particularly eager to organize cultural events highlighting black and Jewish contributions to the performing arts. The couple's exuberance, however, was not always appreciated by their black friends. After a local performance by Paul Robeson in 1951, adoring fan Lillian Shubow threw her arms around the black singer and kissed him. Later that night, black friends called Lillian on the carpet.

"How do you think people will respond to a white woman throwing herself on a black man?" they chided her. "Control yourself. You're endangering the life of a great artist." In 1953 Larry Shubow sponsored a performance of the "Drums of Passion" in Boston, again invoking the ire of black intellectuals. "Larry, what are you bringing these African rhythms here for?" they demanded. "We're not interested in going back to that savagery, that bare-breasted music that you white liberals love so much. We want ballet."[8]

Shubow paid an emotional price for his politics. During the early 1950s, when his name was linked with McCarthy's targets on the front pages of Boston newspapers, his wife was asked to leave a fertility clinic in which she had been seeking treatment. Embittered by such harassments and in need of privacy, the Shubows left Dorchester in 1956, adopted a child, and moved to the western suburb of Newton. There they harbored a sense, which diminished with the passing of years, that perhaps they had jumped ship. But even activists, they told themselves, can enjoy green grass and fresh air.

Shubow ultimately shared Lewis's view of the Lubavitchers. As a young Labor Zionist, he had learned to condemn the rigid and religious right. Like Rosa Luxemburg, the patron saint of many left-leaning assimilating Jews, he found it difficult to show the same sympathy to economically deprived Jews as to the poor of other races or religions. He had found it necessary to cross into black culture to avoid rotting away in what he contemptuously described as the "Eisenhower cotton candy period." Shubow remembers the "fierce, burning, passionate energy" coming out of the early movement for black civil rights. The rest was a wasteland. Years later, in the late 1970s, Shubow would passionately defend the communal rights of the Mashpee Indians, many of whom were as assimilated into American society as he was, in their efforts to regain from Cape Cod developers tribal lands sold by their ancestors centuries before. But Larry Shubow had little concern for the Jewish stake in inner-city neighborhoods.

Both Shubow and Lewis were largely unaware of the class war between local and suburban members of Mishkan Tefila that finally led to the sale of the property to the Lubavitcher group. And even if they had been aware of it, how could it possibly compare with the great civil rights struggle of the 1950s and 1960s? The series of events that mattered began in 1955 when Rosa Parks, a seamstress, awakened the American conscience when she refused to give up her seat at the front of a public bus in Montgomery, Alabama. In 1960 four black students from North Carolina Agricultural and Technical College requested service at a Woolworth's coffee counter in Greensboro, North Carolina, and were arrested for their efforts. By 1963 more than nine hundred public demonstrations for civil rights had taken place in 115 cities in eleven southern states. Shubow, like other Jewish progressives nationwide, was captivated with the voter registration drives, Martin Luther King's March on Washington in August 1963, and the growing demand for Black Power as evidenced by H. Rap Brown of the Student Nonviolent Coordinating Committee (SNCC). Not since his heady days in the radical American Youth Congress—or, later, in the protest against the death sentences for convicted spies Ethel and Julius Rosenberg—had life seemed charged with such meaning. For Shubow, dirty little wars in the Jewish community could never measure up to the historic struggle for black rights.

Shubow and Lewis knew that it would take a methodical plan to convert the temple into an Afro-American center for the arts. The Jewish community was awash in organizations and committees. But it was difficult to know who spoke for the Jews. That task was generally assigned to the Jewish Community Council. Local Jewish community councils had formed in the 1940s, in the wake of the comprehensive MacIver report, to reduce duplication of effort and resources across the communal agenda. The result was the creation of a centrally funded National Community Relations Advisory Council to coordinate the efforts of local and national groups. Local community relations councils soon mushroomed. Boston's council also formed during this period of communal reorganization. Its longtime director, Robert Segal, had struggled to finance the organization independently, fearing political pressure from federation philanthropists. But, in reality, the council's funds came from the same large donors who supported the city's Combined Jewish Philanthropies.

Throughout the 1950s and 1960s, the community councils came to serve as the political action arms of those Jewish federations that directly, or indirectly, funded them. Because it was unseemly for a president of the Combined Jewish Philanthropies to complain strongly to an editor about press coverage of the

Jewish community or to hash out areas of mutual concern with labor unionists, these jobs fell to the council directors. The councils were also encouraged to take strong civil rights stances. In Topeka, Kansas, the local council played a key role in supporting black parents in Brown v. Board of Education, *the landmark case that would later lead to the 1954 Supreme Court decision ordering the desegregation of American public schools. In San Francisco an interracial and interfaith group met regularly for planning sessions in the offices of the council, leading to the creation of the San Francisco Human Rights Commission.*

Larry Shubow felt confident that Bob Segal and the Jewish Community Council in Boston could be counted on in the local civil rights struggle. His confidence was not misplaced. The diminutive and energetic Segal received Shubow and Lewis warmly in his office in the Combined Jewish Philanthropies building at 72 Franklin Street on the edge of Boston's financial district. He listened intently as Shubow described the underutilized buildings in the Jewish community and as Lewis set forth her dream of a national center for Afro-American artists. Lewis was no stranger to Segal, who was proud of his close working relationships with many of Boston's prominent black leaders, including U.S. Senator Edward Brooke, Model Cities director Paul Parks, and Freedom House founders Otto and Muriel Snowden. Together they had worked on many of the decade's most contested issues: fair housing opportunities, job discrimination, and quality public education.

Segal, like many Jews sympathetic to the struggle for black civil rights, had seen his share of racism and discrimination. He retained a strong memory of his first sing-along at a boy scout meeting in the 1920s in a small Ohio town just north of the Mason-Dixon line: "Who's been here since I've been gone?" bellowed the scoutmaster, a question to which the scout pack would sing in turn, "A great big nigger with a gattlin' gun."[9] In 1944, eager to set up a new home in the suburbs of Boston, Segal had phoned a broker for a large real estate company. "Are you an American?" she asked. "Yes, I am," he replied. "You know what I mean, are you a Jew?" the broker queried. "I am," replied Segal, who was left listening to a dial tone.

Segal was impressed with Lewis's argument for mobilizing the organized Jewish community in support of the arts center. "I know Jewish people as well as I know black people," she'd told him. "We had the same problems and we fought along together. But as soon as Jews had the opportunity to be part of the establishment, they took it. Now blacks want the same opportunity. Can you appreciate that our gifted youngsters in the black community are being lost? With Mishkan Tefila I can turn that around."[10] It all seemed so familiar to Segal. Two decades earlier he had fought for the rights of Jews to compete fairly for jobs in Massachusetts banks and utility and insurance companies. Great strides had been made in those areas as well as in opening housing opportunities in the restrictive suburbs surrounding Boston. One need only look at men like Eli Goldston, the head of Eastern Gas and Electric, and Lew Weinstein, who had penetrated the world of downtown law firms, to see that Lewis was correct. Blacks, Segal believed, had yet to get their breaks. "It's an old story," he thought to himself as he listened to Lewis's appeal. "Help your brother's boat across though you've reached the shore yourself."[11]

Like Larry Shubow, Segal was compelled by the drive and energy emanating from the black community, a feeling of excitement and promise in which he longed to share. Back in the 1940s he'd experienced similar excitement working for the rights of Jews. In those days Rev. Charles Coughlin, a scurrilously antisemitic priest, broadcast his hate messages on a nationally syndicated radio program; Segal earned a national reputation through his public denunciations of Coughlin. Boston's Jewish leaders recruited Segal to head the city's first Jewish Community Council when friction between Jewish and Irish Catholic youths in Dorchester was giving the entire city's reputation a black eye. In those clashes Jews invariably ended up on the wrong end of the nightstick in Boston's Irish-controlled police stations. Segal wasted little time convincing parish priests and Archdiocese officials alike that pitched battles in Franklin Park served the interest of no one. He also convinced then-Governor Leverett Saltonstall to form a commission of inquiry regarding partisan law enforcement by police and court officers, putting the city on notice that repercussions would follow the trampling of Jewish rights.

When Segal arrived in Boston in 1944, he'd been told that more than one hundred thousand Jews lived in Dorchester, Roxbury, and Mattapan. Less than half that number remained in the old neighborhoods when Lewis and Shubow came to seek his help regarding the potential for transfering Jewish institutions to black hands. As head of the Jewish Community Council, Segal had done nothing to stem the flow of Jews from Roxbury and Dorchester. Years later he acknowledged that urban renewal and the relocation of poor blacks into Jewish neighborhoods had never been perceived as a Jewish issue; the opposite, in fact, was true. With Jewish Community Council officers like Lewis Weinstein and federation honorees like Eli Goldston in the vanguard of urban renewal policy, it was unthinkable to challenge the reshaping of the city's ethnic landscape.

Segal promised Lewis to use his offices to help secure the temple. During the months that followed, Lewis met on numerous occasions with Greater Boston's leading Jewish lay and professional leaders. The arts patroness came across as competent but brash to federation executives like Ben Rosenberg and Simon Krakow. "You can't cut a people off from beauty for 300 years and expect us to come up beautiful," she told them.[12] Wealthy local philanthropists, like supermarket magnate Sidney Rabb and do-it-yourself building material executive Bernard Grossman, did not escape the Lewis needle. "What was considered good enough for us isn't good enough," she told them. "I'm going to get mine, too."

Throughout the winter of 1967 and shortly after the new year, the federation continued to send feelers to the Lubavitcher community regarding the prospects for vacating Mishkan Tefila. What they heard in return was that the Lubavitcher rebbe strongly encouraged his followers to remain in the inner cities and that even if they were to move, it would cost many thousands of dollars to start over in the suburbs. Segal and others gently suggested to Lewis that she should begin fund-raising in the black community. The timing, however, was awkward. Early in 1968 Student Nonviolent Coordinating Committee leader James Forman and other radical black leaders called for reparations from synagogues and businesses operating in the black community. Jews were shocked at the concept of reparations being applied to the inner city. In the Jewish lexicon, reparations were synonymous with the payments made by the German government to survivors of the Nazi Holocaust. It was one thing to give a helping hand and quite another to imply that Jews were responsible for setting their "brothers' boat" adrift. Boston would not be the last city where black–Jewish cooperation would be sacrificed to semantic subtleties and efforts to establish blame.

For Lewis, the thought of blacks raising money to facilitate a move by Hasidic Jews to the suburbs was too preposterous to be taken seriously. To complicate matters further, Lewis reported back to the federation leaders that the property was falling rapidly into disrepair. The roof of the main sanctuary/performance hall had sprung a large leak, which the Lubavitcher group could ill afford to mend. The Lubavitchers, too, were removing fixtures, furniture, and other useful items from the main sanctuary to supplement their needs in the smaller school building. At the same time, small, mysterious fires were breaking out with regularity on the temple grounds. According to the Lubavitchers, the fires, like the increasing number of threatening phone calls, were messages from the area's blacks that the Jews should leave or face deadly consequences. The blacks countered that the fires were caused by "Jewish lightning" for insurance purposes and that the building would be despoiled if the transfer was not affected immediately. Jewish officials began to lose faith that some accord could be reached between Lewis and the Lubavitchers.

Rabbi Joseph Shubow approached his nephew when he learned that he was taking a leading role in the effort to secure Mishkan Tefila for Lewis. Although they had never seen eye to eye politically, there was a deep respect and understanding between the two men. Larry Shubow had convinced his uncle in the 1950s to help elicit support for a public protest and petition against the witch-hunts of Sen. Joseph McCarthy. Furthermore, Larry Shubow had always suspected that his uncle had pulled not a few strings to help a favorite nephew through the labyrinth of the Harvard admissions office. But the rabbi was infuriated that his nephew now wanted to strip the synagogue from Jewish hands. "What is happening to my Roxbury?" the rabbi asked. "Are the people down there animals? We never had these muggings and robberies when the Jews lived in Roxbury. And now you want to give them a beautiful synagogue so they can destroy that too. Don't ask for my help to displace my own people."[13]

Larry Shubow protested, firing back that it was the Lubavitchers who had neglected the site and were responsible for the decaying condition of the synagogue. "Elma Lewis will restore that building as a holy site," he told his uncle. "The Jews have abandoned Roxbury. Give the blacks a chance to make it right."[14]

Larry Shubow convinced his uncle to tour the site with him on a Sunday morning in March 1968. Together, nephew and uncle climbed the granite steps and made their way to the back of the main sanctuary. Prayer books, many tattered, were strewn about on the pews; prayer shawls, too, were scattered about the sanctuary. Rabbi Shubow picked up a battered prayer book. "These deserve a decent burial," he whispered. "Don't blame this on Elma Lewis," the younger Shubow said. "She hasn't set foot in this place. It's those goddamn Orthodox hypocrites."[15] Larry Shubow was silenced by a sharp look from his uncle. The rabbi walked toward the front of the sanctuary intent on examining the holy ark, which would ordinarily contain Judaism's most precious treasure — the Torah scrolls. For observant Jews, the Torah, the divine body of knowledge and law, is on a par with human life. If a Torah scroll is damaged beyond repair, it is mourned and buried as if a person had died. Both men were conscious of a slimy substance beneath their feet as they climbed the few steps of the raised platform on which the ark rested. The door to the holy ark was ajar. The rabbi opened it gently, praying all the while that he would not find a ravaged Torah. Both men leaped back suddenly as a pigeon flew from the floor of the ark. Other birds huddled inside on a bed of decomposed excrement and feathers. There was no Torah to be found.

The men did not speak again until they were back outside on Seaver Street. "The Lubavitchers say that Elma is threatening to burn them out if they don't leave," said Larry Shubow. "What a joke. What the Jewish community proposes to sell to Elma isn't even worth burning down." Rabbi Shubow stared back at his nephew. "Pigeons in the holy ark," the rabbi muttered.[16]

On Thursday, April 4, 1968, at 6:02 P.M. a lethal shot fired by James Earl Ray, a white supremacist, felled Rev. Martin Luther King, Jr. The King who died on the balcony of the Lorraine Motel in Memphis was a different "dreamer" than the one who had challenged segregated public transportation in places like Montgomery, Alabama. During the year prior to his assassination, King had begun to move beyond the "safe" issue of civil rights into the murky area of class lines that divide Americans. To the dismay of his political advisers and the delight of his detractors, King was not only posing public challenges to America's military adventures in Vietnam but challenging the very nature of capitalism. Although NAACP leaders warned that it was a serious tactical mistake, King was adamant that the civil rights movement address issues like the disproportionate numbers of black soldiers serving in Southeast Asia. Closer to home, King was ready to throw his moral weight behind full-employment policies, guaranteed annual incomes, low-cost housing, and even the nationalization of major industries. In 1967 he had told his staff, "We must recognize that we can't solve our problem now until there is a radical redistribution of economic and political power. This means a revolution of values. We must see that the evils of racism, economic exploitation and militarism are all tied together, and you really can't get rid of one without getting rid of the others. The whole structure of American life must be changed."[17] The message was not meant only for internal distribution. Speaking the same year to a New York group, King said, "Something is wrong with capitalism as it now stands in the United States. We are not interested in being integrated into this value structure."[18]

King did not limit his analysis of American ills to the white and powerful. He loathed the trappings of wealth and power and lived in a modest home in a working-class section of Atlanta. Nor was he afraid to confront the failings in the black community that, he believed, shared responsibility for drug abuse, burgeoning rates of crime, school dropouts, and illegitimate births. King, however, would never get to implement his broader agenda. Within hours after the assassination, inner-city neighborhoods would be plunged into a feverish nightmare. The catch phrase "roving bands of Negro youths" would be repeated the next day by hundreds of reporters on major metropolitan papers across the country. In Boston, Washington, D.C., Detroit, and Los Angeles, "roving bands of Negro youths" stoned cars, beat whites, burned and looted stores, and toppled police vehicles.

Like his counterparts nationwide, Massachusett's Acting Governor Francis Sargent ordered a National Guard alert on the day following the assassination. Ten thousand air and army Massachusetts guardsmen reported to their armories. City Councilor Tom

Atkins, Paul Parks, and the NAACP's Ken Guscott were not confident that they could contain the rage swelling in the city's black community.

A dozen whites had been injured in stoning incidents on Thursday night, April 4, and street intelligence pointed to a major uprising on Friday morning. Hoping to direct some of this diffuse energy, the black leadership of Boston hastily organized and publicized a march from the statehouse to the city center's Post Office Square. The orderly march drew five thousand participants. Several hundred demonstrators, however, broke off to join up with about four hundred others who were planning strategy at the YMCA in Washington Park. Ominous messages waited in the form of pamphlets distributed by Operation Exodus. The pamphlets read, in part: "When the riot starts, you can expect martial law which will confine you to your home for as long as a month or more. We must unite now for the attacks upon our communities from the police, the armed forces and the white communities." The pamphlet further advised residents to stockpile food, water, guns and "plenty of ammunition." At 1:00 P.M., two hundred black youths surged out of the YMCA onto Dudley Street and began to march south toward Blue Hill Avenue. Small groups broke off from the main body of marchers and entered the largely Jewish-owned businesses beneath the elevated line along Washington and Dudley Streets. White shopkeepers were ordered to close their businesses in honor of King. Black business owners, on the other hand, were permitted to stay open. The mob had grown to eight hundred by the time it marched out of Dudley Station into Grove Hall. At the Jeremiah Burke High School the marchers tore down and burned an American flag that had been lowered to half mast in King's memory. Police officers hustled teachers out of the building into waiting police cars.

The mob continued south to the corner of Washington Street and Columbia Road, the site of a vast Stop & Shop supermarket. The Stop & Shop stores were the pride of Jewish Boston. Back in 1914 the Rabinovitz brothers had opened the small Economy Grocery Store in Grove Hall. Sidney, Irving, and Norman shortened their surnames to Rabb and expanded their Stop & Shop empire to more than a hundred stores in New England and New York. Stop & Shop founder Sidney Rabb was a man with a generous spirit whose charity extended to cultural, black, and Jewish causes. "No pockets in shrouds," he would tell business partners who felt his philanthropy was excessive.

To the mob, the Stop & Shop was simply another white-owned business exploiting black shoppers. Scores of protesters swarmed through the aisles of the supermarket and squared off with Boston police. By 2:30 P.M. black leaders had convinced the managers to close the store and send their employees home. The mob's progress south was suspended for a time in the enormous supermarket's parking lot. Only a few blocks east lay the border of the working-class Irish neighborhoods. Schools were just now letting out and there were sure to be hundreds of turf-conscious youths waiting to see if the blacks dared make a frontal assault on the sanctity of their neighborhoods. Only a few blocks to the south lay the Jewish neighborhoods with scores of businesses clearly operating in violation of the slain King's memory. Younger, more radical members of the mob urged the rioters to continue southward down the Avenue. Several adult leaders, bullhorns pressed to their lips, exhorted the protesters to follow them northward back into the heart of black Roxbury. Most followed, leaving the police to disperse those youths intent on pressing forward. It was a scene that would be repeated many times in the next twenty-four hours—mature black leaders, distinguishable by arm bands and walkie talkies, rushing to a trouble spot to diffuse a potentially life-threatening situation. Forty businesses would be looted and burned but Boston would not see the kind of carnage and loss of life experienced that day in other major urban centers like Washington, D.C., where thirteen people would lose their lives and a thousand would suffer serious injuries.

Thomas Atkins was again at the forefront of black leaders trying to restore peace to Roxbury. The city councilor had his hands full on the Friday following King's murder. Atkins was not only making radio appeals for calm and urging black rioters off the street but also negotiating with James Brown, the "Godfather of Soul." Martin Luther King may have ruled the pulpits in the black community but rhythm-and-blues giant James Brown ruled the airwaves. King could inspire his listeners with extraordinary eloquence and unsurpassed depth of feeling, but during the last years of his ministry he had increasingly lost touch with younger radicals in the black power movement. James Brown, however, never broke contact with his fans except when they fainted from the intensity of his trademark blues notes.

On Friday night Brown was scheduled to appear in concert at Boston Garden. Atkins was among the first to learn that the arena officials had decided to cancel the concert because they anticipated violence. He immediately called city hall. The new mayor, Kevin White, had been up all night monitoring the situation in Roxbury and was just stirring from a catnap. Atkins begged the mayor to intercede and tried to convince him that not only should the show go on but that the local public broadcasting station should broadcast the concert live so that Roxbury youths could at least have an incentive to keep off the streets. "It's too late to cancel," Atkins warned. "There'll be thousands of black teenagers down at the Garden this evening and when they find those gates are locked they're going to be pretty pissed off. . . . We'll have an even bigger riot than last night—only this time it will be in the heart of downtown."[19]

The mayor, exhausted from the tense hours glued to his police radio, could hardly argue with Atkins's logic and promised to use his offices to keep the concert alive. Throughout the day Atkins raced between Roxbury, city hall, police headquarters, and various of the city's media outlets. Over the airwaves of WILD, the city's most popular black radio station, he pleaded with parents to keep their children off the streets throughout the weekend. Mayor White expressed confidence in the peace-making ability of the black community's leaders and urged police restraint. Nevertheless, at a 3:30 P.M. meeting with police officials, he decided to close off downtown to all traffic, even though the mobs showed no predilection for turning north. It was one thing if enraged blacks were going to set fire to white-owned small businesses in their own community. It would be something else again if any of the hotheads got the urge to expand the war into the city's financial district.

With Atkins's assurances that the black cause would be better served by a smaller than capacity audience—and with further assurances of a guaranteed gate—the James Brown concert was saved. Only fifteen hundred fans were on hand to greet the singer, many thousands more opting for the safety of their living rooms. Music and politics mixed easily as Brown and Atkins took center stage together. Before launching into his first set, Brown asked the crowd to acknowledge Atkins as a "black man in the driver's seat." The fans roared with approval. Atkins in turn called Mayor White out from the wings—the first face-to-face contact between the mayor and a group of black citizens since the start of the riot. White peered past the footlights at the scattered audience. Sensing that the mayor might lose the crowd before he even opened his mouth, Brown decided to give White's solo a boost. "Give him a big round of applause ladies and gentlemen. He's a swingin' cat," the singer enthused. The crowd immediately warmed to White. "I'm here to ask you to stay with me as your mayor and to make Dr. King's dream a reality," White told the audience. "This is our city and its future is in our hands . . . Let us look at each other, here in the Garden and back at home, and pledge that no matter what any other community might do, we in Boston will honor Dr. King in peace."[20] Relieved, White stepped back from the klieg lights as the "godfather of soul" tore the roof off the Garden.

Black leaders and youth workers again asserted their presence following the Brown concert. More than two hundred and fifty volunteers met concert goers at subway stations and urged them to stay calm and go home. On Saturday night fewer outbreaks of violence were reported. On Sunday, as large metro papers across the nation continued to report death tolls and property damage figures from rioting in major urban areas, the Boston papers were churning out articles on the innovative and effective steps taken by city leaders, black and white, to head off violence. Mayor White had weathered the first crisis of his new administration, and Tom Atkins had proved that black elected officials had much to contribute to the governance of the city. Just how much was noted by Barney Frank, an aide to White who would later go on to the U.S. House of Representatives. Queried by reporters as to whether the Boston Police had been given explicit orders to keep a low profile, Frank answered, "Last year Tom Atkins was clubbed and arrested. This year he's coordinating efforts at police headquarters."[21]

Mel Goldstein, known among his customers as "the Hat Man," often boasted that he enjoyed such good relations with the black community that it was not necessary to put security grates on his windows. Goldstein, a powerfully built man with a quick, ingenuous smile, had been operating his haberdashery in lower Roxbury at the corner of Dudley and Warren Streets since 1950. Back then he sold hats in almost equal proportions to Jewish, Canadian, and black customers. During the days preceding the Jewish High Holy Days, Goldstein always did a brisk business in smart narrow fedoras with low crowns. In the early 1960s Kangol caps with stiched-down brims were great sellers with the Irish and Nova Scotian roofers who worked on the neighborhood's rehabilitation projects. Mostly though, Goldstein stocked wide-brimmed styles for his black customers, the favorite being the top of the line Borsalino velours. By the early 1960s, when white customers were growing scarce in lower Roxbury, the "Hat Man" was more than satisfied to track the preferences in crown heights and brim curls of his loyal black clientele. For customers who couldn't afford the $50 price tag on the Italian Borsalinos, Goldstein developed his own line of high-quality look-a-likes, which he labeled, after a discreet vowel change, Barsalinos.

On the morning after King's assassination Goldstein received visits from black friends urging him to close shop and go home for a few days. Roxbury, they assured him, would be no place for a white man once the initial shock of the murder wore off, leaving only an exposed core of hot rage. Nobody wanted to see the Hat Man come to any harm. He had always provided the neighborhood with quality goods at a fair price and seemed genuinely interested in his customers and their families. During the 1967 disturbances in Grove Hall, surrounding stores had been looted and torched, but the Hat Shop stood untouched. Goldstein had not only weathered the welfare mothers' riot but prospered in the process. In fact, the Hat Shop did record sales on the day after the Grove Hall riot. Goldstein had sold out his entire selection of straw hats on that day, more than he could normally sell in six months. "Guys were walking in here like their feet were ten feet off the ground," he recalls. "They were jubilant. They'd made their mark and wanted to look good."[22]

Like many businessmen and police officers who witnessed riots in Roxbury, Goldstein was totally convinced that they were finely orchestrated proceedings rather than spontaneous bursts of rage. He claimed to have witnessed cash awards to schoolboys from leading members of the city's black radical organizations for, as he called it, "outstanding performances in the category of urban rioting." Since the welfare mothers' riot, however, Goldstein had kept a two-foot length of pipe fitted with a bamboo handle near his cash register. Things had seemed particularly ominous since the Black Panthers had taken over a former dry cleaning store on lower Blue Hill Avenue for their headquarters. The storefront was plastered with revolutionary posters, including one labeled "Target No. 1: the Pig," depicting a pig in a police uniform superimposed on a bull's eye. The Hat Man had always maintained civil relations with his most radical customers, but he couldn't abide the Panthers. With the Panthers, everything had turned upside down. Here, he believed, was a group of hoodlums who engaged policemen in deadly gun battles while their ridiculous white supporters prattled on about the pancake breakfasts the Panthers served to poorly nourished schoolchildren. In Panther lexicon, some hophead picked up for robbing a ma-and-pa grocery store was a "political prisoner." The worst of it was that the Panthers had chosen his corner to sell their journals filled with antisemitic poetry: "Jew land, On a /summer afternoon/Really, Couldn't kill the Jews too soon/Now dig, The Jews have stolen our bread/Their filthy women tricked our men into bed. . . ."[23]

Goldstein moved instinctively for the length of pipe whenever one of the Panthers came into the store. He had vowed never to be shaken down by the antisemites. Once, they had threatened to burn him down and he had insouciantly tossed them a book of matches. One Panther seemed to take particular delight in trying to intimidate Goldstein. "Hat Man, one day I'm going to take care of you," the Panther said, placing his hand threateningly in the pocket of his coat. "When you pull your hand out of your pocket it better be a handkerchief," Goldstein shot back. "If it's anything else, they'll carry you out of here feet first." The Panther came out empty-handed. "I was only funnin' Hat Man," he said. Mel Goldstein wondered how long his nerves would hold out.[24]

At noon on the day after King's assassination, a longtime customer, with ties to several black radical groups, walked into the shop. There was none of the usual small talk, only a hard glare. "One chance, Hat Man. Close it up and go home. Today is serious business." Goldstein looked out onto normally crowded Dudley Street, which was all but deserted. Across the street, an Irishman who had been a steady customer for years was crossing toward the store. Four black youths were suddenly on him, throwing punches and kicking wildly. With several well-placed blows, the burly customer freed himself from his assailants, dashed back to his car, and sped away. This would not be a day for record sales of straw hats. Mel Goldstein did what he had never done in eighteen years of business. He closed his shop up at midday and drove home.

Joe Cohen, who owned National Radio and Television around the corner on the 2000 block of Washington Street, did not receive any warning callers on that Friday morning. Cohen had opened his appliance store back in 1951 after successive failures in suburban dress shops. "The big conglomerates killed me . . . put me right out of business," he recalled in a refrain voiced by many of the area's shopkeepers who had not originally intended to open businesses in the inner city.[25] For a while, he'd gone to work for his brother-in-law, E. M. Loew, who had made a fortune in local movie theatres, nightclubs, and harness racing. But Cohen yearned once again to own his own business. It seemed, at least, that whatever risks were involved in opening a business in a poor neighborhood, they did not include competing with the resources of a chain store. And Cohen had made a go of it. By the early 1960s he had made enough selling small and large off-brand appliances in Roxbury to buy the building.

On the day following King's murder, Joe Cohen was returning to his store from a coffee run when he heard windows shatter behind him. One block down Washington Street, a mob of club-wielding blacks, both youths and adults, were smashing the plate glass windows of the small businesses underneath the elevated. Cohen sprinted for his store and frantically dropped the door grate. He had time to secure only three of the five window grates before the mob reached the store. As glass shattered around him, scores of black hands reached out for blenders, radios, portable televisions, vacuum cleaner attachments, and other small appliances. The mob rushed past Cohen as if he were invisible and stormed the store's foyer in the quest for bigger and better items. Untouched, Cohen rushed to the store's back office and grabbed his shotgun. He walked determinedly to within five yards of the looters and leveled his weapon. One looter dropped his booty and cried out a warning to the others. Some ran away empty-handed; others sauntered away, arms laden with merchandise. Joe Cohen

stood with his shotgun shouldered until the riot-helmeted police
arrived fifteen minutes later.

Bernard Grossman, the chief executive of Grossman's Lumber
Company and the lay president of the Combined Jewish Philanthropies, was asleep in a downtown hotel early in the morning
after King's assassination. Grossman had recently begun to curtail
some of his civic and business interests in Boston and had moved
to the island of Nantucket off Cape Cod. Business, however,
frequently drew him back to the city. At 5:00 A.M. Grossman was
awakened by a loud knock at his hotel door. He shuffled to the
door and opened it, revealing three black men he had never seen
before. Only one man spoke. "We get the temple mortgage free or
else we burn, baby, burn."[26] The men left abruptly, leaving
Grossman shaken and confused. Later that day Grossman huddled
with officers of the Combined Jewish Philanthropies and Jewish
Community Centers of Greater Boston in a meeting room at the
Brighton Jewish Community Center to discuss the threat and their
response to the riots. Led by Al Rosen, the federation's public
relations director, the leadership discussed the harsh anti-Jewish
sentiments that had boiled to the surface in recent days. All were
aware of the growing antisemitic statements emanating from the
Student Nonviolent Coordinating Committee, which attempted to
place the blame for America's internal problems on Jewish landlords and for its external problems on Zionism. Jews had grown
accustomed to antisemitic attacks coming from the right, but few
had anticipated the escalating hate rhetoric from the progressive
left. Grossman learned that he was not the only federation leader
to receive threats regarding the fate of Mishkan Tefila. Others in
the room had received similar messages that day, such as "Put the
temple in the hands of the black community or we'll burn it down
with Jews in it." The Jewish leaders did not believe the threats
were emanating from anyone involved with Elma Lewis. More
likely, they believed, the source of the threats came from the Black
Panthers or other radicals whose publications of late had been
filled with openly antisemitic articles and cartoons reminiscent of
Nazi propaganda.
    Boston's Jewish leaders were convinced that a sweeping
gesture of goodwill would be necessary to keep the peace between

Jews and blacks in Boston. They were also scared. Any further delay in securing the temple for Elma Lewis, they believed, could prove disastrous. During the next week the Jewish federation leaders began their work on two fronts. Since the riot, the Lubavitcher group had become far more receptive to the possibility of relocating in Brookline or another suburb. Parents were reluctant to send their children to school on Seaver Street, and the Lubavitcher staff accepted that their days on the site were numbered. Top executives of the federation contacted ten of the city's leading Jewish philanthropists about the possibility of raising $25,000 from each to relocate the Lubavitcher school. It was an extraordinary plan in that up to that time federation policy did not include direct grants to day schools. The plan called for the money to be given to the federation rather than directly to the Lubavitcher group. In that way, the Combined Jewish Philanthropies could score a double public relations coup: first, through its relocation of the besieged Lubavitcher Jews and, second, by transferring an unencumbered building to a respected agent of the black community.

Bob Segal was given the task of contacting Lewis to see if she would assume some financial responsibility during the transfer. The Mishkan Tefila complex had been assessed for more than $1 million, and a $25,000 mortgage on the property was still outstanding. The federation leaders assumed that Lewis would provide but a small fraction of the outstanding mortgage but nevertheless felt it was important that some remuneration come from the black community. Segal called Lewis after the federation strategy session and asked her directly how much the black community was willing to put on their side of the table to effect a quick sale. "It's traditional in a transaction like this that you make some contribution," Segal told her.[27] Before Segal could explain further about the fiduciary responsibility of Jewish leaders in such situations, Lewis exploded. "You're asking us for money?" Lewis shouted. "The greatest black leader in America was just gunned down by a filthy racist, and you're asking us for money. Your people turned and ran from this neighborhood. Your people let this synagogue slip into disgrace, and now you want money from us. You owe us this building. You owe it to us. And we're not paying a dime." Sheepishly, Segal reversed himself, saying that the federation was looking for nothing more than a token payment. "A five-dollar bill," he sputtered. "Something like that." The concession only served to unleash a fresh stream of invective from Lewis. "No payment," she shouted. "Nothing. Not a dime."

A shell-shocked Segal reported back to the Combined Jewish Philanthropies leadership. Grossman and Executive Director Rosenberg agreed that the transfer must go ahead immediately with or without financial contributions from the black community. Public relations man Al Rosen started to call his contacts in the metropolitan press, explaining to them that a historic and beneficent gesture would take place on April 16. Fearing that the reporters would call attention to the shabby condition of the main sanctuary, the transfer ceremony was arranged at a nearby site on Columbia Road. Greater Boston's leading black and Jewish citizens formed a united front for the cadre of reporters. Liquor flowed freely and the atmosphere was carnival-like. Several of Lewis's young ballerinas moved joyously among the politicians, businessmen, lawyers, and journalists. As the parties prepared to sign the transfer agreement, Lewis's attorney, Larry Shubow, suggested to her that she present Grossman with one dollar to symbolize the legally binding nature of the transaction. Lewis made a show of searching her bag for the bill before coming up empty. "I haven't got a cent on me," she told Shubow, smiling broadly. Bernard Grossman then reached into his billfold for a dollar and handed it to Lewis, who in turn handed it back, raising a round of good-natured chuckles and guffaws from the assembled. Grossman then rose and praised the motives for the transfer. "These buildings have long stood as a majestic expression of our religious heritage," Grossman stated. "We sincerely hope that they will continue to serve as a symbol of the common bond that unites all men, that they will be a source of pride, and their future use a source of inspiration to our entire community."[28] Lewis did nothing to jeopardize the public relations coup. "It seems singularly appropriate that buildings which had symbolized the proud heritage of Boston's Jewish community should now announce to the world the proud heritage of Boston's black community," she noted.

Combined Jewish Philanthropies public relations chief Al Rosen did an effective job of communicating the federation's message to the media. On April 18 the lead story in the *Jewish Advocate* shouted out in unusually large type, "Jewish Gift for Negroes." Boston's major news media joined in to praise the transfer. The *Boston Globe* called the gesture "grounds for prayerful and universal rejoicing." The *New York Times,* too, took note of the extraordinary generosity of Boston's Jews. Congratulatory letters and telegrams poured in from the NAACP, the United Front, the Urban League, and scores of Jewish organizations. The Combined Jewish Philanthropies, the nation's first Jewish federation, had charted new territory once again.

On the Line

Liberals Confront the Boundaries of Moral Concern, 1968

It had always been difficult for the card players to find acceptance at the Golden Age Club at the Hecht House Jewish Community Center on American Legion Highway. Poker and pinochle were considered incompatible with the tenets of Judaism, at least according to the pious club members who preferred to pass the afternoons watching television, reading Yiddish papers, and listening to cantorial music on an old Victrola. As far back as anyone could remember, the social workers had scolded their regular clients for freezing out the card players. "These men are respectable people, just like you," the club advisers pleaded, pointing to the retired sheet metal workers and storekeepers milling awkwardly in the lobby. The regulars were adamant: "What will people say if this turns into a gambling place? It will be a shame for us all." Soon, they argued, the center would be thick with bookies and numbers runners—as ungodly a crowd as one might find at

153

Cutler's pool room or Ye Ole Brown Jug Chinese restaurant on Morton Street and Blue Hill Avenue.

The question of propriety regarding card playing masked more substantive differences between the groups of elderly. The card players, for the most part, preferred the English press over the Yiddish journals and favored Conservative synagogues over Orthodox *shtibels*. To the center's social workers, however, the two groups were virtually indistinguishable—working class men in their sixties and seventies who were seeking respite in a "Jewish place among Jewish people."[1] Neither the pious nor the pinochle players easily engaged in hobbies. Each group balked when the staff at the Jewish community center introduced crafts kits for hand-stitched leather wallets, picture frames, and copper ornaments. Workers who had spent decades mastering the mass production process scoffed openly at recreational crafts. "It's a waste of time," they protested. "I don't do handwork. I'm a machine stitcher. If I could only earn even a few cents extra, I'd be a different person."[2]

Generations of Jewish Bostonians passed through the Hecht House. A constituent agency of the Combined Jewish Philanthropies, the facility had been founded in 1890 as the Hebrew Industrial School for Girls and later named for philanthropist Lina Hecht. The center's first location was on Hanover Street in Boston's North End, where newly arriving Jews from Lithuania were settling in a wedge-shaped district bounded by Endicott and North Bennet Streets. During this early period of Jewish settlement, the Russian Jews crammed into tenements in the nearby West End and the more established German Jews living in South End brownstones curled their lips in disgust at the shabby appearance of the greenhorns. In 1934 the Hecht House followed Boston's Jews to Dorchester and occupied a protective red brick three-story building on American Legion Highway, a leafy boulevard noted for plant nurseries and back wards of the Mattapan State Hospital for the mentally ill. The center, in the 1940s and 1950s, earned a reputation as a first-class social and cultural facility for the more than sixty thousand Jews living within a one-mile radius.

In acknowledgment of its role as an absorption vehicle for new immigrants, the first stated goal of the Hecht House was "to foster an appreciation of American ideals of democracy and citizenship."[3] The center hosted scores of clubs and programs rivaling in content those of today's palatial suburban Jewish community centers. Nursery school children could be found in playgroups supervised by teachers utilizing the latest educational theories while older siblings shot hoops in the gym or practiced the manly arts in the boxing room. Club offerings included dramatics, woodwork, science, Brownies, and community gardening. Musical adults founded a community orchestra and performed symphonic and popular works for their appreciative neighbors in the main auditorium. Special events included performances by popular folk headliners like Pete Seeger and Tony Saletan.

It was the services for the elderly, however, that most impressed a visitor. With limitless patience, workers listened to the litany of complaints and insights from aging Dorchester Jews who felt increasingly alienated from their acculturated children. "For my children, life hangs on the ball game, the television set, and the card table. Do they need books? Do they—God forbid—think about anything but new ways to make money?"[4] Many of the community's elders perceived their children's flight to the suburbs during the 1950s and 1960s as a pathetic attempt to escape Judaism. Men who had worked a lifetime for a pittance struggled to convince one another that they had not misdirected their energy into socialism or Orthodoxy. Surprisingly few, when speaking with their cronies, expressed pride in the material accomplishments of sons and daughters. What good, they asked, was a split level in Sharon or South Brookline if it was not a Jewish home? A millionaire's home meant nothing if the wife did not light the Sabbath candles and the husband did not revere the Torah.

Oddly, it was a young writer, not a social worker, who had managed to break down many of the social and ideological differences between the Jewish elderly at the Hecht House. It was a task well-suited to Sylvia Rothchild, a woman of extraordinary energy and insight. She would display those traits again in service to the cause of black community control. That her two passions would prove irreconcilable exemplifies the tragedy of good intentions that was beginning to take shape in Dorchester. Sylvia Rothchild was in her mid-twenties when she arrived in Boston with her scientist husband in 1949. The couple had been shown a dozen apartments in Dorchester's triple-deckers but had found none to their liking. They settled instead in a suburb south of Boston. But something was missing for Rothchild, a native of

Brooklyn who felt alienated in her new neighborhood of split-level homes. She found herself traveling several days each week into the city to frequent the Jewish shops and services along Blue Hill Avenue. She felt particularly compelled by the stories and recollections of the elderly residents who dawdled over glasses of tea in the local delicatessens. Hours passed while she sat and kibbitzed with her new friends. The young writer's devotion to the neighborhood's older residents quickly came to the attention of Hecht House officials. Rothchild quickly accepted their suggestion that she structure a comprehensive outreach center for the elderly.

When Rothchild arrived for work on that first day in 1951, she found her clients sitting silently in the Hecht House lounge, staring silently at a flickering television screen, its sound turned off so as not to compete with the phonograph in the corner. Surveying her new domain, Rothchild at first was startled by the handsome on-screen actor who seemed to be delivering a buoyant version of the Yiddish folk tune *"A Khazand'l af Shabbos"*; on closer inspection, and out of range of the Victrola, she discovered he was endorsing a brand of soap suds.

Rothchild was determined to find challenging activities for her new friends and clients. In the weeks to come she scoured the branches of local libraries for works in Yiddish—and uncovered translations of Shakespeare, Chekhov, and Jack London. Before long, members had broken away from the television and began to meet her at the door to inquire about the success of her latest literature search. Even the conflict between the card players and TV watchers was deflected by the addition of these new intellectual activities. The most popular events included lectures by guests and experts. Club members, most of whom lacked formal schooling, were anxious to prove their intellectual worth to the visitors, scorning fellow members they felt had lowered the level of discourse; one elderly man, for example, had the nerve to ask an expert in Jewish philosophy whether it was permissible according to Jewish law to open a refrigerator on the Sabbath.

The programs doomed to fail included those that drew on the members' own expertise or life experiences. When Rothchild suggested that one of the members relate his experiences of growing up in Bialystok, the members, grumbling, returned to the television. An appeal to a former craftsman to divulge his techniques to fellow members brought instant rejection. "I'll teach young people if you want, but *those* guys—what's the use? They'll be in their graves before they learn anything."[5]

Nevertheless, under Rothchild's guidance the male membership of the Golden Age Club increased exponentially. But, with the exception of a widow or two on the lookout for potential mates, it was difficult to motivate women to join in the activities. A few times each year, usually around the time of a festive holiday, the wives would arrive at the Hecht House on the arms of their elderly husbands; They would interact little, preferring to arrange the herring, chickpeas, and uncut *hallah* (bread) on the paper tablecloths and pour sweet wine into tiny Dixie cups for their men. Determined to expand membership, Rothchild and other group workers spread out along Blue Hill Avenue's shopping district, buttonholing elderly women and collecting addresses for future mailings. Many of the elderly women pushed away the social workers' pens and pads, insisting that they had forgotten their glasses or were suffering a bout of arthritis. Others rummaged through their pocketbooks for crumpled paper on which their names and addresses were already written. It didn't take long for Rothchild to discover that many of the elderly women in the community were illiterate.

By the mid-1950s the responsibilities of a growing family made it impossible for Rothchild to continue her work at the Golden Age Club. Her duties back in Sharon, a quiet and scenic town south of Boston, now included shuttling her three children to art, music, and dance lessons, Little League practice, and Hebrew school. She still found time to teach a class for the local Hadassah chapter and to write stories, essays, and book reviews. But Rothchild could not shake the feeling that she was living in the hinterlands of Jewish creativity. To overcome the alienation, she became the eyes and ears of the newly founded *Commentary Magazine,* reporting to New York intellectuals about that world of questionable reality beyond the Hudson and East Rivers. Rothchild's intelligence reports on Jewish communal life in the suburbs quickly gained popularity with *Commentary's* readers but drew ire from her neighbors. Her own rabbi denounced her from the pulpit as a *moyser,* a collaborator with unknown forces of enmity, causing Rothchild to head for the cover of a pen name. For several years, she continued to record the materialistic failings, as well as the unexpected signs of vitality, seen in Jewish suburbia.

(Rothchild's column did not, however, survive the ascension of Norman Podhoretz to the editorship of *Commentary*. The magazine of the new editor, who would later entitle his memoirs *Making It,* did not include the observations of a literary housewife writing "From the American Scene.")

By the early 1960s Rothchild longed once again for the intensity and density of urban life. Once or twice a month, she would drive to Boston to see a concert or play. When her route took her through Roxbury and Dorchester, she noted with sadness the physical deterioration of Blue Hill Avenue and her former haunts. For her, as for most liberal-thinking Jews in Greater Boston, the center of Jewish life had shifted away from Roxbury and Dorchester toward the western suburbs, where the Rothchilds had bought a beautiful home. She did not stop to think why the old neighborhood was undergoing such profound racial change, nor did she consider with her usual analytical depth the fate of the tens of thousands of Jews still in the area. When Dorchester again began to draw her back and nag at her conscience, she focused on the plight of blacks and their escalating cries for economic and social justice. Many of her friends had been engaged in the civil rights struggle when she was raising her family. "I was a suburbanite, tending my own garden, raising my own children, preoccupied with the problems of my town," she would reflect some years later.[6]

Rothchild started to think, worry, and write about suburban responses to inner-city black communities. Her stories and essays, however, failed to interest publishers. "Too sad," came back the rejection letters. "Too abrasive . . . too controversial." Rothchild was starting to feel that she was on the sidelines of the most compelling issue of the day. "My unhappiness about racial injustices was one of many discontents and angers that I nursed privately," she noted, "infections that kept me from contentment and suburban smugness."[7]

On the afternoon following the assassination of Martin Luther King, Sylvia Rothchild stood on the lawn of a school in suburban Chestnut Hill clutching a box of cold chicken, a tin of cookies, and several cans of Coca-Cola. She and other white parents had prepared a picnic for students from the Metropolitan Educational Council for Opportunities (METCO) and their parents. The experimental program, which had started two years earlier, placed promising black students from the inner city in high-quality suburban school systems on a voluntary, competitive basis. The program demanded a high level of commitment from the entire family. Parents often needed to rouse their children from bed as early as 5 A.M. to ready them for the bus ride to a school as far as twenty miles away. For students who engaged in after-school clubs and sports activities, the arrival home would not take place until after their suburban counterparts had already finished supper and were starting on their homework.

The white parents and their children stood patiently for more than an hour waiting for their guests. Rothchild pushed away thoughts of the urban rioting taking place just a few miles to the east. Instead, she worried that the Cokes would be warm before the guests arrived. Just when the suburban hosts decided that their guests could not make it through the riot-torn areas, the METCO buses rolled in. The black parents said nothing of the rioting or their difficulties getting to the picnic. Their children immediately joined in the games and congregated with their classmates around the free ice cream stand. No one, black or white, spoke of the assassination or the unrest that followed the riots. "We smiled a lot," Rothchild later recalled.[8]

No one was smiling politely on the following day when almost five thousand of the city's blacks gathered in the Franklin Park stadium for a voice vote on a list of demands drawn up by leaders of the Black United Front. With no whites present, they approved a lengthy list of demands, including the following:

> All white-owned and white-controlled businesses will be closed until further notice, while the transfer of the ownership of these businesses to the black community is being negotiated through the United Front.

> Every school in the black community shall have all-black staff, principals, teachers, and custodians.

> All schools within the black community are to be renamed after black heroes. Names will be selected through the United Front.

The black community must have control of all public, private, and municipal agencies that affect the lives of the people in this community.

The Mayor's office is to mobilize the Urban Coalition, the National Business Alliance, and the white community at large to immediately make $100 million available to the black community.[9]

The leaders of the Black United Front covered all the bases in their demands. The order to close white-owned businesses in the black community, they knew, would strike directly at Jewish business owners. The insistence on $100 million from the mayor's office would deeply embarrass Mayor Kevin White, who, in the manner of New York Mayor John Lindsay, had been working the streets in his shirtsleeves trying to engender trust and accessibility. The demand for an all-black work force in the local schools was a direct challenge to the Boston Irish, whose maiden daughters had successfully climbed the ladder as teachers and administrators. Even school custodian jobs, well remunerated by city standards and a favorite tidbit in the political pork barrel, had not escaped the attention of the black radicals.

The demands of the Black United Front, even in the chaos following King's murder, were deemed irresponsible and unrealistic. Many local store owners refused the demands to close. "I don't tell the blacks to close on Jewish holidays," one market owner said by way of explanation. Some even slept in their stores with baseball bats and firearms at the ready. The teachers and custodians, too, scoffed at the very notion that the city jobs that they had taken decades to win would be given up based on threats from dashiki-clad radicals. Mayor White at first tried to keep relations civil between his staff and the Black United Front but later lashed out at the Front when he realized they were serious and not merely searching out the high ground for a round of political bartering. "I will not by one word or one act add to the delusion that it [the list of demands] is rational, workable, or dignified for either black or white," he responded.[10]

The demands of the black group, however, resonated among suburban liberals whose level of guilt almost matched the level of rage in the black community. Sylvia Rothchild found herself not only listening to the words of each report on King's assassination but listening as well to how the words were used. More so than at any other period in her life, she felt "sensitive to the consequences of guilt, fear, love, empathy, and the lack of it."[11]

Rothchild's neighbor, Sheldon Appel, a successful paper box manufacturer, was also feeling what he would later describe to a reporter as the "guilt of centuries."[12] Appel had been particularly impressed by news reports of black leaders like Tom Atkins who had risked their own lives to save whites trapped in the riot area of Roxbury. He was determined to give something back to the black community. Appel spoke of his desire to help the city's blacks with several friends and business acquaintances, including Ralph Hoagland, a young entrepreneur and founder of the Consumer Value Stores (CVS), a chain of discount pharmacies. The cut-rate drugstores popularized by Hoagland were, in many senses, the antithesis of the neighborhood pharmacies that dotted Blue Hill Avenue. Recently licensed pharmacists, with no roots in the community, worked behind intimidating counters where they could keep an eye on long aisles of health and beauty products. The older neighborhood pharmacists complained bitterly that they could not compete with the cut-rate drug emporiums; if the junkies didn't drive them out of business, they complained, the new CVS stores certainly would.

In mid-April, Appel and Hoagland met several times to discuss the demands of the Black United Front. The demand for $100 million, no strings attached, was legitimate, they believed—and what's more, could be raised. The businessmen settled on a plan of 7:00 A.M. breakfast meetings with potential donors, whom they would ask for a minimum gift of $1,000 and a contribution of time for a skills bank for their newly formed Fund for United Negro Development (FUND). Appel and Hoagland quickly organized dozens of breakfast meetings and succeeded initially in attracting donors beyond their own liberal Jewish circles. From the outset, FUND's organizers shunned publicity so as not to offend the sensibilities of black leaders, who were increasing their demands for community control. But local dailies quickly reported on the initiative when Appel managed to attract financial support from established Yankee families, including Mrs. Henry Cabot Lodge and Robert Saltonstall. Sylvia Rothchild was one of the earliest members recruited by FUND. The solicitation was direct and professional. She would later recall that she had never felt so vulnerable to a recruiter, with the possible exception of the solicitations she received from the Combined Jewish Philanthropies. Within weeks FUND was able to present the Black United Front with $75,000, no strings attached. With little fanfare Appel and Hoagland suddenly had changed the rules in Boston's philanthropic circles. Boston boasted almost nine hundred charitable foundations, the second largest number of any city in the United States. Most were administered by law firms, banks, and corporations, and few focused their attention on the problems of the inner city. The Massachusetts Bay United Fund, the city's largest charitable organization, was also under criticism for neglecting the needs of blacks. Barely $500,000 of the $14 million raised annually by the United Fund went directly to black-run social agencies, a point that Appel and Hoagland were quick to exploit. The mainstream charitable group countered that many blacks were served indirectly through the 225 social agencies constituting the group's United Community Services, which received more than 50 percent of the group's allocations. But black leaders, like the Black United Front's Chuck Turner, scoffed at the distribution policy, stressing that uniquely black organizations should receive direct allotments in the same manner that funds were made available to the Salvation Army, the Red Cross, and Combined Jewish Philanthropies.[13]

Appel and Hoagland continued to broaden their appeals to wealthy benefactors who agreed that the decks were stacked against black advancement in Boston. At several large membership meetings they offered their vision of a new Boston based on economic justice and introduced members of the Black United Front to potential donors. "All over this country people like ourselves are concerned with injustice, but they see the problem as a black problem. FUND sees it as a white problem," Appel told a group of potential donors during a breakfast meeting. "I think the most important thing, though, was we based our entire philosophy on community control, establishment and determination of priorities by the black community, and the commitment of catalyzing the democratic process of unifying a community."[14] Appel further distinguished FUND's operation style from that of more mainstream charities: "We don't study our concepts to death, we don't spend months analyzing every program to root out every potential consequence of our actions, we don't delegate basic functions to staff assistants, we do it ourselves."[15]

Appel made it clear that he was breaking with all traditional methods of philanthropic fund-raising. He warned potential donors that they should not expect any publicity from their donations and that he'd even hired a black-run public relations firm to suppress publicity about the organization on the principle that ego gratification could only inhibit the job of finding the truly committed. Reporters were admitted to membership meetings but only for background purposes and on the condition that they not write a word about the meeting. The ban on publicity was considered particularly unusual for Jewish philanthropists, who had grown accustomed to being feted at special Jewish organization dinners and to seeing their generosity praised in publicity photos in local newspapers.

The city's political and business leaders were deeply suspicious of both the Black United Front and the suburban liberals in FUND. While prominent individuals found the message compelling, Hoagland and Appel had little success when they attempted to crack major institutions for large gifts and political support. Robert Slater, the volatile and politically ambitious president of the John Hancock Insurance Company, saw red when he was approached by Hoagland and theologian Harvey Cox. "No I won't and I'll tell you why. The people you are dealing with are Mafia and Communists."[16] In a meeting at city hall, Mayor Kevin White also lashed out at FUND members, charging that the organization was infected with ex-convicts and garden-variety hustlers. "You're picking the wrong black cats," the mayor warned. "If they go out and buy machine guns, I'm holding you people personally responsible for the bloodbath that ensues."[17]

The blunt rejection of FUND by many of Boston's prominent business leaders and politicians masked a deep fear of the initiative. How, they wondered, had a group of new players from outside the circle of traditional philanthropists suddenly seized the moral high ground? It was increasingly obvious to Mayor White's advisers that FUND's organizers, despite their naïveté, had simply recognized a gaping hole and rushed in to fill it. The city's nerves were starting to fray. John Hancock's Slater and other business leaders were besieging the mayor to address the social problems in the city before further rioting could irremediably poison the business climate. Mayor White's new team, including aides Barney Frank and Hale Champion, were called on to manage the crisis. Champion, who in 1962 ran California Governor Edmund Brown's winning campaign against Richard Nixon, was best placed to sense the city's mood from his new position as head of the Boston Redevelopment Authority. Invariably, when Champion entered the mayor's suite, one prominent business leader or another would be nervously pacing the waiting area. "Another quivering mass of money is waiting for you," Champion would inform the mayor.[18] The mood threatened both the style and substance of the city. In the weeks following King's assassination, Champion had even begun to receive architects' plans for buildings that resembled windowless fortresses. At one point he grew so tired of the panic atmosphere that he disgustedly tossed a set of blueprints into Boston Harbor.

Mayor Kevin White was ecstatic. An extraordinarily savvy politician, he recognized that the threat of a massive black uprising presented a wonderful opportunity to assert his authority over the city's corporate powers. Even the efforts of the upstarts at FUND, he believed, could be used to his advantage if managed correctly. White was growing openly contemptuous of the nervousness displayed by business leaders in the wake of the King assassination riots. Two decades later, White would term the fear of a black revolt an "overwhelming advantage" for an ambitious politician bent on proving his abilities under fire.[19] Unlike the bank presidents, utility heads, insurance chairmen, and the directors of major retail stores from the Vault, Kevin White had little to lose. A first-term mayor, he fancied himself a populist and was not about to jeopardize his image by placating jittery financiers. It was time to show them just who was in charge. Like John Collins eight years earlier, Kevin White decided to pay a visit to the Vault.

In late April White and Hale Champion called the city's most powerful business leaders. "I'm your new mayor," White said. "My budget won't be in until next year. I want to be able to walk into a school yard and put up a new basket. I want to do that right now and I want to do it with private funds."[20] Vault members knew that Kevin White had more on his mind than basketball hoops in the ghetto. A full ninety seconds of silence ensued. "How much?" asked Eli Goldston, president of Eastern Gas and Fuel Associates and the only Jewish member of the Vault. "I'd like about one million dollars. Put it in a separate checking account." With that, White bid the businessmen good day and walked back to city hall. Minutes after returning to his office, the mayor took a call from Charles Coolidge. Coolidge said the Vault members would put $100,000 in the mayor's Special Fund and that it would be replenished as needed.

White's chief aide, Barney Frank, immediately set to work applying the Special Fund to the city's trouble spots. Frank expanded the list of summer jobs in the black community and contracted popular entertainers to perform for kids in Roxbury. Frank, a New Jersey Jew with sound political instincts who would go on to become the first Jewish congressman elected from Massachusetts in more than a hundred years, was an anomaly in Boston's city hall. "Barney was a freak but he was engaging and he was Harvard," White recalls. "He represented the liberals but he could talk to the (Irish) pols. That was his great skill. He looked like he was talking their language."[21] While much of the city's Special Fund went to high-profile projects, portions were kept back to be used as incentives for operatives and informants in the black community willing to serve as White's eyes and ears in Roxbury.[22]

No one at city hall, however, believed that basketball nets and entertainment funds would be enough to satisfy Boston's black community. The Boston Redevelopment Authority's Hale Champion, in particular, believed that only a comprehensive affordable housing program would contain black rage and offset the political advantages being won by the free-lancers at FUND. What Boston's blacks needed was a stake in the system, and nothing provided firmer grounding in establishment values than a home of one's own. Champion had documentation to back up his beliefs. Early in 1968 an independent study presented to the Boston Redevelopment Authority had found a "long-standing and hitherto frustrated desire for home ownership in the Model Cities Area—a desire recently strengthened by the concern of poor people for the control of their community."[23] According to Champion, housing, and nothing less, was the answer to the inner city's woes.

White and his aides also knew that flash money from the Vault could never offset decades of disinvestment. Roxbury and parts of North Dorchester, like so many aging urban neighborhoods across the nation, had been all but disconnected from mortgage lenders by "redlining" (a term derived from the common bank practice of marking off areas of maps in red that were believed to present bad risks), and redlining took both blatant and subtle forms. Outright refusals to grant mortgages in specific areas were not uncommon but ran the risk of community ire and negative publicity. Often loans would be available—but at higher interest rates, shorter terms, and with requirements of higher down payments. Particularly clever loan officers would cite building age as the major criterion for refusing loans, thus isolating older, central neighborhoods. Insurance companies used a similar practice to designate areas for higher premiums. The FHA itself rarely insured mortgages on homes in the inner city, preferring the familiarity of the suburbs.

For decades this practice of institutional disinvestment had seemingly sealed the fate of Boston's black neighborhoods. Conventional mortgage lenders, like their counterparts nationwide, had systematically refused to grant conventional mortgages and home improvement loans to qualified buyers owing to the belief that the very presence of minorities was a precursor to blight and decay. Real estate appraisers, too, could be counted on to advance the self-fulfilling prophecy. The belief in the eventual deterioration of inner-city neighborhoods was almost a religious tenet among appraisers. Official training manuals spoke of "life cycles" of neighborhoods in much the same way rabbis and priests accepted the inevitability of births, marriages, and deaths. "Neighborhoods pass through three life stages similar to the life cycle of all nature:"[24] At birth, neighborhoods subdivide and improve with street work and the addition of public utilities; dwelling construction continues through adolescence and slows as middle age approaches. The custodians of billions of federally insured dollars for mortgages and renovations were warned to be on the lookout for "infiltration of lower user groups" and "inharmonious land uses." Their presence, they believed, were harbingers of a city's death.

By the time White took office, however, urban rioting had both aroused conscience on the part of the public for the plight of

blacks and terrified government officials and business leaders. The
restrictiveness implicit in appraiser manuals was rejected, at least
in theory, by a growing number of Americans. Few, however, were
ready to risk their own property values for integration. It was clear
to White and his aides in the weeks following King's assassination
that the urban riots were in the process of radically redirecting the
thinking of both government and private industry. The head of the
FHA had summoned his regional directors to the nation's capital to
dress them down for their reluctance to insure loans in the inner
city. A national commission was forming to analyze the problem
and would later decry the "tacit agreement among all groups—
lending institutions, fire insurance companies, and FHA"—to
"redline" certain areas of cities and thus deny the residents access
to insurance and loans. "Up until the summer of 1967," the
commissioners revealed, "FHA almost never insured mortgages on
homes in slum districts, and did so very seldom in the 'gray areas'
which surrounded them. Even middle-class residential districts in
the central cities were suspect, since there was always the
prospect that they, too, might 'turn' as Negroes and poor whites
continued to pour into the cities, and as middle- and upper-
middle-income whites continued to move out."[25] Institutional
racism's cover had been blown under the intense light from urban
flames in Watts, Detroit, Harlem, Washington, D.C., and Boston.
Kevin White knew that he could be burned by that fire or bask in
its light.

In late April, their success at the Vault in their hip pockets, the
mayor and his aides convened a series of meetings with the chief
officers of the city's major savings banks in the hope of persuading
them to bring dramatic housing opportunities to the city's poorest
residents. The plan was relatively simple: resuscitate the moribund
Boston Banks Urban Renewal Group (B-BURG), the five-year-old
bank consortium used by former Mayor Collins and former BRA
chief Ed Logue to pump badly needed capital into the Washington
Park urban renewal area.

White and Collins could barely abide one another, but the
new mayor had to tip his hat to his predecessor this time. Back in
1963, a full two years before the first major urban riot in Watts, the
ever-pragmatic Collins had sensed that blacks needed some stake

in the system if his administration was to usher in the New Boston. But it had been a tough sell. Equally pragmatic bankers and insurance providers were uneasy about investing in an area that they perceived less as a neighborhood and more as an advertisement for arson-for-profit. Assured by Logue and Collins that the worst of the arson-prone deteriorating buildings would disappear under the federal bulldozer, the banks reluctantly agreed to commit $2.5 million for rehabilitation and home ownership loans in the Washington Park area. As a designated urban renewal site, the loans would be insured under the Federal Housing Administration Section 220 program. FHA-insured loans seemed the perfect vehicle to bring a greater number of poor and lower-middle-class people under the umbrella of home ownership. In the early 1960s FHA rules limited lending institutions to a rate of interest not to exceed 5.25 percent. Although low yield, the FHA insurance made the loans virtually risk-free to the banks, removing the major stumbling block from investing in poorer neighborhoods.[26] Property owners received similar assurances. By refinancing at the low FHA interest rate, money was freed up for rehabilitation, with the promise that monthly payments would remain the same or in some cases even diminish.[27] The plan seemed logical and just. The FHA was responsible, in large measure, for the creation of black ghettoes nationwide. Who better than the FHA to reverse the process? In Boston, with B-BURG, the mechanism was already in place. All that was necessary was to increase the amount of money in the loan pool.

By 1968 the dormant B-BURG consortium consisted of twenty-two savings banks, cooperatives, state savings and loans and federal savings and loans—collectively known as thrift institutions. The B-BURG banks boasted assets of approximately $4 billion, a figure that represented over 90 percent of the combined assets of the area's thrift industry.[28] The largest of the thrift institutions—including the Provident Institution for Savings, the Boston Five Cents Savings Bank, the Suffolk Franklin Savings Bank, and the Charlestown Savings Bank—represented the lion's share of the portfolio. The Brahmin-controlled thrifts also wielded considerable power over the city's commercial banking industry, in which they bought stock and kept large deposits for traditional banking services, including payroll, mortgage, and teller's checks. It was a simple task to keep an eye on their investments, given the network of interlocking trusteeships that were then still legal in Massachusetts; for example, on the board of the First National Bank of Boston, the city's largest commercial bank, sat trustees of the Boston Five, Charlestown Savings, and Provident Institution for Savings.[29]

The thrifts, unlike the commercial banks, maintained at least a veneer of director diversity. At least two Jews headed smaller B-BURG banks—Phil Wernick at Home Owners Federal Savings and Loan and A. Murray Ginzberg at the Grove Hall bank. In contrast, Boston's commercial banks throughout the 1950s and early 1960s were dominated so totally by Brahmin interests that a Jewish financier, Phil Fine, had created quite a stir when he sought a charter to open a commercial bank. Fine wrote directly to the head of Boston's Catholic Archdiocese, Cardinal Richard Cushing, explaining that his would be the only commercial bank with Catholics, Jews, Greeks, and a woman on the board. The cardinal was suitably impressed. On opening day he sent an emissary to deposit $500,000 of the Archdiocese's money in the new bank. Any commercial bank not linked directly to the Yankee network of boardrooms and social clubs, the cardinal rightly surmised, needed all the help it could get.

The mayor and his aides believed that their best chance of stimulating the banks into action rested with winning the confidence of Boston Five Cents Savings Bank President Robert Morgan and Suffolk Franklin Savings Bank President Joseph Bacheller. Each of the executives had a long history of civic activities at the head of their institutions, which controlled $750 million and $500 million in assets, respectively.

Morgan, a Dartmouth graduate and arguably the city's most influential mortgage banker, was a popular figure in both social and financial circles. Unlike many of his colleagues in banking, Morgan had made peace with federally mandated sub-market interest rate programs aimed at benefiting the inner city. Business editors focused on his infectious optimism, particularly his support for the partnership between the FHA and private industry. Society editors loved to drop in at the beautiful Morgan home in the genteel town of Wayland, where Mrs. Morgan held court over the "ladies committee" of the Boston Museum of Fine Arts.

The officers of the Suffolk Franklin took equal care with appearances, desiring particularly to project the image of big bank efficiency combined with the hometown touch. The bank's president, Joseph H. Bacheller, was a Princeton graduate who favored home mortgages over commercial and industrial loans. More than 80 percent of Suffolk Franklin's outstanding loans were on small residences, that is, one- to four-family units. "The last thing a man will give up is his home," Bacheller was fond of saying. "He'll cut back on his food first."[30] Bacheller traveled the corporate route from Ivy League to bank presidency via the boardroom at the Prudential Insurance Company of America. Silver-haired and partial to bow ties, he cut an impressive figure as a public speaker. Massachusetts Governor John Volpe had been suitably impressed and in 1967 appointed Bacheller to the five-member board of the Massachusetts Housing Finance Agency, a group that sought to develop housing possibilities for low- and middle-income families. But Bacheller was not one to sit on boards that lacked either power or substance. In January 1968 he resigned from the finance agency, along with MIT President Howard Johnson, when the state legislature failed to appropriate $300,000 in program costs.

Over the course of several meetings in late April and early May, Hale Champion reviewed the findings of BRA housing studies with Morgan, Bacheller, and other key representatives of the city's thrift institutions. The potential homeowners, he explained, generally had incomes below $5,000 and little or no savings. Many had bad credit histories and no history of home ownership in their families. Champion even pressed the idea that recipients of public welfare should not be excluded from the American dream of home ownership. To his surprise, he received only encouragement from Morgan when he suggested that "a welfare check is as good as any other check" when it came to sustaining a steady level of payment on a mortgage. The mayor's aide stressed the contingencies necessary for a low-income housing program to succeed— protection against default, short-term exemptions from real estate taxes, tenant/owner cooperatives for maintenance, and a three-month homeowner training and counseling program. The bankers, Champion later recalled, seemed concerned mainly that the loans for low-income families not be extended into the surrounding suburban communities, where, they feared, an influx of poor blacks could create a depositors' revolt in their suburban branches.[31]

In spite of the urgency to go public with a meaningful

program, the mayor and the bankers stopped short of detailing the precise conditions for the loans. Uppermost in their minds was the determination of a sum that could immediately be applied to help solve urban ills. On the advice of his aides, White told the B-BURG chairmen that he wanted to raise $50 million to reinvest in the inner city, primarily in housing. White, who had come up with only 10 percent of his request from the Vault, wasn't sanguine; nonetheless, he threw the figure on the table. The bankers barely blinked. White believed he was starting to get the hang of the business community. "They're shaking like quivering boys," he thought to himself. "The riots are foreign to them. The one thing they want is clarity."[32]

On May 13, 1968, just five weeks after King's assassination, Mayor White announced "a major new urban program for Boston which teams private capital and expertise, governmental coordination and planning and self-directed economic development by the poor." It was a well-timed message, coming as it did at the beginning of what city officials feared would be a long, hot summer. Although B-BURG was not mentioned specifically by name, the key feature of the plan was to include a $50 million loan commitment by Boston savings banks and life insurance companies to accelerate housing rehabilitation and provide mortgage money for "greatly expanded home ownership in the inner city." The mayor, concerned with the growing impatience in the black community, stressed that more than half the funds would be committed within one year.[33] By all appearances, the B-BURG program looked like a winner. The twenty-two participating banks agreed to assign B-BURG loans based pro rata on each bank's total deposits. Even in the event of sour loans and foreclosures, FHA insurance would protect the banks' experiment in do-goodism.

The officers of Suffolk Franklin and Boston Five Cents Savings, the two banks in the consortium with the longest involvement, agreed to provide the professional manpower necessary to implement the program. Bacheller and Morgan set to work scanning their staffs for mortgage officers with the experience and verve to manage the program. The banker they chose to have the lion's share of responsibility for the B-BURG program was Suffolk Franklin Vice President Carl Ericson. On the surface, Ericson was not the kind of man one would expect to see breaking new ground. A stolid, practical man of Swedish stock, he had served loyally at the Suffolk Franklin Bank for twenty years, working his way from the teller's cage to a vice president's office. Along the way, however, he had developed the reputation as a loan officer with a solid track record of dealing successfully with unconventional mortgage seekers.

It was owing to Ericson's efforts that, after a few martinis, Suffolk Franklin's competitors often referred to the institution contemptuously as "the fag bank." The uncouth description could be traced directly to Ericson's willingness to finance mortgages for openly gay successful men who, in the early and mid-1960s, were discovering the charm of Boston's South End. (Before the signs of gay interest in the area's attached row houses, few banks or real estate companies maintained offices or encouraged business in the predominantly minority area at the southern edge of the downtown business district.) The "lower user groups" in the South End were primarily blacks and Hispanics with middle-class aspirations. (Along Dover Street, at the neighborhood's frayed edge, poor Indians and an admixture of transients sought daily wage work at one of several manpower agencies that competed with the area's bars and brothels.) Longtime South Enders looked on with curiosity as the new gay "gentry" directed their savings and energy into rehabilitating decrepit shells and run-down rooming houses. Few had reason to fear the advent of these newcomers who seemed genuinely neighborly when not preoccupied with finding a hanging plant or handcrafted rattan capable of holding its own in rooms where ceilings reached inspiring twenty-foot heights. Many narrow-minded mortgage bankers had difficulty getting past the nontraditional jobs and eccentric references that came with some gay clients. But the gay urban pioneers looked like straight business to Carl Ericson whose main concern was lending out depositors' money at a safe return. "I financed harlots, lesbians, anyone that would pay the bill," Ericson later recalled.[34]

Suffolk Franklin's South End strategy would pay off in a big way less than a decade later. Upscale, dual-income white professionals followed the gay pioneers. For considerably less than the price of a modest suburban home, one could refurbish a five-story New York–style brownstone and still be but a ten-minute walk to

Boston's downtown offices and shopping districts. Soon the competition grew ferocious for the neighborhood's attached row houses, complete with marble fireplaces. Rooming houses were sold and gutted to restore their former elegance. Minority families living in rented town houses were pushed south toward Roxbury to make way for music rooms, skylights, and roof decks. Additional B-BURG banks, including Home Savings Bank and Workingmen's Cooperative Bank, quickly rediscovered the South End as a fertile loan market, but Suffolk Franklin always remained in the forefront—whether for enthralled yuppie mortgage-shoppers or enraged tenant activists who considered gentrification as synonymous with the destruction of working-class minority neighborhoods.

Ericson rejected out of hand the charges that fat-cat bankers were cashing in on the backs of poor people. He had come up the hard way, dropping out of high school to join the service during World War II. After the war he cut timber in Maine and Vermont before succumbing reluctantly to his wife's desire for a return to city life. Ericson had signed on at Suffolk Franklin as a bank teller and moved his way up methodically through the mortgage loan department. Shy and practical, he had no taste for community affairs, preferring to spend his free time in the woods on hunting and fishing trips. Although not given to ideological pronouncements, Ericson was quietly proud that he implemented the message explicit in the national housing policy announced by Congress back in 1949 of "a decent home and suitable living environment" for every American family. Ericson, though not one to buck the system, had been disturbed by how rarely the bank's investment committees approved loans in inner-city neighborhoods. He had seen firsthand the demoralizing effects of the policy: in the early 1960s a black barber walked into Ericson's office and asked loudly, "Do you finance niggers?"[35] The obvious cynicism and unexpected use of street parlance might have sent most jittery bankers in the direction of their security buttons. Instead, Ericson examined the man's South End property, provided a rehabilitation loan, and picked up a haircut in the process. "I felt that anyone who needed mortgage financing should get it. . . . Life is as simple as ABC," Ericson later explained.[36] But life would cease to be simple for Carl Ericson once he became involved in the Boston Banks Urban Renewal Group.

The B-BURG bankers planned a gala opening of their new mortgage-processing office for late July. The selection of a site at 306 Warren Street, in the heart of the black community, was considered highly innovative, sending the message that the financial industry was no longer afraid to do business at the community level. Bacheller and Morgan had requested that Mayor White and BRA chief Champion participate in the ribbon-cutting ceremony and press conference. But Barney Frank, White's politically wily chief aide, was already anticipating problems. Frank insisted that the mayor's participation depended on an agreement by the Boston banks "to encourage and support loans by suburban savings banks to persons from . . . low income areas who desire to purchase in the suburbs."[37] The demand flew in the face of every established mortgage banking practice. Bank appraisers, despite official warnings, were still using the touchstone of a homogeneous population as a key factor in the stability of a neighborhood.[38] Conventional wisdom still dictated that a black shift to the suburbs would invariably weaken the mortgage portfolios of suburban banks and branches through the inevitable reduction of appraisal values. Barney Frank's demand went unanswered.

On July 31, 1968, the banking consortium held a ribbon-cutting ceremony at the new B-BURG office. The bankers, although hungry for publicity, had to settle for the presence of the deputy mayor and a smaller media contingent than hoped for. Bacheller told those present that loans would be made at the prevailing FHA rate of 6.75 percent plus 0.5 percent insurance premium. The mayor's representative made a point of stressing that the loans were not limited to the needy in the Model Cities area. Mortgage seekers in other areas that had suffered under urban renewal, including Irish Charlestown and Italian East Boston, were also welcome to apply to the new consortium. But any reporter who had even the vaguest knowledge of the insular nature of Boston neighborhoods knew that few poor whites would be traveling to Warren Street for mortgage counseling; the program was obviously intended for blacks. White's absence clearly showed that a strain was already developing between city officials and the B-BURG banks (better that the administration not get too close to a situation where blacks might be denied an affordable home in a nice suburb with a terrific school system). What was ominously unclear, however, was just where the lucky B-BURG shoppers might finally settle down.

During July and August of 1968 the chairmen of the B-BURG consortium and city officials held several discussions at Suffolk Franklin and Boston Five to refine the program, particularly regarding its geographic scope. Bacheller was quick to remind all present that profits still came first. "Every once in a while someone turns up who seems to feel that we are a combination of charitable and social organizations. We are not. We are a group of banks owned completely by our depositors," Bacheller would remind them.[39] Champion and others continued to press for a suburban loan plan, stressing that the mortgages would be insured by the federal government and present no risk. The bankers countered that FHA-insured mortgages were, at best, a mixed blessing. Regardless of the race of the recipient, they argued, the very utterance of FHA was associated with a greater risk of foreclosure and abandonment.[40] It was simple human nature. With the government assuming the risk, screening standards always seemed to diminish. Adhering to a social agenda was one thing, but the B-BURG banks would be damned if they were going to accept tiny down payments (at most 3 percent) and throw themselves open to a depositors' revolt in their suburban branches.

No one had to spell it out for Carl Ericson. He intuitively understood the concerns of the banking consortium. He was not, as he would later say, concerned with anything other than the task at hand—"making houses available for people"[41] within the guidelines established by his supervisors. In mid-August, during a meeting with the B-BURG chairmen at the Boston Five Cents Savings Bank, Ericson approached an enlarged wall map showing the Model Cities area and its contiguous neighborhoods. The mortgage banker had both a blue and red pen in his jacket pocket; he chose the red, hoping it would be more easily visible to his colleagues. Ericson began to trace along the contours of the map. Pressing hard along Walk Hill Street, at the southern tip of the Mattapan State Hospital grounds, he continued past Wellington Hill and across Blue Hill Avenue, turning sharply north at Norfolk Street, pressing on past Morton Street, north still past Woodrow Avenue until Franklin Field, where the red line curved east along Harvard Street, crossing Blue Hill Avenue once again at the southeastern border of Franklin Park and eventually looping down across the grounds of the State Hospital. Within the Model Cities area north of the red line, Ericson explained, there was insufficient attractive housing to justify a program as grandiose as the one now touted by the consortium and the city fathers. A contiguous neighborhood, with an attractive housing stock, was clearly needed to make the program a national model. The South End, which lay directly to the north of the Model Cities area, was already showing signs of gentrification. Prices were being driven up by the growing interest in brownstone restoration by affluent white urban pioneers. To the west of Model Cities lay Jamaica Plain, long the most stable of Boston's neighborhoods. Mayor Curley had lived in a sprawling mansion along Jamaica Pond, and the neighborhood was still a favorite for Boston politicians, police, and city workers. From the perspective of the bankers, Jamaica Plain had a large "do not disturb" sign hanging from its doorknob. To the east of Model Cities lay the largely working-class Irish sections of Dorchester. A broad boulevard, Columbia Road, served as the unofficial border between the black and Irish communities. The very presence of a black face in parts of Irish Dorchester was considered sufficient provocation for a chase and beating; the sanctity of the neighborhood and parish was of paramount importance. (In Dot, as Irish youths referred to their section of Dorchester, the direct way was the only way: black encroachment of any kind would be met with hard, fast fists—or, better yet, a length of lead pipe.) What remained was the red arc drawn by Ericson that, almost to the house, corresponded to the precise inner-city locus of one ethnic group—Boston's Jewish community of roughly forty thousand people. It was there, and only there, that low-interest, small down payment loans would be made to the city's minority home-seekers.

Almost two decades after drawing a red line on a wall map in order to establish the loan boundaries for the B-BURG consortium, Ericson said he had no knowledge at the time that he had essentially walled off the city's Jewish community. Instead, he said he had used his skills as an outdoorsman to seek out topographical features, such as Franklin Park and the open cemetery areas along Harvard Street. City planners and historians, however, hold a different view. "The Irish lines are regarded as the hardest, Italian lines are regarded as the next hardest, and the Jewish lines are regarded as softer in terms of people being more willing to accept the problems of minorities,"[42] revealed former redevelopment chief Hale Champion.

In late August Bacheller sent a memo to the top officers of the twenty-two B-BURG banks declaring that the boundaries for loans had been established and that maps would arrive shortly. The banker used the opportunity to shore up his troops. "It is too early to predict with any exactness just how this program will fare, but from all indications it should be a rousing success and distinctly a feather in the cap of each bank involved," Bacheller gushed.[43] Bacheller's enthusiasm was not unwarranted. Home seekers, community leaders, and editorial writers welcomed the program. During the first three months of operation, the consortium assigned 171 mortgages for inner-city families to member banks, considerably more than they'd assigned in the previous six years.[44]

At first, Carl Ericson alternated days at the B-BURG office in Roxbury with a Boston Five Cents Savings Bank vice president. But as the demand for the loans grew, bankers' hours became a thing of the past. Soon there was need to add support staff, and on many days the two vice presidents found it necessary to arrive well before 9 A.M. and to leave well after 5:00 P.M. Ericson didn't mind the hard work. Driving to the office from his home in Framingham, twenty miles west of Boston, Carl Ericson was secure in the knowledge that his decision to leave the woods for the white-collar world had not been foolish. Other mortgage bankers saw only their return on investment; in his own quiet way, Carl Ericson had combined profit with the opportunity to help people. Carl Ericson was "doing well by doing good."

The B-BURG program flourished into the winter months, traditionally a slow time for real estate transactions. By December the number of loans had increased to 314, with a total mortgage commitment of $4,582,850.[45] Even as the snow fell and Boston began to dig out from under a traditional northeaster, the real estate business remained brisk. Ericson recalls processing mortgages in his Roxbury office when he was distracted by the ceaseless high-pitched whine of wheels spinning on ice. He went down to the basement of the B-BURG office, grabbed a large shovel from the corner, and scooped up a large pile of loose dirt from around the foundation. Carefully balancing the load, he walked out onto Warren Street. A black driver in a large commercial van was

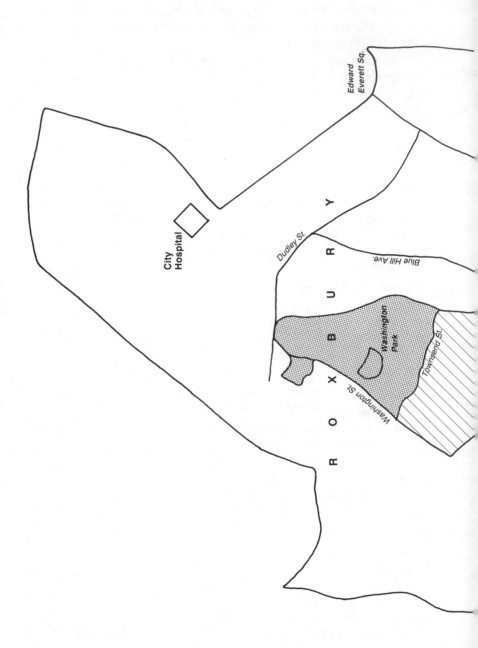

City Hospital

ROXBURY

Dudley St.

Blue Hill Ave.

Washington St.

Townsend St.

Washington Park

Edward Everett Sq.

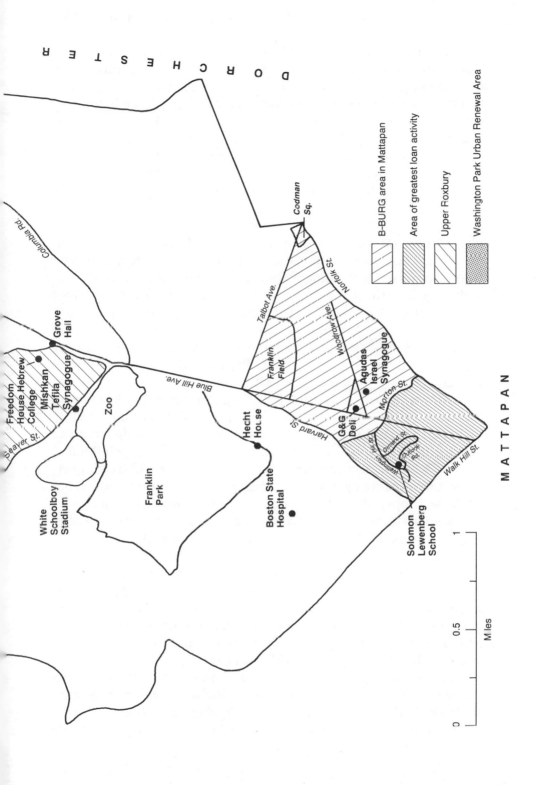

D O R C H E S T E R

D O R C H E S T E R

MATTAPAN

Codman Sq.

Columbia Rd.

Grove Hall

Freedom House Hebrew College

Mishkan Tefila Synagogue

Beaver St.

Zoo

Blue Hill Ave.

Talbot Ave.

Norfolk St.

Woodrow Ave.

Franklin Field

Agudas Israel Synagogue

Morton St.

Harvard St.

G&G Deli

Wellington Hill St.

Ormond St.

Outlook Rd.

Walk Hill St.

Hecht House

Franklin Park

White Schoolboy Stadium

Boston State Hospital

Solomon Lewenberg School

B-BURG area in Mattapan

Area of greatest loan activity

Upper Foxbury

Washington Park Urban Renewal Area

0   0.5   1

Miles

accelerating continuously, which only served to push his nearly bald tires deeper into their icy grooves. Ericson flung dirt under the spinning wheels until there was sufficient traction to free the vehicle. Since momentum on Boston streets in winter is imperative, the driver dared not stop to offer formal thanks, but as he slid past the banker the driver of the truck offered a smart salute. It occurred then to Carl Ericson, who was not particularly inclined to metaphors, that it was time to go back inside and shovel some more money at Boston's social problems.

The 350 FUND members who gathered on December 14, 1968, for a breakfast meeting in the Grand Ballroom of the downtown Hotel Somerset had come expecting to hear an address from Stokely Carmichael, the chairman of the Student Nonviolent Coordinating Committee and the black leader who popularized the phrase "black power" two years earlier at a civil rights march in Greenwood, Mississippi. Carmichael, however, failed to appear and was replaced by local organizer Bryant Rollins, the community activist who had shouted down HUD Secretary Robert Weaver at the Boston Urban Rehabilitation Program press conference at Freedom House the previous December. Rollins immediately launched into a disorganized attack on subjects ranging from the management style of American corporations to the psychological basis of white racism and liberal guilt. He told the FUND supporters not to expect any gratitude, giving them credit only for being "a little hipper than the average honky."[46] Rollins's speech, if intended to motivate the crowd, backfired. His open hostility angered many of the potential donors. "Don't call me whitey," shouted a man from the back of the ballroom. "I resent being called whitey as much as you resent being called nigger."[47] For fifteen minutes members of the audience and Rollins sparred over semantics before Black United Front organizers closed down the question-and-answer period and introduced other Front speakers, who spoke in more measured tones about the need for start-up loans for black entrepreneurs in Roxbury.

Sylvia Rothchild was excited and perplexed by the sharp exchanges. In just a few short months, she had gone from hosting METCO picnics to taking an active leadership role in FUND. Now a writer and book review editor for Boston's *Jewish Advocate* weekly newspaper, Rothchild found great significance in the language used by the white and black speakers. Reviewing the transcript of the meeting, she found that white speakers like Appel and Hoagland used language to mollify, soften, and explicate: "White people are moving toward an education that can let them make a serious commitment to repay a debt"; and "The grandfathers of the black speakers didn't earn a cent for their work" (a reminder that many members of FUND were thriving on inherited income). The language of the black speakers seemed designed to disturb—"It is a fruitless task to tell whites to eliminate or deal with [their] racism"—or threaten—"If we can't communicate to you then that is your loss and maybe you can get yourselves together so if there is a next time you can understand what we are saying."[48]

Sometimes, not often, Rothchild was allowed to glimpse the vulnerability of the black radicals. After being on the receiving end of a particularly vituperative harangue at a FUND meeting, she went home exhausted and depressed. Several hours later, the speaker called her. "Are you a soul person?" he inquired. Satisfied with her response, he asked if she would consider reviewing the grammar and spelling for a paper he was distributing to a black student group.

Rothchild had thrown herself into FUND activities with the same passion she had once brought to the Hecht House elderly outreach center. The communication breakdown at the December membership meeting had convinced her and other FUND members to try a different approach. They organized smaller seminars at which Black United Front speakers were paid fees simply to sit around and talk to FUND members and potential contributors. The meetings were generally held in the small storefronts rented by the Front along lower Blue Hill Avenue. Invariably, the black speakers came at least an hour late, leaving Rothchild and other FUND members sitting in their cars outside the locked storefronts. Rothchild, who had covered the Avenue a decade before to recruit Jewish elderly for the Hecht House outreach program, would now sit for hours and not see a single white passerby.

The storefront forums, too, degenerated into sessions for venting black rage. At one seminar Rothchild and her suburban friends probed a member of Boston's Black Panther party for concrete ways to advance the causes of racial justice. They were told that whites were hopeless because they lacked love and compassion, spent their time listening to operas that invariably ended in mass stabbings, and waited in line to see movies about homosexuals. The voices of the black radicals reminded Rothchild of the irrational views of *goyyim* shared by many of her parents' generation—eating pork turned humans into pigs, eating lobster made people grow claws, and only Jews were capable of compassion and love.[49] Now, as an adult, she was being told that blacks alone possessed positive character traits. Rothchild refused to take the words of the Front speakers at face value; she found herself translating their remarks in her head. "We want absolute control over our community" became "We absolutely cannot bear any longer to have no control over our community." "If I were white, I would commit suicide" came through the filter as "If white people understood our trouble and their responsibility for it, they would feel enormous guilt."[50] Rothchild and other FUND members pressed forward with their fund-raising efforts. All donations were given without strings and ranged from a $54 grant for tuition at a barber school to loans up to $10,000 for equity capital in ma-and-pa businesses. FUND supporters clung to the belief that they wanted nothing more than to provide for inner-city residents what suburbanites already took for granted—the opportunity to affect their local government. Suburbanites, Rothchild would later recall, "tend to be more optimistic about change than their totally powerless city counterparts. Able to reach a selectman, a school committee, a department of sanitation, they know the importance of being able to complain where it can do some good."[51]

Rothchild's phone rang often. Jewish residents of Dorchester who knew her views through her writings in the *Jewish Advocate* called to complain about their black neighbors:

Last night they broke into my husband's pharmacy, the people you help.

My people came to this country without a penny and they pulled themselves up. We worked for everything. Nobody helped us. Let them do the same.

What's the matter with you people in the suburbs? All you want is a tax deduction. You don't know how we suffer from them.[52]

Not prone to defensiveness, Rothchild would mumble to her critics something about how their verbal outbursts simply proved how much work there was for FUND to do. Decades later, however, she would think again about how much intensity she'd heard in the voices of black America, voices that oscillated between unrealistic optimism and despair so profound that destruction seemed just a moment away. But why did the Jewish voices sound so hollow to her ear?

"Acceptable Before Thee"

Slumlords and Rabbis,
1968

The liturgical chanting of Israel Mindick filled the sanctuary of Congregation Beth El on Fowler Street in North Dorchester, a once-proud but fading Orthodox synagogue. Most Dorchester synagogues, including Beth El, were long past the period when they could afford to hire trained professional cantors. The responsibility of leading the congregations in prayer had fallen to laymen, like Mindick.

Israel Mindick and his brothers, Joseph and Raphael, were among the largest property owners in the South End, where they managed forty-four multifamily buildings with almost eight hundred tenants, mostly black and Hispanic. Unlike the Jewish BURP developers, who unwound with games of golf and tennis at suburban country clubs after mulling over ways to get the FHA to streamline multiproperty rehabilitation packages, the Mindicks preferred the bustle of Blue Hill Avenue. Israel Mindick lived in a modest house in Mattapan not far from Congregation Beth El. Joseph "Inky" Mindick kept his head in the business. "Inky" had no compunction about making his living from slum properties. He lived the role, invariably arriving for work attired in polyester pants, a floral shirt, and a porkpie hat, a fashion statement from a man who cared little for the *goyyim,* smart-alecky Reform Jews, and civil rights do-gooders.

The phrase *housing code enforcement* had no place in the Mindicks' vocabulary. For several months the Mindicks' tenants, led by leaders in the radical South End Alliance, had compiled a long list of building code violations on the brothers' properties. It seemed, however, that each effort to serve papers presented code enforcement officers with a meandering paper trail leading to yet another extinct holding company. To the socially striving members of the Jewish community, the Mindicks were more than a liability. They were, in fact, a walking confirmation of the prescience of local German Jews who, back in 1882, had successfully turned back a boatload of Boston-bound Eastern European Jewish immigrants, believing that no good could come from the *Ostinden* (East European Jew). Prominent Boston Jews saw slumlords like the Mindicks as a clear threat to the conventional image of the American Jew standing shoulder-to-shoulder with blacks at the forefront of the civil rights movement. The image of the Jewish slumlord was so strong, in fact, that it could not even be erased by the Jewish "checkbook warriors," who contributed almost 75 percent of the operating expenses of CORE, the Student Nonviolent Coordinating Committee, and the Southern Christian Leadership Conference.

The issue of the Jewish slumlord was always close to the surface. In 1965 Boston's CORE chapter published and distributed a list of largely Jewish property owners cited for state and city code violations. Sol Kolack, the head of the New England region of the Anti-Defamation League of B'nai B'rith, dashed off a memo warning his national office that slum housing "loomed as a major cause of tension between the Boston Jewish and Negro communities."[1] Kolack further tried to convince the leadership of the Realty Lodge of the Boston chapter of B'nai B'rith, which represented many of the city's Jewish landlords, to express to Mayor Collins their disapproval of "slumlordism" and their support for strong building and sanitary codes. The lodge members rejected

Kolack's request, protesting that such action would place Jewish landlords unfairly in the limelight. Jewish politicians at the statewide level, however, were quick to distance themselves from their *landsmen* (coreligionists) in the real estate business. Two state representatives from Brighton, Arnold Epstein and Norman Weinstein, threw their weight behind several bills emanating from the legislature's Joint Committee on Mercantile Affairs, which aimed to set limits on slumlords and housing code violations. Only Dorchester's State Representative Julius Ansel went to bat for the landlords, suggesting that the city encourage compliance by capping assessments following renovations.

These legislative and communal efforts were clearly inadequate to offset the escalating hostilities between black tenant activists and Jewish property owners. At almost precisely the time that Mayor White and the presidents of Boston's thrift organizations were launching the B-BURG program, black and Hispanic tenants were organizing a major action against the Mindick brothers. The tenants' campaign would capture the attention not only of local Jewish leaders but of national leaders as well.

Convinced that city inspectors could not help them, the South End tenants mounted a noisy demonstration on May 5, 1968, in front of Israel Mindick's home in Mattapan. Mindick, however, was not there. Led by a radical black social worker, Ted Parrish, the tenants huddled together to plan an even larger demonstration at a site where the landlord would have to take notice. The tenants saw great significance in Mindick's leadership role at Beth El; although he had never been ordained, they referred to him simply as "the rabbi." How, they challenged, did a man of God square his religious beliefs with responsibility for roach-infested substandard housing? The next demonstration, they decided, would take place beneath the copper dome of Beth El during Sabbath services.

For almost five years the largely working-class congregants of Beth El had been under siege. Like those in Roxbury's Mishkan Tefila, the wealthier and more prominent members of the congregation had relocated in the 1950s to Newton, where they built an imposing synagogue just off fashionable Commonwealth Avenue. Beth El's spiritual leader, Rabbi Abraham Koolyk, commuted between the well-appointed homes of his Newton congregants and those of their poorer cousins who remained in Dorchester. For decades the pride of the Orthodox congregation had been its five-day-a-week afternoon Hebrew School, where the children of struggling tradesmen were at least assured an intensive Jewish education. By the early 1960s, however, Beth El and other Jewish institutions in North Dorchester came under pressure from incoming black refugees who were fleeing the federal bulldozer in Roxbury. With increasing frequency, Jewish children leaving classes at dusk were attacked by black street toughs. Parents searched frantically for alternative Hebrew Schools. So great was the exodus of children from Beth El's classrooms that each week students at the Hebrew School of nearby Conservative Temple Beth Hillel, on marginally safer Morton Street, bet on the number of Beth El students who would show up in the Beth Hillel class that week.

As early as September 1965 the beleaguered board of Beth El had met with representatives of the Boston School Committee to discuss the possibility of the sale of the synagogue to the city. Surrounding public elementary schools, including the Endicott, Gibson, and Greenwood schools, were predominantly black and overcrowded. Black leaders were strongly opposed to the sale. Many considered the building substandard and the classrooms too small, but, more importantly, black leaders objected to the establishment of yet another largely black school in the district. Instead, they urged an expansion of a voluntary busing program that would bring black students to schools with predominantly white enrollments. The sale of Beth El to the city, they concluded, would only further institutionalize the segregation of the Boston public schools.

The city's Jewish leaders sided with the black community on the controversy. No self-respecting Jew, after all, could accept the "separate but equal" standard for black and white schoolchildren. Prominent Jewish lawyers, like Jack Greenberg of the NAACP Legal Defense Fund, were calling northern municipalities to account for subtle segregation methods based on gerrymandered districts and selective transfers. In the larger context, the city's mainstream Jewish leadership contended, the proposed sale of Beth El was essentially an outright assault on the exalted values of Jewish justice. "The gravity and shamefulness of this offer cannot be underestimated and its implications for the future of the Jewish community are ominous and portentous," said one prominent Jewish physician. "This offer was wrong, evil, sinful. It was betrayal of neighbors. It was betrayal of little children."[2] So great and uniform was the outcry that Robert Segal, the director of the Jewish Community Council, issued a statement deploring the proposal, thereby aborting the sale.

Beth El's board members were furious at the actions of the Jewish Community Council. A decade had passed since the wealthier congregants had departed. Break-ins, vandalism, and assaults had made Beth El's name a frequent entry on the police log. In March 1965 black neighbors had even marched in front of the stucco synagogue demanding that "whites get out."[3] The congregants maintained that their only sin had been to remain in an inner-city Jewish neighborhood during the early 1960s when others were abandoning their roots for the suburbs. Now that those who remained saw little hope for the continuation of Jewish life in North Dorchester, the sale of the synagogue was being blocked to appease the consciences of suburban Jews. Where were the leaders when there was still a chance to stabilize the neighborhood? Where were the voices of the Jewish Community Council now that Beth El's Jews were bearing the full brunt of the relocation of poor blacks from Roxbury's urban renewal areas? Only one voice pierced the silence—the liturgical chanting of Israel Mindick.

Rabbi Judea Miller was the first Jewish clergyman to learn that blacks planned to picket Mindick during Sabbath services at Beth El. An energetic Reform rabbi from the nearby city of Malden, Miller had participated in the early civil rights marches in the South and was proud of his contacts in Boston's politically progressive community. Miller first learned of the picket plans from an Episcopal priest with ties to the tenants' movement in the South End who had met the rabbi at several interfaith events. The priest explained that the Mindicks' tenants were increasingly desperate and he feared the consequences. "Why have they singled out this person to picket?" demanded Rabbi Miller. "There are slumlords who are Catholic, Protestant and nonbelievers."[4] The priest responded that the Mindicks were the largest landlords in the South End and had consistently refused to respond to appeals to improve their properties. Miller, however, remained skeptical until the priest suggested that he meet with the Mindicks' tenants and tour the properties. Later that week Miller and social worker Ted Parrish climbed several flights of broken stairs, examined a dozen broken toilets, stomped cockroaches, and stepped gingerly over dangerous electrical wiring in Mindick-owned properties. Appalled, the rabbi offered to intercede.

Miller called Israel Mindick the next day and asked him to meet with tenant representatives. The landlord wanted no part of it. "It's a business matter—it's no concern of the community," Mindick retorted sharply. "Your tenants are entitled to dignified living conditions," the rabbi responded, asking, "Does not Judaism teach us that Jews should be distinguished for their compassion?" Mindick was not impressed. "They're *shmutz,*" he uttered, describing his tenants with the Yiddish word for dirt.[5] The rabbi then warned Mindick that the synagogue would be chosen as a demonstration site and that the entire Jewish community could wind up being judged by the actions of one man. Mindick thought the arguments hollow. "They are a bunch of ignorant antisemites," he said of the protesters; they could do their worst for all he cared.

Miller reported back to the priest that Mindick would not agree to meet with the tenants. The priest responded that the tenants had no choice; they would picket Beth El on Saturday. Miller made an impassioned plea not to target an entire Jewish congregation for the misdeeds of one of its members. If the tenants would cancel their demonstration at the synagogue and concentrate instead on Mindick's residence, the rabbi said, he would join the protesters himself. The rabbi kept his word. Not only did he join subsequent demonstrations at Mindick's home but he brought along members of his temple's youth group. Thus, Israel Mindick was not only treated to the spectacle of black and Hispanic tenants denouncing the conditions of his buildings but in addition was forced to accept the ignominy of being the target of signs with warnings from the Prophet Jeremiah being waved by Jewish youths: "Woe unto them that build their houses with injustice, their palaces with unrighteousness."

At the conclusion of one early morning protest, the tenants regrouped in a South End storefront to drink coffee and plan further tactics. Miller sat apart from the group, concerned mainly with keeping the demonstrators from directing their frustrations at synagogues. As he sat half-dozing, he heard one of the tenants complain of the elaborate use of straw companies used by the Mindicks to keep one step ahead of code enforcement. Each attempt to trace ownership and assign responsibility was met by a new holding company. Property managed by Fee Realty suddenly turned up under the ownership of the Imrei Co. Another protester said that his inquiries regarding violations in Mindick-owned properties were referred to a Shem Company, which he was unable to track down. Miller sat up startled. "Is there a Ratzon Company?" Miller asked. "There is a Ratzon Company," came the reply. "And a Leebee Company?" Miller asked. "Yes," one tenant responded. "How did you know about the Leebee Company?"[6] The tenants immediately gathered around Miller, pressing him for more information on the straw companies. He assured them that he had none. As the group broke up, Miller repeated to himself in Hebrew the final verse of Psalm 19: Yihiyu, Leratzon, Imrei, Fee, Vehegyon, Leebee, Lifaneha, Hashem, Tzuri, Vigoali ("May the words of my mouth and the meditations of my heart be acceptable before You, O Lord, my rock and my Redeemer"). Miller was sure that the psalm had been used by the Mindicks as a mnemonic device to remember their straw companies for easy reference.

The following day Miller went to see Rabbi Samuel Korff, the head of Boston's *bet din,* or religious court. Korff was one of the city's respected and better known rabbis, having combined Jewish scholarship and political savvy since the 1930s, when James Michael Curley had appointed him the first Jewish chaplain to the Boston fire department. Korff was the spiritual head of Congregation Kehillath Jacob on Fessenden Street in Mattapan. With more than eight hundred members, Korff's congregation was the most influential in the district. Sam Korff relished all of his roles in the community. At both the state and national levels, he had earned a solid reputation for the certification and supervision of kosher caterers and packaged foods. But one was just as likely to find him providing chaplaincy services to Jewish inmates at Deer Island Prison as to find him discussing the intricacies of the laws of *kashrut* among his learned colleagues.

Miller first told Korff that the Mindicks were creating an interfaith nightmare at a time when Jews and blacks were working so carefully to advance civil rights. But Korff, an Orthodox rabbi, was not as captivated by the cultural zeitgeist as was his Reform colleague. "Why make this a Jewish issue? Are there not slumlords who are Catholic and Protestant?" Korff asked, echoing Miller's own response to the South End priest. But when the younger rabbi described the ten dummy corporations based on the biblical psalm, Korff's demeanor changed. *"Un zei? Zei vissin?"* Korff asked, switching instinctively into Yiddish as if the gentile world were listening in with disapproval. "And they? Do they know?" *"Nokh Nisht,"* Miller responded. "Not yet."[7]

A week later Korff called a special session of the five-member rabbinical court to determine if the use of sacred text to denote dummy corporations warranted communal intervention. He assigned Miller the task of serving an order on Israel Mindick to appear before the religious tribunal at its downtown headquarters. Although the rabbinic court carried none of the punitive weight of secular court, devout Jews found in contempt of a rabbinic court were subject to a loss of religious privileges and risked being shunned by their Orthodox brethren. It was not a fate Israel Mindick would easily accept.

Miller called on Mindick at the landlord's Mattapan home. He was not invited in and had to issue the request to appear before the court from the doorstep. Mindick, annoyed that the situation had reached the tribunal, refused at first to expose his private business dealings to the scrutiny of the rabbis. "You don't understand," Miller explained in a hushed tone. "This order is not in regard to the Fee Company alone. But for the Yihiyu Company, Ratzon Company, Imrei Company," he stated, completing the Hebrew verse.[8] Mindick blanched and said he needed to call his business partners and discuss the summons. When he returned, after thirty minutes, he replied curtly that all partners in the real estate consortium would honor the summons.

For the better part of the summer, the rabbis heard testimony from the tenants and landlords in a dingy rabbinic courtroom at the Associated Synagogue Building overlooking Boston Common. The tenants recited familiar ills of exorbitant rents paid for substandard dwellings crawling with rats and roaches. The Mindicks countered that they could hardly be expected to take responsibility for tenants who threw garbage out of windows and damaged apartments faster than one could hope to repair them. For weeks the two sides aired their complaints across the bargaining table. During sessions when both the landlords and tenants were present, Israel Mindick remained subdued. When alone with the rabbinic judges, however, he lashed out at the tenants, claiming that their slovenly habits, not improper maintenance, were at the root of the problem.

Rabbi Korff never directly criticized the landlords, preferring instead to work through parable. "A rabbi approached the door of a wealthy man to seek a charitable donation," he told the Mindicks. "The wealthy man's servant announced the rabbi and invited him inside. The rabbi, however, explained he would wait on the doorstep. The servant insisted that the rabbi come out of the cold, but the rabbi would not budge. Soon the wealthy man himself approached the rabbi and beseeched him to come inside for refreshment. 'No,' the rabbi insisted. 'You come outside. I want you to know what it feels like.' "[9] Israel Mindick suffered the long sermons in silence. Often, however, his lawyer would complain of the length of the proceedings. But Korff quickly quieted him, explaining that "there are times when divine providence requires great sacrifice."

Leonard Fein, a supporter of liberal Jewish causes and associate director of the Harvard–MIT Joint Center for Urban Studies, followed the courtroom testimony in almost total amazement. He had always considered the rabbinic court, which was used almost exclusively to adjudicate family matters, as an Orthodox throwback to an earlier era. Years later he would joke that he dared not breathe too hard during the proceedings for fear that the entire scene would "crumble into dust."[10] The unique proceedings, however, challenged his vision of the *bet din* as a sleepy and unprogressive institution. He quickly recognized that even if the tenants' complaints were familiar, the arbitration of social problems through ancient religious laws was unprecedented. National magazines and newspapers shared that view. On August 8, the day scheduled for a final agreement between Mindick and his tenants, reporters from the *Wall Street Journal, Look Magazine,* and scores of others were on hand. The final agreement offered concessions to both tenants and landlords. The landlords agreed to repair, maintain, and paint the apartments in accordance with city codes. They also promised to provide adequate heat and hot water, daily janitorial service, more trash cans, and locks on all hallway entrances. The tenants, in turn, signed a pledge to help maintain the properties once repairs were in place and to drop their demands for private security guards at each building. The contract further stipulated a five-member board of arbitration to settle questions of overdue rents and other disputed claims.

While the court strove for balance in terms of the settlement, it was unequivocal in regard to its sentiment, holding that

> a landlord who would do business in a low-income area must accept the special hazards of such areas. . . . If his resources will not permit him, for example, to maintain the buildings in a non-hazardous condition, then he has no right to be a landlord. . . . The tenant, typically, has no financial reserve with which to fend off calamity; the landlord, typically, can accept temporary reverses. . . . Our aim is clear, it is justice for all concerned. "Justice, Justice, Justice, shalt thou pursue. . . ."[11]

Suddenly, a unique approach had been found for the seemingly intractable problems between Jewish landlords and black tenants. Even "Inky" Mindick looked happy. "In the past, whenever I repaired something it would be destroyed again," he told reporters. "But now the tenants have responsibilities, too." And Ted Parrish, the tough-talking and radical social worker, was suddenly sounding like a communal relations specialist. "The Jewish community," he intoned, "has taken a significant step in its effort to be responsive to the expressions of injustice and inequity voiced by poor blacks, whites and Puerto Ricans of the inner city."[12]

But even as the media touted the unprecedented nature of the court's ruling, the Mindicks made few improvements to their properties. Tenants in twenty of the brothers' buildings went on a rent strike that winter, charging that the landlords had failed to live up to the terms of the rabbinic court's agreement. The rabbis concurred and slapped the Mindicks with a $48,000 fine to be distributed among the affected tenants. "Justice, Justice, Justice, shalt thou pursue," was ringing in the Mindicks' ears. But better, they decided, to pursue it in Florida, where a landlord could still make a living. The Mindicks sold off thirty-four of their buildings to the Boston Redevelopment Authority, which placed them under the control of the South End Tenants Council for management and repair. The price of doing business in Boston, at least as far as the Mindicks were concerned, was growing much too steep.

Blockbusting Mattapan

Bankers and Brokers

At first the junk mail circulars and dinnertime phone calls were just an annoyance for the residents of Mattapan's Wellington Hill:

> Cash for homes—limited offer.

> Good evening, sir. I understand many of your friends and neighbors have their homes up for sale. I would imagine that you might be thinking about doing the same thing yourself. Our brokers can help you get a good price now. If you wait, of course, there is no guarantee.

In the summer and fall of 1968, after the announcement of the B-BURG program, the unsolicited calls from real estate brokers to

Mattapan residents not only increased in frequency but took a decidedly different edge:

> The value of your house is dropping $1,000 every month.

> You have a 12-year-old daughter. What if she was raped. You'd have a mulatto grandchild.

> If you still want to live here, fine. Just take a ride through the [predominantly black] Columbia Point housing project. Then come back and say you want to live here.[1]

Blockbusting, the general term used to describe the scare tactics used by commission-hungry real estate brokers to force the quick sale of homes, was not unique to Boston. During the same period, unscrupulous brokers in Flatbush, Houston, Chicago, Philadelphia, and other major metropolitan centers were poised to break up middle-class Jewish neighborhoods on the basis of the cynical but largely accurate perception that Jews would offer minimum resistance to neighborhood incursion. Whether the excessive solicitations occurred in one of the thousands of two-family homes stretching for fifty blocks east of Flatbush's Ocean Avenue apartment corridor or in the triple-deckers along Boston's Woodrow Avenue, the scenario was usually the same. Postcards, letters, phone calls, and even small armies of brokers knocking on doors generally arrived with the same message: "Cash for homes—sell now before it's too late."

Twenty years after the blockbusting of Mattapan, an anonymous practitioner described his duties during the period for the readers of the *Metropolitan Real Estate Journal:*

> We were told you get the listings any way you can. It's pretty easy to do: just scare the hell out of them. And that's what we did. We were not only making money, we were having fun doing what we were doing. We all liked selling real estate—if you want to call what we were doing back then selling real estate. And it got to a point that to have fun while we were working, we would try to outdo each other with the most

outlandish threats that people would believe, and chuckle about them at the end of the day. . . . I had fun at it. I'd go down the street with the [black] buyer and ask, Which house do you want? He'd pick one, and I'd ring the doorbell and say, these people want to buy your house. If the lady said no, I'd say the reason they're so interested is that their cousins, aunts, mother, whatever, it's a family of twelve, are moving in diagonally across the street. And they want to be near them. Most of the time, that worked. If that didn't work, you'd say their kid just got out of jail for housebreaking, or rape, or something that would work.[2]

Before 1968 and the decision by the FHA to bring the American dream of home ownership to poor and middle-class minorities, blockbusting took more complex forms. One of the clearest explanations of the motives behind pre-1968 block-busting was provided by New York's Secretary of State John Lomenzo during testimony before the Senate Judiciary Committee. The key, he said, to winning at the blockbusting game was multiple mortgages. "Let's say the market value of the house was $15,000. The speculator would offer to buy it for $10,000, all cash, with the homeowners readily accepting as they became panicked," Lomenzo testified. The next step was to offer it at double the price or more to a minority family with the incentive of an automatic mortgage qualification with no money down:

> The speculator would then take back a first purchase money mortgage of $10,000 to $12,000 covering the cost of his purchase of the house. Then he would take a second purchase money mortgage for 60 percent of the balance— $6,000 or $8,000—and a third purchase money mortgage for the remaining 40 percent of the balance.
>
> Now he would turn around and sell these three mortgages (to banks, finance agencies, insurance companies). You see he would sell the first one usually at a 10 percent discount. When he did that, he got all his money back plus about $800. . . . The second one . . . usually would be sold at a 20 percent discount. And the third . . . at a 50 percent discount. . . . And if you put all these figures together, you get an approximate

profit of about $9,000 on the original sale by the white homeowner for the price of $10,000.[3]

The multiple mortgage scam, however, had one major flaw. Weighed down with mortgage payments far in excess of the property's worth, many of the minority buyers soon found themselves in default. Multiple mortgages were suddenly no longer attractive to the secondary market, setting a natural barrier against further speculative practices. That barrier, however, would be easily overturned in 1968 when the FHA declared its intention of guaranteeing loans in the inner city—a decision that would all but seal the fate of Boston's inner-city Jewish community.

The pignut trees that once dominated the crest of Wellington Hill had long since been cleared away when Sumner and Janice Bernstein arrived in Mattapan. Back in 1963 the Bernsteins and their two young children had outgrown their small North Dorchester apartment. It seemed logical to move a few blocks south to more expansive but still familiar Mattapan. Their two-family home on Ormond Street, near the top of the hill, provided a perfect balance between urban life and more pastoral pleasures. From the sun porch on the second floor, the couple could watch the bustle of Blue Hill Avenue. The pressures of the city, however, were easily forgotten when they retreated to their ample backyard for pleasant hours digging earth, spreading fertilizer, and planting grass seed. The Bernsteins thought they had it all. While just a stone's throw from the Jewish shops and meeting places along the Avenue, they could still walk out their front door and be greeted by the lovely fragrance of their lilac bushes. Sumner Bernstein, a longtime city worker, had never put much stock in suburban master plans. For Bernstein, like thousands of other Mattapan residents, it was more important to have a ground floor apartment available for the comfort and security of aging parents.
    The Bernsteins simply fit in on Wellington Hill, a neighborhood that realtors as early as the turn of the century had described as a "clerical" rather than an "executive" neighborhood. On warm evenings the Bernsteins could be found sitting in their walkways on chaise lounges, nursing drinks and gossiping with friends. Janice Bernstein was a classic *halabuste,* a heavyset,

energetic housewife with seemingly endless warmth and energy for her own family and the scores of neighborhood youngsters who passed through her kitchen. The couple spoke with thick New England accents, chain-smoked, and had difficulty controlling their weight. Gruff exteriors, however, did little to mask a keen intelligence and a well-developed sense of fairness. Janice served, unofficially, as the information gatekeeper for Wellington Hill; she had even purposely put off buying a clothes dryer for fear she might miss one of the terrific tidbits that came her way while hanging clothes in the yard. But Janice Bernstein was no mere gossip. Her curiosity extended beyond the affairs of her neighbors to the Park and Recreation Department, nearby schools, neighborhood services, the Police Department, and any other agency that affected the lives of the people of Mattapan.

It was while hanging out her laundry on a balmy summer day in 1967 that Bernstein overheard a neighbor, Jack Vetstein, discussing the formation of a new community group, the Mattapan Organization. Street crime had been increasing in recent months. Neighbors attributed the rise in purse snatchings and housebreaks to the movement of poor black families out of renewal areas in Roxbury into North Dorchester. Bernstein was discomforted by the conversation. She had lived on an integrated street in Dorchester and had little patience for those who sought to lay the world's problems at the doorsteps of blacks. Like many of Boston's Jews, she was familiar with the sting of antisemitism; it required only a small leap of her imagination to put herself in the place of an average black working family. She was wary, therefore, when her neighbor spoke of the need to prevent panic sales as blacks continued to seek housing further south down the Avenue. She felt more optimistic on learning that newly arriving black families also had shown interest in the fledgling Mattapan Organization and that the group was sponsored by religious groups in the area.

The concept of a neighborhood-wide organization was new to Mattapan. Unlike other sections of Boston, which were plagued with institutional expansion, insufficient parking, or high crime, there had never really been a compelling reason to organize in Mattapan. City services were reliable, the streets safe and well lighted, and communal instincts were generally channeled into synagogue or parish activities. But the racial changes just a few blocks north in Dorchester, particularly the decline in property values, threatened to change all that. Two popular Mattapan personalities, Albert Schlossberg and Mildred Kaufman, were among the first to approach the Jewish Community Council to ask for help in starting the Mattapan Organization. Neither was the type to be easily dismissed. For decades Kaufman, a librarian, had literally plucked the bored and recalcitrant youths of Mattapan off the street corners and introduced them to the joys of the reading room in the branch library on Mattapan's Hazelton Street. Schlossberg, the owner of a successful funeral home on Blue Hill Avenue and a high-ranking officer in the Jewish War Veterans, was carrying on the city's tradition of activist funeral home proprietors. Although he'd moved to the suburbs a few years earlier, Schlossberg's world still revolved around the delis and shops on the Avenue, where his opinion and analysis on national and neighborhood affairs was eagerly sought.

Schlossberg and Kaufman had approached Robert Segal, the head of the Jewish Community Council, and asked for his organization's help with staff and start-up costs for an organization to deal with the issues of a racially changing neighborhood. At stake, the pair told Segal, was Jewish survival in Boston. For Segal, there was something profoundly atavistic about the survival concerns of Mattapan's Jews. When he'd arrived in Boston in the 1940s, domestic antisemitism and neighborhood issues had been high on his list of concerns. Since that time, however, the concept of Jewish survival had evolved. The survival needs of Israel had become the primary focus of Jewish defense agencies, including the community relations agencies. On the American front, the battles that remained to be fought, as evidenced by the work of the American Jewish Committee and American Jewish Congress, focused on eliminating prejudice in the executive suite and in setting limits on expressions of Christian religion in the public schools.[4] Segal feared that the organization proposed by Schlossberg and Kaufman, if improperly managed, could threaten the precious black–Jewish alliance. Would these Jewish activists suddenly erect barriers to fair housing for blacks? Did he hear in this request subtle resistance to the moral power of the civil rights movement? His own supervisors had recently made it clear that there would be no breach with the black community. A policy statement widely disseminated by the national office of the Jewish Community Relations Agency had warned its affiliates not to abandon the civil rights struggle and to press forward despite reports that overt antisemitism had poisoned the more radical civil rights organizations. The agency's planners had even urged Jewish leaders to understand the roots of such feelings:

> Often the sole contacts between Jews and Negroes are those between landlord and tenant, employer and employee, or creditor and debtor. Under these circumstances it is easy for the Jew to be identified as an exploiter and it would be unrealistic to expect black demagogues to be more scrupulous than their white counterparts and to shun anti-Semitism, the historic weapon of political demagogues everywhere. . . . Anti-Semitism breeds in ignorance, want, frustration and alien-ation; and the most effective counteractive approach to it is through the amelioration of those conditions. For the Jewish community to be deflected from its support and advocacy of equality for Negroes on the ground that Negroes are anti-Semitic would not only be self-defeating, exacerbating precise-ly what we mean to combat; but would be to repudiate a fundamental tenet of Jewish tradition—equal justice for all.[5]

The librarian and undertaker would not, however, be put off. Controlling street violence in Jewish neighborhoods and protect-ing equity in one's home, they argued, were issues at least as compelling as fighting bigotry in the boardrooms of major compa-nies. The argument was effective. From their first day on the job, community leaders were taught that Jewish survival was never to be taken for granted and that no greater issue confronted the Jewish people or its leaders. Segal agreed to take the funding request to his board and assigned a young assistant, Mark Israel, to continue discussion with the concerned residents. Younger com-munity workers, like Mark Israel and the Anti-Defamation League's Fred Kasner, found the Mattapan story far more compelling than did their supervisors. In subsequent conversations with residents, they became convinced that there was an abiding love for the neighborhood and that, with proper planning, Mattapan presented a unique opportunity both to maintain the integrity of the Jewish community and to advance the cause of peaceful integration. That goal, however, would require a truly interfaith effort.

Although working-class Jews predominated in the triple-deckers along Blue Hill Avenue and the handsome two-family houses on Wellington Hill, the southwest section of the neighborhood was home to many middle-class Irish families who lived in single-family ranch homes built by speculative builders before World War II and in the garden development apartments popularized in the late 1950s and early 1960s. Mark Israel sought, with limited success, to absorb parishioners of Mattapan Square's St. Angela's Catholic Church into the Mattapan Organization. As a Catholic stronghold in a predominantly Jewish neighborhood, St. Angela's parish was always something of an anomaly. Although the parish borders reached east into a narrow strip of largely Catholic Hyde Park and south into suburban Milton, most of its territory was circumscribed by the heavily Jewish neighborhoods in the vicinity of the Mattapan State Hospital. "Being in a neighborhood largely inhabitated by inmates and Jews," quipped one former parishioner, "it was never too tough to find a seat in St. Angela's."[6]

Throughout the 1950s St. Angela's had been led by an aging and frugal priest whose reluctance even to install brighter lights in the vestry had earned him the nickname "Nine-Watt Donahue." In the early 1960s, however, a new priest, Father Paul McManus, had revived the parish with adult education classes, couples clubs, and youth dances. By the mid-1960s St. Angela's had become known, in the parlance of the church, as "a good house to live in." Father McManus agreed with Mark Israel that it would take neighbors working in concert to prevent the kind of housing deterioration and decline in city services that were now plaguing North Dorchester. His parishioners, however, were not enthusiastic about linking up with the Jewish residents. Many believed that the Jews "talked a good game" but would be the first to sell to blacks; hence, they were reluctant to commit their time to the interfaith effort. Better, they thought, to organize among themselves. Parishes, after all, don't just up and move away, but one needed to look no further than Roxbury to see the ease with which Boston's Jews had abandoned their once-glorious religious institutions. Other members of St. Angela's, however, saw immediate value in the goals of the Mattapan Organization. One parishioner, Francis McLaughlin, was particularly eager to see peaceful integration come to Mattapan. McLaughlin, a deeply religious man, took seriously the notion in St. John's Epistles that in Christ there is neither Jew nor gentile, slave nor free man, Greek nor barbarian.

And like many of his Jewish neighbors, McLaughlin felt a moral responsibility on the race issue. "There is a radical equality in Christianity," he would later note. "I felt it would be wrong for me to discriminate against someone, and I felt I had a responsibility not to move away from city problems."[7]

From the earliest meetings of the Mattapan Organization, it was clear that its founders would not tolerate racist harangues or black-baiting. One participant glibly referred to the newcomers as a cancer in the neighborhood and was immediately upbraided by a diminutive postal clerk named Louis Yoffee.

Nothing made Yoffee angrier than to hear people refer to human beings as cancer; whoever could say that knew little about people and even less about cancer. Yoffee knew about both. In 1958 he had been diagnosed with bladder cancer; his doctor told him to begin to put his affairs in order to make his passing as easy as possible for his wife and three small children. But a specialist at Massachusetts General Hospital had offered Yoffee the opportunity for experimental surgery, which, against all odds, stopped the spread of the runaway cells. After his discharge from the hospital, Yoffee had asked his doctor what he could do to return the favor. "No amount of money would ever be sufficient to pay back what this hospital has given you," Yoffee was told. "What we need the most are volunteers to spend some time each week in our pediatrics ward. We need your time."[8] Following that conversation, Louis Yoffee visited the children's ward every Thursday afternoon for more than a decade. Distributing gifts and sweets to small patients from all of the city's neighborhoods, he soon came to be known as the "Candy Man" by both the youngsters and staff. At just five feet, Yoffee stood only slightly taller than many of the charges, but with his shock of prematurely white hair he looked to many like a modern-day Santa Claus. "I may have snow on the roof," he'd tell the nurses, "but I have fire in my heart."

Like all members of the new organization, Yoffee was fiercely loyal to Mattapan. He loved his single-family home at the crest of Wellington Hill Street, where he'd lived since 1952. A talented handyman, he was constantly painting, paneling, and wiring. Like his next-door neighbor and close friend Harry Sklar, Yoffee could not imagine life outside the neighborhood. Yoffee's devotion to his neighborhood could at times border on the irrational: when his son, Dov, passed the entrance examination to the competitive Boston Latin High School, Yoffee challenged the boy's decision to seek education outside the neighborhood. "Why do you want to jump on two buses and a train and go all the way downtown when you can stay right here at the Lewenberg School?" the father demanded. "Latin's the best school in the city, Pa," his son remonstrated. "Nothing wrong with the Lewenberg," Yoffee shot back.[9]

Spurred on by a $3,000 grant from the Jewish Community Council, the Bernsteins, McLaughlins, Yoffees, and other members of the Mattapan Organization formed special committees to provide a balanced approach to community building throughout 1968. Participants on the beautification committee focused their attention on the increasing numbers of abandoned cars and littered empty lots in the vicinity of Blue Hill Avenue and Morton Street; in the first few months alone they would file more than 150 complaints with the Mayor's office. Members of the police committee made personal contact with desk sergeants and area commanders to urge an increase in foot and car patrols.

The education committee of the Mattapan Organization concentrated its efforts largely on the Solomon Lewenberg Junior High School at the top of Wellington Hill. For decades "the Lewenberg" had been considered the premier district junior high school in the city. For decades the student body was composed primarily of Jewish youngsters who had not passed the competitive test for admittance to the seventh grade at the public Latin schools. The Latin school curriculum was so demanding, however, that almost 30 percent of seventh and eighth graders flunked out, resulting in another competitive exam for ninth graders. Lewenberg parents pushed their fourteen-year-old sons and daughters relentlessly in the hope that they would fill those seats ignominiously abandoned by youngsters sent back to the less demanding district high schools.

Since 1965 blacks had been bused to the Lewenberg under the city's open enrollment policy, an early attempt to address issues of racial segregation in the Boston public school system. By 1967 the nine hundred–member student body was equally composed of blacks and whites. White parents perceived a rapid decline in academic standards. Relations between students were strained. Jewish parents suddenly saw their children growing more adept at wisecracking than at conjugating verbs. The Mattapan Organization's education committee members immediately sought out independent experts to conduct on-site seminars and report their findings to the school superintendent. Mattapan's future, they were convinced, was inextricably tied to the educational quality at the Lewenberg.

The brunt of the Mattapan Organization's work, however, involved the real estate committee. A few weeks after the first meeting, Yoffee had addressed an open letter to all Mattapan homeowners and residents. A meticulous writer who had published poetry in *Stars and Stripes* magazine during tours in Okinawa and Korea, he carefully chose his phrases for both substantive and emotional impact:

> The arrival of new neighbors in our midst has caused a decline of interest by many of our friends and neighbors, who, without proper thought and consideration, have suddenly put their homes up for sale and appear to be seeking what they think are greener pastures. . . . It is the studied and reliable opinion of our expert committee that these new residents represent a high caliber of people and should not be considered as detrimental to our area. Indeed we welcome our new neighbors as persons capable of contributing much to our community. . . . Keep your lovely home as you always have as this is where your children have grown and received their education. Here is where your fondest and happiest memories lie. Keep faith in Mattapan.[10]

Yoffee also warned his fellow Mattapan residents to beware of unscrupulous real estate agents who often exploited the common fears of home owners that a decline in property values would always accompany the arrival of blacks. "These real estate people have a single interest in expanding their own business without humane thought for those around them," he warned. "Do not make a move haphazardly." Yoffee proudly presented his letter for approval to members of the Mattapan Organization. Pleased, they authorized that it be sent to three thousand of Mattapan's home owners.

During the summers of 1967 and 1968 Yoffee, Sklar, and other members of the real estate committee made a point to visit the real estate offices along Blue Hill Avenue to explain their commitment to the area and to dissuade brokers from using heavy-handed practices in trying to generate sales. Sklar and the others were familiar with the scare tactics used by unscrupulous brokers in the nation's gray areas—the seemingly innocent circular stuffed in a mailbox describing the new customers willing to pay top dollar for a house, or the phone call alluding to undesirable neighbors. On the plus side, the real estate committee figured, there was little economic incentive on the part of Mattapan homeowners to move: most, after all, owned their homes outright or carried fixed-interest mortgage rates of only 5 percent or less.

In the summer of 1968, the members of the fledgling Mattapan Organization had no idea that the Boston Banks Urban Renewal Group had selected their neighborhoods as the site for $29 million in low-interest, federally insured mortgages for minority home buyers, becoming in the process the major financier for speculators. They knew only that a dozen new storefront real estate offices had opened in recent months along the Avenue; most of the brokers had no roots in the area. Longtime family businesses and even synagogues were closing their doors. Dorchester and Mattapan's only growth industry, it seemed, was real estate commissions.

Sklar and Yoffee showed the brokers the letter they had mailed to all of Mattapan's homeowners. Residents in North Dorchester, they explained, were old and easily manipulated. Mattapan homeowners, they warned, were younger and wealthier and would not sit still for the kinds of real estate travesties played out a few blocks north. The activists said the newly formed organization would pay careful attention to reports of blockbusting. The brokers protested their innocence, claiming they were only minor players in the decay–rebirth cycle characteristic of all of America's inner-city neighborhoods. Sklar countered that brokers could and did employ tactics that compressed a century of community evolution into a few short years or even months. Pointed references by realtors to the growing presence of blacks in a neighborhood were often sufficient to generate fears about property values in weak-willed or racist homeowners. The linking of blacks to escalating violent crime rates, whether specious or not, was often enough to destabilize a neighborhood of homeowners who harbored no racial animosity. Then Sklar gave his own familiar sales pitch on Wellington Hill: "I like it on Wellington Hill. I'm not going to move. I like being near everything. It's convenient. I like the air up there. It smells good."[11]

Back in their living rooms and the social halls of the neighborhood's churches and synagogues, members of the Mattapan Organization continued to pound away with their message, one based on class, not race. The incoming black families, they reasoned, must be middle-class families with values identical to their own. On what rational grounds could one stand in the way of racial integration provided the new neighbors shared their vision of a thriving, safe community? "I want to stay," the argument went. "You like to live on your own economic level. People want to buy a house that they can afford and have the same type of families around. We have the same ideas. We want to give our children a good education. No one here wants to lose any money and this is where our money is. In these houses."

The realtors along Blue Hill Avenue didn't need Sklar to tell them where his money, or that of his neighbors, was located. The B-BURG maps that adorned their walls made that perfectly clear. While members of the Mattapan Organization naively prepared for peaceful integration, brokers continued to swarm into Mattapan, setting up shop in any space big enough to hold a few desks with telephones. Despite their protestations of innocence, their blockbusting campaigns would later attain the intensity to become the focus of an investigation by the Committee on the Judiciary of the United States Senate. City officials were suspicious from the start. Shortly after the opening of the Boston Banks Urban Renewal Group (B-BURG) office, Frederick Paulsen, a legal officer for the Boston Redevelopment Authority, pressed Bacheller and other B-BURG bank officers on the geographic distribution of the loans. The response was curt. "We do not know just why you seem to feel that you are in a position to set up procedures and impose rules and regulations upon our Group," Bacheller responded. The chairman of the board of the Suffolk Franklin Savings Bank then instructed Paulsen that further communication should be interpreted not as an opportunity "to accept or reject our thoughts but rather to advise you just what we are and are not willing to do."[12]

The law was laid down. The city could accept the geographic terms of the loan or it could find solutions to Boston's urban ills without help from the private sector.

As the head appraiser for the Federal Housing Administration in Boston, Joseph Kenealy, together with his staff, was responsible for performing the appraisal on homes that were to be sold to buyers with the benefit of FHA-insured mortgages offered by the Boston Banks Urban Renewal Group. According to a civil suit filed in 1971 by the Justice Department, Kenealy "blatantly engineered" the appraisals in order to enrich himself and members of his family by almost $350,000. As an FHA inspector, Kenealy had direct access to confidential information on upcoming house sales. Much of this information, according to subsequent investigations, was passed on to Kenealy's wife, Anna, and son, Michael, who operated the Mt. Bowdoin real estate office and two additional realty corporations at the corner of Blue Hill Avenue and Morton Street. In one typical transaction, Michael Kenealy, then twenty-five, bought a house on Mattapan's Hazelton Street in October 1968 with an $11,500 mortgage from his father. Four months later the building was appraised by Joseph Kenealy's FHA staff for $22,500, with a notation that there was no need for outstanding repairs although a Model Cities study estimated that 65 percent of the houses needed major repairs at the time of purchase.[13] In another case Kenealy acted through members of his family to purchase a house on Dorchester's Elmhurst Street for $5,000 that was sold only four months later for $17,000, with an FHA approval for a $16,500 mortgage.[14] Members of the Kenealy family were listed as the sellers of property or the borrowers or lenders of mortgage money in the area more than four hundred times during the 1960s. In many of those cases, a Justice Department lawyer later charged, Joseph Kenealy "directly influenced the sale price" by determining the amount of the FHA appraisal; the higher the appraisal, the higher the amount of the mortgage approved.[15]

FHA "windshield inspections," in which appraisers would peer from their cars and approve the mortgages, proved disastrous for both buyer and seller. Testifying in 1971 before the U.S. Senate Committee on the Judiciary, Janice Bernstein would compare an FHA inspection to a Keystone Kops routine. "It took exactly ninety seconds," she testified. "[The inspector] passed by all the rooms and only glanced at the bathroom and kitchen. I tried to show him all the improvements we had made in the last eight years. It did not seem to matter to him. It was quite obvious to me that the FHA appraiser had put a price on my home before he entered the property."[16] For first-time black home buyers, the "windshield inspections" were equally harmful. One B-BURG bank, East Boston Savings, withdrew its support for the program after sending an independent appraiser to check on the FHA report that a two-family home was in ideal move-in condition. The independent inspection, however, revealed one apartment with major leaks in the bedroom ceiling, broken electrical outlets, worn-out bathroom fixtures, and a dangerously rotted porch floor.[17] A later sample survey conducted in 1971 found that 65 percent of the houses sold under the B-BURG program needed major repairs within two years of purchase.[18]

Throughout the latter part of 1968 and all of 1969, the brokers' objectives remained the same: scare away the approximately fifteen thousand Jews who were living within the B-BURG line and get as much of the action before the $29 million minority mortgage pool dried up. Janice Bernstein remembers aggressive calls and sales pitches from Aaron Realty, Mt. Bowdoin, Morton Real Estate, Woolf Realty, and London Realty during this period. "Do you want your child killed by those colored hoodlums?" one realtor asked her in a typical sales pitch. "Move to a nice suburban area where you will not have these problems."[19] The response on the part of the members of the Mattapan Organization was to redouble their efforts on their neighborhood safety and beautification programs. Members even tried to operate their own no-commission house-hunting service after learning that brokers in Mattapan were receiving not the usual 5 or 6 percent commissions on sales but 10 and even 15 percent. They were determined to try anything to stop the profiteering that, they believed, was costing them their neighborhood. Nothing they did, however, seemed to be enough to stop the juggernaut propelled by a consortium of banks of which they still had no substantive knowledge.

By March 31, 1970, more than thirteen hundred families, largely minorities, had bought homes with B-BURG mortgages, with the vast majority steered into the Jewish neighborhoods of

Mattapan. An estimated fifteen thousand people found new residences, many in triple-deckers, during the first twenty months of the program. The 1970 census figures show how rapidly the boundaries of the black community were extended. Only 473 blacks were listed in Mattapan in 1960. By 1970 that figure had increased to 19,107.[20] A study of individual census tracts showed the trend most clearly. From Uphams Corner–Jones Hill (11 percent black) to the south, the black population grew larger in each neighborhood. In the Columbia–Blue Hill tract, near the Franklin Park Zoo, 95 percent of the residents were black. In the Woodrow–Norton tract, once thick with Jewish shops and Orthodox *shtibels,* blacks now made up 69 percent of the population. In the Wellington Hill–Blue Hill tract, the focal point of the Mattapan Organization, the black population grew to 48 percent.[21]

It would not be until the mid-1970s, however, well after Boston's Jewish neighborhoods had been absorbed into the sprawling black ghetto, that housing analysts/researchers would provide powerful evidence of racial discrimination in the city's housing market. Few studies before that time addressed the study of price differentials between white and black submarkets or sought to determine whether racial discrimination played a role in housing prices. Once analyzed, however, the data revealed that blacks nearly always paid more than whites for the same bundle of housing attributes at the same location, that all households in transitional areas experienced markups, and that whites paid more for otherwise equivalent housing located further from black residential areas.[22]

The difference in relocation patterns between blacks and whites was also profound. They could be most easily discerned by comparing the urban renewal traumas of the West End during the late 1950s and Roxbury's Washington Park area just a few years later. The predominantly Italian West Enders resettled in a shotgun pattern: roughly the same number of relocated families could be found in each of the first five-mile rings surrounding the West End; additionally, some 38 percent of the relocatees found new homes outside the city of Boston.[23] But the figures looked very different in Roxbury's Washington Park: of more than fifteen hundred black families relocated from the area in 1966, a full 80 percent had moved within two miles of their previous homes. Few, if any, blacks had managed the passage into outlying suburban areas. The B-BURG bankers and blockbusters, it seemed, had made sure of that.

During the late 1960s, young children whose homes abutted the Solomon Lewenberg Junior High School at the top of Wellington Hill collected tattered textbooks and smashed school supplies in the same manner that other kids collected charms or baseball cards. Pickings were always good on the coal tar schoolyard. Ripped-out textbook pages with pictures or details of colorful maps had trade value superior to broken rulers, pencil stubs, or other pieces of educational dross. (The honor code among the little memento seekers dictated that any intact textbooks would be handed over to parents for return to one of the teachers monitoring student arrival on the next morning. Everything else was fair game. After school the little ones were always careful to wait until the middle school students were well out of range before picking over the battlefield. All feared being swept up in the midafternoon surge of adolescents down Wellington Hill. On a sick day or early dismissal, small faces peered from bedroom windows on Outlook Road at the U-shaped red brick school complex, each hoping for the instant neighborhood fame that might come with the most desired of all sightings—a Lewenberg student dangling headfirst from the window of a second floor classroom, legs presumably held by trusted friends or, worse, relentless torturers.

Residents of Wellington Hill, including Janice Bernstein, also surveyed the school area in the late mornings to see for themselves if the chatter of the children was true; did students truly hang one another out of windows as casually as housewives hung laundry out to dry? Like much of what was happening in Mattapan, it was growing increasingly difficult to sort the authentic from the apocryphal.

When it first opened in 1929, the Solomon Lewenberg Junior High School served a student body drawn largely from immigrant and second-generation Jews. The school was named for a local jurist who, though a loyal Republican, had formed a fast friendship with James Michael Curley, the ferociously Democratic mayor of Boston. Throughout much of the 1960s the school continued to

Roxbury's Temple Mishkan Tefila (above, in 1925) was Boston's *stadt shul* until the early 1950s when the board of directors decided to transfer its assets to a distant suburban community. The building was eventually sold to an African-American arts group and subsequently abandoned. In the 1989 photograph below, shrubs and grasses sprout from the temple's once well-trodden steps.

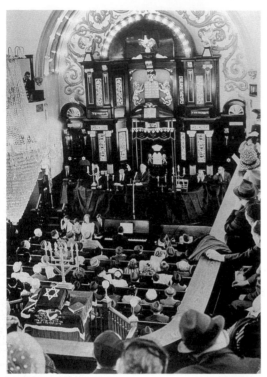

Congregants of the Agudas Israel Synagogue on Woodrow Avenue in Dorchester commemorate the Warsaw Ghetto Uprising in this 1964 photograph. By the early 1970s, increasing crime and violence in North Dorchester would prove too much for the largely elderly congregation.

BOSTON GLOBE PHOTO

The G&G Delicatessen on Blue Hill Avenue, shown in this 1969 photo, served as a political and social center for Boston Jewry for four decades.

AMERICAN JEWISH HISTORICAL SOCIETY

By the mid-1960s, Boston's swelling black population was seeking new housing opportunities because urban renewal had created massive displacement. Most were moving into traditionally Jewish neighborhoods. These photographs of street signs and pedestrians on Dorchester's Blue Hill Avenue reveal the changing nature of this neighborhood. As the level of integration increased, tensions rose betweeen the Jewish community and its new black residents.

BOSTON GLOBE PHOTO

BOSTON GLOBE PHOTO

State Representative Julius Ansel (above left, in 1963) was the consummate Ward 14 politician. Ansel's antics were second only to his devotion to constituent services. Samuel "Chief" Levine (above right, in 1980) was a protégé of Boston's legendary Mayor James Michael Curley. Levine doled out favors across Ward 14 and expected unswerving loyalty in return. Eli Goldston (left, in 1967) was the head of Boston's Eastern Gas and Fuel Associates. He convinced the city's leading citizens that they could "do well by doing good." It was a policy, however, that would backfire on many of the city's blacks and Jews in Roxbury, Dorchester, and Mattapan.

BOSTON GLOBE PHOTO

In June 1967, a protest by welfare mothers escalated into a
major urban riot. City officials
would later respond to black rage
through the formulation of controversial housing policies, which
did little more than extend the
geographic boundaries of the
black ghetto.

BOSTON GLOBE PHOTO

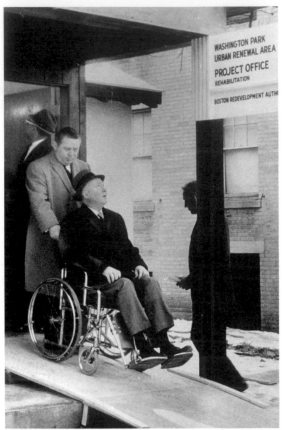

Boston's Mayor John Collins (left, in wheelchair) surveys a Washington Park Urban Renewal Area site in 1963. Boston would boast several of the nation's largest urban renewal programs during the Collins administration. Arts mogul Elma Lewis, shown below in Dorchester's Franklin Park in 1966 with her young dance students, was determined to create the premiere center for Afro-American arts. The transfer of the Mishkan Tefila building for this purpose, however, would drive a wedge between Boston's inner-city Jews and their largely suburban leadership.

BOSTON GLOBE PHOTO

BOSTON GLOBE PHOTO

BOSTON GLOBE PHOTO

Thousands marched peacefully through the city streets following the April 4, 1968, assassination of Martin Luther King, Jr. New housing and banking policies to expand home ownership for blacks were announced shortly after King's murder. The creation of a discriminatory line within which blacks could buy homes, however, would permanently destabilize several Boston neighborhoods. In the photo at right, City Councilor Thomas Atkins (left) convinced Mayor Kevin White (right) that tensions would escalate if the city cancelled a James Brown rock concert scheduled for the day after the King assassination. Shown in the center is James Brown, the "Godfather of Soul."

BOSTON GLOBE PHOTO

BOSTON GLOBE PHOTO

The last members of Congregation
Chevra Shas (above) pack away ritual
objects in 1971. An arson attack in
May 1970 and subsequent assaults
convinced the remaining synagogue
members that they were no longer
safe to pray on Ashton Street in
Dorchester. Rabbi Mordecai Savitsky
(right) buries the scorched torahs
that were destroyed by arsonists in
the May 27, 1970, attack on the synagogue.

BOSTON GLOBE PHOTO

offer a demanding curriculum and strict disciplinary code with but one overriding goal: to funnel as many graduates as possible into the downtown public Boston Latin High School, the system's premier high school.

Latin, as it was commonly referred to, had been founded by Puritans in 1635 as a feeder school for Harvard College. More than three hundred years later a disproportionate number of graduates continued on to Ivy League colleges and rare was the college admissions officer who did not admire the academic achievements of a student from the nation's oldest public school. The Latin Schools were segregated purposefully by gender and de facto by race. In 1968, for example, fewer than ten of the school's three hundred graduates were black. Entrance to the six-year Latin School program was strictly by competitive examination. The quality of neighborhood elementary and junior high schools, therefore, was essential; without a sound education from them, Boston students were destined for one of several mediocre district high schools. In a strange and unseemly ritual, elementary school principals stood before classes of sixth graders and predicted who would and would not likely pass the Latin School exam. In predominantly black schools, few students were encouraged to apply. Hundreds of Jewish youngsters from Dorchester and Mattapan and lace curtain Irish from West Roxbury, on the other hand, bore down each year for the demanding admissions test in mathematics and language skills. The final and often deciding component of the examination was the written essay, in which eleven-year-olds would struggle with weighty topics such as "How communication networks contribute to the concept of our shrinking world." Parents awaited acceptance letters with the nervous anticipation associated with college applications. Rejections meant an uncertain future for their children. Acceptance letters brought unrestrained joy from parents but ambivalence from students. The kids knew that there would be little free time after school for the next six years. Stern Latin "masters" seemed to delight in assigning lengthy chapters of Virgil and Cicero on the very days that their overwhelmed students were cramming for exams in algebra, Greek, and chemistry. A school day, it seemed, never passed without a major test or project falling due. Those who could maneuver the academic obstacle course with a grade

*of 70 or above in all subjects earned the prized certificate of
"approbation with distinction." Few, however, ever saw such a
certificate. Latin School students broke down into three categories: the majority who actually hit the books each night for four
or five hours to maintain a passing grade of 60; a small group of
creative cheaters who shared homework and test results at the
risk of censure or expulsion; and a third group, roughly 25 to 30
percent, who were neither sufficiently adept at academics nor
cheating and simply flunked out during the first two years and
were ignominiously returned to their district middle schools.*

It was the flunkouts from the Latin School, or, more accurately, their empty desks, that most interested the students at Solomon
Lewenberg Junior High School. The city allowed late bloomers
who failed the entrance examination in the seventh grade to try to
replace the fallen ninth graders. (Never mind that those who
entered Latin School in the second round were generally segregated in their own homerooms, an easily identifiable underclass.
Far better to be a second-class citizen on Louis Pasteur Avenue, in
the very shadow of Harvard Medical School, than to be shunted off
to a district school.) Preparation in the seventh and eighth grade at
the Lewenberg, therefore, was vigorous. Unlike much of the rest of
the city, the streets of Mattapan were not filled with the playful
noises of children in the late afternoon. The younger children
were in afternoon Hebrew School while their older brothers and
sisters were at home studying to break into or stay in Boston Latin
High School.

Throughout the early 1960s there was a growing belief that
inferior schools in largely black sections of Roxbury and Dorchester were incapacitating an entire generation of minority children.
In April 1965 a committee appointed by the state Education
Commissioner issued a report on racial imbalance in Boston's
public schools. The committee reported that half of the city's
twenty thousand black students attended schools that were at least
80 percent black. The situation, the committee reported, "does
serious educational damage to Negro children, impairing their
confidence, distorting their self-image and lowering their motiva-
tion." The committee went on to promote legislation to counter
de facto segregation and to make recommendations regarding new
school sites and the drawing of school attendance lines. In the

wake of the report, Governor John Volpe introduced a bill that gave the commissioner of education the power to withhold state funds from any school system in the state that was found to have racial imbalance. The one notable exception to de facto segregation was the Lewenberg, touted not only for its academics but as a rare example of successful integration at work in Boston during the mid-1960s. Black parents in Roxbury knew their children might be greeted with taunts, fists, or worse in schools in South Boston, East Boston, and Charlestown, but in Mattapan they would be free to learn. Jews would not throw rocks at their children.

The attitude of the Jews toward the increasingly black enrollment at the school was significantly more complicated. In Boston —unlike New York City, with its largely Jewish-led United Federation of Teachers—Jews were not well represented either in teaching or administrative positions in the public school system. Control had never been the issue. Everybody knew that patronage and promotions rested squarely in the hands of the Irish, but no politician could keep a Jewish child out of Latin School if he or she scored a sufficient grade on the entrance exam.

To a small but growing number of Mattapan's Jews, the advent of black students at the Lewenberg and the increase in house sales just north of Morton Street and Blue Hill Avenue confirmed their belief that Mattapan was destined to become a geographic extension of the black community. For-sale signs were beginning to sprout like poison mushrooms after a wet spring on the neat side streets off of Blue Hill Avenue. Each school year the advent of a larger group of black students to the Lewenberg precipitated lower overall student enrollment, more early teacher retirements, and staff transfers: in 1965 twelve hundred students attended the Lewenberg, with a minority enrollment of 10 percent, and the following year minority enrollment increased to 22 percent and enrollment dropped to eleven hundred. School integration efforts in Boston seemed to create their own mathematics: each 10 percent increase in black students equaled a dozen teacher transfers and one hundred white student defections. Suddenly Jewish parents, demanding the right to use the same open enrollment policy for their youngsters that black parents were using, withdrew their children and sent them to predominantly white junior high schools in the contiguous neighborhood of Hyde Park.

Black parents, particularly those who had chosen the Lewenberg for its academic reputation, were quick to level charges of racism.

Each day after school Allan Cohen maneuvered his Porsche 912 down Wellington Hill and drove at top speed back to his bachelor apartment on Beacon Hill. Cohen had considered himself lucky to land a position teaching civics and geography at the Lewenberg School, a decent enough job, he figured, while he studied part-time for his law degree at downtown Suffolk University. Other than a few basic education courses, the 25-year-old Connecticut native had no formal teacher training. He did, however, begin to feel a special calling to the field. It was a calling so resonant that Cohen would years later be a primary architect of the cabinet education position created under the Carter Administration. Cohen's students sensed a kindred spirit in the teacher who drove a tad too fast and wore his hair a bit too long. Cohen believed that he'd reached a lot of the kids during the 1967–1968 school year. He particularly liked working with the black students who had chosen the Lewenberg under the city's open enrollment program, which allowed students to choose a school with empty seats regardless of district. Cohen relished the opportunities to take his students on field trips. For many of them, it was their first experience outside of Boston's insular neighborhoods. The naïveté of city kids amazed the young teacher who had always equated big cities with sophistication. On one class trip outside Boston, Cohen had asked his ninth grade civics class if anyone had thought to bring a radio. Several students looked at him quizzically. "Our radios only pick up Boston stations," explained one youngster.[24]

When Cohen returned from summer vacation for the start of the 1968–1969 school year, he was shocked both at the school's new racial composition and the behavioral changes in the students he had known the year before. From the first day of school it was clear that the teachers had lost control. Veteran teachers stood in silent shock as young blacks raced through the corridors trying out the black power slogans they had learned over the summer. The overall student body had shrunk to 754 students, of whom 32 percent were white. It had seemed, over the summer, that the great Lewenberg promise of integration had shattered. Drugged students fell off their chairs and were carried to the nurse's office. White students huddled together for protection against roving extortion rings; fifty cents was the going price to avoid a beating. The largely inexperienced faculty and its principal, Luke Petrocelli, were at a loss. Of fifty-eight teachers, thirty-nine, including Cohen, had not taught long enough to receive tenure from the Boston School Department; nine faculty members were in their first year of teaching. Throughout that winter an average of nine teachers called in sick each day. Without teachers, students often sat all day in the auditorium and watched movies. In one fifteen-day period alone, school administrators counted 718 tardy students; average absenteeism was 178 students each day, roughly one out of four. Like the panic selling in the center sections of Mattapan, these disruptions defied explanation.

During that second year of teaching, Cohen began to see himself more as a security guard than a teacher. He wanted to talk about his frustrations but none of his law school friends seemed interested in the problems of a junior high school at the southern reaches of Boston. Cohen, therefore, started to talk to himself. Settling into his armchair in the late afternoon, he would switch on his tape recorder and begin to verbalize his frustration:

> Today is May 15, 1969, the end of a grueling day. Right before recess, at 10:25, a girl I didn't know entered my class and "called out" one of my students, Melissa, for a fight. The girl jumped on Melissa. What seemed like a hundred other students gathered around. I separated the girls. A girl named Beverly kicked and punched me. . . . Next period I substituted for an absent teacher in a low math class and heard the sounds of fighting next door. I got there just in time to take a bottle away from a boy who was about to swing it at Miss Sullivan . . . (audible yawn). I went in to monitor lunch period. Miss Flynn was leaving with an injured hand. . . . Students were standing on lunch tables, breaking plates, and fighting. . . . The mechanical drawing teacher injured his hand trying to protect himself from a student . . . (audible yawn). Today I broke up five fights. I asked the principal, Mr. Petrocelli, to call the police in. He told me to get back to my room.[25]

Allan Cohen came to believe that adaptability was an essential trait for a good teacher. He resolved, therefore, to find teaching value within the chaos. On a Friday afternoon in late May, Cohen was lecturing an eighth grade civics class on the individual's responsibilities in a civilized community when he heard shouts and cursing in the next classroom. Entering the corridor, he came upon a ninth grader with a vise-like grasp on the doorknob of a classroom. A woman teacher, who had clearly lost control of the class within, frantically pushed on the door in an effort to escape. Cohen demanded that the student release the door as the sobbing Latin teacher rushed from the classroom. "Report now to the principal's office," Cohen demanded.

"Fuck you," the student retorted.

"Down to the office now or I'll see you suspended," said Cohen, holding his ground.

"I'll get your ass, Cohen," the student threatened before sauntering off.

The following day, Cohen confronted the student. "I'm pressing charges against you for assault," Cohen told the student.

"You're crazy, man, I never even hit you," the disbelieving student shot back.

"If you'd hit me, I'd press charges for assault and battery. Since you only threatened me, I'll only charge you with assault. There you go. You learned something today—the difference between assault and assault and battery."[26]

Throughout 1969 a school day rarely passed without violence or mayhem. City editors hungry to fill gaping holes in the newspaper knew that they could always pick up a story at the Lewenberg. On average, a reporter's two-hour-long meandering in the Lewenberg revealed three fistfights, a cafeteria food fight, a superficial injury to a teacher, and a host of exasperated quotes from shell-shocked administrators. None, however, ever reported that most rumored Lewenberg event: the sight of students hanging upside down from windows twenty feet above the schoolyard.

Among the visitors to the school that year was Rabbi Gerald Zelermyer, a young Mattapan rabbi who decided that he must see for himself if the Lewenberg horror stories told by his congregants were indeed true. Zelermyer had little trouble getting access to the school through his friend Allan Cohen. Zelermyer identified himself to one of the three police officers assigned to the junior high school. As he entered the building, he immediately heard sharp bursts of what he mistakenly thought was gunfire. "Only firecrackers," said the impassive beat cop. Sensing the rabbi's nervousness, the officer gave Zelermyer the guided tour. First was an overturned and shattered piano in the school auditorium, a fallen monument to music appreciation class. Close by the principal's office a veteran teacher was calling a cab; only moments earlier he had entered his classroom to find his desk overturned and his chair smashed. Zelermyer then heard a woman unleash a storm of profanity that stung his ears. *(The police officer explained that the woman was the mother of a female student who had been suspended two weeks earlier for assaulting an art teacher. The girl, who had interpreted criticism of her work as racist, had splattered her teacher with paint, torn her dress, and broken her glasses. On the day of Zelermyer's visit the girl's mother, accompanied by a lawyer, had come to demand an end to her daughter's suspension.)* At noontime Zelermyer stopped at the cafeteria. He had barely passed the first table of students when pandemonium ensued; groups of students hurled plates of food and sandwiches at each other.

The Lewenberg appeared beyond repair and redemption. As he left the cafeteria, stepping gingerly over a plate of "American chop suey," the rabbi thought ironically of the biblical command upon which traditional Jews recite the grace after meals: "And you shall eat and you shall be satisfied and you shall bless the Lord your God upon the good land he has given to our fathers."

The mayhem was not confined to school grounds. At the end of the school day, the Lewenberg open-enrollment students burst down Wellington Hill toward Blue Hill Avenue. Nothing, it seemed, was safe along their path—tricycles were smashed and carefully planted rows of flowers were tramped upon; those unlucky enough to get caught in their path were fortunate to escape with just a shower of verbal abuse. Along the Avenue, vendors scurried to remove their goods from sidewalk stalls and dropped their iron grates before the Lewenberg wave broke over them. Those who moved too slow could expect to spend the next few hours salvaging fruit from overturned carts or trying to match left shoes with right.

Mattapan's Jews could not have known that they were running through a dress rehearsal for the desegregation crisis that would rock Boston in the middle 1970s. Hamstrung by raw fear and intimidation, black parents dared not choose schools in any but the Jewish neighborhoods. Most already knew instinctively what they would learn by experience six years later: Irish, Polish, and Italian neighborhoods preferred blood in their streets to blacks in their classrooms. For bigoted whites, the decline in standards of learning and behavior at the Lewenberg School served only to confirm their fears of what might be expected of integration. But in the chaos on Wellington Hill, a valuable lesson about America's seemingly dirtiest secret, discrimination by class, was lost.

The Racial Imbalance Act of 1965 was from the start a tool designed for use only in working-class inner-city neighborhoods. The act defined the school in a state of racial imbalance as one in which "the percent of non-white students in any public school is in excess of fifty percent of the total number of students in such school."[27] Analysts of the Boston schools, notably Pulitzer Prize–winning journalist J. Anthony Lukas, have noted that the wording of the act had essentially exempted every school system in the state's 351 cities and towns with the exception of Boston, Springfield, and Cambridge. Only these three cities boasted black populations sufficient to unbalance an average-sized school even theoretically. School and residential segregation reinforced each other. There were no provisions, for example, for dealing with the intrinsic imbalance of the almost entirely white school systems in the nearby suburbs of Brookline, Milton, and Dedham, all relatively short commutes from Dorchester and Roxbury. Rarely had a piece of legislation, Lukas noted, so nakedly betrayed its class bias.

There was little surprise, therefore, when the Racial Imbalance Act was embraced by suburban legislators despite protests from the Boston School Committee. Among the bill's chief supporters were Father Robert Drinan, the dean of the Boston College Law School, Brookline state legislator Beryl Cohen, and Lt. Gov. Elliot Richardson. The supporters represented, in essence, an invincible cross-section of traditional northeast power structure. Drinan, a priest who spoke out for liberalized abortion laws, had many friendships with progressive Jewish leaders in Boston's western suburbs; they would later help elect the outspoken Jesuit to the U.S. Congress. Beryl Cohen, like his friend and fellow Brookline legislator Michael Dukakis, was a good-government reformer who shunned ward politics as unseemly. Lieutenant Governor Richardson, a Yankee Republican who would later resign in righteous anger from his position as attorney general in President Richard Nixon's administration, rounded out the team.

The bill's backers had little trouble silencing the objections of the Boston School Committee and its chairwoman, Louise Day Hicks. Suburbanites found it easy to scoff at Hicks, a large, physically graceless native of Irish South Boston who favored dresses of kelly green and shocking pink. Hicks, an attorney and the daughter of a judge, was supercilious by "Southie" standards, but she never opted for the "Irish Riviera" on the south shore of Massachusetts and she never lost touch with her working-class neighbors. The chairwoman may have easily topped the ticket for Boston School Committee, but she wouldn't have been elected dogcatcher in any of the Commonwealth's wealthy suburbs and towns. Supporters of the Racial Imbalance Act were quick to label Hicks and her School Committee colleagues as mindless bigots. Rarely, though, did these critics influence their own selectmen or town meetings to build significant tracts of affordable housing in their own tightly zoned communities. As Lukas revealed, the standard liberal position on de facto segregation in Boston echoed the support extended to all of the nation's civil rights legislation up to that point: "The probability of support for such legislation is inversely related to the proximity of its potential application."[28] The same message, stated less elegantly, was being delivered by Louise Day Hicks. But liberal suburbanites could only snicker at the thought of Louise Day Hicks's harangues against the "small band of racial agitators, non-native to Boston, and a few college radicals who have joined in the conspiracy to tell the people of Boston how to run their schools, their city and their lives."[29]

The state would indeed make good on its threat to withhold education funds from the Boston Public Schools, but this would not affect the racial composition of the schools. In 1965 at least forty-five Boston schools were deemed to have racial imbalance; after the passage of the Racial Imbalance Act, the number only increased. Blame was placed squarely at the doorstep of the Boston School Committee, which, critics claimed, had either stepped up its efforts to steer middle school students into high schools based on race compatibility or had located new annexes in neighborhoods that were either overwhelmingly white or black. The only school that became racially "balanced" seemed to be in the Jewish section of Mattapan. This likely resulted not only from perceptions of black–Jewish compatibility but from the ambivalence with which most Boston Jews eyed the chairwoman and her School Committee activities on Beacon Street. There would be few votes and little love lost between Hicks and the Jewish voters. In 1967 Hicks's popularity at the polls had prompted her to mount a mayoralty campaign. For a campaign slogan she decided on the trenchant phrase "You know where I stand." The slogan seemed to inspire equal discomfort in blacks and Jews. Blacks interpreted Hicks's slogan as the battle cry of a candidate who stood on the side of all-white neighborhood schools, segregated housing projects, whites-only beaches, and Irish control of the best municipal jobs. Jews felt an atavistic sting when Hicks derided "the rich people in the suburbs," "the outside power structure" and "the forces who attempt to invade us." Boston's Jews, who shared class characteristics with Hicks's supporters, nevertheless could not shake off their nervous feelings that these remarks were directed at their wealthier cousins; for them, there was more than a grain of truth in the adage that when one Jew stubs his toe, all Jews cry out in pain. Lower-middle-class Mattapan Jewry was doubly isolated: from their gentile neighbors, who were making antisemitic accusations, and from their fellow suburban Jews, who were indifferent to their plight.

Mattapan had no equivalent of Louise Day Hicks to erect barricades around neighborhood schools. In fact, it wanted none. Members of the Mattapan Organization continued to state that their goal was peaceful integration. But by the winter of 1968 its members were convinced that their efforts to stop panic sales in Mattapan would fall short if neighborhood residents lost confidence in the neighborhood schools, particularly the Lewenberg. As cochairpersons of the organization's education committee, Lewenberg parents Arthur Bernstein and Gloria Werman were insistent that educational standards at the school not decline. Toward that end, they met frequently throughout the 1968–1969 school year with Allan Cohen, who had formed a new faculty committee that was determined to do more than send get-well cards to ailing teachers. Cohen and the members of the Mattapan Organization grew increasingly close throughout the school year. Werman would supply the young bachelor with her favorite recipes for baked chicken, and Cohen would provide advice on effective measures to deal with the Beacon Street bureaucrats. The key to reversing the chaos at the Lewenberg, Cohen told his new friends, was to gain the confidence of Principal Luke Petrocelli.

From their first meetings, however, the members of the Mattapan Organization and the embattled principal managed only to alienate one another. Like the cops at District 3, Petrocelli had always considered Mattapan to be an ideal posting for a public servant with just a few more years to put in before collecting retirement benefits. The arrival of unmotivated and disruptive black students had caught Petrocelli unprepared, and his management style grew increasingly erratic. A strict disciplinarian who favored using the switch on recalcitrant students, he seemed at times unaware of the demoralizing effects of unchecked unruly behavior. A cheerful boss who enjoyed bowling after classes with his faculty members, Petrocelli could also turn a studiously cold shoulder to those he even vaguely suspected of disloyalty. As reports of racial turmoil at the Lewenberg increased, the principal presented a puzzling public persona. Petrocelli and members of the Mattapan Organization could not find even the smallest patch of common ground on which to initiate a dialogue. Jewish parents insisted that the ratio of blacks at the school be rolled back to 50 percent. The Lewenberg, they believed, had gone beyond "the tipping point," a sociological term indicating the maximum percentage of minorities, usually cited as 25 percent, present in a neighborhood or institution before the advent of white flight. The Jewish parents pleaded that their concerns not be entangled in charges of racism; middle-class black parents, they noted, were also withdrawing their children, opting for programs that bused a limited number of promising youngsters to suburban schools far from the city. The Mattapan Organization members pressed for permission to serve as teacher's aides, hall monitors, and library aides. Despite the increasingly chaotic situation at the school, Petrocelli said he would brook no interference.

Lewenberg parents stepped up their initiatives. They requested a public meeting about the school's situation, an analysis of the school by independent experts, and the transfer of Petrocelli if conditions did not improve. After several months of stalling, the School Committee agreed to a public hearing during the spring of 1968. For a site, it selected a high school auditorium in the contiguous neighborhood of Hyde Park, a largely Irish section considered openly hostile to blacks. For a date, it chose a day during Passover week despite the protestations of outraged Jews. Few were there to hear Principal Petrocelli field softballs from members of the School Committee. Jewish parents felt that they had no one to whom they could turn; one parent, it was reported, even brandished a pistol at the principal and threatened to shoot him should any harm befall his daughter.

Confused and under pressure, Petrocelli alternately accused black parents and activists of taking over his school and chided the Mattapan Organization and white parents for caring only about declining property values. The problem at the Lewenberg, he told a reporter, was "a conscious plot on the part of the blacks to imbalance the school, a plot to appropriate a good facility."[30] At other times he would state publicly that the school would be "better off all black. We'd have only half the discipline problems if the students were all one color."[31] Members of the Mattapan Organization were coming to believe that the work of their education committee was turning out as fruitless as that of their housing committee.

Throughout 1969 the blockbusting of Mattapan and the crisis at the Lewenberg were taking their toll on Janice Bernstein. Once the first to arrive at the door of new neighbors with a platter of fruit, she had recently taken to walking the streets of her own neighborhood with her son's Louisville Slugger baseball bat. Bernstein was particularly enraged by the school dropouts who had taken to lounging on the lawns in front of homes on Ormond Street and Outlook Road. The loud radios and litter were a constant annoyance to the homeowners. Requests to move off their property were generally met with profanity and insults. Calls to police assured nothing more than window breaking and increased harassment.

The recalcitrant teenagers, however, were only part of the problem. Far more frightening for Bernstein was the growing number of for-sale signs on the hill. Neighbors who had once proudly declared their intention of never leaving the neighborhood were now showing clear signs of panic. Neighbors once eager to chat over a fence or during a shopping trip on the Avenue suddenly averted their eyes whenever Bernstein approached. Bernstein became accustomed to seeing black neighbors move in, but she rarely saw her white neighbors move out; the mystery was solved when another member of the Mattapan Organization told her that the moving vans were ordered to arrive late at night after the neighbors had already gone to sleep.

Like many white parents with children still at the Lewenberg, Bernstein had taken to carpooling with friends: extortion and assaults had become too common to allow children to walk home from school. When it was Bernstein's turn to drive, she frequently pulled up at a popular hamburger joint on Blue Hill Avenue at the foot of the hill where the kids could grab an afternoon snack. While waiting in the car for her son on a spring day in 1969, Bernstein noticed that he was being jostled as he stood in line for his milk shake. Three black youths, only a year or two older, bumped Bernstein's son from side to side as he walked out to the parking lot. One assailant kicked the boy in the buttocks; amused, the other two quickly joined in. Bernstein had tried to teach her children self-reliance, but she was suddenly seized with a terrible fear that the incident would escalate beyond a schoolboy fight. Instinctively, she grabbed for the baseball bat at her feet and dashed toward the youths; they were at first startled and then amused by the large, red-faced woman, bat at the ready, who jumped from her car swearing and sputtering. Bernstein slowed her pace a few yards from the youths and raised the bat above her head. She remembers seeing red, literally: the three taunting youths appeared to be standing in a strange crimson glare. She was swearing heavily but felt a strange calm. "Come over here, you," she called to each in turn. "Come over here." The youths stood their ground, smiling inanely. "Stay there, then," she said softly. "Just stay there." Bernstein edged forward. She knew that the moment she was in reach of the first youth who had kicked her son she would take a full swing at him. Although the bat was still above her head, she could see the swing, could feel it connect. At that moment her gaze locked with that of one of the youths. The sight of the overweight housewife with the Louisville Slugger was no longer amusing—she had murder in her eye. The youth broke the spell and fled out of the parking lot onto Blue Hill Avenue, his companions right behind. Bernstein gave chase, sweat soaking through her dress. Long after the youths were out of reach, she continued the chase; Janice Bernstein, the welcome wagon lady on Wellington Hill, wanted to hurt someone.

The next morning Bernstein made an appointment to see the principal of the Lewenberg. She was determined to identify the three students who assaulted her son and to seek their suspension or expulsion from the school. Her reputation, however, preceded her. "That's the bat lady," a student whispered as she climbed the stairs to the Lewenberg. "That's her. The bat lady."

"Lead the Jewish Racists
Out of Mattapan" .

The Agony of a Reluctant Hero,
1969

The parsonage at 41 Glenhill Road in the southern section of Mattapan was the last outpost of civility before the descent into the ragged wood. Snow-choked in winter, overgrown in spring and summer, the ten-acre wood was a favorite hiding place for neighborhood Jewish youngsters playing hooky from the rigors of afternoon Hebrew school.

For decades, Jewish boys had slid cautiously past the rabbi's ranch-style home at the edge of the wood and played at danger. They were usually heading for Black Rock, a low-browed slab visible from the rabbi's side study. There they re-created favorite fight scenes from popular television westerns of the 1950s and 1960s, such as "Have Gun Will Travel" and "Wagon Train." The boys were equally unenthusiastic about their social studies units on the early American settlers in Massachusetts and their Hebrew teachers' endless drone about the pioneers of a new Jewish state.

225

They would likely have been impressed, however, if told that their feet retraced an Indian trail dating back 300 years which began at the upper falls of the nearby Neponset River.

Exhausted by their rough play, the Boston "cowboys" leaned back against Black Rock and eagerly tore off the tops of packages of processed cheese and crackers. "This is good hardtack," they mumbled as they wolfed the snacks. The meal was followed by Chesterfield cigarettes, purloined earlier from the nearby Stop & Shop supermarket. Lightheaded and hiccoughing from nicotine, the prepubescent boys, some the sons of East European immigrants, discussed the merits of the sidearms favored by their Western heroes. Looking down the knobby sights of dead-brown sticks, they took aim at the window of the rabbi's study. Hours passed as the youngsters uttered popping sounds embellished with the backthroat noise of errant ricochets. But not so much as an acorn ever landed on the rabbi's picture window facing the woods.

During the early 1960s, Jewish youths perceived two major threats when traversing the Mattapan woods. First were the bands of Irish boys from the nearby Gallivan public housing projects. Depending on the season, the Jewish and Irish boys would hurl crab apples, snowballs, or rocks from distances that generally discouraged direct hits. The project kids, many the sons of Boston policemen and firemen, would have hell to pay at home if they were to inflict injuries serious enough to invite police inquiry. The Jewish boys seemed satisfied to retaliate with volleys at least five yards off their marks.

The second danger recognized no ethnic boundaries. On the southern side of the woods was the Mattapan Hospital for Infectious Diseases, a sinister building of yellow brick. Recuperating patients passed through the woods on social and shopping errands. To the neighborhood's youth, each figure represented shadowlike death. Young eyes constantly scanned the paths for gobs of sputum left behind by careless or—who knew?—insane patients. Passing too close to a dollop was sure to infect the entire scouting party. Nine thousand miles away in Vietnam, American troops scanned the ground for trip wires no more diligently than did Mattapan kids for tubercular phlegm.

The dread of infectious disease was sufficient to send more than one Jewish boy scrambling back to the study of *humash*—the five books of Moses—at nearby Temple Beth Hillel. The aging and kindly teachers, like Saul Goldman and Rabbi Ben-Zakkai, accepted wayward students with a stern warning and a gentle twist of the ear. In other places, other times, the teachers too had confronted mysteries beneath a growth of overarching trees.

In the spring of 1968 Rabbi Gerald Zelermyer took up residence in the parsonage at the edge of the Mattapan woods. Newly ordained and unmarried, the 28-year-old rabbi represented both a solid performer and a potential match for the daughter of some lucky congregant. He had been pursued by well-to-do suburban congregations nationwide, but the young rabbi had no interest in becoming a spiritual leader of a sumptuous temple in Scarsdale or any other smug enclave. He opted to serve the inner-city congregation dubbed "the Dor-Mat," the humble moniker for Temple Beth Hillel, a two-story structure of yellow brick set off among the hundreds of wooden triple-deckers crowded along Morton Street, the thoroughfare separating Dorchester from the marginally more upscale Mattapan. Ministering in a "changing neighborhood" would have its own rewards, Rabbi Zelermyer believed. His heart would be revealed in deeds, as his revered seminary teacher, Abraham Joshua Heschel, so often suggested. Zelermyer's first year in his first pulpit confirmed his choice of vocation. A partnership with God suited him to a greater degree than a law partnership or medical practice. The only missing component in an otherwise fruitful life was romance. Single rabbis were looked upon as oddities, and he was eager to meet the right woman, one who would share his enthusiasm for children and traditional Judaism.

On the morning of June 27, 1969, Zelermyer attended a special meeting of black and white clergy from Mattapan and Dorchester for the purpose of discussing disturbing trends that they believed posed a threat to the sanctity of all of their congregations. As usual, the conversation focused on the panic sales of homes by whites who feared the incursion of black families struggling to stay ahead of crowded conditions in Roxbury and gentrification in the South End. Zelermyer listened attentively as the clergymen described the work of venal realtors who would stop at nothing to sow panic in a neighborhood, leaving their blockbusting agents in a position to swoop down on terrified homeowners with offers for houses at a fraction of their market value. The priests from the largely Irish Catholic parishes in the southern sections of Dorchester seemed determined to keep their congregations intact. Some were openly contemptuous of Mayor Kevin White, who one year earlier had won office on a strong neighborhood platform but now seemed more interested in the governor's office than in elderly crime victims and falling property values. The black ministers dealt directly with issues of race and class. They did not gloss over their own suspicion of the largely uneducated migrants arriving from the south. If the status quo could be maintained in the neighborhoods, the black and Irish clergy felt, they could begin to make progress on trying to inculcate a vision of peaceful integration among their congregants. Both groups stressed to the rabbi that the area's middle-class Jews must stand fast against blockbusting in the Jewish neighborhoods. Zelermyer felt accusatory stares with each reference to blockbusting or unscrupulous realtors. He was well aware of the panic sales among his congregants who lived north of the synagogue, and he had confirmed with his own eyes the conditions at the troubled Lewenberg School, where several Temple Beth Hillel children still attended classes.

To the best of Zelermyer's knowledge, the neighborhood south of Morton Street, where the majority of his congregants resided, had not yet experienced the late-night calls of brokers who initiated their inquiries about houses for sale with references to "changing neighborhoods." Zelermyer was not prone to conspiratorial theories, nor did he view the "establishment" as a leviathan. A handful of dishonest brokers, he was sure, could not decimate a solid middle-class neighborhood. Legal safeguards were surely already in place to deal with any aberrations. Driving home, he felt disturbed and excited from the effects of the long but productive meeting. Pulling into his driveway, he noted but paid no mind to the car parked on the edge of the unpaved road at the woods that bordered his home.

Shortly after arriving home, Zelermyer called his mother on the telephone, a daily ritual; that practice, he often thought to himself, would probably change once he married. The conversation was interrupted by the chimes of the front door bell. Placing the receiver aside, Zelermyer, quite accustomed to unannounced visits from congregants, strode quickly to the door and swung it open. The two young men facing the rabbi were not congregants. One of the black youths, whose age Zelermyer estimated at seventeen, shoved a clumsily scrawled note into his hands. Zelermyer made out the words "lead the Jewish racists out of Mattapan" before the other youth, his face turned guardedly to the side, flicked what appeared to be a vial of white powder into the face of the startled rabbi. Zelermyer's head snapped back from frightful pain. The assailants, having never uttered a word, dashed away as the rabbi, engulfed in blinding dust, leapt back and slammed the door shut. Struggling to control his mounting panic, the rabbi stumbled to the telephone table and picked up the receiver. "Ma, I have some people here who need my attention, I'll call you back," he said numbly.[1] Zelermyer hurried to the bathroom and applied a cold washcloth to his face. Whatever he was hit with did not, thank God, blind him; he could see. Squinting out from the side of the compress, he saw blood trickle from the seared skin on the right side of his face. Applying pressure to the wounded area with one hand, he flushed his burning eyes with cold water with the other.

After several minutes of frantic flushing, Zelermyer drove to the office of a nearby doctor. The physician dressed the wound and drove the rabbi to an eye specialist in the southern suburb of Quincy. There the specialist cleansed the rabbi's eyes and tested his vision. By the look of the wound, the doctor said, the substance was a strong and corrosive acid. It hit with greatest damage one-quarter inch below the rabbi's right eye. The doctor wrapped the rabbi's face in bandages, leaving only his left eye exposed. During the fifteen-minute ride back to Mattapan, Zelermyer thanked God numerous times for his hairbreadth escape.

Zelermyer felt more lonely than frightened when he arrived home. He crossed the threshold over which the acid had been thrown just hours earlier—the threshold over which he hoped one day to carry a bride. The *mezuzah*, the encased parchment scroll affixed to the doorposts of Jewish homes, caught his eye. *"Shomer Yisrael* ('guardian of Israel')," he whispered prayerfully. Zelermyer reached out to pat the sacred object, which commemorates God's passing over the homes of the ancient Israelite slaves, thus sparing them the deadly plagues showered upon their Egyptian overseers. The rabbi caught himself in midgesture and withdrew his finger from the *mezuzah*. A dusting of powdery white acid still clung to the doorpost.

Zelermyer's mail had been pushed through the mail slot and was on the floor in the hallway. It included the usual bills, missives from fraternal and rabbinic organizations, and a current copy of the *Jewish Advocate* newspaper, "the weekly newspaper that no Jewish home can be without." There was also an announcement of a recently opened real estate office that promised clients "eager to buy your home."

Zelermyer's home had been built by the congregation eighteen years earlier but clearly not with a bachelor rabbi in mind. The low ranch style was chosen to stand out from the two-family houses and crowded wooden triple-deckers along Morton Street. This was a house that could give a man the sense of providing something special for his family, all the more important because many ambitious rabbis, moving from congregation to larger, more affluent congregation, led itinerant lives that often precluded home ownership. Zelermyer, however, was the type to sink roots. The main level of the house consisted of three bedrooms and a living room, dining room, and study. The kitchen, with modern appliances and ample counter space, seemed ideal for a rabbi's wife, a modern *rebbitzin* who, under the adoring gaze of children and husband, might roll out and braid the dough for festive loaves of Sabbath *hallah* bread. It was the kind of home in which the children, homework accomplished, might rush exuberantly downstairs to the finished playroom, raising a smile of satisfaction from their father as he searched the Torah portion of the week for a clever and relevant insight with which to edify or impress his congregants.

At times, Zelermyer could not help but feel vaguely foolish living alone on Glenhill Road in a house obviously built for a family. Even at the Jewish Theological Seminary in New York City, where each student lived in a room approximately eight by eight feet with a small adjoining sitting room, he had never wanted for space. Within those walls amazing vistas opened for the thin, meditative student who contemplated the lofty Jewish concepts of mercy, kindness, justice, wisdom, and truth. During Zelermyer's years at the seminary, the student "uniform" was blue jeans and work shirts. Zelermyer, however, favored conservative suits or, at

the least, dress slacks, jacket, and tie. His serious demeanor gave
the appearance of one on the way to a funeral. Nevertheless, he
was popular with fellow students because of his intelligence and
fairness and, especially, the wry wit with which he surprised
friends at unlikely times. During his seminary period he was
elected three times to the presidency of the seminary's student
body, but in the freewheeling 1960s Gerry Zelermyer was a
definite anomaly.

The seminary's symbol, a burning bush, was inscribed on the
side of a tower that rose above neighboring institutions —
Columbia University, Union Theological Seminary, and the
Juilliard School of Music. Atop the library tower shone an eternal
beacon. Zelermyer spent long hours in the library poring over
tractates of Talmud, the authoritative body of Jewish law and
tradition. Unable to study any more, he would wander across the
seminary's courtyard, pausing under the arches on which were
inscribed the names of the spiritual founders of Judaism's Conservative movement. From the courtyard Zelermyer could look back
at the tower and see the beacon clearly. "A light unto the nations,"
he thought to himself.

The seminary was on the edge of Harlem, which, just prior to
World War I, was home to almost two hundred thousand Jews. In
subsequent years Harlem would become New York City's largest
integrated neighborhood, composed primarily of blacks and Jews.
But by 1930 only three thousand Jews remained in Harlem, the
exodus attributed by social scientists to deteriorating housing
stock, fear of street crime, and Jewish upward mobility. During
Zelermyer's student days, Harlem's last rabbi lived on campus in
dormitory space provided by the seminary. Rabbi Philip Alstadt
was an elderly bachelor who shared his room with piles of
yellowed newspapers. He served as a living reminder to rabbinic
neophytes of the past glory of inner-city Jewish communities —
and of the dangers of staying single too long.

It was a tradition at the seminary for favored students to walk
their professors home after classes, out of concern for their safety
on New York's unpredictable streets and for informal contact with
mentors. Zelermyer, like his fellow students, particularly cherished contact with Rabbi Abraham Joshua Heschel, a profound
scholar and social activist who was revered by theologians,
Christians and Jews, but looked upon with suspicion by jealous

colleagues. Heschel, a friend and confidante of Dr. Martin Luther King, held great moral influence over his students on matters of civil rights and social ethics. And like King himself, Heschel would not be satisfied with mere lip service to the movement. "It is in deeds that man becomes aware of what life is," he often advised his students. "What he may not dare to think, he often utters in deeds." Heschel, European-born, was relentless both in his defense of American civil rights and his attacks on what he called the "monstrosity of inequality." He urged, harangued, and compelled his students to do justice and not abdicate to courts or government the task of eradicating segregation. "It was easier for the children of Israel to cross the Red Sea than for civil rights legislation to pass the floor of the United States Senate," he often lectured.[2] In March 1968 Heschel introduced Martin Luther King to a convention of rabbis in upstate New York with the following words: "Where in America today do we hear a voice like the voice of the prophets of Israel? Martin Luther King is a sign that God has not forsaken the United States of America. . . . I call upon every Jew to hearken to his voice, to share his vision, to follow in his way. The whole future of America will depend upon the impact and influence of Dr. King." Less than one month after that introduction, Heschel would walk alongside of King's coffin through the streets of Atlanta.

Resting on his living room couch, Zelermyer wondered how his compassionate teacher would have reacted to a splash of acid. Heschel had said that the truly religious would take a "leap of action" in demanding justice for the victims of racial discrimination. Clergymen, through their deeds, would reveal the possibility of stable, integrated neighborhoods. But what of unprovoked, vicious assaults on Jews? Zelermyer thought again of the threatening note. "Lead the Jewish racists out of Mattapan," it had demanded. The threat, though crude, had almost an epic connotation: for a moment, the rabbi saw himself leading Boston's Jews past the aging wooden triple-deckers along Morton Street to a golden land. But the glory quickly faded as he contemplated the next Jewish target. Zelermyer sat up stiffly and began to move from the couch toward the phone to report the assault to the nearby district police station. He was stopped by the thought of the publicity likely to follow the incident. The image of his assailants at large seemed, at that moment at least, less threatening than the panic that might ensue among his congregants. Zelermyer would play no role in a modern-day exodus. He resolved neither to be intimidated by the assault nor to be forced to act in any way complicit with the evil messengers. The approach of Sabbath would give him time to rest and think.

Three hundred families worshipped regularly at Beth Hillel when Zelermyer assumed the pulpit in 1968. When Mishkan Tefila, the *stadt shul* of Boston, moved to the suburbs, it fell to Beth Hillel to serve the more Americanized and better-educated Jews who were not at home in the rigidly observant Orthodox synagogues, where many of the congregants jealously guarded the immigrant ambience. Most congregants of Beth Hillel felt far removed from the *shtetls* of Eastern Europe for which many of the Orthodox synagogues were named. And they clearly did not appreciate Yiddish-speaking rabbis whose only multisyllabic English word was "delicatessen."

The pride of Temple Beth Hillel was its five-day-a-week Hebrew school, the last of this intensive type in Boston. Serious proponents of Jewish education, like Zelermyer, believed that imparting the lessons and obligations of Judaism to youngsters required classes five days a week. But most suburban congregations in the 1960s were happy if they could attract students for two afternoons a week, and many managed only Sunday school programs. When Zelermyer arrived, 125 students were enrolled in the afternoon school. Some of the students had started their Jewish education in the programs of synagogues further north toward Blue Hill but had transferred when schools closed due to street violence and falling enrollment. It was painful to see the closures, but the dedicated rabbi and teaching staff were quick, nonetheless, to glean the Jewish youngsters from poorer neighborhoods in North Dorchester.

Temple Beth Hillel students reported at 3:00 P.M., almost immediately after their public school studies, and remained at their desks until 5:30 P.M. Wisely, the principal and staff tried to develop personal relationships with their charges, even acknowledging that baseball games, dance, or music lessons could compete with Hebrew education. To gainsay this would only mean an increase in the truancy rate. A parent's note indicating that a son was to be the starting pitcher in a Little League game or a daughter the prima ballerina in an upcoming performance was usually sufficient for early dismissal.

Temple Beth Hillel was situated halfway between Zelermyer's home and the enormous intersection at Blue Hill Avenue and Morton Street. On many days during his first year on the job, the young rabbi would walk out the temple's front door and feel the pull in both directions. Zelermyer was fond of the Avenue with its cheerful hucksters, barrels of pickled herring, Hebraic bric-a-brac, and protruding sidewalk vegetable stands. After dropping off his shirts each Friday at a Chinese laundry on Woodrow Avenue, he'd venture onto the thoroughfare. "Great lox today, rabbi," a proprietor would greet him. Mindful of his role in the community and cautious not to offend any of the shopkeepers, the young rabbi would enter one appealing store after another, on many occasions returning home with two or three times the needed amount of smoked fish, fresh rolls, and *halvah.* Zelermyer had also taken special delight in observing the friendly interaction of blacks and Jews who were drawn to the better shops on the southern end of the Avenue. At popular stores such as Prime Market and American Kosher, black housewives from Roxbury, like their Jewish counterparts, knew how to cajole the cigar-chomping butchers into bringing out the freshest meat from the back cutting room. Zelermyer enjoyed watching the black matrons and Jewish *balabustes,* their shoes covered with sawdust, compliment one another on their purchases. Integration, he believed, took just a modicum of effort.

On the Friday of his attack, however, Zelermyer had no appetite for Blue Hill Avenue. His face hurt, his eyes itched, and he foamed with fury that his attackers had tried to rob him of his sight. The dose of acid had eaten away at Zelermyer's sense of security about his neighborhood. Nevertheless, he held tenaciously to the belief that it was here in Mattapan that he could live a truly authentic Jewish life. Zelermyer resolved to lead the next day's Sabbath services at Temple Beth Hillel despite the need to explain his bandaged face. He walked his usual route down Doone Avenue to Lorna Road, streets consisting primarily of well-kept two-family and occasional small single-family ranch-style homes. To the north, on Morton Street, the housing stock changed quickly to the wooden triple-deckers. Zelermyer's route brought him past a large corner drugstore, a small variety store, a butcher shop, a dry cleaners, and a newly opened real estate office. One block further on, at the crest of a small hill overlooking the Midland commuter railroad tracks, was the District 3 police station. Unlike so many of Boston's clergy who were called on to intercede on behalf of young parishioners, Zelermyer was a stranger at the police station. The children of his congregants, thank God, were too busy with homework and Hebrew school to have much time left over for malicious mischief. Zelermyer, still in a quandary over whether or not to report the attack, wanted to walk up the steps of the police station and seek out a sympathetic detective. The young men who had attacked him were not simple muggers. He had a vague suspicion that blockbusters were behind the attack, but with no evidence he knew that his theory would be dismissed as paranoid. Though fearful that other prominent Jews might find themselves victims of assailants whose aim was both to terrorize and to disfigure, Zelermyer believed that a police report would surely lead to sensationalism, panic his congregation, anguish his parents, and serve the interests of his attackers. "There will be no police reports," he resolved as he walked the three additional blocks to his place of work and worship.

As he approached Temple Beth Hillel, Zelermyer thought of the great rabbis like Joseph Soloveitchik who had left the area before he'd even arrived. Why had these great leaders failed to use their influence to strengthen their communities? The suburban exodus surely left thousands behind, and now those remaining were in danger of losing their communal institutions as well. Although his worldview had not been shaped in the Lithuanian *yeshivah* of Brisk but at Buckingham, Browne, and Nichols, an exclusive private school in Cambridge, and at Middlebury College in Vermont, Zelermyer was still certain that the intensity of Jewish life had something to do with density. Jews, he believed, were entitled to their share of the city. Growing up in the affluent suburb of Newton, Zelermyer knew well the attraction of real estate in the towns west of Boston. Cities and towns like Newton and Brookline—with their large parks, progressive public schools, and reform-minded Democrats (like Michael Dukakis, then state representative, and his Jewish wife, Kitty)—attracted the upper class of Boston's Jews in the period after the Second World War. The son of a successful physician, Zelermyer acknowledged the lure of the suburbs for his parents' more assimilated friends. A fashionable address and spacious lawns were more valued than the old neighborhood with relatives close by. In the suburbs Jews were free of peculiar peddlers, nosy neighbors, and interruptions from a seemingly endless procession of bearded old men collecting everything from worn clothing to pennies for the blue and white tin *pushkes,* or charity boxes, distributed by the Jewish National Fund. Toiling over their tulips, suburban Jews congratulated themselves on the resourcefulness that enabled them to move from the old neighborhoods (nevertheless, the rabbi retained childhood memories of grown men throwing aside garden hoses and impulsively jumping into cars to drive the five miles to the Avenue's G&G delicatessen for a lean brisket sandwich).

Zelermyer would have liked to have served his inner-city community when the wooden triple-decker represented the possibility of both family and economic stability. Now, he feared, the typical Dorchester housing unit was in danger of becoming a stultifying symbol for those who longed to follow the clarion call of the suburbs and to shut out the voices of elderly parents who beckoned from the rickety porches. The rabbi refused, however, to believe that Dorchester and Mattapan were finished as Jewish communities. Some of his own congregants, who simply preferred the tight-knit neighborhood, earned as much money as their cousins who had fled to the suburbs. Others worked in the same trades in which their parents forged fierce union commitments, or inherited cherished family businesses with loyal clientele. The news of an acquaintance's desire to relocate to the western suburbs still brought sarcastic responses from those who formed the backbone of Beth Hillel. *"Gai gezunt ahait,"* they'd say in Yiddish. "Go in good health to Newton and Brookline with the garden clubs and U.S. Open golf tournaments."

Even in 1969 a healthy sense of reverse snobbery seemed to be working in favor of Dorchester and Mattapan. The "real Jews," most Bostonians believed, still lived in the old neighborhoods. The very mention of Blue Hill Avenue conjured images of families walking together to synagogue and of ward heelers shoring up Ward 14. Newspaper columnists and irate callers to Boston's plethora of talk radio programs kept the suburbanites from getting too smug through their continuous attacks on "those people out in Brookline and Newton" whose affluence and education were to little avail when it came to understanding the problems of real Bostonians. It took talent and style to live in the Italian North End, Irish South Boston, black Roxbury, or Jewish Dorchester; it only took money to live in the suburbs. Each of Boston's tightly guarded ethnic enclaves was thought to yield certain mysteries only to those who knew its streets, bookie joints, restaurants, and parks. And Zelermyer was learning, perhaps more than he would care to know, about this one.

When Zelermyer arrived at the synagogue on the Sabbath after the attack, several officers and regulars were preparing the sanctuary for the service. The modest facade of yellow brick gave little indication of the beauty within of the eight hundred–seat main chapel with its long, highly polished benches, handsome windows of stained glass, and imposing *bimah,* the dais on which rested the holy ark with the cherished Torah scrolls. The synagogue's basement level consisted of a smaller chapel for children's services in addition to a function hall and kitchen, which were used to raise revenue for synagogue activities. In the suburban temples of Zelermyer's youth, professional caterers moved in their wares before the end of the Sabbath, transforming the function halls into cabarets, a development that caused great unease among the older, more traditional congregants. At Temple Beth Hillel, however, the do-it-yourself spirit prevailed; sisterhood members cooked and served full kosher meals for bar mitzvahs and wedding parties, turning the entire proceeds over to the synagogue and school administration.

The first congregants who saw their gauze-swathed rabbi rushed to his side. "Were you in an accident, rabbi?" "Will you be all right?" Zelermyer refused to be specific about the nature of his injuries except to assure his congregants that he would be fine in a matter of weeks. He tried to defuse the situation by resorting to wry humor. "I had a knock-down-drag-out fight with the cantor," he told a group of concerned temple officers. "I got caught looking down the wrong end of a hard matzoh ball," he joked to sisterhood members. None of the rabbi's quips that day raised a single smile. At the conclusion of the service, Zelermyer woodenly assured the curious that he was on the mend and hurried home.

Like all new rabbis, Zelermyer spent much of his first year

finding his way in the bruising world of temple politics and learning both how to confront and how to assuage the temple's *makhers,* the officers and chairmen who by virtue of ego, economics, or energy play an inordinately powerful role in the community. In Jewish communal life *makhers* run the gamut from persuasive captains of industry to dimwits who wield power like a meat hook. In traditional Jewish civil rights organizations such as the American Jewish Committee, *makhers* generally are rich and powerful individuals who also hold prominent positions in professional and secular charity circles. At the synagogue level, however, the movers and shakers, sometimes referred to as *balabatim,* are more often men and women of more modest means for whom the synagogue leadership roles represent a rare opportunity to hold and exercise power. It was necessary for Zelermyer to quickly learn the art of synagogue politics, something his scholarly teachers at the Jewish Theological Seminary had never taught him.

The toughest of the *balabatim* at Beth Hillel was Samuel Gaffer, chairman of the board of the temple and an assistant attorney general of the Commonwealth. Gaffer, silver-haired and six feet tall, had developed a stern visage designed to intimidate everybody from the rabbi to the temple secretary. Despite a lingering limp from a childhood illness, Gaffer cut a regal figure. His dream was to be appointed to one of the Commonwealth's judgeships, a dream unfulfilled when he died in 1986.

Zelermyer was always wary during his conversations with the temple's chairman of the board. Notwithstanding his impressive demeanor, the chairman had the instincts of a mobster. Gaffer particularly relished entering into contract and salary negotiations with rabbis. Gaffer and Temple Beth Hillel President Saul White, a distributor for a chain of groceries, prided themselves particularly on making sure that rabbis never got the better of the congregation. Gaffer and White respected Zelermyer but thought of him at times as an *alte bubah,* or old grandmother; to the rough-hewn officers, the young rabbi's conciliatory and soothing tones— which helped establish the excellent rapport with elderly congregants of which he had always been proud—seemed to lack a certain manliness. Nevertheless, the officers were happy with their choice, at least for the present time, and they were determined that he not abandon the congregation under false pretenses. *(That had happened once before with a clever rabbi by the name of*

Sidney Steiman; citing ill health, Steiman had asked to be released from his contract only to resurface shortly after in a prestigious pulpit in Indianapolis. Gaffer and White were determined never again to be hoodwinked by a rabbi.)

Early on the Sunday morning after the wounded rabbi's appearance in synagogue, Samuel Gaffer arrived at the rabbi's home. "I know what happened and I want it in every paper in the country," he shot out. Zelermyer shook his head; the man before him, he thought, not only lacked tact but rarely showed up for services. "No newspapers," the rabbi firmly responded. Gaffer's agitation escalated and he demanded the rabbi do as he was told. "This will kill the synagogue," Zelermyer explained. "If a rabbi is this vulnerable, who will want to go to *shul* here anymore?"[3] Gaffer's response hit Zelermyer with more force than had the acid just forty-eight hours before. "Don't worry about that, rabbi," Gaffer said in a tone of sarcastic reassurance. "The synagogue has been sold. The city of Boston bought it for a public school." Zelermyer was suddenly aware of an acutely painful tightening of his facial muscles beneath the bandages. He stared through his uncovered left eye at the wall past Gaffer. By an enormous effort of will, the rabbi fought back tears of rage.

Bernard Hyatt, managing editor of the *Jewish Advocate,* a Boston weekly newspaper published since 1902, was staring at a mountainous stack of mail when his Mattapan source called in the report of the attack on Rabbi Zelermyer. Hyatt thanked the caller for the information and proceeded with the task at hand. Sliding a silver-colored letter opener into the creases of one manila envelope after another, Hyatt extracted a seemingly endless succession of publicity photos clipped to news releases and began arranging them in piles on his desk. The *Advocate,* as it was known throughout the community, boasted in its promotional ads that it published more photos each week than *Life* magazine. The photos, however, were almost without exception "grin and grab" shots of wealthy philanthropists presenting checks to the grateful representatives of Jewish organizations and charities; temple brotherhood members standing three or four abreast at an award ceremony; or ladies auxiliary members seated with a guest speaker around a samovar or some other unusual centerpiece.

Control of the news in the Boston Jewish community was largely in the hands of *Advocate* publisher Alexander Brin and executive editor Joseph Weisberg. At the age of nineteen, Brin had made a name for himself as a reporter on the old *Boston Traveller* with his extensive coverage of the 1913 lynching in Georgia of Leo Frank, a Jewish pencil factory manager wrongly accused in the murder of a young female employee, Mary Phagan. Impressed by the young journalist, Justice Louis Brandeis, America's premier Jewish jurist, handpicked Brin for the top slot at the *Advocate*. Alexander Brin, however, never seemed to apply to the Jewish world the rules of aggressive news gathering that he had learned as a general assignment reporter. Once at the *Advocate's* helm, he traversed the chasm between journalism and public relations with one cheerful and profitable leap.

Bernard Hyatt and his office mate, *Advocate* city editor Lou Brin, were two younger journalists with a lot more to offer than their ability to cut and paste. Hyatt, the Annapolis-born son of a wealthy and devout businessman, had been a paratrooper in World War II and later earned a law degree at Harvard. Brin, a rugged and quick-witted iconoclast, was an expert on the Massachusetts criminal justice system, respected for his fairness by both warders and cons alike. But Brin checked his keen observations and political savvy at the door of his uncle's newspaper. With the exception of an occasional trenchant editorial, neither man was able to put his vision into the paper.

The dilemma facing the *Jewish Advocate* was the same one facing the editors of the roughly one hundred Jewish weekly newspapers across the country: with half of the publications owned and published by the local Jewish federations, there was little likelihood that independent journalism could flourish. The situation was often no better at the independently owned papers (like the *Advocate*), which depended heavily on the advertising revenue of the Combined Jewish Philanthropies (CJP) and its constituent agencies. When it came to reporting Jewish news, it was understood, community leaders wanted publicity, not substance.

One prominent Jewish editor described the continual Catch-22 faced by his colleagues in the field:

An important person arrives at the editor's office with a photograph of himself and press release on his appointment to the presidency of a local country club and demands it appears in the next issue. "Do you subscribe to the paper?" the editor asks. "No," the man replies. "It's full of all this PR junk." Thus the dilemma. If you don't print what the local *makher* wants you to, he won't subscribe. If you do print what he and his friends want you to, he won't subscribe. In the first case he's angry at you and in the second case he has no respect for you. Either way you lose. And so does he. And so does the community.[4]

Alexander Brin trusted Hyatt, his son-in-law, to be prudent despite his close friendship with the iconoclastic Lou Brin. The unwritten rule at the *Advocate* was that no local story was important enough to alienate the major contributors to the federation. (Reports on controversial events in Jewish communities in Israel, Europe, or other American cities were fair game for all the Jewish weekly newspapers, but local news was generated in the publicity departments of the local Jewish communal and charitable organizations, such as the Anti-Defamation League of B'nai B'rith, the Jewish Community Council, and the American Jewish Committee. In that way, no major donor need ever suffer embarrassment in the hometown Jewish newspaper.) The very location of the *Advocate,* on Causeway Street at the edge of Boston's Little Italy, was, tellingly, miles from the Jewish population center.

Throughout 1967 and 1968 Hyatt had received daily phone calls from Dorchester and Mattapan residents detailing the plight of Jews in the neighborhoods. Elderly victims of assaults and purse snatchings by black adolescents were quick to accuse the mainstream Jewish leaders of turning their backs on lower-middle-class Jewry. But each caller, Hyatt recalled years later, would conclude his tale with an appeal *not* to publicize the account. "Don't put this in the paper, but a Hebrew school teacher at Beth El was beaten up by *schwartzes* after class today," a typical caller would say. With each call, Hyatt's inner conflict was deepened. How precarious was the position of Mattapan's and Dorchester's Jews? Were these simple acts of vandalism or were greater forces at work in the community? To what extent was racism within the Jewish community responsible for the neighborhood's travails? Why did the victims themselves not want to publicize the dangerous conditions? These questions and many like them gnawed at managing editor Hyatt as he passed his mornings and afternoons processing photos and captions of mostly suburban Jews bestowing one honor or another upon themselves for charitable works.[5]

Hyatt was deeply disturbed by the news of the acid attack on Zelermyer. The young rabbi was a frequent visitor to the *Advocate* newsroom and was well liked by the staff, particularly the paper's society editor, Cecille Markell, whom the editors hoped to fix up with the unattached rabbi. If a vicious antisemitic daylight assault on a dedicated rabbi wasn't news for a Jewish community newspaper, then Hyatt believed he had no right making a living in the newspaper business. The reticence of Boston's Jewish community would only lead to greater losses and suffering, he later remembered thinking. One need look no further back than one generation to see the dreadful effects on European Jewry of the *"sha sha"* ("hush hush") mentality.

Hyatt's phone call to Zelermyer caught the rabbi in a similar state of mind. The days following the attack had been a time of soul searching. During the early evening hours he continued to walk the streets of Mattapan in order to "show the flag." "Is that really you?" neighborhood youngsters queried the bandaged clergyman. "We heard you'd quit." The rabbi chucked the curious children under their chins and reassured them. "I'm staying right here with you," he told them.

Hyatt convinced Zelermyer to prepare a statement on the incident for the paper's next issue. It would be printed prominently, he assured him, regardless of resistance from community leaders, including his own publisher. "Has the organized Jewish community done its job as far as Mattapan's Jews are concerned?" Hyatt asked the still-reluctant rabbi. "If not, it's your moral obligation to tell people about it."[6] The editor and the rabbi agreed to meet two days later at the *Advocate*'s office to review the report.

Zelermyer woke early on July 1, the day he was scheduled to deliver his article. He had ruminated the night before about placing a courtesy call to Rabbi Samuel Korff, spiritual leader of Congregation Kehillath Jacob, Mattapan's largest Orthodox synagogue. Korff was a powerful rabbi and he would likely be angered if he were to read the report in the *Advocate* without prior knowledge of the incident. Since 1947, when he was appointed the first Jewish chaplain to the Boston Fire Department by Boston's irascible Mayor James M. Curley, and as the force behind the Rabbinical Court of the Associated Synagogues of Massachusetts, Korff had shown a penchant for rough-and-tumble politics. His prominence in seeking justice for the South End tenants in their battles with the Mindick brothers had also convinced the Jewish community's liberal elite that Korff was no garden-variety Orthodox right-winger. In Boston many a bleary-eyed rabbi had reached for a telephone receiver at some ungodly hour only to hear the customary Korff greeting, "How are you, my friend?" Korff never felt the need to introduce himself; instead, he would launch into a spiel about the need for a nationally recognized program to certify packaged foods as kosher or about some other project for which he needed support. Zelermyer, therefore, felt a certain sense of satisfaction as he dialed Korff's number shortly before 7 A.M. "Rabbi, I have something of great importance to discuss with you," said Zelermyer. "Who is this?" demanded Korff. "It's Gerry Zelermyer, rabbi. I need to talk to you," said Zelermyer, smiling to himself. "It's you, Gerry? It's important? Come right over," said Korff.

Korff's home at 573 Norfolk Street was less than a five-minute ride from Zelermyer's. Most of the buildings on the approximately three-quarter-mile-long street, which ran perpendicular to Morton Street, were two- and three-family homes. Korff, however, lived in a spacious, twelve-room single-family house. Korff, who looked ten years older than his age of fifty-six, answered the bell wearing the long prayer shawl and phylacteries traditionally worn by observant Jewish men during morning prayers. He ushered Zelermyer into the living room and then turned, by custom, to the east to continue his morning prayers. "You talk while I *daven* (pray)," Korff stated to the startled rabbi. Feeling awkward and snubbed by having to describe his assault to a praying man, Zelermyer nonetheless recounted the incident and his decision to write about it in the *Jewish Advocate*. Throughout, Korff continued the Hebrew murmur and rhythmic sway characteristic of devout Orthodox Jews at prayer. The ritual completed, Korff removed his prayer shawl and turned to the younger rabbi. "Gerry, I know about this attack on you. My wife was shopping on the Avenue and everybody was talking about it," Korff said in his still discernible Eastern European accent. "I told her, 'I must call Gerry.'" Korff then stood silently for a moment staring at the younger rabbi. "So you're going down to North Station now with your article for the *Jewish Advocate*. Their office is right near Mass General Hospital. Could I get a ride with you? I have an appointment."

The rabbis spoke little on the drive downtown. Zelermyer dropped Korff at the hospital's main entrance on Cambridge Street. Korff's first stop was a public phone; he rang up the *Advocate* and demanded to speak with the managing editor. Dispensing with his usual "How are you, my friend?" Korff got right to the point. "How dare you take an article about Mattapan from Zelermyer?" he challenged. "I've been a rabbi in this community for thirty years and you take an article from a *pisher*—an upstart!"[7] But Hyatt was in no mood for intimidation.

The July 3, 1969, issue of the *Jewish Advocate* carried a page-one article under the headline "Attack on Mattapan Rabbi in Home." The piece, under Zelermyer's byline, gave a brief description of the event and a longer analysis of what was taking place in the neighborhood. The article attacked Jewish leaders for treating the area's lower-middle-class Jews as "flagging stepchildren" and went even further: "The sad fact is that the community beyond has sounded a requiem for our area through almost wholesale indifference to our plight."

The article sent immediate shock waves through the leadership of the Boston Jewish community. Zelermyer's first call was from David Pokross, a corporate attorney and the new president of the Combined Jewish Philanthropies. Like most Jewish agencies, the federation had an insatiable need for positive publicity. Successful fund-raising was based on the ability to project an image of caring and compassion, and Zelermyer's charge of indifference was an embarrassment. Boston, in particular, didn't need the aggravation; in terms of fund-raising, Boston's Jewish federation had long been a weak sister among its counterparts nationwide. Pokross invited Zelermyer to lunch at the CJP headquarters at 72 Franklin Street on the edge of Boston's downtown financial district. Expecting a private conversation with Pokross, Zelermyer was surprised when he was ushered into a conference room with about a dozen Jewish community leaders and heads of constituent agencies. Some presented documents explaining the vocational and family services available to Jews of Mattapan and Dorchester; others described the quiet negotiations under way with city and black leaders to facilitate a peaceful transfer of Jews from the neighborhoods. Not one leader, Zelermyer later recalled, addressed the need to stabilize Jewish institutions, particularly synagogues, already in the area. A sullen anger rose in the 28-year-old rabbi as he listened to the litany from the Jewish leadership. According to Zelermyer, Pokross then asked him if he would care to retract the statements made in the *Advocate*. A calm descended on the young rabbi, not unlike the feeling he'd experienced shortly before the arrival of the Sabbath. "Not one syllable," he said.[8] Years later, Pokross would recall the meeting in different terms, stressing that it was convened to discuss substantive issues of safety in regard to the welfare of the Jews of Mattapan and Dorchester.

July and August were months of confusion for the congregants of Beth Hillel. Some details of the secret negotiations between temple officers, led by Samuel Gaffer, and the Boston School Committee, which was struggling to solve its classroom shortage, began to filter down to the grass roots. With little or no hard information available, rumors began to circulate; most frequently repeated was a report that a black power group had threatened to bomb the synagogue if it was sold to the city rather than handed over to the black community. No one seemed to have sufficient information to confirm or quash rumors. Zelermyer felt helpless and chided himself for not seeing signs that a handful of temple officers, with virtually no guidelines from the rabbi or general membership, had for months been planning the synagogue's disposition. Back in April Zelermyer had come upon a man taking measurements of the floor space of the main chapel and Hebrew school annex. He had immediately called Gaffer, who instructed him harshly that he was not to speak to any people found surveying in the synagogue. Foolishly, the rabbi had complied.

During this period of secret negotiations, Gaffer, White, and other temple officers remained tight-lipped about the sale of the temple and the future of the congregation, with the exception of assuring members that there would be services for the High Holy Days of *Rosh Hashanah* and *Yom Kippur* in early September.

Zelermyer, who had faced down the entire leadership of the federation over the importance of maintaining long-term commitment to the Jewish community in Mattapan, was totally ineffective in trying to pry loose further information from the officers of his own temple.

Much of the mystery was cleared on August 20 when a semitrailer loaded with school furniture pulled up in front of the synagogue and began unloading desks, chairs, files, and boxes of supplies. A reporter from the *Boston Globe* observed the process along with shocked Jewish residents of the triple-deckers along Morton Street. Zelermyer was thankful for the presence of the reporter; along with the rest of Boston, he would at least be able to learn of some of the details of the sale. That evening, an agitated Zelermyer drove to a news kiosk in Harvard Square, one of the earliest drop-off points for the evening *Globe*. The lead paragraph of the story read: "The arrival today of a truckload of furniture was the first indication to most of the congregation of Temple Beth Hillel that the temple had been sold to the City of Boston for $450,000." The report attributed to Samuel Gaffer the statement that the decision to sell was based on the "changing neighborhood."[9]

Zelermyer went immediately to the temple. Although the news report had indicated that congregants would be able to use the chapel for several more months, he no longer believed that his papers or documents were safe in the temple office. He packed his diplomas and personal effects in a cardboard box. As he walked out the front door of the temple, his eyes scanning the heavily trafficked street, he paused not only to consider what would become of Mattapan—but what would become of him.

Zelermyer sleepwalked his way through August and early September. Increasingly uncomfortable in the parsonage, he moved his clothes and books to his parents' summer home at Nantasket Beach, twenty miles south of Boston. His somnambulance was broken with the news of the death of Rabbi Joseph Shubow, a popular rabbi who'd served Temple B'nai Moshe in the Brighton section of the city. Members of the Brighton synagogue approached Zelermyer, asking him to conduct the *Rosh Hashanah* services for the bereft congregation. When Zelermyer explained that Beth Hillel would remain officially open until December and that his first obligation was to his temple, the board members beseeched him to apply for the pulpit at B'nai Moshe. Zelermyer had two years remaining on his contract, at $9,500 each year. "I should just move to Miami Beach and let them pay my salary for a couple of years," the young rabbi joked with friends. But quietly he began to open the lines of communication with the new synagogue.

Gaffer and White were infuriated when they learned of the offer from the Brighton synagogue. Again, without consulting the rabbi, they had made arrangements to transfer the assets of Beth Hillel to Temple B'nai Torah in West Roxbury, a stable neighborhood on the western fringe of Boston. They insisted that Zelermyer go along to minister to the hybrid congregation despite the fact that the West Roxbury temple already had an experienced rabbi. Zelermyer flatly refused, causing several nasty exchanges between board members of the Brighton, West Roxbury, and Mattapan synagogues.

In September 1969 *Rosh Hashanah,* the Jewish new year, which marks a day of reflection and repentance, found the congregation of Temple Beth Hillel spiritually enervated. The ledger books kept by the temple officers proved far more compelling that year than the book of life in which God inscribes the Jewish people. With great fanfare Gaffer and the officers announced the purchase of $300,000 worth of Israel Bonds with a portion of the proceeds from the sale of the temple building. But angry members of the congregation, including congregant Benjamin Resnick, a private detective, insisted on seeing all documentation related to the sale. Who would redeem the bonds and what were the plans for the additional $125,000? the congregants demanded to know. Gaffer tried to assuage the fears and suspicions of the congregation, explaining that the monies now belonged to the West Roxbury congregation. Resnick and others swore they would call in the Commonwealth's attorney general to scrutinize all aspects of the sale. No investigation ever took place and no charges were ever brought.

Zelermyer had hoped, as his final act at Beth Hillel, to turn his congregation back toward spirituality for the High Holy Days. On *Rosh Hashanah* he stood on the temple's *bimah* and began the opening hymn of *Yigdal,* a liturgical poem that emphasizes the foundation of divine faith and Torah. Zelermyer chanted the final verses of the prayer—"God knows all the acts and thoughts of man . . . He rewards and punishes . . . Messiah will come . . . There will be resurrection''—when he heard a commotion at the back of the chapel. Peering over the pews, he made out the figure of Samuel Gaffer and another congregant. Here on *Rosh Hashanah,* the birthday of the world, the congregants of Beth Hillel were exchanging punches.

The "Dirty Little Secret"

Class Conflict,
1969–1970

Activities in the rambling yellow house on College Avenue in Somerville, just a few miles northwest of Boston, were on the cutting edge of Judaism in the United States. When it was founded as a "community seminary" in 1968, young Jews from Greater Boston, many of them studying in prestigious local institutions, were searching for an authentic community that would not reflect in any way the materialistic trappings of the suburban synagogues of their childhoods. Havurat Shalom, as it was named by its founders, was the physical home for just a few young people, but it was the spiritual home for scores of others from local universities who attended intimate weekly services and study sessions there. Havurat Shalom would become an influential model for changes in the American synagogue in the following years. Rather than accept the large edifices and formal services in plush auditoriums led by remote rabbis, the Havurah set an example for more personal prayer and study groups within synagogue life.

The devotees of Havurat Shalom seemed to reject the lifestyle of their parents in favor of that of their grandparents—pouring hot wax for Sabbath candles, kneading dough for ceremonial loaves of hallah, and testing the weight and lay of cloth for prayer shawls. Young rabbis throughout Greater Boston, particularly those drawn to the countercultural values of the late 1960s, taught courses at Havurat Shalom and participated in the spirited singing and dancing on Jewish festivals. They took special delight that Jewish students were being drawn more deeply into their own mystical roots than into the Eastern religions championed by many segments of the counterculture.

Many of the students involved in the renewal movement had a deep suspicion of the Jewish communal power structure. On the lighthearted festival of Purim, the students created elaborate spiels poking fun at mainstream Jewry's organizations and catered social affairs. But unlike their more assimilated contemporaries, they also yearned to be accepted by their elders. They acknowledged the good work performed by federations and their Jewish hospitals and social services but remained convinced that "the Jewish establishment" could never provide identity, inspiration, or leadership for them. Many of the city's brightest and most energetic students, including Reconstructionist Rabbinical Seminary President Arthur Green and author William Novak, were among the Havurah's earliest members. Most had grown up outside of Boston. Others, like Michael Strassfeld, whose rabbi father had left his Dorchester congregation in disappointment and moved to wealthy Marblehead, had apparently chosen to repopulate the ghetto of their youth but this time with like-minded colleagues rather than the denizens of Blue Hill Avenue.

The problems faced by Jews in Mattapan and Dorchester were seemingly invisible to both the community elite and the young intellectuals who vowed to act as their conscience. For those who sat cross-legged on the pillow-strewn floor of Havurat Shalom, the emphasis on spirituality defined the lines of the Jewish community. For the federation leaders who frequented the boardroom of the Combined Jewish Philanthropies, the Jewish community was organized along the lines of different categories of "givers" and "takers." Mattapan's Jews, with their houses and paid-up mortgages, were not "takers"; nor were they likely to be found in the category of major benefactors. The Jewish poor of Dorchester more closely resembled an earlier immigrant generation than a category of Jews calling for new understanding and the allocation of resources. When it came to Mattapan and Dorchester Jewry, both federation and Havurah leaders had developed their own boundaries of moral concern and in so doing ignored the "dirty little secret" of class division within the Jewish community.

In mid-November 1969 the Council of Jewish Federations and Welfare Funds was scheduled to convene in Boston. Major Jewish leaders from across the country would be arriving for plenary sessions on scores of topics relating to the needs and future of American and world Jewry. Members of Havurat Shalom and other groups committed to Jewish renewal approached the organizers of the conference and asked for an opportunity to express their concerns. The request was, at first, refused. When student leaders threatened to demonstrate at the site, however, the federation's conference planners conceded.

Hillel Levine, the spokesman of the motley coalition of outsiders who now wanted in, struck a familial tone with the delegates:

> You grew up during the Depression and always wanted us to have what you did not. You worked your way through college with great difficulty. You lived through the difficult years of World War II, knew of the death of six million Jews, for which we cannot envy you. You enjoyed the post-war prosperity, made it to the suburbs, built synagogues and centers. You want us to be a little bit Jewish and bring you a lot of *nahus* [pride and joy]. But perhaps you would be more interested in knowing who we are. We were born during and shortly after the war. The Holocaust made a deep impression on our young minds, as did the new-felt pride in the state of Israel. We had the best set of blocks, the shiniest bicycle, and piano lessons. We did well in school. We went to Hebrew school and occasionally synagogue, but found them dull. There were few exciting models for us in the Jewish community, little opportunity to give expression to our youthful ideals. In contrast, the larger world was exciting, a labyrinth of mystery and challenge. The warmth of an old grandfather, the tranquility of

a Sabbath at home, the moral indignation of a verse from the prophets may have given us second thoughts about our Jewish identity, but on the whole we knew where the action was and where it was not. We went down to Mississippi for summers, marched against the war. The Jewish publicists spilled seas of ink bemoaning our alienation. Rarely, though, was an honest appraisal made of the source of our alienation. Perhaps it was a sign of our health that we were not attracted to a Jewish life devoid of intellectual and spiritual energy.

Levine delivered an appeal for increased monies for Jewish education, a field that received less than 15 percent of federation funds in 1967. He also made a plea for greater support for Jewish campus life and experimental communities that focused on spiritual experiences in imaginative settings. His call for a reconsideration of Jewish priorities and community services reflected the needs of a younger generation of Jews, "at home" in American life. Born after the Depression, they took for granted the American welfare state and were comfortable with its institutions. With fewer personal experiences of antisemitism than the members of their parents' generation, they were fully confident of their ability to succeed in the larger world while establishing for themselves and others meaningful Jewish communities.

The federation leaders at first viewed these intruders as another interest group petitioning for a bigger piece of the pie. They countered that they were already doing everything imaginable for students. "We truly care about Jewish students," a New York delegate told Levine. "We have 256 agencies in my city including those where a student can have his appendix removed and a mental hospital where he can be committed." Similar responses from agitated delegates further alienated the student protesters. "It's not our neuroses or our ruptured appendices that we want to share with you," Levine responded. "It is our vitality, our enthusiasm, our vision that we wish to share."

Despite their difficulties penetrating the inflexible mindsets of the federation leaders, the students were heartened by their ability to seize the podium And despite their initial resistance, the federation leaders felt they had spanned the generation gap with the students, perhaps more successfully than they'd managed with their own children. The leaders were truly surprised that the students cared enough to attend the assembly. After some cheek pinching, figuratively and otherwise, declarations about turning points, and a head-spinning proposal for a $100 million fund to provide the seed money for spiritual renewal projects, the delegates went home.

Back at his Harvard office, Levine told of the students' victory to one of his closest and most assimilated friends. The aristocratic-looking student who was to become a distinguished professor, listened attentively to Levine but was singularly unimpressed. "I wouldn't give a dime for your efforts. Jewish renewal? I went to prep school with the sons of members of the Cabinet and Congress and I know what antisemitism is all about. Have you heard about this guy Kahane who is protecting those Jews in Dorchester and Mattapan? He's a real radical rabbi. I just sent five dollars to the Jewish Defense League." Levine was horrified by his friend's support for the violence-preaching rabbi. He did not have the vaguest sense of what his fellow student was talking about. Dorchester and Mattapan? Wasn't that part of Boston, somewhere?

Shortly after dinnertime on the evening before Thanksgiving 1969, knots of elderly congregants began arriving at Congregation Chevra Shas, a modest red brick *shul* on Dorchester's Ashton Street. Muggings had become so common of late that Dorchester's elderly Jews scanned cabinets for household items that might double as instruments of self-defense. Because outrunning the young muggers was out of the question, survival, they believed, might depend on a good *spritz* of hair spray in the eyes of an attacker or a solid *zetz* on the nose with a ring of heavy metal keys. Chevra Shas congregants, like sixty-two-year-old Louis Dickstein, were tired of fear. Back in the 1930s Dickstein had been able to pick up a few extra bucks fighting as a bantamweight under the name Kid Lewis. By 1969 Kid Lewis's legs had been gone for at least three decades; his punch fared only a little better. A few weeks earlier two black teens had taunted and assaulted him on Woodrow Avenue. Lewis instinctively threw a hook—his knock-out punch. It felt good landing one on the jaw of an attacker, but it exacted nothing more than a momentary shock. The boys knocked Dickstein down and kicked him repeatedly. It was one hell of a beating, but he got off easier this time than when another youthful pair had sprayed mace directly into his face and then worked him over.

On this late November evening Dickstein and several dozen Chevra Shas congregants had come to hear the teachings of a Brooklyn-based Orthodox rabbi. This was not, however, to be a lesson on Talmud or on Jewish festivals from a distinguished out-of-town *melamed* (teacher). They came, instead, with the expectation of meeting a *shkotz;* they envisioned a seething wildman with a 38-calibre pistol tucked in his waistband and wearing a trademark blue beret and flyer's jacket with a shoulder patch depicting a square clenched fist on a Star of David. They found instead a 37-year-old rabbi, attired conservatively in suit jacket and slacks, a small knitted skull cap fastened with a bobby pin at the back of his head. Several wondered if this thin, soft-spoken man could really be the ferocious Rabbi Meir Kahane of the Jewish Defense League.

The rabbi was equally unimpressed by his audience. He'd already downed his usual daily complement of eight or ten cups of coffee and appeared jittery and anxious to get started. He looked out over his potential recruits, few were younger than sixty.

"A Jew has a right to be free, just like anybody else," Kahane began.[1] The simple statement was no longer self-evident in North Dorchester. In recent weeks scores of elderly Jews had been beaten and one had been shot. Each week an average of thirty elderly Jews in the neighborhood suffered assaults or robberies. Many knew of neighbors who no longer left their homes, not even to attend the morning or evening services required of the observant. Kahane's simple acknowledgment that they were no longer free men and women was the first such admission from any Jewish leader; someone, at last, was taking notice. More importantly, he offered hope. "We have a reputation that we are Jewish Panthers," he told them. "Never deny it. The more people say it, the safer you are."

On this night, however, Kahane had no intention of pinning the neighborhood's problems on the black community. Like his audience, the rabbi, a Queens native, lived in a changing neighborhood. He was embittered not so much by disaffected black youths who resorted to crime but by Jewish neighbors who panicked and pulled up roots because of the very presence of black neighbors. Kahane urged the audience members to establish a board of responsible leaders—"not kooks and racists"[2]—and to set up self-defense and anti-crime task forces. Race, he stressed, was not the issue. The rabbi's focus caught many of the Chevra Shas congregants off guard. Expecting a reinforcement of their own racial views, they were treated instead to an assault on "establishment Jews" who had failed to organize an effective response to the alarming increase in street crime. It was a message the rabbi had delivered repeatedly in New York, Cleveland, and Philadelphia. "They [Jewish leaders] don't live in areas where there is a nightmare of chaos and crime and violence," Kahane railed. "We are out to help those Jews that do live in those areas, and if we're called names, so be it. We will live with this sin."[3]

Kahane had founded the Jewish Defense League (JDL) just over a year before his appearance at the Dorchester synagogue. Since then the organization had grown to a national membership of seven thousand largely on the basis of a series of headline-grabbing confrontations and publicity stunts in New York City. Despite Kahane's attempts to deemphasize race, the greatest recruitment drive for the JDL had come in the wake of black–Jewish tensions arising from the 1968 United Federation of Teachers strike in New York City. In the Ocean Hill–Brownsville area of Brooklyn black parents had not only refused to support the largely Jewish teachers' union but had formed school governing boards as a way to exert "community control" over the public schools. Among their first acts was the ouster of many longtime Jewish teachers and administrators. Black activists carefully interviewed replacement teachers, probing for any sign of paternalism or other traits deleterious to black pride. Ousted teachers charged that black antisemitism, not educational philosophy, was at the root of the review and firings. As proof, teachers' union president Albert Shanker released to the press blatantly antisemitic handbills that had been stuffed in the mailboxes of Jewish teachers in the Ocean Hill–Brownsville system. The anger over the school strike and "community control" spilled over into other New York neighborhoods where Jews and blacks lived. It was clear that many blacks now perceived former allies in the civil rights movement, like Shanker, as more concerned with maintaining the economic status quo than providing opportunities for black schoolchildren. A growing number of Jews were convinced, on the other hand, that lingering within every black "community control" supporter was another pathological antisemite.

Kahane's troops adopted the guerrilla theater tactics of the left to exploit the perceived threat posed by blacks to the hard-earned economic advances of middle-class Jews. In June 1969 JDL members wearing baseball uniforms and spikes picketed the major league baseball draft taking place in the Americana Hotel in New York. Holding aloft signs reading, "Merit, shmerit, we want our quota," League members launched their irreverent attack on black demands for representative quotas in universities and municipal jobs. JDL spokesmen first demanded that the Mets field a team in which Jews were represented in accordance with their overall population in the city—26 percent. "I want to play second base," shouted one JDL man. "So what if I can't hit. I'm motivated." As other League members urged him on, the man reached for the top: "To hell with second base. No more tokenism. I want to pitch," he demanded.[4]

The hostility between striving blacks and middle-class Jews played perfectly to Kahane's vision of the American city. "The city is polarized almost beyond hope—there's anger, hate, frustration," he had noted. "The Jew is the weakest link in the white chain and the black militant knows that few non-Jews are concerned with the Jew's plight. The Jew has always been more liberal than other white ethnic groups. So now most Jewish neighborhoods are integrated, and the militant blacks there practice terror, extortion and violence."[5]

JDL histrionics would have meant little had they not been backed up with muscle. Kahane had cleverly adopted the phrase "Never again" to symbolize the League's promise that Jews could no longer be slaughtered in silence as they had in the death camps of Nazi Europe. League members backed up their promises with action, such as wading into a neo-Nazi counterdemonstration during an Israel Independence Day Parade on New York's Fifth Avenue, tearing apart "Gas the Jews" signs, and hospitalizing several of the antisemites in the process.

Months earlier Student Nonviolent Coordinating Committee (SNCC) leader James Forman had demanded "reparations" from Jewish synagogues, landlords, and store owners for perceived economic crimes against the black community. The payment of reparations for crimes committed on the basis of race or ethnicity was an especially emotional one in the Jewish community. For decades Jews had debated the moral correctness of the reparations paid by the German government to Jewish Holocaust survivors; some victims had shunned the payments as hush money. But the very notion that Jewish landlords and shopkeepers had done to blacks what Nazis had done to Jews infuriated those with even the most basic understanding of the significance of six million Jews in European death camps. Cautiously worded press releases from major Jewish organizations rejected Forman's demands, but the JDL seized the issue. Reports had circulated that Forman would present his platform at Temple Emanu-El, one of Manhattan's wealthiest and most liberal congregations. Kahane's forces quickly mobilized. On the day of the scheduled appearance, approximately forty JDL foot soldiers took up strategic positions around the synagogue. Some stood silently in position, baseball bats at the ready; others, their fingers clenched around brass knuckles, patrolled the perimeter. Forman, prudently, stayed away.

In subsequent weeks the JDL members trumpeted their victory with a series of subway advertisements showing stern JDL soldiers posed in front of Emanu-El under the legend: "Is this any way for nice Jewish boys to behave?" In response, the printed message read: "Maybe—just maybe—nice people build their own road to Auschwitz." The advertisements shocked the leaders of Jewish organizations who had directed so much of their energies into maintaining positive communal relations.

Later, on a local radio talk show, Kahane said that the message of the ads was intended more for Jews still living in the inner city than for black radicals, who, he believed, were displaying signs of growing antisemitism. "We wanted to get an idea across about that Jewish boy who suffers daily in Crown Heights, or Williamsburg, or Queens, or in the Bronx because he wears the yarmulka, who gets beaten up because he's an easy mark—well baby, there's a new Jew."[6] Kahane refused to relinquish an inch in his publicity war with mainstream Jewish groups. He called for $100,000 from the Anti-Defamation League of B'nai B'rith and American Jewish Congress to set up citizen patrols in changing neighborhoods across the country. The idea was roundly rejected by Jewish groups in a flurry of press releases labeling the JDL as an organization of dangerous vigilantes. A typical response read:

The Anti-Defamation League, in its 56 years of existence, has always worked effectively and successfully with law enforcement agencies. Where crime and violence exist in this country, they are problems which affect not Jews alone but American citizens of every race and religion. If all groups were to form their own so-called "defense" leagues, this country would be headed toward national polarization and violence fast approaching anarchy. The Anti-Defamation League will have no part in the Jewish Defense League's business of hysteria. The Jewish Defense League is a vigilante group and its activities are no less harmful and dangerous because it has called itself "Jewish."[7]

Despite their provocative protests, Kahane and the JDL understood one aspect of the American Jewish community that seemed beyond the comprehension of the mainstream groups: the presence and pressures of class conflict. In Boston citywide class issues would be largely ignored until the 1985 publication of J. Anthony Lukas's *Common Ground,* a book that chronicled the battle over school desegregation in Boston during the mid-1970s. Lukas would place responsibility for much of the city's agonies at the doorstep of successful Irish politicians and judges who had long since abandoned ethnic neighborhoods for the orderliness of town and country. People left behind in working-class Irish neighborhoods, like Charlestown and South Boston, were expected to bear the brunt of school integration while nearby suburban classrooms remained almost entirely white.

Such lessons had been available for learning in Dorchester's Jewish community at least six years before the violent episodes over school desegregation in the mid-1970s. No one, however, was listening. Suburban Jews, free from the crime and conflict of the city, were busy forging civil rights alliances with blacks of equal stature and accomplishment. The brunt of integration, however, was shouldered by poorer Jews for whom issues of basic safety outweighed ideology. The feelings of abandonment, in both Irish and Jewish neighborhoods, quickly turned into bitterness at one's own. At City Hall Plaza, Boston Irish would pelt U.S. Sen. Edward Kennedy, the embodiment of Irish political success, with eggs and tomatoes as he tried to address an anti-busing rally. And in working-class Jewish neighborhoods across the northeast, residents embraced the JDL. Lukas would state the dilemma with ringing clarity during a speech at Boston University in 1988: "The centripetal pull of shared ethnicity may be less powerful than the centrifugal force of social class. Class is America's dirty little secret, pervasive and persistent yet rarely confronted in public policy or judicial intervention."[8]

The JDL could not be trusted to keep America's "dirty little secret." In speech after speech, JDL members stressed that the plight of Jews in Dorchester and other changing neighborhoods was caused, in large measure, by organizational abandonment; their emphasis was almost without exception on issues of class. "Those who sneer at us are often self-conscious Jews who feel more comfortable in their assimilationist environment," charged former JDL national publicity director Samuel Shoshan. "The fallacy in their thinking lies in that they look for acceptance and love of the Jew by the gentile world by painting the portrait of the Jew as 'we are just like you—therefore, love us and take us into your country club.' "[9]

In Boston and other cities, the pull of shared ethnicity with suburban Jewry felt by inner-city Jews weakened with news of each fresh assault by ruffians. The drawing power of the JDL, on the other hand, increased. The crude but largely accurate class analysis of the JDL went unheeded by the major Jewish organizations, who instead rushed to equate the JDL with lawless vigilantism. A policy statement by the National Jewish Community Relations Advisory Council, an umbrella group composed of nine national and eighty-two local Jewish community organizations, condemned "the paramilitary operations of the Jewish Defense League as destructive of public order and contributory to divisiveness and terror." The Synagogue Council of America advised its members to reject Kahane and his followers on the grounds that "lawlessness of vigilantes no more makes for a defense of Jewish or other interests than the [black] riot makes for the rectification of social injustices." On rare occasions, prominent leaders would step gingerly into the class debate raised by the JDL. Rabbi Balfour Brickner and Albert Vorspan, directors of the Commission on Interfaith Activities for the Reform movement, tried to assuage lower-middle-class Jews by urging patience, since "America is going through a difficult period." The eruption of violence in changing neighborhoods, they argued, is directed at whites, not

Jews. "It is much easier for a man to believe that he is the victim of violence because he is Jewish rather than it is for him to believe that he is a victim because he is white, even if the latter explanation may be closer to the truth."[10]

Brickner and Vorspan, both urbane and respected leaders of Reform Jewry, had taken the "politically correct" stance for the 1960s, but in so doing they had clearly ignored escalating black antisemitism in the inner city. Police reports of housebreaks in Jewish homes in Dorchester frequently described antisemitic scrawlings on walls and mirrors. In many cases the messages were aimed directly at the remnant communities: "Move Jew" was painted in three-foot-high letters on the living room walls of ransacked homes; chants of "old Jew, old Jew" rang in the ears of elderly mugging victims. But in their discussions of the problem, the Reform leaders chose to refer to such attacks as "so-called crimes of violence."[11] Inner-city Jews began to wonder if they had to be murdered before they could win even marginal recognition from the leaders of American Jewry.

From its inception the New England chapter of the Jewish Defense League was an odd conglomeration of Jewish mystics, karate enthusiasts, talmudic students, and Vietnam veterans. At its head was Rabbi Marvin Antelman, a thirty-three-year-old Orthodox rabbi and one of the most controversial characters on the local Jewish scene. Antelman was the very antithesis of a mainstream Jewish leader; intense and impolitic, he could jump in a single sentence from an analysis of false messiahs in Jewish history to the threatened existence of inner-city Jewry. His conversational references to arcane Jewish principles and his frequent lapses into Hebrew and Yiddish made him at times comprehensible only to those with the deepest Jewish backgrounds.

For years, New England Jewish leaders had steered a wide berth of Antelman, a man they considered thoroughly unpredictable. A strictly observant Jew, Antelman openly chided the Conservative and Reform movements favored by the majority of Jewish *makhers*. While most American Zionists were aligned with the comforting personalities of Israel's centrist Labor party— including everyone's favorite Jewish mother, Golda Meir—

Antelman agitated on behalf of the right wing Herut party of Menachem Begin. Antelman had even made a trip to Israel to issue a special appeal for resettlement of Boston Jewry and had actually convinced one Dorchester family to opt for the uncertainties of life in the besieged Jewish state rather than risk the likelihood of a pogrom in Dorchester.

The JDL had profound appeal for Antelman. Within the new organization he saw the spiritual heirs of the biblical heroes whose stories he'd devoured as a youth. *(While a ten-year-old in Camden, New Jersey, in 1943, Antelman had been dumbstruck by the news of the murder of several relatives in concentration camps; he would never forget the effect on his usually robust father, who sank into a lengthy period of depression. The gassing and starvation of millions of Jews in Europe was incomprehensible to young Antelman, who fantasized about biblical heroes such as Judah Maccabee, a leader who refused to bend his knee to foreign invaders. Jews, he had been taught, were fighters.)* Antelman hurled himself into recruiting for the New England chapter of the JDL by visiting suburban synagogues, college campuses, religious schools, and local businesses to explain the goals of the new chapter. At the end of November 1969 Antelman and the JDL decided to show the flag at the G&G delicatessen. Several black youths, mostly between the ages of twelve and sixteen, had been targeting customers for muggings and sauntering by their tables uttering insults and threats. Several JDL members, including Antelman and Sol Sidman, a Newton judo expert, made a big show of arriving at the G&G in berets and dark glasses, walkie-talkies in hand. The JDL members took up positions at the delicatessen's entrance. Curious passersby stared at the JDL members as if they had just stumbled off some strange B-movie set. Within minutes, however, a few black youths arrived to taunt the newcomers. With considerable bluster Antelman raised his walkie-talkie to his mouth and called for "armed reinforcements." Unbeknownst to the street gang, the nascent JDL chapter had neither a communication system nor a central headquarters. Sensing apprehensiveness on the part of the black youths, other members of the small JDL squad began a karate drill, complete with ferocious shouts and air kicks. The black youths backed up slowly at first and then, perhaps believing that these middle-aged

Jews were totally mad, broke into a run. Antelman and his troops jumped into a sedan and, siren blaring, pursued the youths down Blue Hill Avenue.

Within a few days word had circulated throughout Jewish Dorchester and Mattapan that the JDL had routed troublemakers from the G&G. With each retelling the number and ferocity of the black teens grew, as did the reputation of the League. JDL members did nothing to set the record straight; the apocryphal tales were bringing in new members. Suddenly, there was belief that something could be done for the city's weak, disorganized Jews. The JDL chapter grew quickly to 150 members. Antelman, who many in Boston Jewry had dismissed as a madman, confounded his critics by insisting that new recruits pass strict psychological tests to determine their ability to handle high-stress situations. Even reporters who requested "ride-alongs" on JDL patrols had to submit to an interview with the JDL psychiatrist.

Antelman's recruitment efforts were tracked carefully by Iz Zack, a former military intelligence officer and "fact finder" on the staff of the local office of the Anti-Defamation League (ADL). Dogging fellow Jews was a new experience for Zack. He'd earned his stripes tracking the local America First followers of Gerald Smith, neo-Nazi George Lincoln Rockwell, and hatemonger Father Charles Coughlin. "I knew them but they didn't know me," was operative Zack's standard response to those on whom he maintained voluminous files. Suddenly, on the request of the directors of the Jewish Community Council, he was gathering data on a group of Jews whose agenda seemed no more ominous than protecting a group of elderly residents.

In early 1968 Zack had visited scores of Jewish merchants along Blue Hill Avenue to gather data on the reports of escalating crime in the neighborhood. Almost all had reported threats of arson and other intimidation by black militants in the neighborhood. Zack turned his report over to both the ADL regional chief Sol Kolack and to Robert Segal of the Jewish Community Council. He'd expected significant action but received only a vague instruction from Segal to go down occasionally and "hold hands" with the merchants and residents.[12] But Zack's bosses were not so indifferent to the activities of the JDL. Segal, in particular, was becoming "a little bit paranoid" about the activities of Kahane's local followers.[13] So long as the JDL recruits limited themselves to marginal issues in the community, the Jewish leaders felt that there was little to fear in the public relations arena. But Antelman, despite his tendency toward obscurantism and his florid personal style, was making unexpected inroads. Community patrols had received the quiet blessing of the widely respected Boston rebbe Levi Horowitz, who encouraged his Brookline congregants to come to the aid of fellow Jews in North Dorchester and Mattapan. For several months a core group of students from the Massachusetts Institute of Technology had volunteered to attend evening services in the small *shtibels* to ensure the quorum of ten males required by Jewish law. They, too, were quick to answer Antelman's appeal.

The major strength of the Boston JDL chapter, however, was its ability to draw in Mattapan residents who supported neighborhood integration efforts but felt alienated by the class structure of mainstream Jewish organizations. The Jewish Community Council, for example, took special note when Arthur Bernstein signed on as a JDL patrol leader. Bernstein had been a mainstay of the Mattapan Organization's education committee and was, in the eyes of the council, a responsible liberal who could be counted on to further integration efforts. His involvement in the JDL perplexed Segal and others in the city's Jewish leadership.

Bernstein, his wife and two children lived on Mattapan's Savannah Avenue, a quiet side street of modest single-family ranch-style homes. Bernstein managed a local lumber business; with his thick limbs, athletic neck, and eyes that rarely looked away, he himself seemed rooted to the spot. There was, however, little in Bernstein's early life that would suggest such rootedness. While still a teenager, he had shipped out as a merchant seaman during World War II. His main links to home were the news clippings his mother sent from the Anglo-American and Yiddish press that described the conditions of European Jews who were being deported with frightening efficiency to Nazi death camps. Gazing from the deck of bulk cargo ships in the mid-Atlantic, Bernstein tried to picture the fate of his European coreligionists. Back in Boston after the war, the 21-year-old seaman was expected to settle down in a shoreside trade.

Bernstein's first stop was the offices of the Jewish trade unions—of carpenters, bakers, garment workers, cap and hat makers—in rented space over the Morton Theatre on Blue Hill

Avenue. Bernstein looked down the row of offices, but baking *hallahs* or fashioning fedoras did not fulfill the adventurous inclinations of a young merchant mariner. Captivated by reports of the Haganah, the Jewish underground army fighting in Palestine before the founding of the State of Israel, Bernstein asked around the Zionist network in Boston as to how he might best volunteer his sea skills to the fledgling movement. Within days he was in Baltimore aboard a ship flying a Honduran flag, which by midwinter had set sail for Sweden to pick up approximately eight hundred teenage survivors of Nazi concentration camps who had been rescued by the Swedish Red Cross. The Haganah ship made its way into the Mediterranean and picked up more refugees in Italy. By then the ship housed more than sixteen hundred potential recruits for the underground Jewish army. With the exception of the largely American crew, most of those aboard ship had been near death just months before from starvation or disease. British mandate leaders in Palestine, concerned about their own "tipping points," were determined to block the influx of Jewish immigrants into the territory. But Bernstein and his crew were equally determined. With the British navy in hot pursuit, the crew ran the ship onto the beach north of Haifa while scores of refugees jumped overboard to seek the protection of the Haganah. For his trouble Bernstein was arrested and shipped to a British detention camp on Cyprus, where he was imprisoned with fifteen thousand other Jews.

After his release, which was arranged by prominent Zionist leaders in Boston, Bernstein returned to Boston to learn the lumber trade. Like thousands of Boston Jews who came of age in the 1940s, his residences followed a predictable pattern over the next two decades: an apartment in Roxbury, a wooden triple-decker in Dorchester, and eventually the small neat home at 160 Savannah Avenue. A nonbeliever, Bernstein had little use for the synagogue activities that flourished throughout Mattapan and Dorchester. He preferred the offerings of the Workmen's Circle on Blue Hill Avenue, an organization that promoted Yiddish culture and strong secular Jewish identification through films, readings, and lectures. Like his brother Julius, who for many years headed the city's Jewish Labor Committee, Arthur scorned the forces of suburbanization within the Jewish community. Mattapan was good enough for Arthur Bernstein and always would be.

Had Bernstein ever entertained the idea of becoming involved in mainstream Jewish activities, such thoughts were dashed in 1961. In January of that year American Nazi party Führer George Lincoln Rockwell decided to return to his native New England and pay a visit to Boston. The occasion was the local premiere of the film *Exodus,* the romantic Hollywood version of the founding of the state of Israel, scheduled to open at the popular downtown Saxon Theatre on Tremont Street. Rockwell and his twenty-two-year-old cook checked into the Hotel Touraine directly across the street from the theater. (In keeping with his macabre sense of humor, Rockwell registered under the name of Nathan Ginsberg.) He immediately began inviting New England sympathizers to join him on a picket line for the January 15 opening, where Rockwell promised to expose Israel's links to "international communism." Leaders in the Anti-Defamation League and Jewish Community Council had decided to "quarantine" Rockwell—essentially, to use all of their influence to ensure that neither counterdemonstrators nor the press be on hand to meet Rockwell and his contingent. Mayor John Collins told Segal that he could not deny Rockwell and his followers the right to picket the theater, but, on the Jewish Community Council's urging, he appealed to Boston's Jews to ignore "the trouble-making intruder." After the mayor's announcement Bernstein and a handful of American veterans of the Israeli army insisted to the Council that the "quarantine" would be viewed as a sign of weakness. They asked, instead, that Segal help them mobilize Jews throughout Greater Boston to stage an enormous counterdemonstration to the Nazis. Emotions, they explained, were running particularly high among Jewish concentration camp survivors, who vowed that Rockwell would not disrupt the opening of *Exodus.*

During several meetings at the Council's Franklin Street office, Segal insisted that a large counterdemonstration, particularly one with the potential for violence, would be a public relations fiasco for the entire Jewish community. Bernstein countered that nothing could be more disastrous for the community's reputation than allowing Nazis in jackboots to march in the streets of downtown Boston. The two groups could find no common ground. In anger, several survivors accused the Jewish Community Council of acting like the *Judenrat,* the Jewish bureaucrats appointed by the Nazis in Europe to oversee Jewish community affairs before the mass deportations. "The Council, the police, everyone told us to trust them to take care of the situation," Bernstein recalled. "Our attitude was that the son of a bitch [Rockwell] shouldn't walk."[14]

On the afternoon of the premiere, Bernstein and two thousand other Jews converged on the theatre district. The mob turned the corner at Boylston and Tremont Streets and began a noisy anti-Nazi demonstration in front of the Saxon Theatre. The demonstration continued for a few minutes beneath the grotesque gargoyles that festooned the Saxon's facade until Rockwell and a single follower emerged from the hotel across the street wearing khaki uniforms, black ties, and red arm bands with black swastikas. Within seconds a phalanx of police formed around the two Nazis and the crowd responded with a fusillade of rocks, eggs, and tomatoes. Jewish demonstrators clashed with police officers in their frenzy to reach Rockwell. Bernstein rushed at the Nazi, determined to give him a welcome that he could ponder for a few days from a traction bed at the nearby Massachusetts General Hospital. But as he reached out to grab the self-styled American Führer, Bernstein was tackled by a burly police sergeant. The police officers managed to get Rockwell into the lobby of the Saxon and shoved him out through an alley door to a waiting police cruiser. Shortly thereafter, he was at Boston's Logan International Airport, where he was unceremoniously put on a flight to Washington, D.C.

Less than a decade later Bernstein repeated the *Judenrat* charges against the community leadership during the blockbusting campaign in Mattapan. Was the community leadership using the same "quarantine" approach to offending realtors and bankers, namely, no public exposure and no direct confrontation? He was convinced it was the case. Bernstein went to work clearing out a portion of his basement in order to set up maps of Dorchester and Mattapan that highlighted the location of synagogues and Jewish institutions. He also installed a police and citizens band radio, which he could use to dispatch other JDL members to trouble spots. Arthur Bernstein's home on Savannah Avenue had become JDL Central.

Kahane was quick to recognize the special qualities of the Boston chapter of the Jewish Defense League. On December 16, 1969, the anniversary of the Boston Tea Party, he convened an executive meeting of the new Boston chapter to present the JDL's platform. A taped recording of that meeting presents a portrait of a leader far different from the one who would become infamous two decades later for his calls to expel Arabs from Israel and the occupied territories. "No one in JDL thinks the ultimate threat to Jews comes from blacks," Kahane told the Boston organizers. "There is no place for racism in this organization and that's it. . . . All you need is one nut to get up and shout 'nigger' once—aside from the fact that it is a reprehensible thing to say—and the whole organization is smeared."[15] Several of the Boston organizers also challenged the League's national agenda, particularly well-publicized attempts at infiltration of the Students for a Democratic Society and JDL's open support for a combat role for the United States in Vietnam. Kahane, however, urged them to adhere to the platform of the New York–based national organization. "I know that JDL was formed in Boston for a local, parochial reason—Mattapan," he said. "But Boston is not an island."[16]

The smashed wall clock of Chevra Shas showed 12:40 A.M. The city arson investigators, who had arrived a short while later, were gingerly picking over pieces of singed velvet and burnt parchment for clues. The fire, which had been ignited in the Holy Ark on the eastern wall of the red brick *shul,* had burned itself out after destroying the holy Torah scroll. The shock reached every corner of Greater Boston Jewry. Even the nonobservant had been taught to approach the Torah—containing the Five Books of Moses—with awe. For the observant, who are taught to "study the Torah again and again for everything is contained in it,"[17] the desecration was like a violent death in the family.

The Chevra Shas fire was not the only one set in the early morning of May 27, 1970. According to investigators, the arsonists struck moments later around the corner at Agudas Israel. In purely monetary terms, the second blaze was more serious: $10,000 in damages to the front sections of the handsome synagogue. But it was the news of the desecration of the Torah at Chevra Shas that was on the lips of Dorchester Jewry the following morning. "To burn the Torah?" the old men asked. "Were they Nazis?"

The synagogue arsons brought the media out in force to North Dorchester. Although the B-BURG banking programs and resulting neighborhood turmoil had rated barely a nod from editors, the spectacle of a desecrated Torah in a plain pine coffin surrounded by wailing Jews set newsrooms abuzz. Photographers snapped away as Chevra Shas congregants entered the synagogue for the funeral. Much of the attention was focused on Rabbi Mordecai Savitsky, one of the country's leading Talmudic authorities but a man little known outside of traditional Jewish circles. "Sioux City" Savitsky, as he was dubbed by the denizens of the G&G, maintained a virtual lock on the certification of kosher meat at several of the nation's largest Midwest slaughterhouses. The rabbi was also renowned for a steel-trap mind that, local legend maintained, enabled him to memorize pages of Talmud at a single sitting. Savitsky, however, usually shunned the spotlight, living modestly and usually speaking only in Yiddish, particularly when IRS agents came around to inquire about his Midwest business interests. After the Chevra Shas arson, however, Savitsky found his tongue. Clutching a charred portrait of a Jewish sage, the rabbi delivered a stunning eulogy over the desecrated Torah scroll:

> Like Eli the high priest we suffered in silence when we were robbed, assaulted, beaten and killed. And like him we will not remain silent any longer, now that they have burned our Torah.
>
> Boston officialdom cannot say "we did not see the killings that have taken place". . . . They noticed. Boston knew. The mayor knew, everyone knew what was happening in this section. Tens of times they were literally begged to put on extra patrols in this neighborhood. . . .
>
> And so we are in this neighborhood without honor. Look at our shattered windows marked by years of stone throwing. Look at our members who have been robbed and beaten near death in this neighborhood and in this synagogue itself.
>
> And for what?
>
> All they wanted to do here was to be left alone to pray to God in peace.
>
> This neighborhood and her synagogues were once packed. Today we are forced to scrounge for ten people to make up our quorum.
>
> If our enemies think that they can drive us out of here, then, God forbid, the curse upon us will be worse upon them for they will have utter desolation.[18]

The gaunt rabbi broke into tears as congregants carried the pine box containing the Torah remains to a waiting hearse. "We have appealed time and time again to the mayor and police," the rabbi told reporters. "But there is nothing I can do. I have no power." Then, gesturing to his elderly congregants, his voice rose in anger: "And now we must be soldiers in guarding ourselves."[19] Other Orthodox rabbis added their voices to the charges of official neglect. The country's only American-born Hasidic rabbi, Levi Horowitz, who had moved his congregation out of Dorchester five years earlier, noted the absence of Mayor Kevin White. He charged that "the Mattapan–Dorchester Task Force, operating with the Mayor's Office of Human Rights, met frequently and at length, but produced no tangible programs to alleviate the progressively worsening situation."[20] Rabbi Israel Goldberg, who had conducted services on the steps of his own damaged Agudas Israel, targeted mainstream Jewish organizations. "This lesson is very clear," he said, "and yet very difficult for our people to understand. As Jews we collect funds for causes and we've given ourselves to civil rights. Now we ask for our own to be with us in our tragedy."[21] Boston Mayor Kevin White did not attend the funeral for the Torah at Chevra Shas in the spring of 1970. The mayor and his aides, in fact, were so totally focused on securing White's Democratic nomination for governor that concerned insiders at City hall feared that the city was rudderless. It was a fear confirmed years later by the mayor himself: "You know where my mind was in 1970," White revealed. "You know where [chief aide] Barney Frank's mind was. . . . I was going to be interplanetary leader. The next step is the governorship." What little attention his administration paid to city matters, White reflects, was designed to accomplish short-term objectives. "It's the potholes," the ex-mayor explained. "It's the potholes. There was no long-range thinking. . . . I know a guy will say, 'Jesus Christ, my wife walked out last night. I never saw it coming.' "[22]

There is ample evidence that White, indeed, never saw it coming. The mayor's most solid political support was precisely in those black and Jewish neighborhoods most adversely affected by blockbusters in pursuit of the Boston Banks Urban Renewal Group largesse. From White's perspective, it was the Irish, not the Jews, who were fleeing the city for suburban lifestyles. As late as

November 1968, when NBC News was preparing a report on big city mayors, White had chosen to be filmed among the fruit carts and small Jewish businesses along Blue Hill Avenue. There, he believed, he was assured of an appreciative claque. "I was comfortable with the Jewish community. I was one of theirs. If the Jewish community was still there, I'd still be carrying it. I'd carry it to my grave," he said.[23] White insists that no one—not Jewish state representatives, civic leaders like Eli Goldston, or prominent Jewish supporters from the Combined Jewish philanthropies— ever asked him to intervene on behalf of the stricken neighborhoods. "I didn't know the neighborhood was dying. I wouldn't have let that happen. The Jewish community was not making noise. Such swift change and they were not making noise. I missed this completely like you would a child off to the side in a large family."[24]

Members of the White administration might have had little success capturing their boss's attention on any subject unrelated to higher office, but the more prudent among them saw political trouble in the B-BURG plan, particularly the banks' decision to limit available mortgage funds for low-income buyers to the largely Jewish sections of Mattapan. A few months after the announcement of the program in May 1968, reports of blockbusting and other scare tactics already had begun to reach White's aides. Every official in northern municipalities knew that the greatest political dangers lurked on the residential borders between black and white neighborhoods.[25] It was openly assumed that incursion into Irish and Italian neighborhoods would be met with open hostility; what, precisely, would be the fallout in a Jewish neighborhood was still unclear.

Barney Frank, in particular, was discomforted by the reports he was hearing from the field. The increasing violence in Mattapan, he believed, could not be understood without considering the effects of the B-BURG mortgage program. Frank requested Frederick Paulsen, the Boston Redevelopment Authority (BRA)'s assistant administrator for physical and economic development, to review the documentation related to B-BURG and to determine why the bank consortium was refusing mortgage loans outside the increasingly destabilized narrow neck of Mattapan. The answer, in the form of a lengthy memo, showed clearly that the banks had never had any intention of expanding the loan opportunities for low-income blacks to surrounding suburbs. Paulsen produced a July 23, 1968, memo in which city and BRA officials had requested that "loans to low-income persons who desire to buy a home outside of the above [B-BURG] areas will be made in cooperation with suburban banks." But banker Joseph Bacheller, chairman of the Boston Banks Urban Renewal Group, would not buy in. In a August 13, 1968 memo, the Suffolk Franklin chairman responded curtly: "I think you have been advised on at least three or four occasions that we are not willing to process applications for relocatees outside of the area which the Group is prepared to serve."[26]

City Councilor Tom Atkins was also disquieted by the reports he was hearing about the Boston Banks Urban Renewal Group. Atkins's political career had advanced considerably since the time he'd knocked the wind out of an overzealous cop with a karate chop during the Grove Hall welfare mothers' riot. Back in 1967 he had been barely able to capture a seat on the council. During his latest reelection campaign, however, Atkins had placed a strong second on the nine-member board—bested only by South Boston's Louise Day Hicks. By 1969 people were promoting Atkins as the candidate who could be elected the first black mayor of Boston.

In March of 1969, hoping to learn more about B-BURG, Atkins requested a meeting with Robert Morgan, the president of Boston Five Cents Savings Bank. Atkins was ushered into a conference room where the civic-minded Morgan and several staffers waited in front of an easel that held an enlarged map of the sections of Roxbury, Dorchester, and Mattapan where mortgage funds were available.

"Why did you start this program?" Atkins asked.

"We've been accused of taking something out of the community and not putting anything back into it," explained the affable Morgan. "This is our way of improving community and developing housing opportunities."

Atkins was still unsure of what he was looking at. "How was the area chosen?" he queried.

"To have an impact we wanted to concentrate in a relatively small area so we just chose an area," Morgan replied. The banker's assistants shifted uncomfortably.

"What happens if somebody meets the criteria but the house happens to be a street or two outside the line?" Atkins asked.

"We'd have to deny the loan," said Morgan.

"Is that legal?" asked Atkins, trying to sound as nonconfrontational as possible.

"We don't have to give this money up, you know," the banker replied.

Atkins thanked his hosts and reached for his jacket. "I'll be needing to explain your policy to my constituents," he told the bankers. "Would it be possible for me to have a copy of the map?"

Morgan dispatched one of his assistants to retrieve a copy. "Glad to help," the banker replied.[27]

Atkins felt dizzy as he walked out onto School Street. I can't believe they think they can do this, he later remembered thinking to himself. Heading back to the council office, Atkins tried to digest what he had just heard. He'd heard of redlining—the practice of denying mortgage loans in predominantly minority areas—but never before had he encountered it in this variation— where federally insured mortgage money was provided to minorities only on the condition that they buy where the bankers told them to. The blockbusting in Mattapan suddenly made perfect sense. The insult against blacks was obvious, but the effect on the Jewish neighborhoods, he realized, was equally profound. A fragile community, with many elderly residents, would now be submitted to relentless pressures.

Initially, Atkins was reluctant to challenge a program that was publicly linked to black home ownership. He began to change his mind, however, when a black constituent asked him to intervene with the banks on his behalf. The man had located a house on Whitman Street, a few blocks east of the B-BURG line in a predominantly Irish neighborhood. The mortgage officers in the B-BURG office, however, had told him that he qualified for a loan only within the prescribed area. Atkins kept the pressure on the B-BURG banks with follow-up letters to the B-BURG office in Roxbury, including one in which he promised to file a formal complaint with the Massachusetts Commission Against Discrimination on behalf of his house-hunting constituent. On March 25, 1970, he received a lengthy reply from Suffolk Franklin's Joseph Bacheller, the chairman of the B-BURG Steering Committee. Bacheller indicated that the banking consortium would offer the loan for the Whitman Street home "strictly on an exception basis" and advised Atkins that further inquiries regarding the B-BURG line were not welcome:

Today we, together with most of the thrift institutions in and around the city, are lending only to our depositors or other customers of the bank for the purchase of homes. There is one exception that we make and that is B-BURG. To put this in another way, the people we are serving in the area which we have defined are getting special privileges. Your reference to discrimination and your threat to take us before the Massachusetts Commission Against Discrimination are obviously not well founded upon the facts as they are.[28]

As one of the country's prominent civil rights attorneys, Atkins would go on to see his share of discriminatory housing practices. In 1981, while serving as counsel for the NAACP, he would file the original suit against the city of Yonkers, New York, that led to a federal judge's order that the city council pay stiff fines for failing to endorse a court-mandated housing desegregation plan. But B-BURG, he later noted, was one of a kind. "Rarely," he said, "do you see blockbusting and redlining join in such spectacular fashion. But I've never seen the two joined with the official imprimatur of local, state, and federal government."[29]

The B-BURG bankers were not blind to the unintended consequences of their experiment in socially aware banking. As early as February, 1969, Morgan and Bacheller were hearing disturbing news regarding speculative buying from the B-BURG field office in Roxbury. Bacheller sent a memo to B-BURG bankers regarding "some abuses [which] seem to have crept into our operation in the B-BURG areas."[30] In an attempt to set limits on the already rampant speculative buying, Bacheller ordered his fellow bankers to reject any cases where ownership had not been established for a minimum of twelve months. More disturbing were reports that several local racketeers had eschewed their traditional business interests in illegal numbers and prostitution in order to go into the Mattapan real estate trade. The situation worsened in the late spring of 1970 when several assaults took place against B-BURG employees staffing the Warren Street office. Community leaders, who only two years before were arguing for the presence of the bankers in the black community, were now suggesting that the bankers "get back downtown where they belong."[31]

In June 1970, fearful that their grandiose scheme in public

relations would fail, the B-BURG banks closed their Warren Street office. The loans, however, would continue through a subcontract with a community-based, nonprofit organization, the Association for Better Housing (ABH). At first glance, the agency seemed like a perfect choice to polish up B-BURG's increasingly tarnished image. It had first formed in 1967 to guide black families through the maze of mortgage borrowing, closing costs, and appraisals associated with first-time home ownership. The organization's president, Jesse Sargent, was the wife of Massachusetts Governor Francis Sargent, a consummate New England Brahmin and the great-grandson of the hugely successful Yankee banker Henry Lee. Sargent, though a Republican, had long been dedicated to progressive politics. As acting governor, he had ordered the statehouse flag flown at half-mast for the students killed at the Kent State demonstration. Members of his own party chided the governor for placing key Democrats in powerful positions in the state government. The governor's wife had never been content to conduct social teas in their hometown of Dover. Instead, she sought out contacts in Boston's black community and formed partnerships with political leaders to open up housing opportunities for black citizens.

The day-to-day operations of the Association for Better Housing was run by its executive director, Harold Ross, a self-described "simple Baptist minister."[32] In conversations with Morgan and Bacheller, members of the ABH staff explained that black buyers were at the mercy of blockbusters and unprincipled FHA inspectors. First-time white home buyers, the argument went, always brought along more experienced friends to search for problems missed by building inspectors. Blacks, they explained, did not have such resources to draw upon. Ross proposed to provide "social service banking" to the B-BURG clients, including mortgage counseling, legal advice at closing, appraisal help, and liaison services between clients and brokers. The B-BURG chairmen were convinced and contracted with the ABH to originate and service all B-BURG loans for 1 percent of the principal amount of each loan.

Ross estimated that as many as two hundred brokers were actively working the B-BURG area out of approximately twenty-five storefronts on Blue Hill Avenue and the surrounding side streets. One of his first duties was to call each active broker into a meeting at the ABH office on the second floor of Crawford Street's Freedom

House, the original site of Hebrew College. Ross clashed bitterly with Irving Woolf, an optometrist who had branched out into real estate during the speculative buying frenzy in Mattapan. He also clashed with Royal Bolling, the former state senator who now operated a lucrative real estate practice on Blue Hill Avenue. Several brokers, including Bolling and Woolf, soon found themselves pariahs at the ABH; B-BURG mortgages, they were told, were now off-limits to them. Other realtors with reputations for speculative practices, however, seemed to enjoy favored status, which prompted rumors that ABH officials had joined Boston's FHA inspectors on the take. Ross and the ABH staff denied such charges and countered that they uniformly resisted the almost daily bribery attempts by scores of brokers hungry for B-BURG funds. Even as late as the summer of 1971, B-BURG and the Association for Better Housing were earning rave reviews in the metropolitan press. After almost three years of blockbusting, sales through "straw buyers," and community destabilization, ABH President Jesse Sargent continued to praise the "unusual blend of commitment of the downtown banking industry with social services."[33]

Subsequent evaluations of the period would not prove so kind. Census data from 1970 showed that of all black home owners in the city, 19 percent had purchased their homes between 1969 and March 1970, compared to less than 7 percent for owner-occupants citywide.[34] But unlike home owners in other sections of the city, the B-BURG buyers did not realize the traditional benefits of home ownership; much of the problem related to a decline in city services. Julia Owens, a black Mattapan resident who moved to the area prior to the establishment of B-BURG, testified at a later U.S. Senate subcommittee hearing that she was one of two black home owners on her street in 1967. When she arrived in Mattapan, trash was picked up twice-weekly, and the street was swept on a strict schedule. By 1970 the block had experienced a 90 percent racial turnaround and a steep decline in city services. Trash now was picked up once a week "with more of it left on the street than in the trucks,"[35] and street sweepers were a thing of the past. Broken streetlights, Owens testified, were not fixed for months, and abandoned buildings were neither boarded up nor patrolled by police. Owens had moved to Mattapan to live in an integrated neighborhood. But her sole contact with whites in the neighborhood was reduced to sightings of bat-wielding Jewish Defense League patrols. "It is only a miracle," she said, "that no one has been killed."[36]

Subsequent surveys of black home owners in Mattapan found that they experienced little satisfaction with their new neighborhood. Most felt that, rather than get a fresh start, they had simply taken on the same problems experienced in the urban renewal areas of Roxbury. "I'm in an area that's going down fast," stated one woman in a typical response. "I would like to move, but I'm afraid that I couldn't get my money back on this building."[37] The respondent's instincts were correct. B-BURG buyers were far more likely to lose their homes through foreclosure and abandonment than to realize capital gains on their purchases. With little or no down payment, the new buyers enjoyed no equity. For those who had difficulty meeting mortgage and upkeep costs and who had no reserves to cover the needed repairs that inefficient or corrupt FHA appraisers had failed to report, it was often more prudent to walk away than to persevere. Since the implementation of the program in the summer of 1968, abandonments and foreclosures were on the increase in North Dorchester and Mattapan. Later studies, in fact, would reveal that more than one-half of all B-BURG purchasers would lose their homes by 1974. The effect on the city's black community would be devastating.

The B-BURG loan pool would also have long-range effects on Boston housing patterns, with one study finding that "during July 1977–June 1978, 91 percent of the government-insured foreclosures were in South Dorchester, North Dorchester and Roxbury. In fact, 53 percent of the city's foreclosures were in South Dorchester (which includes Mattapan). Furthermore, 84 percent of the 93 foreclosures in North and South Dorchester were concentrated in the B-BURG program census tracts."[38]

Although both the black and Jewish communities suffered incalculable losses during the B-BURG years, with the program now considered a classic example of racial discrimination in urban housing markets, the banks themselves prospered. Later studies showed how the banks protected themselves from losses by assigning all foreclosures to HUD, thereby incurring no costs from bad loans. Additionally, the 1 percent fee charged by the banks more than covered the costs of processing the mortgages.[39] The process was described as follows:

Interest rates for FHA loans run below conventional mortgages. Thus a point system allows the bank to pay less than appears on paper to compensate for lower earnings. When the mortgage is foreclosed, the bank collects more from FHA insurance than it paid when the loan was originated. To the extent that they banded together, the B-BURG banks also increased their total portfolio in B-BURG neighborhoods from 4½ to 5 percent mortgages to 8½ percent mortgages. In other words, when B-BURG purchasers bought a home from the seller, the change-over represented a loss of a 5 percent mortgage to one bank and the gain of 8½ percent mortgage to another. But adding all B-BURG transactions together, B-BURG banks shifted from a pool of 5 percent mortgages to a pool of 8½ percent mortgages.[40]

Debate on the value of B-BURG swirled through the black community. Some community leaders, like Harold Ross, continued to argue that any program that put blacks in their own homes was by definition a good one. Others, like Tom Atkins, contended that the B-BURG program had merely extended the geographic boundaries of the black ghetto southward into Mattapan, advanced the rate of abandonments, and created a special class of home owners who would never enjoy the benefits of resale value. Quietly and cautiously, Tom Atkins began to put out feelers to acquaintances on the Committee on the Judiciary of the U.S. Senate to see what, if anything, could be done to advance an independent evaluation of the program. Certainly, he thought, leaders within the Jewish community would also be interested in getting to the bottom of B-BURG. He called Robert Segal at the Jewish Community Council and other prominent community figures. They all promised to get back to him; none, he would later recall, ever did.

The Hearings

Congress Plows the
"Mysterious World of Finance," 1971

Sporting the only beard in the U.S. Senate, Philip Hart of Michigan strode across the plaza at Boston's Government Center and entered the John Fitzgerald Kennedy Federal Building at precisely 9 A.M. on September 13, 1971. It was unusual to see Senator Hart on the road. Unlike many of his colleagues who used their committee work as an opportunity to see the nation and the world, Senator Hart preferred to be on hand for floor votes at the Capitol. When not tied to his office duties, Hart could be found with his family at their rented apartment on Mackinac Island in their home state.[1]

But Hart had felt compelled to come to Boston. He had been besieged with requests during the months following his announcement that his Senate Subcommittee on Antitrust and Monopoly of the Committee on the Judiciary would be investigating unholy alliances between the real estate and banking industries. And he was beginning to suspect that the hand of government, in addition to private entrepreneurs, might also be inhibiting competition. Pundits back in Washington were making sarcastic remarks about where this "ferocious Samson" might start his investigation; city officials and civic groups from New York, Philadelphia, Kansas City, Dayton, and other cities were beseeching the senator to visit their cities. The requests from Boston, however, seemed to arrive with the greatest sense of urgency.

A pattern emerged from the shrill and fragmentary reports: neighborhoods where blacks and whites lived together, or contiguously, were breaking up. This "massive turnover," as Hart would subsequently call it, was often accompanied by violence, white flight, and the development of new ghettoes, with even more clearly demarcated boundaries, bearing the familiar signs of deterioration. And all this took place precisely at the moment when the country should have been reaping the benefits of serious attention to the problems of race and poverty. There appeared, at last, a growing responsiveness in white America to the moral challenge presented by the civil rights movement. A growing fear of "long hot summers" and the threat of black violence had led to influential studies such as that of the Kerner Commission, new legislation such as the 1968 Civil Rights Act with its specific Title VIII provision against housing discrimination, and federal programs such as Office of Economic Opportunity spin-offs and expanded FHA mortgage programs directed to the inner city. But despite those earnest efforts of the '60s to put an end to racism and poverty, Senator Hart feared that the problems were simply getting worse.

Hart was no fan of the theatrics and self-promotion that often accompanied congressional investigations; to his press secretary's dismay, he had shunned personal publicity in the course of earlier hearings he had conducted on the Fair Packaging and Labeling Act. Whether analyzing consumer issues or civil rights, his voice was at once modest and passionate. Hart's decision to examine low-income housing programs in the light of antitrust statutes brought him in contact with a commodity with which he was largely unfamiliar—the press. Until the Boston hearing, Hart had been focused on the more general aspects of antitrust inquiries: the growth of conglomerates, industrial concentration, and the relation of corporate size to the maintenance of competition; more often than not, those complex and technical hearings lacked the intrinsic drama that drew the press corps. Hart figured he'd receive as much attention with his latest attempt to explore the connection between racially changing neighborhoods and monopolistic activities. His fellow Democrats, after all, were wedded to solutions based on big spending by big government. His conservative opponents favored the capacity of unregulated markets to correct major social problems. Antitrust problems, Hart had come to accept, were in the middle and hard to explain.

The "Samson" of the U.S. Senate had long been frustrated that his two most compelling issues—poverty and consumerism—were not directly addressed by his committee assignments. In Boston, he hoped, that might finally change. And he was ready to pull the pillars down on anyone foolish enough to challenge the jurisdiction of his subcommittee to deal with racial conflict. Opening the session of the antitrust hearings in Boston, Hart said:

> Any list of major problems which torture this country would have to include the alienation of our people, the deterioration and financial woes of our cities—whether they are on this corner of the east coast or any other corner—and the lack of decent housing. . . . In a way, we plow new ground by translating or attempting to translate what is generally considered the mysterious world of finance into its social implications. Antitrust may strike some as a rather strange vehicle for this text. Yet this impression exists only because at least in recent times antitrust has been somewhat like a Siamese twin—showing only one face, the economic one. But there is a social one also.[2]

After three days of testimony Hart would also find a link with his other passion, consumer affairs: "It made some of us inquire if it would not be possible to put the same kind of useful information on the label of a house for the benefit of the prospective buyer as we have spent hours in Congress insuring be on the label of Post Toasties."[3]

Edward Kennedy, U.S. senator and member of the Committee on the Judiciary from the host state, was conspicuously absent at the Boston hearings. Chairman Hart mumbled a stock apology on his behalf and entered a letter into the record. Senator John

Tunney from California, the only other member of the subcommittee present at the Boston hearings on its first day, was ready to get down to business. In his opening remarks he raised the possibility that "Government is acting in collusion . . . with local lending institutions and real estate agencies in order to develop and maintain ghettoes." Tunney emphasized that the problem was by no means restricted to Boston. Hart quipped that "the test of courage will depend on whether we go to Detroit and whether you go to California. It is easy to come to Boston."

Janice Bernstein, the "bat lady" and a former resident of Mattapan, sat at the front of the hearing room. In her hands she clutched a written statement of her family's experience in the past five years and of the activities of the Mattapan Organization, a group of residents who had supported integrated neighborhoods and who had tried to stem the tide of blockbusting, school and neighborhood deterioration, street violence, and white flight. Though a black housing official testifying at the hearings would later dismiss these efforts as "hypocrisy" and censure the Jews of Mattapan for choosing to leave for the suburbs as blacks moved in, Janice Bernstein knew that under different circumstances she could have lived in harmony with black neighbors. She hoped, over the course of the three-day hearing, to reach some understanding of the change in herself as well: How, she agonized, had it come to pass that a woman who once baked cakes for her new black neighbors subsequently chased their children with a baseball bat?

Allen Hessel, the director of the Laurelton Area Neighborhood Action Program, was also in that Boston hearing room on September 13, 1971. He was thinking not so much of Mattapan as of the changes that had taken place in his beloved tree-lined New York City suburb—"a real integrated Apple Pie American Dream Community."[4] Adjacent to a sizable black community in southeastern Queens, Laurelton's population of twenty-six to twenty-seven thousand residents was 99 percent white in 1960. In the decade that ensued, the black population grew to more than 30 percent. Yet there were abandoned buildings and the crime rate had increased; no one was quite sure why the neighborhood seemed to be deteriorating. At first, Hessel had been chagrined by the responses of his white neighbors to the new blacks on the block. After all, didn't these people have the right to attain "the American dream of owning one's own home"?[5] He observed that the new black resident often "was far more economically advantaged than the person he was replacing. He had made it in a very tough society and he was seeking his just reward."[6] At the same time, he could not find anything objectionable in the attitudes of Laurelton's whites, particularly its Jewish residents, many of whom "were still willing to work together, still willing to remain in an integrated fashion" in an effort to preserve their sense of community and the viability of their neighborhood institutions. Like Boston's Jews, the Jewish residents had felt abandoned by the federations of Jewish philanthropies, the large Jewish institutions that dismissed Laurelton as a "changing neighborhood" rather than see in it the opportunity for integration. Perplexed by this reaction, Hessel and his neighbors became increasingly suspicious; some uttered conspiratorial theories. "How closely involved are the large philanthropic organizations in this type of community destruction?" he wondered.[7] Soon Hessel and his white and black neighbors discovered that the neighborhood was changing not because of the upward mobility of middle-class blacks from the adjacent neighborhoods of Cambria Heights and Springfield Gardens who needed another bedroom or preferred the better public schools of Laurelton. They heard rumors about the arrival of black families from South Jamaica, Queens, from Harlem, and even directly from the South who were unemployed and on welfare and who doubled up in houses they could not afford. A growing number of houses owned for a short time by these unemployed blacks were now abandoned and boarded-up. There was an increase both in the number of real estate agencies on the main thoroughfares and in the crime rate.

Hessel sat engrossed throughout the hearings and, despite his intention to remain objective, found himself suspecting the existence of a conspiracy:

> I didn't realize . . . that there were such things as redlining, that there were certain communities that were designed for black people and they were adjacent to existing all-black communities. I wasn't aware of this but slowly I learned. . . .[8] Somebody is directing money. It is organized. I think somebody is preplanning this. . . . We have a giant monster that has

been created in this city for one express purpose, and that is to make a lot of dollars for somebody.[9]

Hessel left Boston vowing to bring the case of Laurelton to the attention of the Hart Committee investigators. With media attention focused on the Boston hearings, other activists across the country—like Gail Cincotta in Chicago, Walter Brooks in Baltimore, Gloria Lopez in Detroit, and George Gould in Philadelphia —began to demand official inquiry into neighborhood change. All were coming to learn what had transpired in their own neighborhoods through the increasing clarity of the lens focused on Boston.

The first witness in the Boston hearing was Sadelle Sacks, who since 1961 served as director of Fair Housing, a charitable agency that helped families in the Roxbury area find improved housing. Calmly and dispassionately, the wife of Harvard Law School dean Albert Sacks presented a written brief for the record with an oral summary that placed the investigation squarely within the antitrust subcommittee's jurisdiction while providing the historical and ethnographic detail to get things off to a promising start. Sacks described the plight of families, largely black with several children, in the South End and the Washington Park section of Roxbury. During a decade of urban renewal they had to give up their affordable apartments to the federally subsidized programs managed by the city's renewal authority. With no new public housing under construction in Boston since 1954 and with a combined rental and sales rate of less than 2 percent, these large black families who could least afford it paid the heaviest price for urban renewal. "In 1967, there were riots in Roxbury and the building up of this expanding population within the segregated borders of the community created a crisis in the supply of housing, with strong potential for explosion in the future,"[10] Sacks explained. In an interview years later, she would recall dreadful living conditions of the area's residents. She painted sardonic images of Jewish slumlords against whom she organized rent strikes, but she held no fonder memories for the increasing number of black slumlords whose buildings were equally dangerous and unattractive.

It was precisely against this background that Fair Housing began to change in the fall of 1967 from a local charity to a conduit for federal funding for the FHA mortgage programs of the Housing Act, under which families with low incomes could purchase houses with little or no down payment. "We thought we had finally found an answer for low-income families and welfare-recipient families," recalled Sacks. Fair Housing counseled the families on their financial capabilities and the costs of home ownership, helped them locate a suitable house, and assisted them with the abundant paperwork in applying to the banks, the insurance companies, and the like. These efforts were followed by ongoing support for the new homeowners. It was customary for Fair Housing to send a vacuum cleaner as a housewarming gift and to maintain a tool-lending library for the proud new do-it-yourselfers. Fair Housing was becoming a comprehensive program to usher newcomers into the world of equity and help them cross the line into the American middle class.

But Fair Housing, averaging fifteen hundred client families per year by the late 1960s, was interested in more than helping poor whites and blacks escape being "trapped in substandard and often uninhabitable apartments." Sacks also deemed it important to expand the areas into which her clients could move. She began with her own all-white community of Belmont, west of Boston, by assisting a black family to purchase a home. Her neighbors were outraged, "horrified that the blacks would cross over." She turned to the revered Cardinal Cushing for support in finding housing for her families in Irish neighborhoods. "When the Irish were trying to get housing, no one let them in," he'd responded. "Now they're not going to let anyone else in."[11] No sooner had Fair Housing successfully utilized its newly available instruments to enable one of its client families to move into "predominantly white communities of their choice" than Sacks and her colleagues noted some new agencies arriving in the area with home ownership programs.[12] These included the Boston Redevelopment Authority (BRA), the Association for Better Housing, and, by the fall of 1968, a coalition of twenty-two Boston banks, B-BURG.

Sacks was deeply suspicious from the outset. When no government guarantees had been available, these same institutions had refused outright to finance housing in "changing areas." With the advent of FHA insurance, they adopted a plethora of self-serving rules and administrative procedures, punctuating every memo with self-righteous proclamations of their commitment to the black community. Sacks was chagrined by the 1 percent service charge imposed by B-BURG banks on the applicants even though most of the paperwork and all of the risk were covered by other agencies. And soon enough, she testified, the coalition of banks began to control the situation by forcing applicants into specific mortgage programs and geographic areas. The banks refused to administer the FHA 235 program, which subsidized interest payments as well as VA loans. Under the guise of stabilizing the Model Cities area, the banks in fact were destabilizing that area and an adjacent area populated largely by Jews by creating "a perfect climate for blockbusting, speculation, and price gouging."[13] "Every local, state, and federal housing agency knew about the discriminatory line set up by the B-BURG coalition," Sacks testified.[14] But when these concerns were raised at a meeting convened by the BRA with B-BURG bankers Robert Morgan and Joseph Bacheller, the latter threatened to terminate the mortgage loan program if such complaints persisted. The Association for Better Housing, with its comfortable relationship with both the banks and the realtors, soon received an exclusive contract for counseling all applicants, further limiting the benefits that black home hunters could enjoy through access to free markets. Poor whites and other ethnics, Sacks added, were virtually excluded from any of the benefits of B-BURG financing.

Two decades later Sadelle Sacks recalled that she was prepared to take on her Belmont neighbors but reluctant to take on the banks. "I didn't get into that whole field. I thought of them as the WASP establishment downtown. . . . Someone might need a loan," she said, laughing at herself and registering surprise in recalling her own timidity. That there were Jewish lawyers, staff, and directors in the B-BURG banks who were privy to what the banks were doing in establishing their "discriminatory line" never dawned upon her, she said.[15]

Throughout that first day Senators Hart and Tunney and their staffs heard testimony from people, mostly blacks and Jews, aggrieved by B-BURG. The distressed citizens attested not only to their personal losses of beloved neighborhoods and homes but of a lost national opportunity to achieve integrated neighborhoods. The most depressing testimony came from Ethel Jean Farrell, a

black mother of four whose husband, Charles, had been killed in
Vietnam three years earlier. Armed with a Veteran Administration
eligibility certificate, Ethel Farrell had gone on a yearlong journey
through HUD and nonprofit and local realtors' offices. All told her
that banks were no longer accepting VA or conventional FHA 235
loans; her best chance, they told her, was B-BURG. Although she
had hoped to live in Brockton, a blue-collar town south of Boston,
with a strong school system, she was told by HUD housing
counselors to set her sights closer to the city. After finally locating
a suitable house on Alabama Street in Mattapan, she was informed
by the broker that a loan could not be approved because it was "on
the wrong side of the line." In frustration, Farrell burst into a
counselor's office at the Veterans Administration and threw down
on the table in disgust her husband's service papers, medals, and
condolence letter from the president. "I don't understand why
there would be a line around the area black people can live in, and
I don't understand why banks should be able to take away benefits
and programs which I am entitled to because of my husband's
sacrifices," she asserted to the senators.[16]

The senator from Michigan decided to bring an emotion-laden
day to a conclusion with some housekeeping activities. The
assistant counsel listed the prepared statements to be entered into
the record. The Jewish organizations, which generally competed
to present well-documented cases of threats to Jews, had by now
relegated the Mattapan issue to the social workers. A letter was
submitted for the record by the Anti-Defamation League of B'nai
B'rith and the Jewish Community Council of Metropolitan Boston,
a letter supporting B-BURG but claiming that "with neither public
knowledge nor approval the Boston Banks Urban Renewal Group
arbitrarily designated an area of Dorchester and Mattapan and
decided that in this area alone would such [low interest, B-BURG]
mortgages be granted."[17] This singular official Jewish response was
sufficiently neutral that neither majority nor minority counsel saw
in it anything useful and it was quietly accepted "for the record."

The search for the origin of the discriminatory boundary line
became the pursuit of the next two days. The Tuesday, September
14, session was convened by Senator Hart at 9:40 A.M. in the
chambers of the Boston City Council. In a spirit of fairness Hart
requested that a brief written statement by former Boston Redevel-

opment Chief Hale Champion be read and entered into the record. Champion, who had recently become the financial vice president of Harvard University, enthusiastically declared that "only the B-BURG undertaking came close to achieving its stated goals, with over $29 million of home loans being placed in the core city areas, providing home ownership for some 2,000 families. . . . A particularly innovative aspect of the B-BURG program has been that it was administered in the neighborhoods where the funds were made readily accessible to the intended borrowers." He concluded with the admission that not everyone saw the results of B-BURG in such favorable terms: "those who were willing to be at least partially responsive are often subjected to greater public criticism than those who offer little or no response."

Champion's picture of a consistent and well-developed program was immediately challenged by Jack Blum, the assistant counsel of the subcommittee. He introduced Champion's own memo written to Mayor Kevin White on May 13, 1969, in which he described his efforts "to work out some arrangement that would ease the Mattapan situation" by getting the Federal Home Loan Bank of Boston and the Massachusetts Savings Bank Association to "take on exposure of the same kind under the same conditions [as B-BURG]." By including other banks in the loan program, the theory went, B-BURG's competitors would also be tying up their capital in the inner city and would not gain a competitive edge in the suburban real estate market. Under those circumstances, Champion believed, the B-BURG banks would be less concerned with how they might be undermining their own business beyond the inner city and would allow clients the flexibility to purchase homes throughout the metropolitan area.

The subcommittee's assistant counsel was just warming up. Champion had skillfully blurred the issue of the discriminatory line, and Blum tried to bring it back into focus by showing that the issue of the line was a problem from the very onset of B-BURG. Memoranda from the White Administration in the summer of 1968 had clearly challenged the "take it or leave it" attitude of the banks, yet a year later White's director of redevelopment was taking the banks' position in helping them reduce their alleged risk and avert potential competition.[18] Hart was getting into the investigative mood, and the first in-person witness testimony of the day heightened his interest. Walter Smart, a former member of Champion's staff, was one of the few blacks to rise to a middle-level administrative position in city hall. Director of the Family Relocation Department for the BRA in the late 1960s, Smart painted a very different picture of the impact of B-BURG from the one presented by his boss:

> My initial understanding of the function of that office proved to be incorrect. I thought the function would be similar to that function carried out in Washington Park. Upon seeing a map of the boundaries of the program I wondered why a section of Mattapan was included, an area I believed to be outside the Model City's boundaries. I did not question anyone about the boundaries at that point, thinking that no harm could come in an expanded rehabilitation program. I became concerned, however, on learning that the bulk if not all of the B-BURG activity was related to sales (transfer of ownership) rather than to rehabilitation.[19]

Furthermore, Smart "learned the startling fact that B-BURG would not grant mortgages (not even government-insured mortgages) unless the family purchased a home within the boundaries established by B-BURG."[20]

According to his testimony, Smart attempted to deal with the situation directly by getting the banks to offer mortgages for families with low and moderate incomes under Section 221(d)(2) and Section 235, with their minimal down payment requirements and the subsidies that they offered through a reduction of the interest rate. "We could not find any banks that would issue a mortgage under either of these programs," he later testified. The banks, he recalled, claimed that there was too much paperwork. As early as August 8, 1968, Walter Smart tried to blow the whistle on B-BURG by writing the assistant legal officer of his agency, Fred Paulsen, criticizing B-BURG for not approving any mortgages under Section 220 of the Housing Act for absentee owners. "At the least, this appears to have some illegal elements when an industry acts in concert to defeat a certain program [monopoly]," Smart claimed, anticipating what Senator Hart and his subcommittee would have to establish. Hale Champion was sent a copy.

The intra-agency response came from the legal department of BRA more than a year later. Counsel Terrance Farrell responded to Smart on August 25, 1969, by claiming that B-BURG should not be criticized "for not meeting its commitments for we have been judging it according to a standard which may not have been envisioned by the banks when the operation began." Smart responded to Farrell the very next day. "There is one area, however, which I believe that they must change if they are to maintain their office on Warren Avenue in Roxbury," he wrote. "That is, it is totally unconscionable for this group to restrict all black persons seeking to own a home in the limited geographical area that they have outlined." Smart further warned of dire consequences if these policies would persist and suggested "that the Redevelopment Authority should renounce any association with the Group."[21]

Senator Hart quickly focused on the conflict of interests. The banks, he offered, might argue that "there is just so much money to go around; this is the area we have agreed most needs revitalization and for that reason we are simply not going to go beyond that boundary." Turning to Smart, he added, "Your point would then go to the use of the funds to assist the people and they may look on it as the use of funds to help a geographical area. . . . So whatever Congress does about developing programs to enable low-income families to move out of squalor, and on occasion break racial barriers, depends for its success completely on the contribution in both those efforts on the part of private institutions." But Hart had few suggestions as to how Congress might resolve this conflict; nor did he state unambiguously that Congress must manage these programs directly and, because of such conflicts, cannot rely on the private sector to implement public policy.[22] Smart reinforced Hart's musings on the problems of implementation:

> The point was that all of the programs, the 221(d)(2), 235, coming out of Congress were I thought excellent programs. We just could not make use of them for people's benefit in a manner that could have a dramatic impact on housing and environment in the Boston community, simply because certain private institutions had decided, "no."[23]

The hearing's chief minority counsel, Peter Chumbris, finally saw an opportunity to defend the bankers. Returning to Walter Smart's point that the banks refused to lend money for repairs within available rehabilitation programs, he questioned Smart regarding the demography of the area of Mattapan that the bankers included within the line. The houses in the "tip" were "owned by fine Jewish families," Chumbris asserted. "The homes were fine homes, but they were moving out. . . . So," he concluded, pointing to the map, "this area down here did not need revitalization."

Smart retorted rather wistfully, "It makes you question the justification of the program."

Chumbris was caught off guard: "I did not hear you." Smart repeated his challenge. Chumbris responded that "the justification of the program would be to permit black people who are inside of this blue and red line to be able to go down into this tip here and borrow money to buy a fine home."

Smart wasn't buying it. "Black families wanted to go to that tip in other places, too," he retorted.

Chumbris again complained about his auditory problems as he tried quickly to compose a new defense of the bankers. He fell back on the argument that "they wanted to do something about this particular area."

But Smart, now aroused, would not back off: "Sir, I have no quarrel with government or special groups deciding that a certain group requires help, perhaps more than others, at a certain point in time. I have no quarrel with that. I am saying that there is no man that should have the right to determine where I or anybody like me can live. That is my point."[24]

Hart leapt into the discussion. "I am glad that you spoke as you just did, lest we forget the underlying problem of which this is just a part, a critical part."[25]

While discussion focused on the discriminatory lines, the polarization of blacks and Jews as the consequence of B-BURG policies would remain a faint motif in the actual hearings. Those who examined the fiscal policies of B-BURG years later would claim that the banks "in a very subtle manner, imprisoned 80 percent of Boston's black population," including those blacks "funneled" into this area because it was "the only area of Boston where incoming blacks could secure FHA loans to buy houses." The one "anomaly in this reasoning," was the inclusion of one white neighborhood, Jewish Mattapan and Dorchester.[26] This anomaly did not capture Hart's curiosity.

For the remainder of the day an array of realtors, accompanied by their attorneys, and a few officials with their experts in tow told a story that was by now altogether familiar. The realtors presented themselves as entrepreneurial, involved in nothing more than the all-American way of capitalism, buying low and selling high. The officials gave the appearance of being in charge, without assuming too much responsibility. That there was "a line" was indisputable; the reasons and the results still seemed to be elusive.

Reverend Harold Ross, executive director of the Association for Better Housing, testified late that afternoon and suggested that there was a touch of whimsy to the B-BURG line: "blacks are almost shepherded by these circumstances down the narrow corridor into Mattapan and into what is called Milton. The only amusing aspect is that it is a southern movement, and I call it the homing instinct, but it is going down into Mattapan." Jacquelyn Hall, his assistant director, in presenting her testimony, was in no joking mood. She accused the Jews of hypocrisy: "They moved because they wanted to move."[27] Janice Bernstein and other Mattapan Organization members present in the hearing room who had wanted to live in an integrated neighborhood silently recalled the incidents that led to the Jews' moving and were not at all amused by the Reverend's "homing instinct" remark or by his staffer's outburst.

The schedulers of the hearing kept the best for last. The bankers, called to the witness stand on the third day, were led by Joseph Bacheller, who had recently retired from the chairmanship of the board of Suffolk Franklin. To set the stage a statement—just received from Mayor Kevin White—was read and entered into the record; it praised the banks for the B-BURG effort, asking that the hearings not be an occasion "to pillory them for past errors" but at the same time carefully placed distance between White's administration and the banks' drawing of the line and "the subsequent expansion to the south."[28]

Bacheller began by introducing his colleagues and immediately asserted: "We note that testimony during the past few days has distorted the social and economic significance that the privately supported B-BURG program has achieved in our city." Summarizing the history of "twenty two thrift institutions joined in a public-spirited commitment to halt this decadence and assist the disadvantaged," he promptly acknowledged but condemned "in the strongest terms the unethical blockbusting practices of unscrupulous real estate dealers who buy cheap and sell dear, using racial scare tactics."[29] Bacheller further refused to concede any causal relationship between the bankers' boundary line and the blockbusters' activities. In fact, he argued, it was only in January 1971 that the "boundary was made distinct instead of the fuzzy line it had earlier been." This was done because "charges of extensive blockbusting occurring beyond the B-BURG boundaries came to our attention. As Reverend Ross has informed this committee, the B-BURG program was not involved at all in these blockbusting activities. Nonetheless, to remove any illusion that B-BURG mortgages might be fueling such activities, we chose to withdraw entirely from the affected areas."

Documentation in the record refuted this limp effort to blame the blockbusters for the line and indicated that the banks had been confronted with the blockbusting activities within the first year of the B-BURG program and had responded by refusing mortgage money for any house in the B-BURG area that was being resold after an ownership of less than one year. But on that morning in Boston, the senator and his staff did not challenge the banker on what was the cause and what the effect.[30]

Bacheller insisted that there was more than a historical connection between the obligation that the banks had undertaken to rehabilitate the Model Cities area and the population that was to be entitled to B-BURG loans. "Some critics of the B-BURG program say that we should offer a mortgage for this house [outside the Model Cities neighborhood], on preferential terms, to a person who comes from an urban renewal area, and that we should offer a mortgage for the same house to a person from similarly low income from another section of the city on regular market terms less advantageous to the buyer." In an implicit appeal to the American sense of fairness and with a good measure of self-righteousness, he added, "This, we are not willing to do." Then, challenging the evidence to the contrary already presented to the subcommittee, Bacheller asserted that "there is an almost complete absence of demand for houses outside of the present B-BURG area on the part of the residents now living within the area."[31]

As Hart continued his questions on the causal relationship

between the B-BURG boundary line and blockbusting, Bacheller began to squirm and repeat himself. But the senator from Michigan had never been known as a "closer"; rather than tighten his grip, he began to relax. Gently informing Bacheller that he was placing himself out on a weak limb, Hart narrowed the inquiry: "Rather than proceeding through a whole series of questions, let me tell you the one thing that I have a hang-up on, in terms of B-BURG and, of course, it is the line." Bacheller again resorted to his official bankers' history of B-BURG, burying Hart's question in a myriad of irrelevant details and repetition. He insisted that B-BURG from its inception was bound to a specific area, suggesting that the banks, when they "were straying a little outside of the area," received complaints. "But the more serious one was that we were beginning to be painted with the blockbusting brush because these loans were made, at least to some extent, in those areas where block-busting criticism was arising." Bacheller repeated the January 1971 date as the turning point in the bankers' reaction to blockbusting: "We had no knowledge of this, direct knowledge, nor did we contribute to it. But we discovered that blockbusting was being brought up in those areas as a matter of criticism and in some cases we had made a loan in those areas and we decided we had better get out before we were tarred with this brush."[32] Again Bacheller resisted any link between blockbusting and the B-BURG boundary line.

The holes and contradictions in Bacheller's argument were evident. Even the mild-mannered "Samson" began to lose patience with him: "Mr. Bacheller, the record should reflect—and I am reacting quickly to several of the points you made and I will ask staff to follow up. . . ."[33] Hart went on to challenge Bacheller's assertion that blacks did not want properties beyond the line. The line, he noted, had been established without the concurrence of the political leadership of Boston and was unquestionably a "disservice" itself, creating the conditions that fostered block-busting.[34] But what "follow-up" inquiries or measures were made by the subcommittee's staff, or anyone else, has never been made clear.

With all of Hart's efforts to trap Bacheller in his own statements, the former banker appeared to have slipped right through, easing his way with more righteous indignation. "I am very sorry . . . I am very, very sorry that somehow or other someone did not get a group of the satisfied customers that we have got within the area to rebut some of the malcontents who have been before you." Hart backed down: "I have no doubt . . . that two thousand people are in large part delighted and, if you would, appreciative of what you have done. I have no doubt of that." Bacheller made one last chance to strengthen his case: "We could not afford to—we do not have the money in the first place—and we could not afford to make terms more favorable throughout the city of Boston."[35]

Joseph Bacheller, the chairman who had worked so hard to combine big bank efficiency with the hometown touch, concluded:

> The only reason we can justify discriminating in favor of these people is because of a civic sense of duty, in other words, a sense of duty to our environment as well as to our depositors, but we think there has to be a limit to that exception. . . . I think that on sober reflection most anybody will admit that we have to have a line somewhere beyond which we will not go in offering these special terms, for various reasons. . . . So we cannot really see that there is any need to argue the necessity of our having a line somewhere.[36]

Carl Ericson was next to testify. The vice president of the Suffolk Franklin Savings Bank and vice-chairman of the B-BURG steering committee was the bankers' representative who directed the Warren Street office. In contrast with his fellow bankers testifying that day, he did not seem prone to shifting the blame. With disarming bravado he made the following claim: "It was my feeling along with the other people involved in establishing the line that we should create an expanded area beyond the Model Cities area to take in white neighborhoods so that there would be no reference to discrimination against whites." Satisfied with this principled argument, Ericson elaborated on the operational implications: "The streets were just arbitrarily picked because they looked long, they looked conspicuous, and Walk Hill Street was just to the south."[37] The assistant counsel, Jack Blum, pressed Ericson on just how arbitrary was arbitrary. Ericson at first tried to claim that the annexed white area to the south was Irish, but Blum remained unconvinced. Finally Ericson admitted, "Jewish people were living to the south." The assistant counsel further queried Ericson on Mattapan's subsequent destabilization, prompting Ericson to say, with considerably less triumph than when he began, "Oh, it did not enter my mind that there was anything being created that would create the unrest and dissent that does prevail there today."

But this spasm of candor was not to prevail as the assistant counsel continued to examine Ericson and his former boss on their awareness of blockbusting. Blum asked Ericson if anyone complained to the B-BURG office or to him about what was happening in Mattapan.

"I personally had no complaints," Ericson replied. When Blum asked if the bank group had received complaints Ericson responded, "I have read a few letters. We have not had too many letters of complaints of blockbusting. I have seen a couple." The assistant counsel then produced a thick pile of letters from the subpoenaed B-BURG files, asked that they be entered into the record, adding, "I wonder who received those complaints? Were those complaints received by you, Mr. Bacheller?" "To the best of my knowledge, Mr. Blum," the former chairman replied, "at the time that I retired, which is a year-and-a-half ago, I do not believe that we had any complaints about blockbusting. In fact, when the word was first used and I first heard it—perhaps some months after I retired—I did not know what it meant."

Blum began to read from a letter, dated April 23, 1969, from the commissioner on housing and education, the City Mission Society, Association of Massachusetts Conference of United Church of Christ: "However, we also feel upon reflection that the limitation of mortgage placement within district lines by Boston Banks Renewal Group is grossly contributing to the ghettoization of the city. Although it is not the intention of the Boston Bank Urban Renewal Group to do so, it is hastening the flight pattern of the Mattapan section served by that group." Blum turned to Bacheller: "Did that not make you wonder whether or not the program was having the undesirable effect?"

Bacheller countered, "Was the letter addressed to me?"

Blum answered, "It is addressed to [Boston Five vice president] Mr. Robinson. Excuse me. Is there anyone present who was aware of this letter?"

"Did you see it, Carl?" Bacheller asked Ericson, who replied,

"No; I was not involved." "Mr. Robinson must have handled it," concluded Bacheller.

Blum made one last effort: "Was the letter never discussed in your group?"

"No. . . . Some of these things we heard about," Bacheller said carefully. "I say some of these things. Once in a while he would discuss informally with us a complaint and tell us that he had handled it to the satisfaction of all concerned. We did not go further than that."[38]

The brief demonstration of bureaucratic buck passing excited the subcommittee's assistant counsel, Jack Blum. He had succeeded in getting the bankers to exhibit their true behavior regarding the line: hear no evil, see no evil, speak no evil. Now he relished the thought of getting them to admit to their motive in drawing the line. It was not difficult to get Bacheller to pontificate upon his theory of ethnic relations or his theory of changing neighborhoods. "I cannot believe, Mr. Blum, that the elimination of the line would have changed this picture," Bacheller offered. "I think that the ethnic groups would have tended to congregate together anyway. . . . Our feeling is that others would move there to be together and inevitably a pocket would be formed." Blum responded with sarcasm, "And your effort was to help that move which was naturally occurring." "Our effort was to make home ownership available, Mr. Blum," Bacheller snapped back.

The counsel for the banks, Gale Mahony, quickly jumped in:

> Mr. Blum, I might say this. It seems to be implicit in your question that you assume that the existence of the line was a principal cause for the special concentration of movement of black families into this area down in the center part of the map. Now if that conclusion has been reached by the subcommittee, I would suggest it is entirely premature and an improper conclusion . . . the movement that you refer to of black families was entirely unrelated to and independent from the action of B-BURG and the existence of the B-BURG line.[39]

Bacheller was determined to complete the exposition of his theory of ethnic relations, which he had begun before the lawyers' squabble. "I think it is absolutely inherent in the present stage of relationship between whites and blacks, historically, and how soon it can be eliminated I do not know. But at the moment, let us be realistic about it. If blacks move into a white neighborhood, it does tend to decrease value . . . I think very definitely ethnic groups have tended to clan together," he opined.

If several hours of testimony did not prove that Bacheller was an architect of the line, they clearly demonstrated that he was a master of stonewalling. Nevertheless, Hart tried to strike a conciliatory note as Bacheller left the stand: "As you leave, I think it is right that I express at least some awareness of how you must feel. . . . In part you have cooperated with the federal government in seeking to achieve what is a national goal, and that is to provide homes for low-income Americans. . . . I confess that I remain hung up by the drawing of a geographical line which has the effect of—well, it has several effects." But he cut himself short; reassuring the banker that he wanted to avoid confrontation, he thanked him for his cooperation.[40]

Subsequent studies of B-BURG did suggest motives and effects. Stable, well-established Jewish neighborhoods such as Mattapan where elderly Jewish homeowners had paid off their mortgages years before or had 4½ percent loans, available during the 1940s and 1950s, were considered "dead areas" for the banks. The thrift institutions had merely expanded their economic opportunities by directing blacks into such neighborhoods. Although this policy convinced blacks and their supporters that the banks were giving them new opportunities, the financial institutions, arguably, were merely extending the ghetto while protecting the stability of neighborhoods in which they were more heavily invested.[41]

The Boston hearings continued with the testimony of HUD's area director, M. Daniel Richardson, the individual responsible for enforcing Title VIII, the recent congressional legislation against housing discrimination. Internal HUD memoes from the period acknowledged that blockbusting had taken place "on a major scale . . . and it continues to take place" and pointed to the unnecessary bureaucratic and legal obstacles that the agency placed before any citizen who wanted to file a complaint against blockbusting or some other Title VIII violation.[42] But the federal bureaucrat was unwilling to concede even that which the B-BURG bankers had publicly acknowledged:

I do not think the Department can say today, or I can say today, as a representative of the Department, that, you know, block-busting exists or does not exist. We certainly have a lot of information in the public press and there certainly seems to have been a lot of information here indicating from people that blockbusting does exist. They have no formal complaints upon which to base any definition or determination of the fact that the alleged blockbusting does exist.[43]

Howard O'Leary, the staff director and chief counsel of the Subcommittee on Antitrust and Monopoly, resumed the questioning. "Were you aware of the line when you first began to work here in your present position?"

Richardson replied, "Yes; aware of a number of lines, as a matter of fact."

"With respect to the B-BURG line — and if it is not appropriate to ask you, perhaps someone who is accompanying you can answer — it is a fair assumption to say that HUD, FHA, were aware of the lines from the outset of the program?"

"I would say yes."

"What efforts, if any, has FHA or HUD taken to get rid of the line or, in the alternative, is it the position of the agency that the line is a good thing?"

"It is certainly not the position of the agency that the line is a good thing or a bad thing. It is a line that was agreed to originally by the city fathers and the B-BURG banks, which was a loose coalition as is stated in the testimony, which was created specifically to provide assistance to families within the Washington Park renewal area. Second, to provide assistance of that same type to people within the Model Cities area as it was extended. And lastly, to define the area that the banks decided that they would go into and insure mortgages in through their loose confederation."

"Is it your testimony that from the initiation of the program up to the present date the agency simply has not taken a position one way or the other as to whether the line is good or bad?"

"I would say yes, because our position, and as I said before, Mr. O'Leary, I think it is stated in our testimony, was to provide within lines mortgage money of a certain amount that could use available HUD insuring programs which previously were not available in that area."[44]

Senator Hart, who was silent through much of this discussion, could no longer contain himself. "Do you feel at all uncomfortable administering one of the programs that is assigned HUD—a program intended to assist Americans to obtain housing though they are in the low-income bracket—which is restrictive and will not let them locate outside a geographic line drawn not by public authority but by the private sector? You are administering a program around which a line has been drawn. It denies at least some behind the line the opportunity to use a program to locate beyond the line."

Richardson began, "I do not—"

Hart interrupted, "How do you feel about it?"

"I do not in fact think that is true."[45]

Hart concluded his interrogation of the HUD official without his usual reassuring words about good intentions.

Throughout the three-day hearings, middle-class black residents of Mattapan submitted their names to the subcommittee's witness agenda. While acknowledging that the Jewish community had indeed been victimized, they argued that it was hardworking black families who, in the end, would be B-BURG's greatest victims. Robert Fortes, a member of the active Mattapan Neighborhood Block Association, convinced the subcommittee's staff to allow him time to address the hearing:

> I can tell what has happened in the community because I live there. I can testify to you what has happened to the B-BURG program because I have been affected by it. I can tell you what is happening in Mattapan because I see it every day. . . . There are eleven homes for sale on Almont Street alone. Eleven for-sale signs. Every street you turn down there are signs in the window. The atmosphere for the young blacks, the turmoil for your black kids, looking up and down the street seeing what is going on, is shocking. Whites run from fear, a lot of fears from innuendo, a lot of fears from rumor, not facts. Businesses moving out of the city, service decaying, from Walk Hill to Blue Hill Avenue. . . . The fact is that we support 100 percent maximum housing for minorities. Our organization supports that. The price which minorities have to pay for decent housing we do not support. The price which blacks have to be subject to because they want to live in decent

housing, who want to move with their families into something that is up to standards of the housing codes of Boston, they are forced to pay ridiculous prices. . . . We talk about what is going to happen in urban renewal, talk about the costs, what the factors are. . . . Blacks are forced every three or four years to uproot themselves either because of a federal program for urban renewal or because of the fact that the decay in the community has gotten to the point where they cannot send their kids to healthy schools or decent city services are not provided for them or proper education.

My concern is that why does the property value change because blacks move into a community? . . . These are the concerns that the residents in our communities have. Organizations of over 500 people. We often work together trying to deal with this problem. Blacks are more frustrated than ever by the problem because the whites are getting out. Blacks are going to stay there. We want opportunities for our people this time. They are not provided the opportunity by the B-BURG program or any program that the government claims it is supporting in the communities. They are not being given that kind of help. . . . Senator Hart, I hope this committee does not whitewash—I hope this committee is looking into these problems because we are working hard night and day, volunteering our time in this community, trying to combat the problems. We are working hard trying to organize ourselves against the forces that have affected us for a long time. Senator Hart, I just want to say one other thing. We have paid a deep price.

We continue to pay that price. Many, many blacks in Boston, good 90 percent of them, are fighting to live in decent good housing, to bring their children up in a healthy society. The racism in this country is going to destroy all of us. What is happening in Mattapan is an example of what is happening across this country. Hearings like this have got to go on. They have got to go beyond political motives, beyond high-priced salaries, and beyond profiteering. They have got to deal with the sensitivities of the people that are affected by them, and I mean this deeply, because we are paying a deep price and all we see is a lot of talk.[46]

The fervor of the last speaker provided a note on which Hart could now more comfortably make his closing statement:

> Gentlemen, I know perfectly well that the printed record will not reflect the quiet of the room when you spoke. I make no self-serving statement about what the committee may or may not be able to accomplish. I hope you believe I share the same concerns that you voiced and indeed the same aspirations you are speaking of. It may be very well that we close on the note you sound.
>
> The forces that operate to produce the add-on costs of being black, the forces that operate and give rise to the problems you described in Mattapan are in operation. I suppose I would be hard put to find any community where they are not. And even without formal lines, they create walls where decisions are not made in the community, and I do not know whether this society of ours has the ingenuity to develop or the will to deliver on a series of actions which will change the problems that you described.
>
> Sooner or later if we fail to remove lines, whether they are tangible real walls or the consequence of decisions that have the effect of a wall, forces would be unleashed that could destroy us as a people. . . .
>
> I close without being able to state on the record to you or even at home to my own children an absolute lead-pipe certainty in my own mind that as a society we will be able to do that.[47]

Senator Hart had driven his "strange vehicle" as far as he could for now.

The subcommittee reconvened on May 1, 1972, in Washington, D.C. The influence of the Boston hearings on Allen Hessel from suburban New York and a fledgling group of community advocates from around the country would soon become apparent in room 1202 of the New Senate Office Building. The dramatic tension was no longer focused on mysterious perpetrators; identifiable conspiracies lurked all over. ". . . We identified the enemy. We found that it was not us," a Chicago activist would attest.

The Boston hearings had compelled Senator Hart to push beyond the antitrust bailiwick. The true concern of the subcommittee, he said, was "the total social cost to all of us when cities are destroyed, the alienation of the people is magnified, and tax dollars are already wasted."[48] Peter Chumbris, minority counsel, further set the mood by reading from the Congressional Record of the past three days entries made by Senator Taft on housing:

> We have received news of massive housing frauds involving government subsidies from New York, St. Louis, Detroit, Philadelphia, and other cities. At the same time, the expense of maintaining these programs has mushroomed. It is the executive branch of government, rather than the legislative branch, which can and must respond to the housing standards effectively and immediately. Senator [George] Romney has demanded that the administration of FHA programs be tightened up; speculators and other fast-buck artists can no longer be allowed to take advantage of these programs and the low-income Americans that they serve. To get rid of speculators, the FHA will have to upgrade its inspection procedures for existing housing, because home buyers consider FHA approval as proof that a home is in good shape. The agency cannot be content just to appraise these dwellings.[49]

From the first testimony offered by Gail Cincotta, chairman of the Chicago-based National People's Action on Housing, it was clear that the scope of the problem was perceived as national and therefore the sense of urgency was greater.

> What we see in our newspapers is that one day it hits the headlines in Chicago that there is a hearing, that there is redlining, and there is nothing done. For one day it hits in Philadelphia that there was a hearing, and there is nothing done. And it is on and on.
>
> What we did in Chicago was a group of blacks, whites, and Latinos got together and we identified the enemy. We found out that it was not us; that it was the real estate companies, the insurance companies, the savings and loans and banks and the big powers. And, to our amazement, it is the federal government, the FHA, and HUD that is destroying our communities.

Having outlined her thesis, Cincotta was tempted to flesh it out with sad stories of real people who lost their homes and their communities: "We would like to go and tell you about ourselves from the personal experiences, what a changing community means. You know, it is in the headlines, and it is called a natural phenomena." But Cincotta could not let go of her suspicions of lurking, elusive forces:

> We say it is not natural. It is collusion. It is a conspiracy. . . . It is happening in our communities. The government of our country during its War on Poverty has ignored the edge of the ghetto and concentrated instead on feeding its dying center. Yet, this center keeps widening and the edge becomes thinner and will soon disappear if the conspiracy is not stopped. . . .
>
> Either by design or lack of insight, FHA is the largest force in the change and destruction of the neighborhoods of Chicago. It destroys free choice of housing for minority groups and is the tool of the unethical real estate broker.
>
> We need this committee's help to uncover the conspiracy. The testimony you have heard on Boston, the evidence you are uncovering on New York this week all points to the same conclusion—it's not natural for our cities to flourish, then to decay. Because of outside forces, whites believe that they have been driven from their homes at a great loss by the blacks and browns. The minorities in turn believe that all the injustices they have gained are due to the fault of the whites, and both of the victims are reduced to blaming one another. The cause is not racial; it lies in the conspiracy, and to this we and you must continue to address ourselves.[50]

Cincotta in Chicago, like Janice Bernstein in Boston, had come to the belief that elusive forces, mightier than a few realtors on a main avenue, had undermined her community. It was suddenly no longer paranoid to speak of collective forces, including agencies of the U.S. government, being responsible for one's personal suffering.

"The American Dream of owning one's own home," as Allen Hessel now testified, ". . . must be focused on by all levels of government, because it is being replaced by a nightmare of victimization that is leading to bitterness. Bitterness on the part of

the long-time resident who feels he is forced out of a once viable
area and bitterness on the part of a new resident who is forced into
a deteriorating area."[51] Hessel also reported that local efforts at
self-defense were often turned back as politically out of step with a
national liberal agenda. He spoke of a Laurelton rabbi who had
started a nonprofit real estate brokerage to counteract the speed
with which his neighborhood was changing. The rabbi had been
widely denounced by Jewish organizations throughout New York.
Hart was perplexed: "I am troubled by it . . . if it is true that
massive turnover, rapid turnover, is undesirable, undesirable to
those who seek a balanced, integrated community, whether somebody then undertakes to forestall that and finds he is going to get
shot down, as an anti–civil rights force, then you are not going to
have people working to stop the turnover." Hessel, too, was
puzzled by the negative responses, particularly from the New York
Federation of Jewish Philanthropies, deemed a liberal organization
that would support efforts to preserve and stabilize communities.
"When we try to come up with an individual program, it is
criticized severely by those who could possibly benefit most," he
shrugged.[52]

The hearings in Washington yielded impassioned defenses on
the part of bankers as well, defenses far more compelling than
those offered in Boston. Isidore Lasurdo, the executive vice
president of the Green Point Savings Bank in Brooklyn, praised the
soundness of the FHA concept while decrying its poor management:

> While there would appear to be abundant evidence of a
> deterioration of sound evaluation and underwriting practices
> [that has] crept into FHA operations during recent years, it does
> not diminish the fundamental soundness of this excellent
> program created to meet a vast catalog of unfilled housing
> needs in our nation and, more especially, in our hard-pressed
> cities.
>
>   I believe this program has not produced wanted and
> desired results more recently because of inadequate accounta-
> bility and inefficient supervision in FHA regional offices. I
> believe the recent ugly disclosures represent only the visible
> top of a larger hidden iceberg of ineptitude, favored treatment

and flagrant disregard of the public interest and the taxpayer's money.

In my opinion, all that is required to properly and adequately operate this program for the benefit of all is courage and resolve at the top leadership level supported by a staff of officials of high morality, dedication and talent who will devote their energies and resources toward aiding those in our nation in need of shelter to obtain sound housing at reasonable costs and terms, with minimum down payments.[53]

Senator Edward Kennedy, in attendance that day, asked the banker to expand on those "ugly disclosures." Lasurdo speculated that, at least in metropolitan New York, they were

very widespread . . . I would say in the FHA level it ranges from the clerk at the desk to the man at the top, and it does not miss too many people except maybe the maintenance people that come in and clean the building at the end of the day. . . . There are people who will do things and are not aware they are doing something they should not be doing. When somebody hands them something, they take it in the nature of a gratuity. It is not a bribe. It goes on day after day. They are getting gratuities and, I think, that is the way many of them look at it. However, it is not a gratuity . . . they are getting paid for expediting and changing procedures.[54]

Lasurdo's words were prophetic. HUD, more than any governmental agency, would prove, during the Reagan years, to be rife with influence peddling and mismanagement. A top-to-bottom audit in 1989 would reveal massive corruption costing the government millions of dollars in contract overpayments on the Section 8 moderate rehabilitation program. In Boston many of the housing transactions under investigation had their roots in foreclosures from the era of BURP and B-BURG. But back in the late 1960s and early 1970s, Senator Hart's "mysterious world of finance" was still thick in cloud cover. It may indeed have been true, or at least possible to believe, that the elusive forces that provoked a tearful decision to sell a beloved home or led to an unexpected foreclosure on a family's future equity were but tragedies of good intentions.

In Search of New Centers— the 1970s

The largest of the intruders prepared a bed of wet garbage on the floor of Saul and Gertrude Pearlman's living room closet before trussing the elderly couple back to back and tossing them in. "Get in there and stay in there, old Jews," the man had told them. During the previous two hours the same man had held an enormous hunting knife at Saul's throat while his two partners ransacked the eight-room apartment on Dorchester's Kerwin Street. With the exception of a camera and a small amount of cash, the intruders were finding little of value. The discovery of a wall safe had prompted momentary excitement, but it yielded only mortgage and insurance documents and some precious family photos, all of which were contemptuously tossed aside. "Gonna kill you now, old Jews," the disappointed intruder told the couple. The Pearlmans, married more than forty years, did not need words to communicate. In Saul's eyes his wife could read the message to remain silent and not beg for their lives. Earlier, when the knife-wielder had ordered Gertrude to lie down on the couch and had covered her face with a towel, her husband had willed her not to speak. He felt somehow that if they did not speak they would survive.

Despite her husband's protestations that the neighborhood was becoming too dangerous, Gertrude Pearlman had refused to leave Dorchester. Twenty years earlier, when they'd bought the spacious two-family Victorian, they had enjoyed living in the heart of Boston's ninety thousand–strong Jewish community. By 1974, at the time of the assault, they were the only white family on their street. Gertrude had held religiously to the belief that white flight was cowardly and immoral. When the first black family moved in across the street ten years earlier, Gertrude welcomed them to the neighborhood with a basket of cookies and warm rolls. Saul, an oil burner mechanic, gave the heating system a once-over and warned the new family about a neighborhood oil distributor who poked holes in storage tanks and then billed new customers for costly repairs. Within three days of the arrival of the black family, seven for-sale signs were visible on the lawns along Kerwin Street. For Gertrude Pearlman, those who put their houses up for sale were shameless apostates. She was determined to do everything in her power to keep Dorchester integrated. When that failed, she worked assiduously through the local Jewish Family and Children's Service to provide hot lunches and entertainment programs for the elderly Jews left behind, and she joined with predominantly black neighborhood groups to monitor the level of education in the neighborhood public schools from which her own children had graduated decades before.

Pearlman had long since given up trying to explain to suburban friends why she remained in an area of escalating crime rates and declining property values. Each fresh criticism of her choice of residence only prompted her to find new ways to reinforce her decision. One way was to walk the mile from Dudley Station, the deteriorated center of the black community, over to Warren Avenue and down Blue Hill Avenue to her home. The journey took her past the worst of urban blight—the garbage-strewn lots, the burnt-out apartment buildings, and the reeling sidewalk denizens. Rarely, if ever, did she see another white face. Pearlman was forced to abandon these sojourns not because of violent episodes but because passersby invariably fell into step with her and insisted on accompanying her all the way home in order to protect her from muggers and addicts. She had started out to prove that anyone could walk safely through Boston's insular neighborhoods but had merely ended up wasting the time of local samaritans.

For Gertrude and Saul Pearlman, the dream of integration ended as they wriggled on their closet floor to free their binds. The assault, Gertrude recalled, "continued to play like a newsreel in my head." The couple had adamantly refused to listen to the logic of neighbors who had fled to the suburbs. But now even their black neighbors were appealing to them to leave. "You're older, Jewish, and vulnerable. It's over for you here," said a neighbor who had become particularly close to the couple. After the assault, arrangements were made for the Pearlmans to stay with out-of-town relatives. Before leaving, the couple visited the graves of loved ones at a Jewish cemetery west of Boston. After only a few days away, they mustered their courage and returned home. Stepping from their car, they saw three young men hacking away with axes at their basement door.

The Pearlmans moved from their home of more than twenty years in great haste. Much of its contents now seemed tainted. Saul left behind many favorite tools and treasured books, even the birch table he had made himself. The lazy Susan that had provided hours of enjoyment for their grandchildren suddenly seemed awkward and unimportant. Gertrude took her final look at the hand-embroidered Japanese tapestry that rested under the heavy glass top of the dining room table; the couple had bought it on a trip to Japan. Now it seemed useless and inappropriately festive; they had no use for it. Leaving Kerwin Street with what they could carry, Gertrude looked back only once. Her eye fell on the decorative wooden carvings beneath the roofline, which Saul had painted white to set them off from the charcoal-gray exterior. She wanted to walk one more time through the bright red door with its cheerful brass knocker, but Saul was eager to go. "We tried hard," Gertrude told her husband. "We're wasting time," he responded.[1]

The responsibility for dismantling the last vestiges of Boston's inner-city Jewish community would fall to Bernard Olshansky, a native son. Olshansky was on the fast track in the Jewish professional world when he accepted the executive director position at the Combined Jewish Philanthropies (CJP) in Boston in 1970. Previously an assistant director of the Jewish federation in Cleveland, one of the nation's richest and most effective, Olshansky knew that he just needed to keep his somewhat quick temper in check and a top slot in a major federation would soon be within reach. Although bright and talented, he had some difficulty accepting the major component of corporate philosophy in the Jewish world—conflict avoidance.

Sociologist Daniel Elazar, who made a major study of the dynamics of American Jewry, found that the productive use of conflict, a mainstay of American politics, was practically nonexistent among decision makers in major Jewish organizations and federations. "In the aftermath of the Holocaust and because of the continuing crisis affecting the Jewish world, no issue is allowed to emerge as a matter of public controversy in the American Jewish community if it is felt that this might threaten the unity of the community," Elazar wrote. "Especially where voluntary leaders are involved, every effort is made to avoid overt dissension. When issues are likely to provoke conflict there is every tendency to avoid raising them in the first place."[2]

Avoiding conflict had been among the hardest lessons for Olshansky to learn. Growing up in the 1940s in Dorchester, he had discovered that some differences could only be settled with his fists, particularly when engaging Irish antagonists in Franklin Park. Occasionally, the fisticuffs would land him in the hands of local law enforcement officials. The scrapes with the law, however, were not without their incidental pleasures. Some of his fondest childhood memories, he would later recall, centered on the long private chats he had with his dad as the two walked back together from the local police station.

Olshansky studied social work and applied its lessons in Dorchester and the working-class suburban city of Waltham throughout much of the 1950s and early 1960s before landing a plum job with the Jewish federation in Cleveland, an organization from which federations in larger Jewish communities often recruited. After the retirement of the likable but passive Ben Rosenberg from the Boston Jewish federation, Olshansky sought and won the top slot back in his hometown. Dorchester was a very different community from the one he'd grown up in. Only one year earlier, Olshansky had convinced his elderly parents to move out of Dorchester after his father was mugged near the family home on Norfolk Street. A visit to the once-thriving G&G that year had convinced him that Jewish Boston was beyond repair. "It was seedy and depressing. The stuff was lousy," he recalled. "The place wasn't clean. The people were tired. . . . It was clear to me we were past recovery." For a leader who had grown up in a tightly knit Jewish community, Olshansky had surprisingly little nostalgia for the old neighborhood. "There was no way I was going to live in a three-family wooden tenement when I could live in a single-family house," he explained. "The American dream was a house of your own, some land, two cars, good schools for your kids. Living on Blue Hill Avenue was not my aspiration."[3]

In Cleveland, Olshansky had watched dispassionately as Jews headed for the suburbs, leaving that city with almost no Jewish community in the city proper. Like Jewish communal planners in Greater Detroit and other "model" Jewish communities, he perceived the demographic shifts as new opportunities to build massive Jewish community centers with sports and recreational facilities equal to those found at the better country clubs. Olshansky embraced the concept of the suburban Jewish community center with the same enthusiasm that city planners and developers had shown for massive urban renewal projects. Ironically, the concept of "building community" was often used as the justification for the new and expensive centers nationwide. Pulpit rabbis, often fearing encroachment of the federation, preached that the "country club" centers were devoid of Jewish values. Jewish community center officials countered that Olympic-size swimming pools and racket sports would at least succeed in bringing Jews in the door. Once there, they maintained, many would take advantage of classes and Jewish-content programs. For Olshansky, the allocation of communal resources to shore up aging communities like Dorchester rather than building community centers in Boston's western suburbs was a foolish investment. Dorchester's Hecht House was not the only liability Olshansky saw in the federation's constellation. Additional local facilities in the working-class cities of Revere, Chelsea, and Brockton were hardly on the cutting edge, either architecturally or in terms of programming. Even the flagship of the Jewish community center movement, which had been opened in Brighton in 1958, was nothing more than a rowboat in Olshansky's eyes.

Greater Boston's Jewish community, Olshansky believed, was desperately in need of revitalization. By national standards, Boston's Jews had never been considered particularly generous in their giving to Jewish charitable causes. Throughout much of the 1950s and 1960s, there had been little growth in the federation's fund-raising activities. The volunteer hierarchy, too, had been considered weaker in terms of leadership ability than that in other cities. It had not been until the Six Day War, in fact, that New England's Jews began to increase their communal giving and take bolder political action. A demographic study commissioned by the Combined Jewish Philanthropies in 1967 had concluded that only forty thousand Jews remained in Boston proper, barely 20 percent of the state's Jewish population. The study also noted that 40 percent of the Jewish population of Mattapan and Dorchester was over the age of fifty, with teenagers, the next largest group. "Those who are teenagers now will leave the neighborhood in a few years and the youngest age group is insufficient to replace them," the study noted. "The population will decline as death takes its toll in the upper age groups."[4] At CJP headquarters in the financial district, the future of inner-city Jewish life looked bleak.

When Olshansky assumed leadership of the federation three years later, much of his time was absorbed with the plight of the neighborhood devotees in Mattapan and Dorchester who insisted on struggling on. CJP records numbered Mattapan and Dorchester Jewry at less than ten thousand. The counts, however, were met with skepticism by neighborhood residents. Jewish Defense League (JDL) members took particular delight in uncovering scores of Jewish families in North Dorchester, which the CJP insisted had been completely cleared of Jews. The JDL did not limit its criticism to statistical studies. Shortly after the arson attacks on Agudas Israel and Chevra Shas, JDL members had picketed the CJP headquarters demanding that the federation provide $50,000 for a rabbis' discretionary fund to hire security guards at area temples. David Pokross, a successful lawyer and lay president of the CJP from 1968 to 1970, made his best attempt at damage control with the local newspapers. "The Combined Jewish Philanthropies has been carrying on positive programs for the Jewish families remaining in the Roxbury–Dorchester Mattapan areas," he told reporters. "In order to accomplish these programs, we have allocated more than $300,000 in emergency funds for this year. In addition, we expect to open this week a multi-service center at 1421 Blue Hill Avenue which will enable us to be of greater help in the areas."[5] Internal memos, however, told a different story. Wrote Sol Kolack, the director of the New England Regional Office of the Anti-Defamation League, in a memo to his national office:

> Like other ghetto situations, there remains in Dorchester/ Mattapan a remnant of the Jewish community made up of old defenseless people forsaken by their children and, to a large extent, by the organized Jewish community. The whole area is in a state of revolution, hooliganism is rampant, and the Jewish institutions that remain are under constant threat. The Boston Police have not been able to deal with the violence in the area—violence perpetrated against both black and Jewish residents. The Jewish Defense League has moved into this tense situation posing as the protector of the Jews who are left, and playing on the failure of the social agencies within the Jewish community to help the elderly and their institutions that remain.[6]

Olshansky, who had come to Boston hoping to implement a grand new Jewish Community Center in a wealthy suburb, instead found the efforts of his planners and foremost lay leaders focused on counteracting negative publicity that had grown out of the anger and frustration of Mattapan's remaining Jews. There was no help to be found at the national level. A Council of Jewish Federations memo, dated March 16, 1971, shows how clearly out of touch the Jewish leaders had become. More than five years after Mattapan and similar communities nationwide had lost the lion's share of their Jewish population and institutions, the umbrella organization of the Jewish federations seemed to be just discovering the problem. "Since these problems can surface in any community, at any time, with varying degrees of complexity and intensity, and with a variety of options for action," the memo reads, "it is essential that each local Jewish community develop a method for systematically monitoring these developments."[7]

The Boston planners believed that only a centrally located

multiservice center would quell the criticism and provide residents with the security they craved. To Olshansky's dismay, his staff began preparing bids for plasterers and exterminators rather than for swimming pool engineers and landscape architects. Placed at the head of the Combined Jewish Philanthropies' committee to organize the multiservice center was Avram Goldberg, son-in-law of Sidney Rabb, the city's leading Jewish philanthropist and founder of the Stop & Shop grocery chain. Like "Mr. Sidney," Goldberg had penetrated the boards of major hospitals, museums, and orchestras but still felt the greatest draw to Jewish charitable endeavors. Goldberg had a knack for getting along with practically everyone. He had grown up in Brighton during the period of heightened enmity between Jews and Irish. It was not unusual, he recalled, to see elderly relatives spit and cross the street when they passed a church. At Boston Latin School, however, he had found himself drawn to many of his Irish classmates and their celebrations. It was an affinity that continued through Harvard and his business career. By the time he had taken up position as a leading executive at Stop & Shop, many employees referred to him by the nickname "Murph." Goldberg had also developed close ties with leaders in the black community. Unlike those of NAACP president Kivie Kaplan, who many blacks privately believed was paternalistic, Goldberg's motivations were rarely questioned.

Goldberg and his volunteer committee, which included Janice Bernstein and other members of the Mattapan Organization, rejected Hecht House as the site for the new multiservice center. Situated on a largely deserted section of American Legion Highway, it was considered far too dangerous a walk for most residents. Site selection, in fact, proved to be more problematic than originally anticipated. When potential landlords discovered that it was the rich and mighty Jewish federation seeking space, the going price per square foot often jumped to double or even triple the going rate. To complicate matters, several of the federation's planners wanted to locate the facility south of Mattapan Square in an area that comprised mostly single-family homes and was still considered marginally safe. But Goldberg insisted on a site north of Mattapan Square where most of the elderly and less affluent Jews still resided. Goldberg and other members of the committee eventually settled on a two thousand-square-foot reconverted suite of dental offices on the 1400 block of Blue Hill Avenue. For several months the committee planned out on paper an array of hot lunch programs for the elderly, youth programs, and phone networks whereby suburban housewives could check on the safety of elderly residents whose own children, apparently, were too busy to call.

With renewed hope and energy, the center was opened in July 1970. The fanfare, however, did not match reality. From the day it opened the center served more as a testament to the years of inaction of the Combined Jewish Philanthropies than a symbol of caring. It also drew the intense scrutiny of members of the Jewish Defense League who, despite the protestations of the communal leaders, immediately added the facility to its list of patrol sites.

A relatively minor incident in early September escalated into a major confrontation between the center's officials and the JDL patrollers and heightened the internal "class warfare" in the community. Following an assault on two Jewish teenage girls who were on their way to a center activity, and the failure of the Boston Police to make an arrest, a JDL patrol launched its own investigation and apprehended three black teenagers as suspects. When the case came to court, one of the alleged assailants was represented by attorney Lawrence Shubow, who was still resented by many Mattapan Jews for his role in the transfer of Mishkan Tefila to a black arts group. To heighten tensions, a former law partner of Shubow's, Stephen Morse, who served as an attorney for the Jewish Community Council, appeared as a friend of the court and delivered a stinging criticism of the vigilante tactics of the JDL. The incident drew intense coverage in the newly revivified *Jewish Advocate* newspaper and confirmed for most of the neighborhood's Jews the depth of the gulf between the leadership and the community. "From the perspective of Westwood [a suburb of Boston], Mr. Morse warns the Jews of Mattapan of the dangers of the JDL," wrote Arthur Bernstein in the *Jewish Advocate.* "We and not he and the Jewish Community Council brought the young hoodlums to heel. We and not he and the JCC were out at midnight on *Selihot* [repentance service] to escort congregants home safely. . . . These details may not be important in the suburbs but here in Mattapan people do not condemn us for our concerns."[8]

The anger also began to affect the ability of the Combined Jewish Philanthropies to raise funds. An increasingly typical response came from a Newton dentist, Dr. Morris Stone, who had managed an active practice on Blue Hill Avenue for more than a decade. Stone sent a letter to CJP leaders with a $50 check for the Israel emergency fund and a note explaining that he was withholding the remainder of his pledge until the CJP promised to "stop fooling around and do something for the Jewish people of Mattapan and Dorchester." Stone listed crimes against Jewish residents and business owners, including the recent shootings of two drugstore owners and a fellow dentist. "The elderly Jews live in fear for their lives and they are not wrong," Stone wrote. "I know because my office is in Dorchester and I have to repair their broken teeth. I see the closing of the drugstores because of firebombings and severe beatings of the owners. . . . When I see these bumper stickers 'Save Soviet Jewry,' I can't see why we don't give out stickers to 'help Mattapan Jewry.' I feel they are just as bad off and a lot closer to home."[9]

With the possibility of a major public relations fiasco at hand, federation planners and leaders wisely acknowledged the safety concerns of the elderly and even tried to turn it to their favor in the fund-raising arena. Suddenly, the concerns of Avram Goldberg took on a new sense of urgency. During an annual address to the CJP board of directors in 1970, Goldberg ended the official silence of the organized Jewish community:

> No one living in Brookline, Newton or Wellesley—no matter how many articles he or she may read or how many speeches he may hear or even make—can appreciate the severity of the problem without personal contact with the area. . . . The CJP was tragically late—in recognizing and responding to the real problems that existed and trying to do something substantial about them. The people in the area feel abandoned by the power structure of the Jewish community, physically and spiritually abandoned. All of us in this room and outside of it share a responsibility for that feeling of desolation, and it is up to us to try our best to make up for lost time.[10]

What had seemed alarmist and embarrassing just a few months earlier, now seemed of utmost importance. By 1971 the federation's fund-raising literature was urging wealthy Jews to give "sacrificially" to the campaign so as to support the CJP center, a Roxbury elderly outreach program, and, most importantly, the relocation of elderly Jews out of Mattapan and Dorchester. But even when the federation had decided to confront the effects of the Mattapan crisis head-on, they still avoided looking into root causes. None of the federation leaders and powerful members of the Jewish community, including those who sat on the boards of the city's major charitable institutions, dared to muster their influence in city hall. Social workers, they decided, would be chosen to deal with the crisis. Political activists, they reasoned, threatened the underlying mode of Jewish organizational life— conflict avoidance.

Years later former Mayor Kevin White would reflect on the Jewish community's failure to use a great American tradition— complaining to city hall: "I'm not knocking here but I don't remember anybody from the United Jewish Appeal. The Jewish community was not making noise. Swift change and they were not making noise. . . . Why was the opportunity for integration missed? Who was responsible? Was the patient dying anyhow and we accelerated the death?"[11]

Bernard Olshansky would also recall the debate that took place around this issue within the Jewish communal leadership in 1970. Just as it had for more than a decade, the arguments were framed squarely in concern about how the image of the Jewish leadership would be perceived in the black community. "When I first came back to Boston, people were attacking the relocation process as racist," he remembered. "Enlightened liberal Jews attacked us. There were Jews who felt we had to be in the forefront of integration and they didn't realize the degree of danger people were in. They did not see moving Jews out of the area as the appropriate thing to do. Our attitude was you don't force integration on the backs of old, helpless people."[12]

The hardest Zezette Larsen had ever worked was in the summer and fall of 1970. A social planner in the field of aging, Larsen had been hired to staff the elderly services component of the Combined Jewish Philanthropies' multiservice center. What she found from the first day on the job, she recalls, was naked fear. From her tiny office at the center, Larsen attempted to survey and conduct a needs assessment on Dorchester's elderly Jews. Most at risk, she believed, were the several hundred Jewish residents living in the

Franklin Field housing project, just yards away from the wall where Boston's Jews once gathered on the High Holy Days but by 1970 a neighborhood racked with the problems of broken families, drug use, and concomitant violence. The elderly residents who were transported to the center for a kosher lunch program told horror stories of being assaulted and humiliated by young, rootless teens. In describing the problems in their neighborhood, the pejorative term *schwartze* slipped effortlessly from the lips of her clients, a fact that always made Larsen uneasy and conflicted.

Each morning small knots of elderly waited at Larsen's door. Her clients were of two sorts: those who begged for escorts on shopping trips or other outings and those who appealed for the agency's help in finding a safer neighborhood in which to live. "We were at my son-in-law's house in Canton on Sunday but he couldn't drive us home," explained one elderly man who lived on Dorchester's Harvard Street. "We took the bus back to Mattapan Square and then a bus to Blue Hill Avenue and Morton Street. Then two . . . two vicious persons pushed me aside and knocked my wife down and took her bag. They broke her back and they broke her arm. I need to get away from here."[13] For those who wished to remain in the neighborhood, Larsen could offer little but verbal comfort. For those who wished to move, she promised help finding an apartment in Brighton, a middle-class neighborhood of seventy thousand people on the west side of Boston.

Adult children also besieged Larsen to relocate their parents, but few, she later recalled, offered to take their mothers and fathers into their own suburban homes. Larsen patiently explained that help was available for those who wanted to leave but that the worst thing that could happen to an elderly person was to be relocated against their will. Few showed any understanding. Larsen never knew when she would likely be accosted by the offspring of Dorchester residents. Once while shopping in Filene's downtown department store, a salesclerk had rushed up to her and demanded, "When will you find an apartment for my mother? If anything happens to her it will be on your conscience." Larsen was incensed. "You've got that wrong," she shot back. "If anything happens it will be on *your* conscience."[14]

The federation leadership had appealed to Boston's largest landlords, including notorious slumlord Maurice Gordon, to help find available apartments in Brighton. Most were happy to help.

But for the elderly who were accustomed to single-family homes or spacious Mattapan apartments, the tiny studios and one-bedroom apartments they saw in Brighton looked like prison cells. "Couldn't I stay in Mattapan?" they begged. "Can't you find some way to protect me?"[15]

Larsen later recalled the sense of urgency she felt about the relocation effort for Mattapan's elderly, an effort that stirred suppressed but painful memories for her. As a young girl growing up in Brussels during World War II, her own family had been warned to leave before Nazi occupation. Her parents had refused. "How can we leave our nice apartment and nice furniture?" they said. "How can we leave what we know and go to the unknown?" When Larsen was 12 years old, her family was deported to Auschwitz, where her parents perished. Years later she would make the connection between her feelings before deportation and the urgency of her concern for her elderly clients:

> I was replaying something I was unconscious of for many years. Maybe what I was doing was rescuing my parents. I was helping them get away from danger, something I was incapable of doing as a child. Now I wonder how, physically, I did the job I did. . . . Seeing these old people afraid of being attacked. Afraid to make appointments later than two o'clock in the afternoon. Fear of walking in the street. It was so painful that I had an enormous drive to find housing for them. Never in my life did I put so much of myself into something.[16]

Larsen's clients would tell her about the blockbusting and other unseemly real estate practices taking place in Mattapan. These subjects, however, would never be raised at weekly staff meetings with CJP officials. Instead, the organization concentrated on establishing a Jewish census and finding sufficient apartments for relocation. Almost 20 years later Larsen marveled at her own shortsightedness and that of the otherwise dedicated CJP staff. "It appalls me that I didn't ask more questions about B-BURG," she admitted. "Especially because I was a planner. I'd just become so darned emotionally involved in that thing [relocation]. I lost track of other things. In my position I could have asked questions and suggested policy. I don't remember doing that. It sounds so stupid."[17]

The Jewish leadership, by its own admission, had developed a single track policy. "We urged all the Jews to get the hell out of there as quickly as they can," remembered Norman Leventhal, the founder of the Beacon Companies, a major real estate and development firm and a former federation president. Years later Leventhal blamed a lack of "sophistication" and "aggressiveness" for the limited responses of the Jewish leadership: "They don't have the ability to take a problem, analyze it, and solve it. . . . Leaders have to take an aggressive position." Though he recalls being puzzled at the time by the B-BURG bankers' singular choice of the Jewish neighborhood in which to implement their program to expand housing opportunities for blacks, he still believes that their intentions were good: "I will not accuse these people, I may be wrong, of anything immoral. . . . I think the intention was good but it worked in an opposite way than it was intended. They tried to help people but they hurt them. . . . I don't know. It's really sad. I saw some of it happening. It was terrible."[18]

During the height of the relocation efforts in 1971, Leventhal's friend, philanthropist Ben Ulin, came to see him with an innovative proposal: to build housing for the elderly in Brighton. The modest proposal was quickly embraced in local philanthropic circles. Within twenty-four months Boston Jewry would boast the development of more elderly housing than any community other than New York (with its Jewish population larger than that of Boston by a factor of nearly fifteen). With extraordinary speed, building permits and contractors were secured for a massive HUD-funded Jewish Community Housing for the Elderly complex in Brighton. The Mattapan-based Yiddish-speaking group workers who were loved by the elderly were replaced with young master's-level social workers who wrote copious notes on adjustment problems exhibited by the relocatees. By most accounts, Mattapan's Jewish population fell below three thousand by 1972, but little attention was paid to the fact that along with the suffering and dislocation of thousands of Jews and the loss of cherished institutions, Boston Jewry had lost its urban center and with it, perhaps, a spiritual core that would not be so readily retrieved.

The problems were most apparent to outsiders. In late 1971 Yona Ginsberg, an Israeli graduate student at Harvard, set out to interview a hundred elderly Jews in Mattapan and Dorchester for a thesis on changing neighborhoods. Initially, her research was to be part of a team project on blacks and Jews in Mattapan, but her colleague chose prudence over valor and chose another topic. Ginsberg was completely unprepared for what she found. Her difficulties getting into the homes of Jewish residents were exceeded only by her difficulties getting out once her subjects opened up to her. Despite the fact that she had called ahead, many residents at first refused to unlatch their dead bolts and police locks until she'd consent to utter a few words of Yiddish or present an identifiable Jewish object such as a copy of the Yiddish-language daily newspaper, *Forward.* "We live in fear," the residents would say as Ginsberg passed through their doorways and entered dusty living rooms where she would be further treated to a litany of past muggings and street humiliations.

But Ginsberg also found a profound awareness on the part of the elderly of the root causes of their sufferings. Most, it seemed, were versed in the operations of the B-BURG banks and their decision to provide low-interest mortgages almost exclusively in once-Jewish Mattapan. Praise was uniform for close black neighbors and condemnation swift for young thugs who seemed to delight on preying on the elderly, black and white. *"Nishbarti,"* she muttered to herself in Hebrew after completing only five interviews. "I am broken, I have had enough." (Years later she would reflect on her response to the Jewish situation in Mattapan, comparing it with growing up in Israel. "I had experienced many wars since childhood, but I had never experienced physical violence.") Ginsberg quickly regained her determination and decided that she must do something about the situation. She approached various officers and staff of the Combined Jewish Philanthropies to see if they could use their political influence to help her new acquaintances. "The Jewish organizations weren't happy with the idea of my doing this research," she recalled. "Questions seemed to infuriate them. . . . Everything was considered a social work problem. They would deliver hot meals to the elderly but they could never understand them."[19]

Ginsberg began to look for answers from area clergymen. She approached Rabbi Samuel Korff of Congregation Kehillath Jacob, but he had little to offer. The area's most politically astute rabbi, the driving force behind the rabbinic court of justice that had brought down the Mindick slumlord empire, now looked utterly depressed. A few weeks earlier thieves had broken into his Norfolk

Street home while he was out on a condolence call. He'd returned to find his front door smashed in and his possessions strewn about his house. Valuable silver and other expensive items that had been in the Korff family for generations had been stolen, but it was in Korff's study that the greatest damage had been done. "My most sacred documents have been destroyed," the rabbi told police. "Sacred documents."[20]

Ginsberg turned next to Father Paul McManus at St. Angela's church in Mattapan Square. Was she simply watching the results of "succession" by a new ethnic group, which her professors had described in sociology class, she'd asked. And what was all this talk about a banking group? And why, for heaven's sake, did Jewish leaders believe that the answer was a few kosher meals-on-wheels? "Everything that happened here was intentional," answered the blunt priest. "Of course it was deliberate. The Jews were the easiest to move." Ginsberg left the church with one distinct feeling. "I was quite confused by Jewish liberalism," she would later observe.[21] Other foreign visitors in Boston were equally confused.

In May 1972, on the eve of Israel Independence Day, Greater Boston's Jewish community was rolling out the red carpet for Soviet dissident Boris Kochubievsky. Only weeks earlier the Kiev native had been allowed to emigrate after serving a sentence in a forced labor camp. Kochubievsky had been accused of anti-Soviet slander after defying official attempts to silence his support for Israel in the heady days after the Six Day War.

Underground journals in the Soviet Union carried reports of Kochubievsky's trial, including the following exchange between prosecutor and defendant on the rationale of World War II:

PROSECUTOR: You know what we were fighting against?

KOCHUBIEVSKY: Fascism.

PROSECUTOR: And what were we fighting for? Was it freedom?

KOCHUBIEVSKY: Yes.

PROSECUTOR: Did we win?

KOCHUBIEVSKY: Yes.

PROSECUTOR: Well, there you are, then, we have freedom.[22]

Boston's Jewish federation officials, like those nationwide, were discovering the emotional pull of the refuseniks. They also discovered the fund-raising potential of hosting Soviet émigrés. When they heard that Kochubievsky would be visiting the East Coast, they asked him to address the city's Israel Independence Rally on the Boston Common. But the federation leaders were not the only ones interested in the Soviet dissident. The Jewish Defense League's Marvin Antelman also approached Kochubievsky and invited him on a guided tour of Boston's inner-city Jewish neighborhood. Combined Jewish Philanthropies officials tried to convince their guest that it would be an unnecessary distraction, but the dissident jumped at the chance.

Kochubievsky and several JDL members set out on a tour of Blue Hill Avenue and its side streets. Stephen Morse, a staffer at the Jewish Community Council, followed closely behind in his own car. At each stop the JDL members pointed out sites of former synagogues or Jewish specialty shops. At the tiny remaining *shtibels* on Woodrow Avenue, they explained that elderly Jews feared to venture forth for the evening *minyan*. They also catalogued the assaults and robberies visited upon those who had chosen to cling to their neighborhoods. Kochubievsky nodded knowingly. One of his relatives had been shot by the Bolsheviks during the civil war. Another had fallen victim to a Stalinist purge. His own grandparents had been killed by Ukrainian nationalists. Near Grove Hall the JDL driver pulled up in front of an Elijah Muhammad's Mosque. He explained that it was here, on the former site of the Aperion Plaza, that thousands of Roxbury and Dorchester Jews had celebrated their life-cycle events. Kochubievsky was aiming his camera at the building when several Black Muslims rushed out and demanded that the group leave. The JDL members refused and the Soviet émigré continued to snap away. One enraged Muslim slapped Kochubievsky's camera to the ground and started to punch him. The JDL men quickly joined the fray. Morse, who had witnessed the exchange, summoned a police officer, who separated the group. Sputtering that the JDL had endangered the federation's guest, Morse drove away quickly with his charge.

A few days later, on Israel Independence Day, Kochubievsky stood before thousands of celebrants on the Boston Common, where, with the aid of a translator, he was to deliver a speech thanking American Jews for their renewed generosity and support on behalf of the federation's charitable overseas work. To the surprise of the translator, however, the émigré began to relate his experience touring the dissipated Jewish communities of Roxbury, Dorchester, and Mattapan. "Even in the Soviet Union," Kochubievsky related in Russian, "Jews are not afraid to walk on the streets in their own neighborhoods after dark." The translator quickly conferred with federation officials and approached the microphone. "I am so happy to be able to visit the wonderful city of Boston," the translator told the audience. "It is a great honor and pleasure."

It was in 1972, some six months after the Hart hearings, that Boston's metropolitan press at last began to analyze what had transpired in North Dorchester and Mattapan. A *Boston Globe* investigative team concluded that "policy makers played a decisive role in accelerating the movement of the slums along Blue Hill Avenue toward Mattapan Square. They set the stage for the wholesale blockbusting patterns and real estate profiteering that made Mattapan a national symbol of a victimized neighborhood."[23] The report further noted that while the existence of the B-BURG line was not widely publicized, its presence was known to FHA officials, Boston Redevelopment Authority officials, and leaders in both the black and Jewish communities.

Even as the city papers began to assign responsibility for the decay, and subsequent reports pointed to federal investigations of area real estate firms, including the prominent Cummins Real Estate, Inc., an average of thirty white families continued to move from the area each week. Equally distressing were the problems faced by the incoming home owners. With insufficient counseling, many families had bought houses that, unbeknownst to them, were badly in need of repairs. Many low-income B-BURG-era buyers, therefore, were caught between fixing their homes and not paying their mortgages or paying their mortgages and letting their houses fall into disrepair. The first option led to foreclosure, the second to further neighborhood blight.

By 1973 Jewish abandonment of the old neighborhoods left fewer than twenty-five hundred Jewish residents still clinging to their homes in Dorchester and Mattapan. The new B-BURG buyers, too, were walking away from their "dream homes" at a rate of one every two days. Studies would show that new residents were more likely to lose their homes through foreclosure and abandonment than they were to realize capital gains in the event of resale.[24] In triple-decker neighborhoods citywide, property values jumped 13 to 42 percent from 1970 to 1973; in the B-BURG neighborhoods, however, they stagnated or declined. With little or no money invested in down payments and little equity to protect, walking away had become a rational option. Nor did the B-BURG banks take measures to assist buyers prior to foreclosure. By 1974 more than 10 percent of the housing in the B-BURG area was found to be in default or abandoned. Subsequent studies would show that one-half of B-BURG purchasers had lost their homes five years after the introduction of the program. B-BURG banks, however, continued to profit. Interest rates for FHA mortgages ran consistently below conventional mortgages. By charging a 1 percent service fee on every B-BURG loan, banks were able to pay less than appeared on paper to compensate for lower earnings. When the loans were foreclosed, the banks collected more from FHA insurance than they'd paid at the point of the loan origination.[25] Furthermore, by assigning the foreclosures to HUD, the banks were able to avoid the payment of taxes and utilities during the foreclosure process. As a consortium, the B-BURG banks profited both individually and collectively.

In March 1973 Rabbi Samuel Korff would deliver the ultimate requiem for Jewish Mattapan. Although most of his congregants had been relocated to other neighborhoods by the federation's social workers, a handful of congregants at Kehillath Jacob had refused to leave. One congregant, a retired fruit dealer named Charles Shumrack, had repeatedly sought reassurance from Korff. "I hope the synagogue will remain open," Shumrack would tell his spiritual mentor after every morning service. "It will as long as you are alive and come to the synagogue," Korff would tell him.[26] Content, Shumrack would embrace the rabbi and walk back across the street to his apartment, where he lived alone since the death of his wife two years earlier. In mid-March, Shumrack was found murdered in his first-floor apartment. His rooms had been ransacked, and his clothes were strewn across the backyard. In his eulogy for Shumrack, Korff unleashed months of pent-up frustration and anger: "In days of old, when a murder was committed, the civil and religious authorities, the elders and judges, before even searching for the criminal who perpetrated the crime, would re-evaluate their own deeds, and in a special ceremony, would seek to know if 'our hands did not spill this blood.'" Korff then challenged future historians to determine "how it was possible for a Jewish community of 40,000 souls to be emptied in the course of two years and how so much crime was concentrated in the short space of 40 blocks." Resorting to the language of the European Holocaust, Korff further demanded an explanation as to how Mattapan, like Roxbury and Dorchester before it, had become "Judenrein."[27] For Korff, the battle was over. He left Boston and prepared to rebuild a congregation in the western suburb of Newton. The only question was whether Shumrack would be the last Jewish casualty.

Some, however, wanted to continue the fight from their new neighborhoods. Janice Bernstein, the "bat lady" from the Mattapan Organization, had moved to West Roxbury, a section of Boston favored by police, firefighters, and city officials. A lawyer friend told Bernstein that she and other former residents of Mattapan, as well as newly arrived black residents, might consider a class action suit against the B-BURG consortium. The idea intrigued Bernstein, Harry Sklar, and other former members of the Mattapan Organization's real estate committee. If they failed to win money damages, at least they would bring the B-BURG policies to public scrutiny. The group contacted several lawyers who agreed, in principle, to work on a contingency basis. A few thousand dollars would be necessary immediately, however, for research and travel to Washington, D.C., to examine all the documents compiled by the Hart committee. Bernstein and her friends were only able to raise a few hundred dollars, and their lawyers quickly grew discouraged. Family and friends counseled Bernstein to get on with her life and not dwell on the past. The "bat lady" was determined, however, to take one last swing. Bernstein knew that Lawrence Shubow, the attorney who had played a key role in helping Elma Lewis secure the Mishkan Tefila building for her school for African-American arts, had watched the subsequent blockbusting in Mattapan with great discomfort. Back in 1968, when Shubow helped broker the transfer of Jewish institutions into black hands, he'd believed that the black struggle for civil rights and economic advancement was the only front necessary to fight on. The B-BURG program, however, had provided him a sobering lesson.

"It was a horrible thing those banks did," Shubow would later note. "To take two populations and pitch them against each other. . . . Here was the case of two populations at their most sensitive and naked edges being rubbed together. . . . Objectively, the bankers were bastards. They made it impossible to have an integrated community."[28] Shubow was well connected with leaders in the Jewish Community Council, American Jewish Congress, and other local Jewish organizations. He told Bernstein that he would use his persuasive powers to convince the legal affairs committees of these organizations to provide the necessary funds to mount a legal challenge to B-BURG. The idea of a class action suit struck an immediate chord with some members of the Jewish leadership and a decidedly negative tone with others. Justin Wyner, an industrialist and lay president of the Jewish Community Council, had been experiencing pangs of guilt since the Combined Jewish Philanthropies first opened their multiservice center on Blue Hill Avenue in the summer of 1970. A resident of Brookline, Wyner had taken to praying in the last remaining synagogues along Woodrow Avenue. Elderly congregants would surround him at the end of the service and plead for help in stabilizing the community. "We don't want you to help us get out," one man had told him. "We want you to help straighten this mess out. It's not black against white. We want you to help make this a mixed community."[29] But it was a drive through the area with a member of the local Jewish Defense League that had clearly shaken Wyner. The JDL driver was silent as the pair viewed boarded-up synagogues and drove down deserted streets that had once vibrated with commerce and family life. Finally, the driver spoke: "When the president of the Jewish community council in Warsaw finally learned where the trains were going, he hung himself."[30]

The idea of a class action suit did not go over well with other members of the Jewish community's leadership. Lewis Weinstein, who had brokered the deal to move Hebrew College out of Roxbury two decades earlier and who sat on the board of the Boston Five Cents Savings Bank, a leading B-BURG bank, would not hear of it. Aligned with Weinstein were Matthew Brown and Phil Fine, both powerful lawyers with major clients in the downtown business and banking communities.[31] The discussions on the advisability of the suit within the legal committees of the Jewish organizations continued throughout the spring of 1973. Bernstein and Shubow would hear favorable reports and just days later receive news of delays. One by one, the letters began to arrive at Bernstein's door in late March and early April 1973. Some examples:

From the Jewish Community Council: "The Legal Committee and the Council were divided on the merits of the case, but there was a general agreement that the chance of victory at this late date was remote. Given these judgments and the division over the inherent wisdoms of a lawsuit on this matter within the Jewish community, the Council decided not to become involved in an official action against B-BURG.[32]

From the American Jewish Congress: "We have regretfully determined that we can take no action on this matter due to the lack of both financial and personnel resources."[33]

Janice Bernstein was defeated. Only one or two of the brokers who had been responsible for blockbusting in Mattapan had received even minor penalties or temporary license revocations. Now, with no money to challenge the B-BURG banks and their discriminatory line, there was nothing further to be done. Janice Bernstein settled down to life in her largely Irish Catholic neighborhood in West Roxbury. The "bat lady," who had so loathed the assimilationist values of suburban Jewry, vowed never again to live in a Jewish neighborhood. Why even bother, she thought, to seek a place for myself in the Jewish community?

Several black residents of the area who had endured losses that they attributed to B-BURG also thought of bringing a class action suit against the banks. They interested an attorney, Dan Satinsky, in representing them and appealed to the NAACP for support. But the NAACP expressed as little interest as its Jewish counterparts in stirring up old issues.

Others, however, were paying careful attention. Community activist Michael Ansara had moved to a two-family house behind the old courthouse in the Irish section of Dorchester in the early '70s. His friends thought that he was crazy. The area was a bit frayed, but he had confidence in his black middle-class neighbors and the stability of the neighborhood. The house was beautiful, conveniently located, and well priced at $30,000. Ansara's mother had been a community organizer; the recent Harvard graduate had

had his own fling with radical student politics. Impressed by some of the tactics and successes of Saul Alinsky, the neighborhood alliance maker, Ansara decided to turn to community organizing. Distressed by the results of B-BURG, a "pernicious program," Ansara established Fair Share to work with the residents of Hyde Park and other neighborhoods dangerously close to the B-BURG line. He tried to neutralize the blockbusters by organizing blacks and whites to find common ground. He got buyers and sellers to coordinate activities, thereby threatening to completely eliminate the services of the real estate brokers. Those who were intent on continuing their quick turnaround tricks, so refined by the B-BURG experience, soon realized that Hyde Park would be a different situation and branched out in other directions. Other brokers signed agreements on professional standards that were enforced by Fair Share with greater effectiveness than by the state real estate licensing board (which was under the control of the realtors themselves).

"Could it have been stopped?" Michael Ansara asked as he reflected upon the fate of Boston's inner-city Jews.

> The answer is multiples of yes. It did not need to happen. There could have been different outcomes because bankers made different decisions or because there was a real process of organizing the communities that were involved. . . . There was no sense of approaching the organized Jewish community as a vital part of reorganizing a neighborhood anywhere in the city. . . . The Jewish community could have been more supportive of organizing blacks and whites against blockbusting. The banks were only interested in appearances. The bottom line is that they didn't care to really look at the impact of their policies. Does that make you a crook? No! Does it make you a very damaging institution that is not socially responsible? Absolutely.

A decade and a half after the fact, Ansara proudly pointed out that he had managed to build black–white alliances at the moment of the sharpest racial conflicts during the Boston school anti-busing riots. "Were this to be done in 1966–1970, it would have been even more successful," he suggested. "Neighborhoods do not have to acquiesce to their own destruction. It is a singular failure of communal institutional life that a serious program was not mounted to change what was going on."[34]

In 1979 the Combined Jewish Philanthropies purchased twenty acres of land in suburban Newton for the site of a massive Jewish community center on land that had formerly served as both the Catholic Working Boys Home and the novitiate for the Xaverian Brothers. The vision of Bernard Olshansky, the Dorchester boy who had dreamed of building community centers on a par with those in Detroit and Cleveland, was coming to pass. The project would take an enormous fund-raising effort on the part of the Jewish community's leading philanthropists. Major developers like Norman Leventhal decided to take an active role and make it happen. "By building the JCC," Leventhal would say, "I hope we have reconstructed something that brings the Jews together the way Blue Hill Avenue or the Hecht House did in a different way."[35]

On October 2, 1983, the Leventhal–Sidman Jewish Community Center on the Gosman Campus—proudly bearing the names of prominent Boston Jewish real estate developers—was dedicated. It was a rapturous time for Jewish communal leaders, although considerably less so for Olshansky, who had been ignominiously dismissed during the construction period. Notwithstanding problems such as its inaccessibility by public transportation and cries of unfair competition from area rabbis, the center was instantly trumpeted a success for its architecture and its programs. The glossy program of the dedication ceremony declared:

> It is a remarkable achievement. CJP has made accessible, in a central site, an array of essential community services unprecedented in Boston and probably elsewhere in the nation. It is situated in a setting that invites the warmth of belonging and promotes the sharing of Jewish values. In its commitment to the strength and unity of the family and to the generational renewal, the Jewish Community Campus is an affirmation of the future of the Boston Jewish experience. . . . It is more than architecture and landscaping, more than gymnasiums and meeting rooms. It is a strong affirmation of a vision of shared positive values and nurturing institutions. Boston, the first city

in the United States to establish coordinated Jewish communal and charitable services, has once again fashioned a precious service legacy to be passed from generation to generation.

The building had more books of Judaica when it was the site of the Catholic Working Boys Home.

Students of Jewish identity and commitment continue to debate the efficacy of the suburban Jewish community center. Can the smell of chlorine and fresh cut grass evoke the "warmth of belonging" and the "sharing of Jewish values" in a way that scores of neighborhood synagogues, shops, and clubs could not? Is the "strong affirmation of a vision of shared positive values" keener in the eyes of a federation social planner than in the eyes of the sages who populated the *shtibels* along Woodrow and Blue Hill Avenues? Is the cause of "generational renewal" served more by the building of federally subsidized community housing for the elderly than by sharing a triple-decker with one's aging parents?

During the decade in which Boston's Jews were trying to define new centers for themselves, the city's blacks continued to grasp at home ownership options. Statewide "anti-snob" ordinances were duly enacted in area suburbs, but the suburbs of Boston remained overwhelmingly white. As a secretary of communities and development would later note, mixed-income housing had become "counterintuitive."[36] With programs like B-BURG to look back on, it was little wonder. The black community continued to hemorrhage. The same problems that had long plagued Roxbury—street crime, unreliable municipal services, and substandard schools—had merely moved down the avenue, generating wider anger and resentment. Like the Jews before them, middle-class blacks were overwhelmed by the small but significant underclass that preyed on the honest and seemed to delight in breaking them. Unlike the Jews, the blacks had nowhere to go. Communal leaders continued to prattle on about a black–Jewish alliance rooted in the great civil rights struggle of the 1960s. No one was buying it. If the two communities viewed one another at all, it was across a widening gulf of suspicion and fear.

There were no winners. But were there learners?

Conclusion

A Tragedy of Good Intentions

To this day, Jewish leaders like Julius Ansel and Samuel "Chief" Levine are recalled as lovable rogues by former residents of Roxbury, Dorchester, and Mattapan. In truth, they served a higher purpose than fixing traffic tickets. Through Ansel and the other ward bosses, the Jews of Ward 14 could, in Toqueville's words, "practice the art of government in the small sphere within their reach."[1] If Ansel returned to Blue Hill Avenue today he would undoubtedly be pleased by the seventy-five-acre Franklin Park Zoo. "Only the best," Ansel would probably muse. But he would probably find the zoo the only truly improved part of that changing neighborhood. Since the zoo's $26 million renovation in 1989, Happy the Hippo's successors, Clarence and Camille, live in their own well-cared-for pool in the "African Tropical Forest" and are enjoyed by schoolchildren brought in from the suburbs. The large yellow buses park close to the zoo's well-fortified gates. As visitors

331

walk through the entrance and branch out along the veldt, they
observe the remains of Mishkan Tefila that still tower over the zoo
like the ruins of an old German synagogue.

Were Ansel to repeat this stroll down his beloved avenue,
today he would be walking through Boston's highest crime area.
Like many metropolitan areas across the country, Boston is setting
new homicide records. Rarely a day goes by without headline-
grabbing reports of terrible violence. And 80 percent of 1990's
murders were perpetrated in Boston police Areas B and C—
encompassing Dorchester, Roxbury, and Mattapan—home to only
30 percent of the city's population. Two out of three murder
victims were black, many under the age of twenty.

On Seaver Street, Ansel would no longer see mothers looking
out the window watching their children at play. Today, many
mothers keep their youngsters inside for fear of random shootings.
The violence of today's young blacks far exceeds anything former
Dorchester residents can recall. As Hubert Jones, dean of Boston
University's School of Social Work, says, "Taking out a human
being is like taking out a fly."[2] If Ansel continued south down Blue
Hill Avenue, he would probably still find many adolescents sitting
along the wall at Franklin Field. But gone are the parades in High
Holiday finery and the spirited games. Today's youths have established their own symbols, such as the rows of running shoes that
are laced together and hurled over telephone wires to delineate
the "turfs" of the numerous gangs that now plague North Dorchester and Roxbury.

In the early 1970s, more than 70 percent of B-BURG–assisted
homeowners were unable to keep up their mortgage payments,
because those payments far exceeded their earning power or
because they were faced with repair costs about which the FHA
appraisers and the loan officers had failed to warn them. The banks
foreclosed on more than a thousand single-family homes and
multiunit dwellings in the area. The local HUD Office took over
these houses after paying the banks full compensation for their lost
loan moneys. HUD was ill equipped to manage this real estate.
Some feeble efforts were made to repair, rent, or even auction off
some of the houses, but these efforts themselves became the
source of new charges of corruption against federal government
officials. The solution of choice for beleaguered bureaucrats
became condemnation—whatever the actual condition of the

house. Thus, increasing numbers of B-BURG houses received fresh plywood shutters on the very trim that a few years earlier had been freshly painted—the spiffy "cover" that was all that the FHA appraisers ever saw on their ninety-second "windshield" inspections. Vandals and arsonists practiced their craft, for both fun and profit. Demolition crews were kept so busy that they often could not be concerned with the finer details: the favorite story on the Avenue in the middle 1970s was how wreckers were sent to Bowden Street but did their job at the same number house on Bowden Avenue instead.[3]

Rather than exchange greetings with Jewish merchants gesturing from the doorways of their stores, today Julius Ansel would encounter relatively few shopkeepers along Blue Hill Avenue. Of the existing stores that interrupt the plywood storefronts along the Avenue's northern end, many are owned by Asians who live elsewhere; the exertion of "local control" over businesses in the black community still remains elusive after more than two decades. The large supermarket chains Purity Supreme and Stop & Shop, both owned by Jewish families, no longer operate in the area. Although their owners tried to transfer the stores to local, black entrepreneurs, these experiments failed, forcing residents either to travel several miles to shop for food or pay premium prices for a smaller selection at the scattered small stores remaining in the neighborhood.

Walking along the Avenue, Ansel certainly would not come across many branches of Boston's banks or any of the automatic teller machines that proliferate in other neighborhoods. Banks chartered by the state or federal government have only 9 branches in Roxbury and Mattapan, just 4 percent of the 219 branches in the city.[4] As in Ansel's day, the banks are powerful but remote downtown institutions. The Jews, however, did not miss their presence then. Many had financed their home purchases in the years following World War II with long-term and low-interest mortgages. On smaller transactions, many Jews from Boston's inner-city neighborhoods preferred to deal with their own credit unions, where managers like Meyer Finkel were sure to remember their names, their fathers, and their creditworthiness.

For the black community, however, neighborhood banking services are vital. Much hope was put in the Community Reinvestment Acts (CRAs) enacted by Congress in 1977. The Commonwealth of Massachusetts passed its own CRA legislation in 1982. The CRAs were considered a corrective to the problem this book relates. Banks chartered by the state or federal government, as part of the price of doing business were to balance cóncern for preserving their depositors' equity with concern for conserving those depositors' neighborhoods.

Federal insurance would provide depositors a safety net for the prudent investments of their bankers, making more credit available for housing. But in the deregulation environment of the 1980s, the banks were not prone to comply voluntarily with the reinvestment acts, and enforcement of the legislation was wholly inadequate. Moreover, savings and loan banks created hundreds of billions of dollars of losses in speculative and often fraudulent ventures. Taxpayers will have to cover that bill for generations. In this environment, the bankers unabashedly violated their old claim of "responsibility to depositors" (their excuse for not making credit available in black neighborhoods in the 1960s), as well as violating the laws of the 1970s mandating reinvestment in the community.

Leading experts on minority mortgage lending, such as Charles Finn of the University of Minnesota, cast profound doubt on the viability of the Community Reinvestment Acts. Finn notes that the federal and Massachusetts CRAs have been in force for a number of years. Yet there has been little or no enforcement by regulators. The experts hold out little hope for recent revisions to the federal CRA that require regulators to make public their ratings and evaluations of individual banks. Finn notes further that bank regulators "have clearly not carried out their responsibilities under the CRA."[5] He suggests that agencies with fewer personal ties to the banking industry be used to monitor and enforce the CRA.

Julius Ansel, himself no stranger to questionable ventures, would have scoffed at the B-BURG–style government partnership with the private sector. Any system that couldn't be trusted to deliver a hippotamus obviously could not enforce regulations against clever white-collar criminals. He also would have chuckled at the noise the downtown politicians made over catching a few little fish while they let the big ones slip by. During the 1980s, for example, the Massachusetts Commission Against Discrimination routinely sent investigators to ferret out real estate agents who

were steering minority home seekers away from certain neighborhoods, yet in the same period of intensive real estate activity,
Boston bankers were making home improvement loans in minority
neighborhoods for a third of the rate they were offering to
applicants with the same income in the city's white neighborhoods, thereby discouraging stability in those areas. The 1989
study by the Boston Redevelopment Authority drew out the stark
consequences of these findings: "Banks, as an important source of
capital, play a pivotal but often invisible role in determining
whether a community will thrive or decline. Without a steady flow
of credit, neighborhoods deteriorate." The government appears to
be making little more than a symbolic effort to stop housing
discrimination.

But it is not only in regard to sins of omission in Boston's
inner-city neighborhoods that banking policies stand accused and
toward which the politicians are being overly tolerant. In early
1991, at the height of the savings and loan failures and the depth
of the recession, it was discovered that several Greater Boston
banks were colluding with dubious "home improvement" concerns that encouraged inner-city residents to undertake unnecessary repairs, and offered financing through second mortgages,
many with interest rates of more than 15 percent; the banks were
then buying up this paper and foreclosing on many residents who
couldn't make their payments.

Boston again faces the introduction of B-BURG–like programs. The banks once again hold out the hope for equity and the
potential for misery. On January 2, 1991, a lawsuit brought by the
NAACP against the federal government some twelve years earlier
resulted in a "historic agreement" between HUD and the NAACP
in which $450 million would be made available over the next
fifteen years to increase minority access to white neighborhoods in
Greater Boston. This special grant would also support a clearing-
house to make known the availability of state-assisted home loans
and of 500 new rental subsidy certificates to be administered by
the state. But the ink was barely dry on the agreements when a
controversy broke out over the degree to which suburban municipalities would be effectively pressured to participate. Even Boston
city hall, without whose cooperation the settlement could not
work, is sending mixed signals. The city was not the target of the
initial lawsuit, but in the wake of racial tensions stirred up by the

highly publicized murder of Carol Stuart—in which a black man was falsely accused of killing a pregnant, white attorney—the city leaders, like their predecessors after the Grove Hall riots, groped for a way to counter Boston's racist image. The NAACP's legal counsel, Dianne Wilkerson, spoke of the program as an "unprecedented blockbuster." She proclaimed that "this is a very big one not only for the NAACP and the city of Boston but for the entire country. No other housing case in the country has qualified for this kind of money." But old-line Bostonians like District City Councilor James Kelly of South Boston remember the history of similar programs. Deeply mistrustful of the "liberals" in Newton and Wellesley, he is ready to think of this as a "blockbuster" of a different sort. "You cannot compact racial minorities into the city of Boston, because Boston will eventually become a predominantly minority city and that's not in anybody's interest."[6] Moreover, given the 1,500 rental subsidies recently eliminated by the state and the 14,000 families on the Boston Housing Authority's waiting list, 500 certificates will be only a drop in the bucket.

There would be a lot of tongue clucking and shaking of heads among Julius Ansel's old Jewish friends were they to join him on his walk down the Avenue. Many of them still live a short distance down the road in towns like Milton, Stoughton, and Randolph, worlds apart from Roxbury, Dorchester, and Mattapan. "This used to be a nice place to live. What did they do to the neighborhood?" they would ask. "They," of course, would mean the blacks, not the planners, bankers, and real estate agents whose dirty work is still so much in evidence.

Any blacks who overheard the remarks of these Jewish visitors would probably have an equally pained, personal, and accusatory response. They would consider the Jews as having run away just as blacks were beginning to get ahead. Those Jews voluntarily abandoned their cherished neighborhood, its community and institutions, rather than give blacks a chance to be good neighbors. Moreover, the Jews cheated the blacks by selling them houses in disrepair at highly inflated prices.[7] And now these Jews, sitting by the rivers of their suburban Babylons, shed insincere tears when they remember their "lost Zion."

Among the aging black and Jewish leaders who were active in the civil rights movement during the 1950s and 1960s, there would be the type of exchange that takes place among old war buddies who shared critical moments but then avoided each other for a few decades. The backslapping and the friendly banter, the updates on their families and jobs, and the flashing wallet photos of grandchildren would end abruptly before either side expressed its disappointment in the other or hinted at old slights and new interpretations of the "good old days."

The ambiguities of doing good are a profound source of discontent in these times. Even with the best intentions, it is increasingly difficult to remain "on the side of the angels." The actors in our story, even those with highly refined moral sensibilities, often found themselves confounded by seemingly unbearable choices. They both over- and underestimated their power. At the very times when they perceived themselves as victims of circumstance, they were actually in control, but when they thought they were independent moral actors, they were in fact being influenced by elusive forces outside themselves. Many of them later attempted to exonerate themselves by expanding the catalogue of extenuating circumstances from which they made their self-serving claims. They convinced themselves and others that "it never happened," "I didn't do it," and "besides, they deserved it." Their need to feel that they were just, efficacious, and wise, despite overwhelming evidence to the contrary, led to greater destructiveness and delusion.

Many of those interviewed for this book, former residents of inner-city neighborhoods as well as politicians and their expert advisers, expressed their experience of change in familiar neighborhoods, the loss of community, and the decline in property values in the language of natural phenomena: "It was like a tidal wave came over our neighborhood." Others used the imagery of invasion and conquest to describe their displacement. Still others used fragments of fashionable social science theories regarding "succession" or "tipping," which they applied to their personal experiences with a sense of determinism and inevitability—a strange combination of revealed truth and common sense.

These notions about "filtration," or the trickling down of older housing to lower-income residents, have been popularized by journalists and have had undue influence on policymakers as well as on neighborhood residents. In fact, the rates of upward mobility of different ethnic groups and their attachment to neighborhoods vary considerably and unpredictably. "No longer do all neighborhoods seem to follow steady straight line trends as they mature."[8]

While listening carefully to the descriptions and explanations of our interviewees, the authors also used other modes of analysis. Government policies and banking practices are at least as salient to changing neighborhoods as the "lower-middle-class bigotry" that tries to keep "others" out of the neighborhood or prompts "white flight" when this proves impossible. As Everett Ortner put it:

> Wherever I look in the American city I see the work of the federal tinkerer, reenforced by so much power that the movement of one of his fingers blots out a neighborhood, or slashes a scar through it for automobiles to ride on, or pushes down a historic public building, or any one of a hundred urban crimes. . . . In my judgment, a very large proportion of our urban ailments [are] iatrogenic, caused by the ill-advised treatment of our specialists in urban affairs. Dr. Urban Renewal has been treating us all these years. . . . The cities may yet be destroyed by people who play on your compassion for their own ends.[9]

But bureaucrats and bankers are often less colorful and more discreet than bigots, blockbusters, and slumlords who try to interpret and profit from social structural forces. As for the masses of Americans who have helplessly observed the decline of their communities and have been victimized by changing neighborhoods—their concerns with equity, both fiscal and philosophical, have been in tragic conflict. The elusive political and economic forces that rendered the movements of Jews and blacks less than voluntary or natural and that created no winners in either community have not been given sufficient attention by community leaders, social planners, or scholars. In focusing on the hot passions of racism, they have neglected the role of cold logic and economic rationality. By helping to clear away the "structural underbrush" of contemporary racism, the authors of this book have tried to foster understanding and, ultimately, new means of resolution.[10]

At a time when equality is promoted as the supreme value,

this book has argued for a public policy that is respectful of community. Granted, such a policy presents dilemmas for liberals and conservatives alike. The concepts of local control and community have been used by the left and the right with exclusive and ultimately racist consequences.[11] Pro-community rhetoric is used by the libertarian right to limit the intervention of "big government" and to free market forces, and by the egalitarian left to oppose the dominance of the corporate sector and to justify the welfare state. That communities could be subjected to ecumenical nightmares in an unholy alliance of entrepreneurs and bureaucrats seems beyond imagination. The community must therefore be protected from its friends as well as from its enemies, who are evenly distributed across the political spectrum.

In Boston, racist attacks on rabbis and synagogues were perpetrated in the name of "local control." The acid assault on a rabbi and demands to "lead the Jewish racists out of Mattapan" were plausible but perverse and violent dramatizations of the actions of the bankers and policymakers who were fostering black resettlement only within the restricted B-BURG line. Those same bankers and planners were seemingly protecting racial notions of community in Boston's white ethnic enclaves, as well as its suburbs, by restricting to a limited area their federally insured and subsidized low-interest mortgages for blacks only. While it may not be government's role to support the communal aspirations of its citizens, it certainly should not use its power and resources to obliterate existing communities.

If the executive branch and the corporate sector cannot be relied on to protect the community, its defenders may at least be found in two other quarters: the legislative and judicial branches, which might foster and uphold clearer legal definitions of communality as a basic human right, and the charitable foundations and voluntary associations—the Independent Sector—which might lend their financial support. Notwithstanding the deep suspicions of our nation's founders of "factions" and sectional interests— described in *The Federalist Papers* as the "infinity of little jealous clashing tumultuous commonwealths, the wretched nurseries of unceasing discord, and the miserable objects of universal pity or contempt"—some lawyers have tried to find constitutional roots for the community's legal rights.[12] In recent years several significant court cases regarding the redrawing of congressional district lines or the implementation of public housing decisions have forced local and federal administrators to come to terms with the reality of communities. The principle upon which a new mindfulness of community as against individual rights might be supported is that the tax deductibility of mortgage payments imposes some public responsibility. At a minimum, planners should require an environmental impact study for the protection of people and their communities as comprehensive as those required to protect flora and fauna. These "community impact studies" could generate valuable data for both opponents and proponents of specific projects, thereby equalizing opportunities for effective advocacy.

In this book, the criticism of respected representatives of Jewish communal organizations may be somewhat strong. But it derives from the sense of responsibility that these organizations have historically served and a more general concern for the vitality of the Independent Sector. The tax deductibility of the charity dollar clearly bolsters the argument for greater public responsibility. The Jewish community shares the problem that has been acknowledged by other independent institutions: accountability, not merely in the fiscal realm but in the choice of issues they address.[13] These organizations should model themselves less as private clubs of *makhers* and "big givers" and more in accordance with their communal responsibilities, becoming more participatory and more effective.

Leadership that does not reach down to the neighborhood level can never be truly effective. In Dorchester, opportunities did exist to maintain the "patchquilt" pattern of ethnic communities whose residents have a healthy sense of turf and pride. "Parishes" whose geographic boundaries are ever shifting and ethnic enclaves "waltzing" around each other within larger integrated neighborhoods might have provided a basis for stronger alliances between the black and Jewish communities. Instead, their leaders looked on helplessly as larger economic forces intensified the tendency toward conflict and mutual hostility.

We do not suggest, however, that the defection of Jews from the inner cities was prompted entirely by black–Jewish conflict. Jewish suburbanization was prompted by other motives as well. Most American Jews were only a few generations removed from the villages and farms of Eastern Europe. Whether they were drawn to the suburbs primarily by some rustic ideal or by a primordial desire to return to the garden or the not-so-distant homeland, whether they were haunted by the image of the "destroyed city," or whether they were simply bored with the urbane is not at all clear.[14] In addition, reflecting on their own recent successes, Jews believed that middle-class blacks would follow them in moving "up and out." With myopic optimism but certainly without malice, American Jews encouraged blacks to get ahead. Jews failed to recognize the unique obstacles that blacks would face, particularly the intransigence of housing discrimination. This led to Jewish impatience with blacks and black frustration with Jews.[15]

Whatever that golden age of black–Jewish relations really amounted to, the 1960s were a period of optimism. "We shall overcome," "blacks and whites together"; there was a commitment to "get America going again," in the words of Boston's favorite son John F. Kennedy. The American Tragedy would be confronted and resolved, it was believed. But Blue Hill Avenue is a living monument to the new tragedy that was unfolding. Two decades later, blacks feel abandoned and frustrated; whites including Jews feel threatened and weary.[16] Through the late 1960s, the black–Jewish alliance appeared to be of great historical significance; now the barriers between blacks and Jews are more impassable than a banker's red or blue line. The ethnic complexion of America is changing almost daily, a function of political and economic vicissitudes the world over as well as changing immigration laws, factors wholly independent of the relations of blacks and Jews. According to demographic predictions, in 1992 blacks will yield their position as America's largest ethnic group to Hispanics, at least for the time being.

Black–Jewish relations may be changing from being of great historical significance to mere historical significance. The most vitriolic ethnic confrontations in recent years have occurred between blacks and those with whom they have far less in common even than with Jews. During the recent black boycott of Korean grocery stores in New York, a few blacks were quoted as missing their old Jewish shopkeepers. Yet, we have learned to suspect this nostalgia and the rage that it conceals. So busy blaming each other, neither the blacks nor the Jews of today manifest much understanding of the elusive forces that are external to their communities and function independently of both their wills and interests. Entangled as they are in the "social structural undergrowth" of ethnic relations in America, it is no wonder that they are unable to find common cause and common ground.

Notes

INTRODUCTION

1. Anonymous, "Confessions of a Blockbuster," *Metropolitan Real Estate Journal,* May 1987.

2. Edward Banfield, *The Unheavenly City: The Nature and Future of Our Urban Crisis* (Boston: 1970), pp. 15, 80.

3. Nathan Agran, "The Problems of Philadelphia's Jews," *Congress Bi-Weekly,* September 8, 1972, pp. 8–12.

CHAPTER 1.   BLUE HILL AVENUE

1. Mark Mirsky, "The G&G on Blue Hill Avenue," *Boston Globe,* March 7, 1971, p. A2.

2. Interview with Meyer Finkel, March 18, 1988.

3. Internal memo from I. Zack, April 21, 1951, archives of the Anti-Defamation League of B'nai B'rith.

4. Mirsky, "The G&G," p. A2.

5. Interview with Sam Levine's son-in-law, Phil Briss, May 28, 1989.

6. Sally Baler, "The Chief . . . Profile of a Politician," *Hyde Park Tribune,* November 15, 1973, p. 1.

7. Isaac Fein, *Boston—Where It All Began: A Historical Perspective of the Boston Jewish Community* (Boston Jewish Bicentennial Committee, 1976), p. 4.

8. Ibid., p. 7.

9. Ibid., p. 38.

10. Ibid., p. 40.

11. Theodore White, *In Search of History: A Personal Adventure* (New York: Harper & Row, 1978), p. 15.

12. Francis Russell, "How to Destroy a Suburb," *National Review,* October 1, 1976, p. 1063.

13. Ibid. Also see Russell for full description of Wellington Hill.

14. Ibid., p. 1064.

15. For a history of Upper and Middle Roxbury, see Langley Keyes, Jr., *The Rehabiliation Planning Game. A Study in the Diversity of Neighborhood* (Cambridge: MIT, 1969), chap. 5.

16. For a history of Irish Dorchester see *Dorchester: Boston 200 Neighborhood Series* (Boston: Office of the Mayor, 1976).

17. J. Anthony Lukas, *Common Ground: A Turbulent Decade in the Lives of Three American Families* (New York: Vintage Books, 1986), p. 379.

18. See Daniel Elazar, *Community and Polity. The Organizational Dynamics of American Jewry* (Philadelphia: Jewish Publication Society of America, 1976), p. 33.

19. For a description of internecine struggles see Fein, *Boston—Where It All Began.*

CHAPTER 2. MOVERS AND SHAKERS

1. Philippa Strum, *Louis D. Brandeis: Justice for the People* (New York: Schocken Books, 1984), p. 295.

2. Ibid., p. 17.

3. Ibid.

4. Arthur Goren, "National Leadership in American Jewish Life: The Formative Years" (University of Cincinnati, The Ninth Annual Rabbi Louis Feinberg Memorial Lecture in Judaic Studies, 1986), p. 1.

5. Jacob Schiff, *American Hebrew,* March 3, 1916, p. 472. Quoted in Goren, p. 1.

6. Goren, "National Leadership," p. 13.

7. Ibid., p. 16.

8. For discussion see Benny Kraut, "American Jewish Leaders: The Great, Greater and Greatest," *American Jewish History: An American Jewish Historical Society Quarterly Publication* 78, no. 2 (December 1988), p. 207.

9. Strum, *Louis D. Brandeis,* p. 259.

10. "Tribute to Justice Louis Brandeis," in Lewis Weinstein, *MASA: Odyssey of an American Jew* (Boston: Quinlan Press, 1989), p. 311.

11. For a thorough analysis of volunteerism in Jewish organizations see Daniel Elazar, *Community and Polity: The Organizational Dynamics of American Jewry* (Philadelphia: Jewish Publication Society, 1976), chap. 8.

12. Elazar, *Community and Polity,* p. 162.

13. Ibid., p. 167.

14. Interview with Lewis Weinstein, December 18, 1987.

15. Ibid.

16. Ben Halpern, *Jews and Blacks: The Classic American Minorities* (New York: Herder and Herder, 1971), p. 31.

17. For further analysis see Jonathan Kaufman, *Broken Alliance: The Turbulent Times Between Blacks and Jews in America* (New York: Scribner's, 1988), p. 32.

18. Interview with Muriel Snowden, September 16, 1988.

19. Interview with Otto Snowden, September 16, 1988.

20. Paula Hyman, "From City to Suburb: Temple Mishkan Tefila of Boston" in Jack Wertheimer, ed., *The American Synagogue: A Sanctuary Transformed,* A Centennial Publication of the Jewish Theological Seminary (Cambridge, England: Cambridge University, 1987), p. 188.

21. Ibid., p. 188.

22. Ibid., p. 189.

23. Ibid., p. 190.

24. Ibid.

25. Ibid., p. 191.

26. Ibid.

27. Ibid., p. 193.

28. Ibid.

29. Ibid., p. 198.

30. Langley Keyes, *The Rehabilitation Planning Game* (Cambridge, Mass.: The MIT Press, 1969), p. 146.

31. Chester Rapkin, "The Seaver-Townsend Urban Renewal Area," *Boston Redevelopment Authority* (1962), p. 19.

CHAPTER 3.   WHEELING AND DEALING

1. Interview with former Mayor John Collins, March 8, 1988.

2. For an in-depth discussion of Boston's economic woes see Alan Lupo, *Liberty's Chosen Home: The Politics of Violence in Boston* (Boston: Beacon Press, 1977).

3. For analysis see Anselm Strauss, *Images of the American City* (New Brunswick, N.J.: Transaction Books, 1976), pp. 144, 206.

4. For full discussion of FHA role see Charles Abrams, *Forbidden Neighbors: A Study of Prejudice in Housing* (New York: Harper and Bros., 1955), pp. 229–237.

5. For list of "inharmonious" groups see Abrams, *Forbidden Neighbors,* p. 161.

6. For variations on Gresham's Law of Neighborhoods see Henry Hoagland, *Real Estate Principles* (New York: McGraw-Hill, 1940), p. 148.

7. Stanley McMichael and R. F. Bingham, *City Growth and Values* (Cleveland: Stanley McMichael Publishing Organization, 1923), p. 181.

8. Ibid. p. 182.

9. Abrams, *Forbidden Neighbors,* p. 161.

10. Ibid., p. 230.

11. Ibid., p. 234.

12. Ibid., p. 237.

13. For a provocative discussion of suburbanization see Boston Urban Study Group, *Who Rules Boston? A Citizens's Guide to Reclaiming the City* (Boston: Institute for Democratic Socialism, 1984), p. 11.

14. Collins interview.

15. Ibid.

16. See Herbert Gans, *The Urban Villagers: Group and Class in the Life of Italian Americans* (New York: The Free Press, 1962).

17. Collins interview.

18. Ibid.

19. Ibid.

20. Ibid.

21. Lewis Weinstein, "Judicial Review in Urban Renewal," *The Federal Bar Journal* 21 (Summer 1961), p. 321.

22. Interview with Lewis Weinstein, December 18, 1987.

23. Steven Roberts, "Boston's Mastermind in Renewal Weighs Lindsay's Offer for a Post in the City," *New York Times,* May 1, 1966.

24. For further discussion see Langley Keyes, *The Rehabilitation Planning Game* (Cambridge, Mass: The MIT Press, 1969), p. 163.

25. "Synagogue Thronged For Julie's Funeral," obituary, *Boston Globe,* March 16, 1965.

26. Interview with Meyer Strassfeld, March 17, 1988.

27. Collins interview.

28. Jonathan Kaufman, *Broken Alliance: The Turbulent Times Between Blacks and Jews in America* (New York: Scribner's, 1988).

29. Collins interview.

30. Strassfeld interview.

CHAPTER 4.   CARRYING THE MESSAGE

1. Eli Goldston, "A New Look at Urban Priorities" (speech to the National Association of Manufacturers 74th Congress of American Industry, Waldorf Astoria, New York, December 3, 1969).

2. Interview with John Collins, March 8–10, 1988.

3. John Collins and Edward Logue, "The 90 Million Dollar Development Program for Boston," *City Record,* city hall, Boston, September 24, 1960.

4. For discussion of success traits see Richard Huber, *The American Idea of Success* (New York: McGraw-Hill, 1971), p. 94.

5. Interview with Robert Goldston, April 10, 1988.

6. Interview with Thomas Atkins, September 30, 1988.

7. "Sit-in Escalates into Riot," *Boston Globe,* June 3, 1967, p. 1.

8. Ibid.

9. Atkins interview.

10. Herbert Kupferberg, "Their Hard Road to Glory," *Parade Magazine,* March 12, 1989, p. 14.

11. For excellent Parks profile see Jonathan Kaufman, *Broken Alliance: The Turbulent Times Between Blacks and Jews in America* (New York: Scribner's, 1988), p. 52.

12. For recollections of Shag Taylor see Lawrence Carden, *Witness: An Oral History of Black Politics in Boston, 1920–1960* (Boston: Boston College, 1989), p. 22.

13. St. Clair Drake, "The Social and Economic Status of the Negro in the United States," *Daedalus* 94 (Fall 1965), pp. 771–814.

14. For Boston black history see Robert Hayden, *Faith, Culture and Leadership: A History of the Black Church in Boston* (Boston: NAACP, 1983).

15. Ibid., p. 35.

16. Quoted interview with Boston Redevelopment Authority official Walter Smart in Langley Keyes, *The Rehabilitation Planning Game* (Cambridge, Mass.: The MIT Press), p. 150.

17. Diane Lewis, "Roxbury's Rebirth Brings New Hopes and Old Fears," *Boston Globe,* June 12, 1988, p. 1.

18. Quoted in Kaufman, *Broken Alliance,* p. 44.

19. Carden, *Oral History of Black Politics,* p. 9.

20. Ibid., p. 13.

21. Ibid., p. 58.

22. Interview with Royal Bolling, November 29, 1989.

23. For analysis see N. Lemann, "The Unfinished War," *Atlantic Monthly,* December 1988, and January 1989.

24. "Hub Riot: 'Revolution,'" *Herald Traveler,* June 12, 1967, p. 2.

25. Incident witnessed by coauthor Lawrence Harmon.

26. Atkins interview.

27. Interview with former Boston Mayor Kevin White, December 3, 1987.

28. Langley Keyes, *The Boston Rehabilitation Program. An Independent Analysis* (Cambridge, Mass.: Joint Center for Urban Studies of the Massachusetts Institute of Technology and Harvard University, 1970), p. 40.

29. For excellent analysis of the political climate surrounding BURP see prologue in Keyes, *The Boston Rehabilitation Program.*

30. Keyes, *The Boston Rehabilitation Program,* p. 2.

31. Ibid., p. 49.

32. Letter from Robert Tracy to Jay Janis, March 6, 1968 in Keyes, *The Boston Rehabilitation Program,* p. 59.

33. Patricia Pierce, "Preliminary BRP Report. Federal Housing Administration," May, 1968 (Mimeo.) in Keyes, *The Boston Rehabilitation Program,* p. 120.

34. Interview with Norman Leventhal, March 29, 1988.

35. Interview with Allen Moore, Jr., April 6, 1990.

36. Ibid.
37. Ibid.

CHAPTER 5.   THE GIFT

1. Interview with Marvin Gilmore, May 8, 1990.
2. Margo Miller, "Black Boston's Miss Lewis: Art Czarina With a Needle," *Boston Globe,* April 18, 1968, p. 20; interview with Elma Lewis, March 4, 1988.
3. Ibid.
4. Ibid.
5. Interview with Judge Lawrence Shubow, December 21, 1987.
6. Ibid.
7. Ibid.
8. Ibid.
9. Interview with Robert Segal, April 26, 1987.
10. Lewis interview.
11. Segal interview.
12. Miller, *Black Boston's Miss Lewis,* p. 12.
13. Shubow interview.
14. Ibid.
15. Ibid.
16. Ibid.
17. Juan Williams, "How Would America Be Different If King Had Lived?" *Washington Post Magazine,* April 3, 1988, p. 21.
18. Ibid.
19. For excellent description of tensions in the wake of King assassination and Atkins's peace-keeping role see J. Anthony Lukas, *Common Ground* (New York: Vintage Books, 1986), p. 32.
20. Ibid., p. 34.
21. F. B. Taylor, Jr., "Negroes, Whites Respond Quickly to Hub Threat," *Boston Globe,* April 7, 1968, p. 18.
22. Interview with Mel Goldstein, March 27, 1988.
23. *Black Panther Journal,* June 1967.
24. Goldstein interview.
25. Interview with Joe Cohen, January 25, 1989.
26. Interview with Bernard Grossman, October 18, 1989.
27. Segal interview.
28. Alan Lupo, "Negro Art School Given Two Buildings," *Boston Globe,* April 18, 1968, p. 21.

CHAPTER 6.   ON THE LINE

1. Sylvia Rothchild, "Sixty-Five and Over," *Commentary,* December 1954, p. 550.
2. Ibid.
3. Hecht House promotional brochure, circa 1940.
4. Rothchild, "Sixty-Five and Over," p. 551.

5. Ibid., p. 554.

6. Sylvia Rothchild, "A Suburban Response to the Black Ghetto," unpublished manuscript, p. 1.

7. Ibid.

8. Interview with Sylvia Rothchild, February 8, 1988.

9. J. Anthony Lukas, *Common Ground: A Turbulent Decade in the Lives of Three American Families* (New York: Vintage, 1985), p. 39.

10. Ibid., p. 39.

11. Rothchild interview.

12. Lukas, *Common Ground,* p. 38.

13. For analysis of charities in Boston see ibid., pp. 345, 347.

14. Minutes of FUND membership meeting, Hotel Somerset, Boston, December 14, 1968, Leavitt Reporting Service, Weymouth, Mass.

15. Ibid., p. 5.

16. Lukas, *Common Ground,* p. 40.

17. Ibid., p. 41.

18. Interview with former Boston Mayor Kevin White, December 3, 1987.

19. Ibid.

20. White interview and material from Lukas, *Common Ground,* pp. 36–37.

21. White interview.

22. Described in Lukas, *Common Ground,* p. 37.

23. Housing Innovations, Inc., A Home Ownership Proposal for the Boston Model Cities Area (Boston, 1968), p. 68.

24. James Knowles, *Single Family Residential Appraisal Manual* (American Institute for Real Estate Appraisers, 1974), p. 26.

25. "Building the American City," report of the National Commission on Urban Problems, December 1968, pp. 100–102 (analysis available in Rachel Bratt, *A Homeownership Survey: A Report on the Boston Banks Urban Renewal Group,* Boston Model City Administration, 1972, p. 7).

26. *Competition in Real Estate and Mortgage Lending: Hearings before the Subcommittee on Antitrust and Monopoly* of the Committee on the Judiciary, U.S. Senate, Ninety-Second Congress, Second Session, Part 1, Boston, September 13, 14, and 15, 1971 (Washington, D.C.: U.S. Government Printing Office, 1972), p. 256.

27. For analysis see Martin Anderson, *The Federal Bulldozer: A Critical Analysis of Urban Renewal, 1949–1962* (Cambridge, Mass.: The MIT Press, 1965), p. 151.

28. Susan Blanche Soutner, *The Boston Banks Urban Renewal Group Homeownership Program: A Study of Racial Discrimination in an Urban Housing Market* (Department of City and Regional Planning, Harvard University, November 1980), p. 8.

29. *Competition in Real Estate and Mortgage Lending,* p. 308.

30. Dick Miller, "Man Came to 'Pru,' Stayed to Bank," *Boston Globe,* December 2, 1965.

31. Interview with Hale Champion, May 11, 1989.

32. White interview.

33. Press release from Office of the Mayor Kevin H. White, May 13, 1968.

34. Interview with Carl Ericson, March 25, 1988.

35. Ibid.

36. Ibid.

37. Memo on Mayor's Financial Program from Barney Frank to Frederick Paulsen, July 11, 1968.

38. For analysis see *Urban–Suburban Investment Study Group. Redlining and Disinvestment as a Discriminatory Practice in Residential Mortgage Loans* (Washington, D.C.: U.S. Government Printing Office and U.S. Commission on Civil Rights, 1976).

39. *Competition in Real Estate and Mortgage Lending,* p. 264.

40. Soutner, *Boston Banks Homeownership Program,* p. 14.

41. Ericson interview.

42. Champion interview.

43. Joseph Bacheller, memorandum to Boston Banks Urban Renewal Group, August 26, 1968.

44. Statistics from Joseph Bacheller, memorandum to Boston Banks Urban Renewal Group, October 4, 1968.

45. Joseph Bacheller, memorandum to Boston Banks Urban Renewal Group, January 16, 1969.

46. Minutes of FUND membership meeting, December 14, 1968.

47. Ibid.

48. Rothchild, "A Suburban Response to the Black Ghetto," p. 7.

49. Ibid., p. 12.

50. Ibid., p. 14.

51. Ibid., p. 17.

52. Ibid., p. 16.

CHAPTER 7.   "ACCEPTABLE BEFORE THEE"

1. Memo from Sol Kolack to Arnold Forster, Anti-Defamation League of B'nai B'rith, January 27, 1965.

2. Letter from Dr. Harry Kozol to Robert Segal, director of Jewish Community Council, September 14, 1965.

3. Anti-Defamation League memorandum from Isadore Zack to Justin Finger, March 1, 1965.

4. "When Boston's Biblical Slumlords Faced the Rabbis," *Jewish Advocate,* January 21, 1988, p. 13.

5. Recollection of Rabbi Judea Miller, April 28, 1989.

6. Ibid.

7. Ibid.

8. Ibid.

9. Ibid.

10. Interview with Leonard Fein, October 24, 1989.

11. Quoted in J. Anthony Lukas, *Common Ground: A Turbulent Decade in the Lives of Three American Families* (New York: Vintage, 1985), p. 431.

12. Leo Shapiro, "Rabbinical Court Helps Solve Tenant-Landlord Difference," *Boston Globe,* August 29, 1968, p. 50.

CHAPTER 8.   BLOCKBUSTING MATTAPAN

1. Material gathered from Anonymous, "Confessions of a Blockbuster," *Metropolitan Real Estate Journal,* May 1987, p. 14.

2. Ibid.

3. Quote and other excellent information on blockbusting tactics in Geoffrey Stokes and Gary Tolzer, "The Lords of Flatbush: The Economics of Blockbusting," *Village Voice,* December 3–9, 1980, p. 12. Reprinted by permission of *The Village Voice* and the author.

4. For analysis see Daniel Elazar, Community and Polity: *The Organizational Dynamics of American Jewry* (Philadelphia: Jewish Publication Society of America, 1976), p. 288.

5. "A Jewish View of the Crisis in Race Relations in America: An Analysis and a Statement of Position" by the Jewish Community Relations Agencies Comprising the National Community Relations Advisory Council, July 1967, p. 19.

6. Interview with Professor Francis McLaughlin of Boston College, November 12, 1987.

7. Ibid.

8. Interview with Dov Yoffee, son of Louis Yoffee, December 3, 1989.

9. Ibid.

10. Letter from Louis Yoffee to Mattapan homeowners and residents, *Mattapan Organization,* August 3, 1967.

11. Alan Lupo, "The Blue Hill Avenue Story," *Boston Globe Sunday Magazine,* May 4, 1969.

12. Letter from Joseph Bacheller to Frederick Paulsen, August 13, 1968.

13. "FBI Probing FHA Official's Boston Dealings," *Boston Globe,* June 3, 1971, p. 18.

14. The case was heard in Massachusetts District Court in 1980; Judge Andrew A. Caffrey made the decision fining Kenealy (Vol. 487, Federal Suppl., p. 1379). Quotation from "Judge Assesses Appraiser $348,511 in Conflict Case," *Boston Globe,* April 3, 1980, p. 18.

15. Quotation from *Boston Globe,* April 3, 1980, p. 18. The case was appealed, and the lower court's decision was upheld by the First Circuit Court of Appeals in 1981 (Vol. 646, Federal Reporter 2d, p. 699). Kenealy then appealed to the U.S. Supreme Court, which refused to hear the case; thus the First Circuit Court's decision was upheld (Vol. 454, U.S. Reports, p. 941, 1981).

16. Janice Bernstein's testimony in *Competition in Real Estate and Mortgage Lending: Hearings before the Subcommittee on Antitrust and Monopoly of the Committee on the Judiciary, U.S. Senate,* 92d Congr., 2d sess., Part 1, Boston, September 13, 14, and 15, 1971 (Washington, D.C.: U.S. Government Printing Office, 1972), p. 74.

17. Susan Blanch Soutner, "The Boston Banks Urban Renewal Group Homeownership Program: A Study of Racial Discrimination in an Urban Housing

Market" (Department of City and Regional Planning, Harvard University, November 1980), p. 11.

18. Rachel Bratt, "A Home Ownership Survey: A Report on the Boston Banks Urban Renewal Group," Boston Model City Administration, January, 1972, p. 24.

19. Interview with Sumner and Janice Bernstein, June 5, 1987.

20. Soutner, "Group Homeownership Program," p. 18.

21. Ibid., p. 19.

22. Robert Schafer, "Racial Discrimination in the Boston Housing Market," *Journal of Urban Economics* 6 (1979), pp. 176–196; also cited in Soutner, "Group Homeownership Program," p. 5.

23. Joe R. Feagin et al., *Subsidizing the Poor: A Boston Housing Experiment* (Lexington, Mass.: Heath, 1972), Table 4.

24. Interview with Allan Cohen, April 12, 1988.

25. Taped reminiscences of Allan Cohen, May 15, 1969.

26. Cohen interview.

27. The Commonwealth of Massachusetts, *An Act Providing for the Elimination of Racial Imbalance in the Public School,* 1965, chap. 641.

28. J. Anthony Lukas, Kahn Memorial Lecture, Boston University, March 28, 1988.

29. J. Anthony Lukas, *Common Ground: A Turbulent Decade in the Lives of Three American Families* (New York: Vintage, 1985), p. 130.

30. Burt Peretsky, "Mattapan School Example of Troubled Times," *Record American,* December 18, 1969, p. 5.

31. William Cooper, "How School Became 67 Percent Black in Four Years," *Herald Traveler,* January 5, 1969, p. 47.

CHAPTER 9.   "LEAD THE JEWISH RACISTS OUT OF MATTAPAN"

1. Interview with Gerald Zelermyer, October 14, 1987.

2. Abraham Joshua Heschel, *The Insecurity of Freedom: Essays on Human Existence* (New York: Schocken Books, 1972), p. 103.

3. Zelermyer interview.

4. Speech by Gary Rosenblatt, editor of *Baltimore Jewish Times,* at Brandeis University, April 1, 1985.

5. Interview with Bernard Hyatt, December 3, 1987.

6. Ibid.

7. Ibid.

8. Zelermyer interview.

9. Fred Pillsbury, "Boston Buys Temple for School Space," *Boston Globe,* August 20, 1969, p. 1.

CHAPTER 10.   THE "DIRTY LITTLE SECRET"

1. "Attacks upon Elderly Spur Mattapan Action," *Boston Globe,* November 25, 1969, p. 1.

2. Ibid.

3. R. Bongartz, "SuperJew," *Esquire,* August 1970, p. 110.

4. Ibid.

5. Quoted in Jonathan Kaufman, *Broken Alliance: The Turbulent Times Between Blacks and Jews in America* (New York: Scribner's, 1988), p. 157.

6. Bongartz, "SuperJew," p. 110.

7. ADL press release, November 20, 1969.

8. Kahn memorial lecture delivered by J. Anthony Lukas at Boston University, March 28, 1988.

9. Bongartz, "SuperJew," p. 111.

10. January 13, 1971, memo on JDL by Commission on Interfaith Activities (Union of American Hebrew Congregations, Central Conference of American Rabbis, and Jewish Chautauqua Society).

11. Ibid., p. 4.

12. Interview with Iz Zack, May 5, 1987.

13. Zack interview.

14. Interview with Arthur Bernstein, October 18, 1987.

15. Taped interview of Jewish Defense League Boston Executive Session, December 16, 1969.

16. Ibid.

17. Avoth: 5:25, translated in Philip Birnbaum, *A Book of Jewish Concepts* (New York: Hebrew Publishing, 1964), p. 630.

18. "Officials Blamed in Eulogy," *Boston Herald Traveler,* June 1, 1970, p. 7. Reprinted with permission of the *Boston Herald.*

19. Bob Creamer, "Jews Bury Desecrated Torah," *Boston Herald Traveler,* June 1, 1970, p. 1.

20. Ibid.

21. Ibid.

22. Interview with Kevin White, December 3, 1987.

23. Ibid.

24. Ibid.

25. For analysis see Nicholas Lemann, "The Unfinished War," *Atlantic Monthly,* January 1989, p. 56.

26. Frederick Paulsen, "Position Taken by the Boston Banks Urban Renewal Group to Limit Loans to Persons Buying Property Located Within the Model Cities Area and Areas Adjacent Thereto," memo to Barney Frank, June 22, 1970, cited in *Competition in Real Estate and Mortgage Lending: Hearings Before the Subcommittee on Antitrust and Monopoly* of the Committee on the Judiciary, U.S. Senate, Ninety-Second Congress, Second Session, Part 1, Boston, September 13–15, 1971 (Washington, D.C.: U.S. Government Printing Office, 1972), p. 341.

27. Interview with Thomas Atkins, September 30, 1988.

28. March 23, 1970, letter from Joseph Bacheller to Thomas Atkins, cited in *Competition in Real Estate and Mortgage Lending,* pp. 452–453.

29. Atkins interview.

30. February 21, 1969, memorandum from Joseph Bacheller to Boston Banks Urban Renewal Group, cited in *Competition in Real Estate and Mortgage Lending,* p. 530.

31. Minutes of January 14, 1971, housing seminar, MIT Department of Urban Studies and Planning.

32. Interview with Harold Ross, February 28, 1988.

33. Anthony Yudis, "Unique Group Helps Guide Blacks to Home Ownership," *Boston Sunday Globe,* May 23, 1971, B-39.

34. Susan Blanche Soutner, "The Boston Banks Urban Renewal Group Homeownership Program: A Study of Racial Discrimination in an Urban Housing Market," unpublished paper, Department of City and Regional Planning, Harvard University, November 1980, p. 26.

35. Testimony of Julia Owens, *Competition in Real Estate and Mortgage Lending,* p. 45.

36. Ibid.

37. Rachel Bratt, "A Home Ownership Survey: A Report on the Boston Banks Urban Renewal Group," Boston Model City Administration, January 1972, p. 42.

38. Soutner, "Homeownership Program," pp. 31–32.

39. Ibid., p. 33.

40. Ibid.

CHAPTER 11.   THE HEARINGS

1. For Hart biography see Ralph Nader, *Congress Project: Citizens Look at Congress* (New York: Grossman Publishers, 1972).

2. *Competition in Real Estate and Mortgage Lending: Hearings Before the Subcommittee on Antitrust and Monopoly* of the Committee on the Judiciary, U.S. Senate, 92d Cong., 2d sess., Part 1, Boston, September 13, 14, and 15, 1971 (Washington, D.C.: U.S. Government Printing Office, 1972), pp. 1–2.

3. *Competition in Real Estate and Mortgage Lending As It Affects the Housing Crisis—New York, Part 2,* Washington, D.C., May 1 and 16, 1972 (Washington, D.C.: U.S. Government Printing Office, 1972), p. 316.

4. Ibid., p. 94.

5. Ibid.

6. Ibid., p. 81.

7. Ibid., p. 92.

8. Ibid., p. 81.

9. Ibid., pp. 86, 93.

10. *Competition in Real Estate and Mortgage Lending,* part 1, p. 6.

11. Interview with Sadelle Sacks, October 31, 1989.

12. *Competition in Real Estate and Mortgage Lending,* part 2, p. 5.

13. Ibid., p. 26.

14. Ibid., p. 28.

15. Sacks interview.

16. *Competition in Real Estate and Mortgage Lending,* part 1, pp. 29, 78.

17. Ibid., p. 103.

18. Ibid., pp. 119–121.

19. Ibid., p. 121.

20. Ibid., p. 123.
21. Ibid., p. 127.
22. Ibid., p. 128.
23. Ibid., p. 129.
24. Ibid., pp. 130–132.
25. Ibid., p. 132.
26. Martin Healy, Philip Murray, Jr., and Thomas Murray, "You Can Trust the Bankers (to be Bankers)," unpublished paper, Boston College, 1972, p. 23.
27. *Competition in Real Estate and Mortgage Lending,* part 1, pp. 226, 229–230.
28. Ibid., pp. 253–254, 261.
29. Ibid., p. 255.
30. Ibid., pp. 257–258.
31. Ibid., p. 259.
32. Ibid., p. 263.
33. Ibid.
34. Ibid.
35. Ibid., p. 264.
36. Ibid., p. 265.
37. Ibid., p. 284.
38. Ibid., pp. 285–287.
39. Ibid., pp. 291–292.
40. Ibid., p. 310.
41. Healy, Murray, and Murray, "You Can Trust the Bankers," pp. 23–24.
42. Patricia Morse, Sanford Neiman, and Roger Auerbach, memo entitled "Status of Investigation—Alleged Blockbusting Activities in Mattapan," to James J. Barry, Regional Administrator, HUD, circa 1970, pp. 1–11.
43. *Competition in Real Estate and Mortgage Lending,* part 1, p. 318.
44. Ibid., p. 319.
45. Ibid., p. 332.
46. Ibid., pp. 335–339.
47. Ibid., pp. 338–339.
48. *Competition in Real Estate and Mortgage Lending,* part 2, p. 2.
49. Ibid.
50. Ibid., pp. 4–8.
51. Ibid., p. 94.
52. Ibid., p. 103.
53. Ibid., p. 756.
54. Ibid., pp. 759–760.

CHAPTER 12.   IN SEARCH OF NEW CENTERS—THE 1970s

1. Interview with Saul and Gertrude Pearlman, May 15, 1989.
2. Daniel Elazar, *Community and Polity: The Organizational Dynamics of American Jewry* (Philadelphia: Jewish Publication Society of America, 1976), p. 315.
3. Interview with Bernard Olshansky, June 15, 1987.

4. Combined Jewish Philanthropies of Greater Boston, *A Community Survey for Long Range Planning: A Study of the Jewish Population of Greater Boston,* 1967.

5. Tom Murray, "CJP Defends Its Mattapan Aid," *Herald Traveler,* June 3, 1970, p. 3.

6. ADL memo from Sol Kolack to Alex Miller, June 3, 1970.

7. Memo from Martin Greenberg, director of Social Planning & Research Dept., Council of Jewish Federations & Welfare Funds, March 16, 1971.

8. Arthur Bernstein, "JDL Leader Cannot Understand Moves of Jewish Community Council," letter in *Jewish Advocate,* November 5, 1970.

9. Letter from Dr. Morris Stone to Board of Directors of the Combined Jewish Philanthropies, November 9, 1970.

10. Speech by Avram Goldberg to Board of Directors of the Combined Jewish Philanthropies, June 30, 1970.

11. Interview with Kevin White, December 3, 1987.

12. Olshansky interview.

13. Interviews with elderly Georgetown residents.

14. Interview with Zezette Larsen, December 2, 1988.

15. Ibid.

16. Ibid.

17. Ibid.

18. Interview with Norman Leventhal, March 29, 1988.

19. Interview with Yona Ginsberg, July 9, 1989.

20. "Robbers Vandalize Rabbi's Home in Mattapan," *Boston Globe,* May 28, 1971, p. 3.

21. Ginsberg interview.

22. Joshua Rubenstein, *Soviet Dissidents: Their Struggle for Human Rights* (Boston: Beacon Press, 1980), p. 160.

23. "How Men in Power Let Mattapan Area Be Victimized," *Boston Globe,* April 4, 1972, p. 1.

24. Susan Blanche Soutner, *The Boston Banks Urban Renewal Group Homeownership Program: A Study of Racial Discrimination in an Urban Housing Market* (Department of City and Regional Planning, Harvard University, November, 1980), p. 29.

25. Ibid., p. 33.

26. "Murder Victim Eulogized: Synagogue Was His Home," *Boston Globe,* March 21, 1973.

27. Ibid.

28. Interview with Lawrence Shubow, December 21, 1987.

29. Interview with Justin Wyner, June 9, 1987.

30. Wyner interview.

31. Recollections of Janice Bernstein (June 5, 1987) and Lawrence Shubow (December 21, 1987).

32. Letter from Justin Wyner to Janice Bernstein, April 19, 1973.

33. Letter from Lawrence Cohen to Janice Bernstein, March 21, 1973.

34. Interview with Michael Ansara, December 12, 1990.

35. Leventhal interview.

36. Peter Canellos, "Anthony's Housing Legacy Built to Last," *Boston Sunday Globe,* December 30, 1990, p. 21.

CONCLUSION

1. As quoted in Michael Sandel, "A Public Philosophy for American Liberalism: Democrats and Community," *New Republic,* February 22, 1988, p. 22.

2. Derrick Z. Jackson, "Wake Up, African Americans—and Act," *Boston Globe,* December 16, 1990, p. A16.

3. Interview with Michael Ansara, former director of Fair Share, December 12, 1990.

4. Charles Finn, *Mortage Lending in Boston's Neighborhoods 1981– 1987: A Study of Bank Credit and Boston Housing,* (Minneapolis: Hubert H. Humphrey Institute of Public Affairs, University of Minnesota, 1989), p. 38.

5. Ibid, p. IV.

6. "Accord Seen Today on Broad Plan for HUD Fair Housing," *Boston Globe,* January 2, 1991, pp. 1, 23; "HUD–NAACP Pact Praised but Its Impact Questioned," *Boston Globe,* January 3, 1991, pp. 17, 22.

7. Lew Finfer, *Dorchester Community News,* April 30, 1985.

8. Rolf Goetz, *Understanding Neighborhood Change: The Role of Expectations in Urban Revitalization* (Cambridge, Mass: Ballinger, 1979), pp. 2, 36.

9. Fifth Annual Back to the City Conference, 1978, quoted in ibid., p. 129.

10. See Thomas Pettigrew, "New Black White Patterns: How Best to Conceptualize Them?" *Annual Review of Sociology* (1985), pp. 329–346; William Julius Wilson, *The Truly Disadvantaged: The Inner City, the Underclass, and Public Policy* (Chicago: University of Chicago Press, 1987), pp. 3–19, 125–139

11. Sandel, "Public Philosophy for American Liberalism, pp. 20–23; Amy Gutmann. "Communitarian Critics of Liberalism," *Philosophy and Public Affairs,* 14 (1985), pp. 308–320.

12. See Ronald Garet, "Communality and Existence: The Rights of Groups," *Southern California Law Review,* 56 (5), (July 1983), pp. 1001– 1074.

13. Harold Nelson, "Charity, Poverty, and Race," *Phylon: The Atlanta University Review of Race and Culture,* 29 (3) (1968), pp. 303–316; Robert Havighurst, "Philanthropic Foundations as Interest Groups," *Education and Urban Society,* 13 (2) (February 1981), pp. 193–218; Waldemar Nielson, *The Endangered Sector* (New York: Columbia University Press, 1979).

14. See George Steiner, "The City Under Attack," *Salmagundi,* 24 (Fall 1973), pp. 3–18.

15. For a review of how enduring this pattern of residential segregation is, see National Research Council, *A Common Destiny: Blacks and American Society,* Gerald Jaynes and Robin Williams, Jr., eds. (Washington, D.C.: NRC, 1989), pp. 88–91. Black suburbanization in the 1970s often created "mini-ghettos" to which problems of the inner cities were transferred without the benefits of the suburbs.

16. Nathan Glazer, "Frustrated Blacks and Weary Whites," *London Times Higher Education Supplement,* July 20, 1990, p. 15.

Index